HOMOSEXUAL DESIRE IN
SHAKESPEARE'S ENGLAND

HOMOSEXUAL DESIRE IN
SHAKESPEARE'S
ENGLAND

A CULTURAL POETICS

Bruce R. Smith

The University of Chicago Press
Chicago and London

BRUCE R. SMITH is professor of English at Georgetown University. He is author of *Ancient Scripts and Modern Experience on the English Stage, 1500-1700.* (1988).

The University of Chicago Press, Chicago
The University of Chicago Press, Ltd., London
©1991 by The University of Chicago
All rights reserved. Published 1991
Printed in the United States of America

00 99 98 97 96 95 94 93 92 91   1 2 3 4 5

Library of Congress Cataloging-in Publication Data

Smith, Bruce R., 1946—
Homosexual desire in Shakespeare's England : a cultural poetics /
Bruce R. Smith.
p. cm.
Includes bibliographical references and index.
ISBN: 0-226-76364-1
1. English literature—Early modern, 1500-1700—History and criticism.
2. Homosexuality and literature—England—History—16th century.
3. Homosexuality and literature—England—History—17th century. 4. Shakespeare, William, 1564-1616. Sonnets. 5. Desire in literature. 6. Sex inliterature.
I. Title.
PR428.H66S6   1991
820.9'353—dc20   90-47356
                                                              CIP

♾ The paper used in this publication meets the minimum requirements of the American National Standard for Information Sciences—Permanence of Paper for Printed Library Materials, ANSI Z39.48-1984

For
Gordon Davis

CONTENTS

ILLUSTRATIONS

PREFACE

This book began, not as a manifesto, but as a dialog.

Six years ago, when I presented some of the ideas from what is now chapter 6 as a twenty-minute talk before the Lord Byron Society of Washington, D.C., I finished by raising questions. Some of the ideas put forward by other members of the discussion group on that occasion are still to be found here. And some of the questions the discussants asked of me are still not fully answered. I am grateful to Armen Tashdinian, founder of LBS, for providing the forum that set me to talking with other people about homosexuality in English Renaissance literature. In 1984 it was a topic that seemed not to exist.

The breadth and the direction that the subject has assumed in these pages are the result of continuing dialog. Early drafts of the entire book were generously read by Steve Brown, Gordon Davis, Douglas Gold, Joseph Marchesani, Elias Mengel, and Joseph Pequigney. Their disagreements, with me and with each other, were no less important than what they happened to approve. Individual chapters are both more pointed and more circumspect, thanks to close readings by Donald Foster, Margreta de Grazia, Susan Lanser, Alan Price, Michael Shapiro, and Joel Siegel. To Sue Lanser, who offered encouragement and reassurance at a crucial juncture, I owe particular thanks. Several people unselfishly shared research with me before it had been published: Margreta de Grazia, Donald Foster, Michael Hall, and Michael Shapiro. I am grateful also to Victoria Pedrick, who translated passages of Greek for me; to Patricia Tatspaugh, who hunted down reviews of Royal Shakespeare Company productions; and to Laetitia Yeandle, Curator of Manuscripts at the Folger Shakespeare Library, who conferred with me about the Folger manuscript that has come to be known as Richard Barnfield's commonplace book.

The Folger Shakespeare Library has, in fact, nurtured this project from the beginning. Most of the early books and manuscripts I cite come from the Folger's collections. Lectures and seminars at the Folger have acquainted me with facts, theories, and people I would otherwise not have known. Part of my year as a Folger Fellow in 1988-89 was spent carrying out the legal research that figures in chapter 2 and making final revisions to the entire manuscript. To the Folger staff and to fellow readers at the Folger over the past twenty years I owe gratitude so various and so protracted as to be truly incalculable.

I am happy to acknowledge, too, the support that Georgetown University has given my research and writing in the form of a Summer Academic Research Grant, released time from teaching, and funds for preparing the manuscript. In the tasks of printing and duplicating, Lynne Hirschfeld and Joan Reuss of the English Department office have been extraordinarily helpful.

Words set in type can look deceptively final. The dialog that has produced this book will, I hope, continue among those who read it.

B.R.S.
Arquà Petrarca
May 1990

HOMOSEXUAL DESIRE IN SHAKESPEARE'S ENGLAND

CHAPTER ONE

SEXUALITY AND THE PLAY
OF IMAGINATION

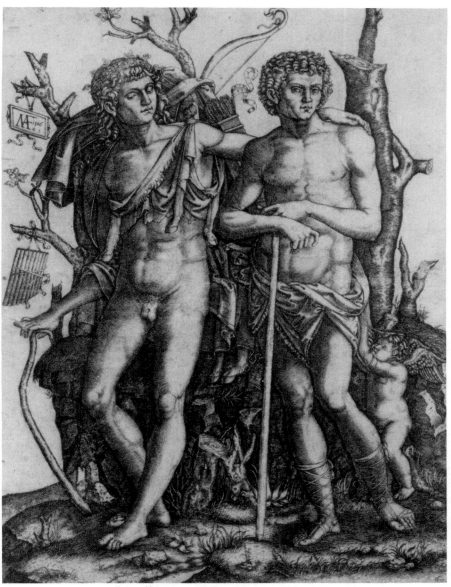

"Apollo, Hyacinth, and Amor" (1506)

Marcantonio Raimondi

What are we to make of a culture that could consume popular prints of Apollo embracing Hyacinth and yet could order hanging for men who acted on the very feelings that inspire that embrace?

Sex is one of the constants in human experience; sexuality, one of the variables. Sexual desire animates human beings in all times and all places, but the forms that desire assumes, the objects to which desire is directed, change from culture to culture, from era to era. The English adventurers who put out to sea in the sixteenth century found at the end of their journeys not only exotic lands, exotic animals, and exotic plants but exotic sexual customs as well. Practices that were anathema in Christian Europe turned out to be commonplace elsewhere. In most other parts of the world, for example, polygamy was a measure of a man's social status, not of his moral depravity. Even more outlandish practices figure in Henry Hawkes's account of his five years as a merchant in Mexico. It took the wine of their Spanish conquerors to set them off, but the Indians in Mexico, Hawkes reports,

> are soone drunke, and given to much beastlines, and void of all goodnes. In their drunknnes, they use and commit sodomie, and with their mothers and daughters they have their pleasures and pastimes.[1]

The voyages of cultural discovery begun during the sixteenth century have continued for the past two hundred years in the researches of anthropologists and social historians. Imagine any form of sexual expression, even incest, and somewhere there are people who have made it a cultural institution. What these activities mean to the people who actually practice them is, of course, something altogether different from what they mean to unacculturated people who observe them from the outside. When we read Henry Hawkes's report that the Mexican Indians "use and commit sodomie," we need to distinguish three things: what *he* means by sodomy, what *we* take the word to mean, and what *they*, the Indians, may have thought they were doing. "Sodomy" may be a single word, but in this instance it refers to three very different realities. For us, it is a precise bio-legal term that denotes one particular sexual act. Hawkes's field of reference is rather broader: his choice of the verb "commit" puts his readers in mind of all the other things a man might commit—adultery, say, or murder—and by linking sodomy with "beastlines" and incest he leaves no doubt that, for him, sodomy is not so much a species of sexual activity as a species of crime. Just beneath the surface of Hawkes's word looms the city of Sodom and the sin that brought down Jehovah's wrath in the form of fire and brimstone. That biblical allusion, the very essence of the matter for

Hawkes, is probably no more present for most speakers of English today than the image of light in the word "illustrate" or the image of something hanging down from something else in "dependent"—images that would have been present for most readers, if not speakers, of English in the sixteenth century. Despite the fact that he uses a word we recognize, Hawkes is not quite speaking the same language we speak. What the Indians were doing to each other physically he may or may not be attempting to specify. What the Indians *thought* they were doing to each other is another thing still: to find that out we would need more to go on than Hawkes's preconceptions—or our own. And so for the sexual desires of Henry Hawkes himself. Can we be so sure that the sexuality of Henry Hawkes and his compeers, if we could know it from the inside, would be any less exotic to us than the sexuality of the Mexican Indians was to them?

Because sex is such a basic part of our humanity, changes in sexuality, changes in the forms of desire across historical time, present a much more difficult challenge to the imagination than do changes in laws, in marriage customs, in literary conventions. Sex, we tell ourselves, is a biological drive, a "natural" given. But for *homo sapiens* it cannot remain just that: the central fact about human sexuality, Roger Scruton proposes, is human self-consciousness. Sex may be rooted in instinct, but that instinct is mediated and transformed by human rationality.[2] What philosophers have had to say about sex is the subject of Scruton's book on *Sexual Desire*. At least one sixteenth-century philosopher has anticipated twentieth-century critics of Scruton's argument in doubting that "rationality" is quite the right word for whatever it is that connects human sexual instinct with human consciousness. We may think about sex and we may talk about sex, but we do not always think about it and talk about it rationally.

Almost never, Montaigne observes, do we approach the subject of sex directly. Instead, we resort to euphemisms. "Why was the acte of generation made so naturall, so necessary and so just, seeing we fear to speake of it without shame, and exclude it from our serious and regular discourses?" Montaigne asks in his essay "Upon Some Verses of Virgil."

> We pronounce boldly, to rob, to murther, to betray; and this we dare not but betweene our teeth. Are we to gather by it, that the less we breath out in words the more we are allowed to furnish our thoughts with? . . . It is an action we have put in the precincts of silence, whence to draw it were an offence: not to

accuse or judge it. Nor dare we [beate] it but in circumlocution and picture. A notable favour, to a criminal offender, to be so execrable, that justice deem it injustice to touch and behold him, freed and saved by the benefit of this condemnations severity.3

Concerning sex, more than any other aspect of our humanity, we use indirections to find directions out. We know it primarily by "picture," through "circumlocution." We may be able to *understand* sex as an instinct only in terms of sexuality, but sexuality is as much a matter of concrete images and emotional associations as it is of intellectual reflection. When we talk about sex, we talk mostly in metaphors. Anyone who claims that Pallas and the Muses are at odds with Venus knows nothing about sexual desire, Montaigne concludes.

> Who-ever shal go about to remove amourous imaginations from the *Muses*, shall deprive them of the best entertainement they have, and of the noblest subject of their work: and who shall debarre *Cupid* the service and conversation of Poesie, shall weaken him of his best weapons. . . . But for so much as I know of it, the power and might of this God, are found more quick and lively in the shadowe of the Poesie, then in their owne essence.4

By separating *poësie* about sexual desire from sexual desire in its *propre essence*, and by attributing the greater power to *poësie*, Montaigne advances an argument that runs just counter to how we have been taught to think about sex for the past hundred years. When it comes to sex, philology recapitulates biology: Charles Darwin and Sigmund Freud leave no doubts about that. Like Montaigne, Michel Foucault sees it all the other way around. Between the widely read introductory volume to his *History of Sexuality* and the three later volumes he managed to complete before his death, Foucault may have changed his mind about just when in western history sexuality became an obsessive object of rational inquiry, but he maintains through all four volumes his fundamental contention that sexuality, like madness, is a construct of human imagination, a cultural artifact that changes with time. Sexuality has no independent existence, Foucault argues, either outside in "nature" or inside within the subconscious mind:

> Sexuality must not be thought of as a kind of natural given which power tries to hold in check, or as an obscure domain which knowledge tries gradually to uncover. It is the name that can be given to a historical construct: not a furtive reality that is difficult to grasp, but a great surface network in which the stim-

ulation of bodies, the intensification of pleasures, the incitement to discourse, the formation of special knowledges, the strengthening of controls and resistances, are linked to one another, in accordance with a few major strategies of knowledge and power.[5]

There could be no clearer illustration of Foucault's argument than the casebooks of Simon Forman, self-taught physician, professional astrologer, irrepressible self-promoter, and in those three capacities the confidant of scores of sixteenth- and seventeenth-century men and women ranging in social station from servants to peers. About them and about himself Forman kept copious notes that cast a suggestive light down dark, unfrequented passages of Renaissance imagination that otherwise would be closed to us. Not only sexual exploits figure in Forman's notes but sexual dreams as well. In those dreams we can discern images, characters, and events that seem universal—archetypal, indeed, in the precise meaning that Jung gives the term—but we discover also a great deal that seems specific to the culture of sixteenth-century England. Forman's own dream about Queen Elizabeth, for example, illustrates graphically how sixteenth-century structures of power and sixteenth-century structures of knowledge shaped sixteenth-century images of sexual desire. In January 1597 Forman

> dreamt that I was with the Queen, and that she was a little elderly woman in a coarse white petticoat all unready. She and I walked up and down through lanes and closes, talking and reasoning. At last we came over a great close where were many people, and there were two men at hard words. One of them was a weaver, a tall man with a reddish beard, distract of his wits. She talked to him and he spoke very merrily unto her, and at last did take her and kiss her. So I took her by the arm and did put her away; and told her the fellow was frantic. So we went from him and I led her by the arm still, and then we went through a dirty lane. She had a long white smock very clean and fair, and it trailed in the dirt and her coat behind. I took her coat and did carry it up a good way, and then it hung too low before. I told her she should do me a favour to let me wait on her, and she said I should. Then said I, "I mean to wait *upon* you and not under you, that I might make this belly a little bigger to carry up this smock and coat out of the dirt." And so we talked merrily; then she began to lean upon me, when we were past the dirt and to be very familiar with me, and methought she began to love me. When we were alone, out of sight, methought she would have kissed me.[6]

The attack by a man—specifically a tall man—with bristling red hair, the white gown that becomes dirtied, the mounting familiarity that proceeds from talking to touching to leaning to kissing: all of these things in the "manifest content" of the dream point to a "latent" sexual meaning (if "patent" isn't the better word in this case) that was as clear to Forman as it is to post-Freudians like ourselves. Witness his erotic pun on "waiting *upon* you." But what about the detail that the attacker was, of all things, a weaver? That, surely, is an aspect of the dream's eroticism that is understandable mainly in terms of Elizabethan structures of power, which replicated Elizabethan structures of knowledge in setting the Virgin Queen at a tantalizing distance above the animality of a rude mechanical. For the original watchers/dreamers Bottom the weaver must have had a *machismo* that eludes twentieth-century analysts of *A Midsummer Night's Dream*. The "reddish beard" of the queen's attacker is another detail that seems partly universal, partly peculiar to the sixteenth century. Samson was neither the first nor the last hero whose virility has been predicated on his hair. But why red? The structure of Elizabethan knowledge established parallels among body fluids, organs of the body, psychological traits, and planetary influences—categories logically separate to us but to the Renaissance mind causatively interlinked as aspects of one grand hierarchical order. Red was the color of the heart's blood, productive of a "sanguinary" humor and controlled by the planets Mars and Venus by association with their namesakes' prowess in love. A red beard was erotic because Elizabethan thinking made it so.[7] The very fact that Forman should have an erotic dream about the queen shows us, in just the terms Foucault proposes, how structures of power in a society help define sexuality in that society: Forman's dream suggests how much of the political success of "Gloriana" consisted in arousing the sexual energies of her male subjects and deflecting those energies toward politically useful goals.

As with the dreams of Forman and his patients, so too with their sex lives: Forman's notes present us with an odd mixture of the familiar and the strange. The exuberant promiscuity of Forman and his patients, even the female ones, is enough to challenge the most sexually liberated twentieth-century reader of his diary, yet Forman's careful notations of the exact times and places of coitus reflect structures of knowledge and structures of power that have little to do with twentieth-century sexuality. The first of several entries about a certain Mrs. Hipwell is typical of Forman's record keeping: "Halek [Forman's private euphemism proves the truth of what Montaigne says about sex and language] prius [on an earlier occasion] Elizabeth Hipwell 15 June 1596, 4.20 p.m. studio [in the study]." Mrs. Hipwell had more reason than most of Forman's sexual partners for seeking satisfaction in beds other than her husband's:

> He is a lewd fellow . . . spends all and keeps ill company and theft, like to have been hanged for robbing. A faint-hearted fellow, a yellowish beard and brown head. Fovit prius pro peccato inter anum et sodomy; illa halek cum duobus del Finchley . . . [He warmed her up on one occasion—for a sin—through the ass and sodomized her; she screwed with two (at once?) at Finchley].[8]

Forman wanted to know precisely when and where he had managed to "halek" so as to give his sexual acts astrological significance: knowing such things made it possible for him to know whether the deed had been propitious and whether he could look forward to further sexual relations with the partner in question. Then, too, dates, times, and places just might come in handy for denying paternity. In either case astrology provided a structure of knowledge and, more especially, a structure of power that shaped Simon Forman's sexuality in ways very different from our own. A sixteenth-century European defined his sexual self against a background as vast as the universe; he synchronized his sexual activities with the movements of the planets and the fixity of the stars. "My father compounded with my mother under the Dragon's tail and my nativity was under Ursa Major, so that it follows I am rough and lecherous. Fut! I should have been that I am, had the maidenliest star of the firmament twinkled on my bastardy." Edmund's contempt for the laws of astrology is one of many ways in which the "illegitimate" son stands sulking outside the Elizabethan order of things.[9]

In Forman's journal we have a particularly intimate example of how every culture has, in Foucault's words, its own distinctive ways of "putting sex into discourse." With that phrase Foucault does not mean, as common sense would have it, that sexuality exists over *here*, that discourse exists over *there*, and that "putting sex into discourse" is a matter of joining the two things together. Quite the contrary: sexuality cannot exist apart from being talked about. *Sex* may be a biological given, but *sexuality* has to be verbalized. "To put sex into discourse" is, in effect, to turn sex into sexuality. Discourse involves not only what is being said (the "knowledge" in Foucault's formulation) but someone saying that something to someone else to produce some effect ("power"). By "discourse," then, Foucault means not so much a set of written documents, a body of texts, as a social process: it is people talking to people, in a variety of situations, for a variety of purposes. Talking about sex, in person or in print, is no different from talking about anything else: it is a means of informing other people but also of controlling other people, a means of being informed but also of being controlled. For Foucault, sexual discourse is finally a political phenomenon.

> Indeed, it is in discourse that power and knowledge are joined together. And for this very reason, we must conceive discourse as a series of discontinuous segments whose tactical function is neither uniform nor stable. To be more precise, we must not imagine a world of discourse divided into accepted discourse and excluded discourse, or between the dominant discourse and the dominated one; but as a multiplicity of discursive elements that can come into play in various strategies.

These "strategies" vary "according to who is speaking, his position of power, [and] the institutional context in which he happens to be situated."[10] That is to say, whenever we examine discourse about sex, we need to be clear about who is speaking to whom, and under what circumstances. Foucault never makes the point explicit, but discourse about sex can also be a person "speaking" to himself. Witness Forman in his private journal. For an individual, sexuality is the interpenetration of external social controls with internal experience.

To think in such terms about sexuality in general is to raise serious questions about "homosexuality" in particular. *Is* there such a thing? Is homosexuality a biological or psychological type, a predisposition that exists and has existed in all times and in all places, or is it a cultural variable that may be specific to our own time and place? Is homosexuality something that is essentially *there*, in the body, in the mind, or is it socially constructed? Concerning this particular version of the nature/nurture debate writers have tended to come down on one side or the other, often without thinking through the alternative. John Boswell distinguishes three types of "sexual taxonomy": Type A, which takes all humans to be "polymorphously sexual"; Type B, which defines "two or more sexual categories, usually but not always, based on sexual object choice, to which all humans belong"; and Type C, which makes "one type of sexual response normal (or 'natural' or 'moral' or all three) and all other variants abnormal ('unnatural,' 'immoral')."[11] By taking sexual object choice as the key category in human sexuality, an "essentialist" like Vern Bullough can write the history of homosexuality as the history of changing attitudes to an unchanging type of behavior.[12] By assuming, on the other hand, that human sexuality is polymorphous, a matter of potentialities that different cultures define and direct in different ways, "social constructionists" like Foucault, Jonathan Katz, Jeffrey Weeks, David M. Halperin, Robert Padgug, and David F. Greenberg maintain that sexual behavior itself, and not just attitudes toward it, is a cultural artifact.[13] Between the essentialists and the constructionists Boswell defines his own position as middling. Distinctions between one person and another based on the sexual objects they choose—men who prefer older women, women who prefer fat men, men who prefer other men—can be recognized and talked about in a society, even if those distinctions do not operate as major categories of social definition. Hence, Boswell can speak confidently of a "gay" identity in the Middle Ages.[14]

Strict social constructionists like Foucault, Halperin, and Padgug would argue that "sexuality" as a category of experience is itself a cultural construct specific to our own time and place. For us, sexual activity is a psychological and sociological phenomenon. That has not always been the case. Psychology and sociology are, after all, structures of knowledge that have been erected in the twentieth century. It was only in the eighteenth century, Foucault proposes, that sexual behavior became the subject of "scientific" inquiry that it remains for us today. In Greek and Roman antiquity sexuality had been largely an ethical concern; in the Middle Ages, a moral concern. Moral and ethical considerations still figure, of course, in our own ideas about sexual behavior, if not about sexuality as a subject of scientific inquiry, but those considerations are complicated by all the ways sex has been thought about—so obsessively thought about—during the past two hundred years: during the nineteenth century as an organic phenomenon, as a concern for biology and medicine, and, before that, during the Age of Reason as a technical, demographic, economic, and political concern.[15] "Sexuality" as a construct involves all these things. With respect to sexual behavior, as to so much else, the Renaissance was a period of transition, a time when sex as a moral preoccupation was changing into sex as a subject for self-reflection and intellectual analysis.

On one particular point of knowledge we need to be absolutely clear: in the sixteenth and seventeenth centuries, sexuality was not, as it is for us, the starting place for anyone's self-defini-tion. Just because sexuality has become an obsessive concern in our own culture does not mean that it has always been so. In early modern England, as in many non-Western cultures today, sexual activity occupied a radically different position than it does for us relative to all the other activities a person pursues, to other social ties, to other ways of thinking about things in gen-eral. No one in Shakespeare's day would have labeled himself a "homosexual." The term itself is a clinical, scientific coinage of the clinical, scientific nineteenth century. "Bugger" and "sodom-ite," the closest equivalents in early modern English, do have Anglo-Saxon earthiness to recommend them, but neither has much exactitude, since "buggery" was also used to refer to besti-ality and "sodomy" could cover a variety of heterosexual acts—as Mrs. Hipwell's experiences attest. For individuals and their self-identity this definition, or lack of definition, had enormous consequences. In his study of *Homosexuality in Renaissance En-gland* Alan Bray puts the case as strongly as possible:

> To talk of an individual in this period as being or not being "a homosexual" is an anachronism and ruinously misleading. The temptation to debauchery, from which homosexuality was not clearly distinguished, was accepted as part of the common lot, be it never so abhorred. For the Puritan writer John Rainolds, homosexuality was a sin to which "men's natural corruption and viciousness is prone"; when the governor of Plymouth col-ony, William Bradford, mused in his history of the colony why "sodomy and buggery (things fearful to name) have broke forth in this land," the first answer he gave was all-embracing: "our corrupt natures, which are so hardly bridled, subdued, and mortified."[16]

The structures of knowledge that impinged on what we would now call "homosexuality" did not ask a man who had sexual relations with another man to think of himself as fundamentally different from his peers. Just the opposite was true. Prevailing ideas asked him to castigate himself for falling into the general depravity to which *all* mankind is subject. For sixteenth- and seventeenth-century speakers of English the words "sodomy" and "buggery" sent the mind spinning toward heterodoxies of all sorts: sorcery, religious heresy, treason. Homosexual acts be-longed to the anathema of this larger whole. The essential fact about homosexuality, so Bray concludes, was that it had no place in the Elizabethan world picture. No one in England dur-ing the sixteenth or seventeenth centuries would have thought of himself as "gay" or "homosexual" for the simple reason that those categories of self-definition did not exist. But that does not mean, Boswell would interject, that there were no men in early modern England whose sexual desires were turned primarily toward other men.

To distinguish "homosexual" men from "heterosexual" men is, then, a distinctively twentieth-century way of constructing sexuality. It takes sexual desire as a point of departure for personal identity. It presupposes a sexual essence in the desiring subject. It insists on drawing distinctions according to the objects of that subject's desires. Nothing in Renaissance theology, philosophy, or jurisprudence suggests that individuals found their identity in this way. Homo*sexual behavior* may be a cross-cultural, transhistorical phenomenon; homo*sexuality* is specific to our own culture and to our own moment in history. Learning to unthink "homosexuality" as a subject of inquiry and "homosexual" as a type of person has several implications for a book like this one. If, first of all, we deconstruct "homosexuality" as a concept, we are forced to search out the other ideologies that formerly gave sexual behavior a vocabulary, a syntax, and a logic. If homosexual activity was not thought about in terms of biology or medicine or psychology, to what categories of knowledge *did* it belong? Second, if there was no such thing in early modern England as a "homosexual," we must question how useful it is to read the history of homosexual behavior in early modern England as the oppression of a sexual minority. Such a model not only overvalues the importance of sex; it may very well blind us to ways in which homosexual behavior served to empower certain men, not victimize them.

How *did* men who happened to desire other men fit into a social structure that defined personal identity in terms other than sexual desire? Gay criticism, Eve Sedgwick maintains, has yet to learn one important heuristic lesson from recent feminist criticism: oppression in a society is structured in different dimensions that intersect in complicated ways. A given individual can be oppressed in one dimension and yet privileged in another.[17] To contradict the title of a recent collection of historical essays, homosexuality is not so much hidden *from* history as hidden *in* history.[18] Until it acquired a definition and a name in the late nineteenth century, homosexuality was not something that had to be masked or covered up. Before it could become classified information, the love that dares not speak its name first of all had to *have* a name. When we try to search out the social reality of homosexuality before the end of the nineteenth century, what we discover is not a dirty secret that has been covered up by a polite fiction but something that has been there in front of us all along, like the figure that lurks within the tangled lines of a puzzle picture in a child's book. To see the pattern we have to know, first of all, what to look for. To decipher the message we have to know the code.

Foucault's model of how sex is "put into discourse" points us to the two things we need to look for: "knowledge" and "power." Concerning "knowledge," the French language allows Foucault to make an important distinction that is sometimes lost in Robert Hurley's English translation. The "special knowledges" that Foucault speaks of in connection with bodily pleasure, controls and resistances, and talk about sex are *connaissances*, knowledge in the sense of acquaintance, familiarity, experience. (Compare our borrowed term *connoisseur*.) The knowledge that Foucault allies with power is, on the other hand, *savoir*, knowledge in the sense of learning, erudition, ideas.[19] In Foucault's formulation, experience (*connaissances*) is a function of ideology (*savoir*). The experience of sexual desire at a given moment in history is shaped by the ideas that people happen to entertain at that historical moment. To avoid confusing these two different senses of knowledge, we should perhaps prefer the term "ideology" as a coordinate with power.

"Ideology" is one aspect of sex put into discourse; "power" is the other. The power implicit in a text is ideology put into action. It is a speaker exerting control over a listener, a writer exerting control over a reader. It is a listener or a reader internalizing the text and exerting control over himself. Power, in Foucault's view, is not just a matter of negative prohibitions, a central authority telling people what they may and may not do, what they may and may not feel. Power is also a matter of positive excitations: it is people, situations, and objects that a particular culture endows with erotic value. That is to say, sexuality is not simply *subject* to power; it *manifests* power. To understand homosexuality in early modern England we need to investigate not just what was prohibited but what was actively homoeroticized. What we discover is a startling ambiguity. The one salient fact about homosexuality in early modern England, as in early modern Europe generally, is the disparity that separates the extreme punishments prescribed by law and the apparent tolerance, even positive valuation, of homoerotic desire in the visual arts, in literature, and, I shall argue, in the political power structure. What are we to make of a culture that could consume popular prints of Apollo embracing Hyacinth and yet could order hanging for men who acted on the very feelings that inspire that embrace?

The importance of what Foucault calls the "institutional context"—who is speaking to whom, and under what circumstances—can be witnessed in two documents from the pen of King James I. In *Basilicon Doron*, the twice-published treatise (1599 and 1603) on right rulership he wrote for Prince Henry, James lists sodomy along with witchcraft, murder, incest, poisonings, and counterfeiting of currency as "horrible crimes that ye are bound in conscience never to forgive."[20] In a private letter to George Villiers, sometime royal cupbearer and afterwards Duke of Buckingham, James takes a rather milder line on the subject:

> I cannot content myself without sending you this present [letter], praying God that I may have a joyful and comfortable meeting with you and that we may make at this Christmas a new marriage ever to be kept hereafter; for, God so love me, as I desire only to live in this world for your sake, and that I had rather live banished in any part of the earth with you than live a sorrowful widow's life without you. And so God bless you, my sweet child and wife, and grant that ye may ever be a comfort to your dear dad and husband."[21]

In discourse about sex, context is all.

The example of King James and the evidence of Renaissance poetry should warn us that, if we are to see desire whole, we must discriminate among various *kinds* of discourse about homosexuality. Legal discourse about homosexuality, what Foucault calls "juridico-political discourse," is only one way of joining together ideology and power—and only one kind of ideology with one kind of power, at that. Moral discourse about homosexuality presents another configuration of another kind of ideology with another kind of power. Foucault's own concern in volumes 2, 3, and 4 of his *History of Sexuality* is with moral discourse, with "conduct books" that consider what one ought or ought not do and why. Particularly in the Roman and Hellenistic texts that Foucault considers, the "why" of moral discourse is usually founded on yet another way of talking about sexual behavior: medical discourse. A similar merging of the moral and the medical is to be found in the books of advice that famous doctors in eary modern Europe wrote for other doctors and for general readers concerned about good health.

There is, however, a fourth way of talking about sexual desire, a fourth configuration of ideology and power that Foucault and most other social historians have distrusted: the kind of discourse we are used to calling "literary," "poetic," "imaginative," or "fictional." Consider Simon Forman's dream about Queen Elizabeth. Readers of *The Faerie Queene* will appreciate how it is not just Elizabethan structures of power and Elizabethan structures of ideology that have shaped Forman's sexual imaginings but Elizabethan patterns of storytelling as well. At one level the scenario of Forman's dream perhaps reflects the literal fact that on Sundays and holidays couples went strolling in the fields north of London—hence the crowds of people that the dreamer encounters—and that walled gardens near the edge of the city were notorious trysting places.[22] At another level, however, it puts the dreamer into one of the great Elizabethan fictions, casting him as the questing knight of neomedieval romance who rescues virtuous damsel from villainous dastard. A lover thinks of himself and his beloved in terms of certain fictional roles; the two of them play out those roles in certain fictional plots; those fictional plots move toward certain expected endings.

We miss this imaginative dimension to sexual experience if all we attend to is moral discourse, legal discourse, and medical discourse, with their narrow interest in sex as a physical act. Clearly, there is more to Simon Forman's dream than adultery (as moral discourse would have it), treasonous assault (as legal discourse would have it), and phallic pleasure (as medical discourse would have it). Sexual acts are acts of the imagination as well as acts of the body. They function as symbolic discourse. The ideologies of moral philosophy, law, and medicine can tell us about particular elements of Simon Forman's dream, but they cannot give us a sense of the whole. Above all, they cannot tell us much about the dream as *Simon Forman's* dream. What did the dream mean to the dreamer? Why did the moral, legal, and psychic elements come together, for him, in just this way? About such questions *The Faerie Queene* can tell us more than the Ten Commandments, the common law, and Freud's *Interpretation of Dreams*. *The Faerie Queene* provides a narrative that gives voice and image to ideology and power.

Sexual behavior is *scripted* behavior. For most people, even sophisticated Freudians, "the assembly of bodies in time and space" remains the defining characteristic of sex. The physical facts of sex are used to judge virtue versus vice, legality versus illegality, health versus sickness. What is missing in this view,

John H. Gagnon and William Simon observe, is the subjective content of sexual activity, what it means to the people who are doing it. With their concept of sexual "scripts" Gagnon and Simon find just such a way of coordinating bodies and meanings. Looked at in one way, a script for a sexual encounter is an external, impersonal matter, "the organization of mutually shared conventions that allows two or more actors to participate in a complex act involving mutual dependence." Looked at in another way, it is an internal, intrapsychic matter, the result of how those socially shared conventions have been selected, elaborated, and personalized by each participant in the encounter. Sexual scripts are the point at which individual experience intersects with social coordinates. Gagnon and Simon go so far as to say that it is sexual scripts that dictate sexual desire and not the other way around. Neurochemistry may cause sexual arousal at the image of a partner; everything that happens after that is culturally scripted in one way or another. That is not to say, however, that culture is in complete control of what happens, how it feels, and what it means. Gagnon and Simon distinguish three "levels" of scripts, ranged according to the greater or lesser degree that they involve other people and the greater or lesser degree that they incorporate individual imagination. "Cultural scenarios" are shared by everyone in a particular culture, and in tightly organized traditional societies they may constitute all that happens and all that is felt in most sexual encounters. The more complex and diversified a society, the greater the possibility for "interpersonal scripts" in which the social actor becomes a partial scriptwriter who selects and adapts cultural scenarios to fit his own situation. At the most personal level there are "intrapsychic scripts," private fantasies that reorganize reality in ways to satisfy the individual's "many-layered and sometimes multivoiced wishes." As an individual plays them out in imagination, intrapsychic scripts seem to come from the deepest self, but even here cultural scripting is at work, particularly as an individual gives play to conflicting desires and to wishes that cannot readily be accommodated in cultural scenarios or in interpersonal scripts.[23]

The mode of discourse that gives us most intimate access to these scripts of sexual desire is not moral, legal, or medical, but literary. There are two reasons why. First, literary discourse, unlike moral, legal, or medical discourse, does not have to be logical and consistent. Fiction is able, in Wolfgang Iser's phrase, to show "the simultaneity of the mutually exclusive." In fiction, as in dreams, logically separate experiences can be "bracketed to-gether" for the space and time of the fiction in a way they can-not be in everyday life—or in the logically rigorous confines of moral, legal, and medical discourse. Fiction is uniquely fitted to address the contradictions that must be covered up to make or-dinary life possible. Second, literary discourse involves a power relationship between speaker and listener that is far more com-plicated than in other modes of putting sex into discourse. In legal discourse, as in moral discourse and medical discourse, the writer speaks from a position of complete authority. The reader's role is assumed to be one of passive acquiescence. In fictional discourse, "authority" is not so absolute: in creating a hypothetical imaginary reality author and reader are, in a sense, *collaborators*. Between them power is constantly being renegoti-ated, as the writer keeps offering new details of the hypothetical world he is constructing, as the reader draws on his own experi-ence to amplify those details and gives or withholds his imagi-native assent. In a word, fiction making is a *performative* act in which the reader or the listener is as much a participant as the author.[24] Since the making of fictions and the enjoying of fictions in early modern England were far from being limited to the writ-ten word, "poetic" is perhaps a better name for this kind of discourse than "literary." "Poesy" is the term that Sir Philip Sid-ney uses to denote what men create when they make a thing out of language, whether they do it in writing (lyric poems, prose narratives, epic verse), in oral speech (ballads), or in something in between (drama on the public stage).[25]

The four kinds of discourse about homosexuality—moral, legal, medical, and poetic—in fact address different subjects en-tirely. Moral, legal, and medical discourse are concerned with sexual *acts*; only poetic discourse can address homosexual *de-sire*.[26] And it is with the fact of homosexual desire that I begin. Questions of etiology, questions about what "causes" homosexu-ality, are beyond my frame of reference here just as they are beyond my competence to answer. Instead, I assume, along with Michael Ruse in *Homosexuality: A Philosophical Investigation*, (1) that homosexual *acts* occur in all cultures and that what varies is the interpretation that different cultures put on those acts; (2) that homosexual *desire* exists in all cultures, that people every-where do, on some occasions, in some way or another, feel sex-ual desire for members of their own biological sex; and (3) that the intensity and frequency of homosexual desire may vary from individual to individual, but that in every culture there are some people whose sexual desire is *exclusively* homosexual.[27] All three of Ruse's assumptions seem to be borne out by David F. Greenberg's encyclopedic survey of cultures in *The Construction of Homosexuality*.[28] By accepting Ruse's points simply as demographic *givens* we can avoid either extreme of the essentialist/constructionist controversy and so negotiate the Scylla and Charybdis that has obstructed academic discourse about homosexuality.

"The crime that ought not to be named among men": when writers of moral discourse use such circumlocutions, we should not necessarily assume, as Bray for example does, that they had only a vague sense of what they were talking about. What is *not* said can be just as exact as what *is* said. William Bradford called sodomy and buggery "things fearful to name"—but name them he did. In order not to say something one has to have a precise sense of what that thing is. "Sodomy" is an action; it can be observed from the outside; it can easily be labeled. Homosexual desire is a feeling; it can be known only from the inside; it needs to be talked about, not simply named. About the physical act of sodomy sixteenth- and seventeenth-century writers could speak in direct, increasingly exact legal terms. "Sodomy" is a topic in moral, legal, and medical discourse; homosexual desire is a subject that only poetic discourse can express. Throughout this book I shall maintain this distinction between acts and feelings, between "sodomy" and homosexual desire, because I believe it is crucial to understanding homosexual behavior in any society, early modern England included, that stigmatizes homosexual acts. For the same reason I shall not be using the term "gay." However old or new the word may be (*gai* in Middle English could denote anyone, male or female, whose behavior was morally unconventional), "gay" is neither a physical act (recognized and named in the sixteenth and seventeenth centuries) nor a state of desire (recognized and acted upon in the sixteenth and seventeenth centuries) but a term of self-definition (current only since the nineteenth century).[29]

Connections between homosexual desire and patterns of poetic discourse are the subject of this book. If sixteenth- and seventeenth-century structures of ideology and sixteenth- and seventeenth-century structures of power shaped homosexuality in certain characteristic ways, what contribution was made by sixteenth- and seventeenth-century ways of creating fictions? In terms of theater, what *dramatis personae* could a writer draw upon? Into what plots could he project his characters and set them to interaction? What kinds of things could those characters say to each other? What distinctive images could they use to express thoughts and feelings? Toward what possible endings could characters and plots move? To put the question another way, what were the "love games" that men who desired other men could play in early modern England? What were the objects of the game? What constituted the rules? From what strategies of play could a poet/lover choose? My purpose in these pages is to define the "imaginative vocabulary" that sixteenth- and seventeenth-century writers possessed for talking about homosexual desire—the repertory of character types, plot motifs, images, and themes that offered ways of conceptualizing homosexual experience and playing it out in imagination. What I hope to isolate and identify are the "myths" of Renaissance homosexuality—"myths" in the sense that Denis De Rougemont uses the term in *Love in the Western World*:

> Speaking generally, a myth is a story—a symbolical fable as simple as it is striking—which sums up an infinite number of more or less analogous situations. A myth makes it possible to become aware at a glance of certain types of *constant relations* and to disengage these from the welter of everyday appearances.[30]

In adopting De Rougemont's term I don't want to invoke all the portentous and pretentious meanings that "myth" has acquired in the past twenty-five years. What I intend is something closer to the literal meaning of the Greek *mythos*: simply, a story.

For the specific activity of fiction making, I am proposing something like the concept that Pierre Bourdieu has formulated for social practices in general. *Habitus* is Bourdieu's coinage for the range of "strategies" open to actors in a given situation, the "dispositions" social subjects have to act in certain ways but not in others, the collective "matrix of perceptions, appreciations, and actions" within which individuals improvise behavior. The point of mediation between material reality and internal consciousness, *habitus* is not a matter of "laws" or "rules" of behavior such as a structural anthropologist might infer, but of possible "schemes of action" that have been so internalized that actors in a given culture seldom or never think about them consciously. In Bourdieu's elegant phrase, *habitus* is "history turned into nature." *Delimited* by past choices, but not *determined* by them, present choices of action become part of a society's accumulated store of experience and thus help to define the range of future choices. *Re* structuring, as well as structuring of experience, is constantly going on. To Renaissance makers of fiction Bourdieu's concept of *habitus* holds out a "conditioned and conditional freedom." To postmodernist writers of social history it offers a handy way out of three modernist dilemmas: the objective/subjective dichotomy in models of social science in general, the question of base/superstructure interaction in Marxist theory, and the problem of accounting for where change comes from in structuralism.[31]

Where Denis De Rougemont sees only one myth, the story of Tristan and Isolde, as the archetype that focuses the conflicting perspectives on love among European writers and readers, I have isolated six separate myths of homosexual desire, each of which involves a different combination of characters and plot, a different set of ideas about sodomy, a different way of enacting homosexual desire in imagination. Though Renaissance moralists saw only Chaos beyond the perfectly ordered heterosexual world of Christian dogma, classical literature offered a range of myths and literary modes for articulating homosexual desire. In identifying each of the six myths with a particular classical text I want to emphasize the complex interplay between ancient and modern in Renaissance culture. Every literary text represents an accumulation of what has been written and thought before. So with the classical texts I cite. Unlike ancient statues, buried beneath the rubble of Rome, the texts themselves were not, on the whole, fresh discoveries of Renaissance writers: many of them had remained well known during the Middle Ages. What *was* fresh was what Renaissance writers discovered they could do with those texts. Each is a repository of centuries of experience—experience that could be used to express a modern writer's own sexual desires. None of the six texts was esoteric knowledge. They were the common possession of all educated persons in the sixteenth and seventeenth centuries. Like other aspects of Greek and Roman culture, the myths contained in these texts interested Renaissance writers and readers less as documents of a vanished civilization than as ways of giving shape and meaning to their own concerns. These texts spoke to Renaissance writers and readers, not from the outside, but from within. In the uses to which Renaissance writers put the six myths we encounter, then, not a one-way influence of ancient texts on modern experience, but a dialectic between the two.

In Foucault's terms, each of these six myths represents a different intersection of structures of ideology with structures of power. As we move from one myth to another we can observe changes in how the "energies" of power and ideology come together, and how those energies shape and are shaped by a conventional set of characters, speeches, and plots. Sexuality, after all, is something that happens between people. It is not a thing but a process. Robert Padgug speaks for Foucault and other social constructionists when he insists that

> sexuality is relational. It consists of activity and interactions—active social relations—and not simply "acts," as if sexuality were the enumeration and typology of an individual's orgasms (as it sometimes appears to be conceived of in, for example, the work of Kinsey and others), a position which puts the emphasis back within the individual alone. "It" does not do anything, combine with anything, appear anywhere; only people, acting within specific relationships create what we call sexuality.[32]

In Gagnon and Simon's terms, each of the six myths that I have isolated constitutes a "cultural scenario" for acting upon homosexual desire. Within these six scenarios, shared by all educated Englishmen, each individual writer can be seen as an adaptor, as the author of one particular "interpersonal script" for himself and his readers. Only in Shakespeare's sonnets do we encounter, perhaps, instances of the "intrapsychic scripts" that Gagnon and Simon see as the most private, most idiosyncratic transmutations of cultural scenarios.

Each of the six myths articulates one particular dimension of the social structure in early modern England; each plays out one particular dynamic of social interaction. Inescapably, the social relations in a culture's constructions of sexuality replicate social relations in that culture at large. To understand homosexuality in early modern England we need to search out, then, not only the dramatic content of sexual experience but the social sites of that experience. The sites of sexuality in early modern Europe are not necessarily ones that would come to mind today. For us, the most significant loci of sexuality are private life and the family. It was during the sixteenth and seventeenth centuries that sexuality first came to be seen as a private concern, but sexuality was located even more solidly within social institutions that strike us today as remote or inappropriate. Each of the six myths that I have identified here is situated within one of these social institutions: within the male power structure in general, within educational establishments, within festival occasions, within religion, within social class, within private life. Only the last is likely to have an immediate connection with our own experience. The relationship that I am suggesting between myth and social structure is in each case an *homology*: the myth enacts in symbolic terms what the relevant social institution fosters in actual behavior.[33]

In addition to its alliances with a particular structure of power, each myth has affinities with a particular structure of ideology: moral, legal, or medical. The relationship among these four modes of discourse was then, and remains today, anything but simple. To assume, as some modernist critics have done, that "official" discourse—moral, legal, and medical—is always in control of poetic discourse is, surely, just as naive as to assume that poets are the unacknowledged legislators of mankind.[34] Rather than dictating or being dictated to, poetic discourse more often *mediates* between the official ideal and the quotidian real. Renaissance critics like Sidney seem to be saying as much when they place poesy midway between the ideal prescriptions of philosophy and the untidy facts of history. Fiction, in this view, is philosophy brought down to earth and history transfigured by philosophy.[35] The function of ideology, Marx argues, is to conceal contradictions and to present a falsely coherent account of how things are.[36] Poetic discourse, I believe, can—under certain conditions, at least—address those contradictions. It is in the nature of moral, legal, and medical discourse to deny contradictions by deciding alternatives one way or the other; poetic discourse need not be so dogmatic.

Each of the six myths of homosexual desire is allotted a separate chapter. Chapter 2, "Combatants and Comrades," is an attempt to read homosexuality in early modern England as one of many indices of male bonding in a society that was rigidly segregated by gender and radically patriarchal in its disposition of power. "Combatants and Comrades" takes up the matter of legal discourse and the, to us, baffling disparity between homosexual acts as proscribed by law and homosexual desire as inscribed by literary texts. Structural distinctions according to gender are replaced by distinctions according to age in chapter 3, "The Passionate Shepherd." Sixteenth-century medical discourse about sexual behavior, particularly the sexual behavior of adolescents, helps us to situate homosexuality in the educational settings that nurtured boys into men. The holiday festivals and literary genres that functioned as licensed occasions for playing about with gender roles and sexual roles are the subject of chapter 4, "The Shipwrecked Youth." There we shall take stock of the forms of androgyny that Renaissance Englishmen read about in romance narratives, applauded in plays like *Twelfth Night*, and knew firsthand in St. George plays, May Day festivals, morris dancing, and Christmas mummings. The border between licit and illicit is crossed in chapter 5. Fired by moral discourse about sexuality during antiquity and the Middle Ages as well as during the Renaissance itself, "Knights in Shifts" summons up for critical scrutiny the lecherous lords and lascivious lads, the drag queens and hermaphrodites lambasted in verse satire, epigrams, and stage comedy. Satire speaks for institutionalized morality, for church dogma and the secular legal code that increasingly was replacing it. Chapter 6, "Master and Minion," addresses the explicit disparities in power that animated homosexual desire in early modern England—disparities in social class, in political power, in the latitude that individuals had for being different. Christopher Marlowe's stage versions of the Myth of Master and Minion show us for the first time in the book the beginnings of a specifically homosexual subjectivity. Through Shakespeare's sonnets the final chapter, "The Secret Sharer," takes up this question of subjectivity and pursues the poet and his beloved as they move beyond the expression of desire into sexual consummation—and into emotional and artistic territory that was largely unmapped before Shakespeare.

The progression of myths from chapter 2 to chapter 7 defines several larger thematic progressions. The most basic one is mimetic. Just what aspect or aspects of sexual desire does each myth depict? In tracing an escalation from sentiment to passion, from metaphors of male bonding to the physical realities of sexual union, the six chapters follow the basic "plot" of human sexual activity. However much the meaning of sexual acts may change from culture to culture, the physiological properties of those acts, what can be observed from the outside, remain the same. On this basis, Masters and Johnson have distinguished four "phases" of human sexual response: excitement, plateau, orgasm, and resolution.[37] As arranged here, the six myths replicate this "cycle." In anthropological terms, the progression from codes of male bonding in chapter 2 to the physical and emotional mutuality of Shakespeare's sonnets in chapter 7 shows us the transformation of a universal feature of human society into one that seems quite specific to its place and time. In chronological terms, this shift from the general fact of male bonding to the particular case of a poet/lover who struggles to read his experience in the idiom of heterosexual love is a move from manifestations of homosexuality that are as old as western civilization to a manifestation that seems distinctively modern. In social terms, the six chapters describe a shift in ways of acting on desire that changes from licit to illicit, from socially inclusive to socially elite, from public to private. In psychological terms, the shift from public to private traces a passage from conscious, carefully controlled ways of expressing same-sex sexuality to ways so probing that they call the writer's self-identity into question. In artistic terms, finally, the book's six remaining chapters map out a journey from well-traveled paths of literary expression toward imaginatively uncharted territory. Stories of male friendship in chapter 2, pastoral fantasies in chapter 3, romance narratives in chapter 4, and verse satires in chapter 5 offered Renaissance writers ready ways of putting sex into discourse; Marlowe in his plays and Shakespeare in his sonnets struggle within and against existing genres in giving homosexual desire a voice. With certain of Marlowe's stage heroes and with the speaker of Shakespeare's sonnets, the fictional character who feels homosexual desire, and acts on it, has changed from "he" to "I." Out of conventions that portray homosexual desire from the outside—as somebody else's feelings—Marlowe and Shakespeare create a homosexual subjectivity.

The "mythic" approach I have adopted to homosexuality in early modern England differs, I believe, from other books on the subject and avoids, I hope, some of the pitfalls that await writers in a field so little explored and so explosively political. Writers about homosexuality have tended to treat literary texts in one of three ways. Documents of social history, first of all, are what Alan Bray seeks in *Homosexuality in Renaissance England*, James M. Saslow in "Homosexuality in the Renaissance: Behavior, Identity, and Artistic Expression," John Boswell in *Christianity, Social Tolerance, and Homosexuality*, and Vern Bullough in *Sexual Variance in Society and History*.[38] Prudently, all of these historians call attention to the discrepancy between the facts we know about from statistics, historical writings, court records, and letters and the visions of experience we read about in literature. Literary texts, after all, can just as well reflect what *could* be or what *ought* to be as what *is*. Indeed, Renaissance critics like Sidney would have put the stress on the former, not the latter.[39] That is not to say, however, that poetic discourse has nothing to tell us about homosexuality in early modern England. Bray makes a point of discounting "purely literary" evidence on the same grounds he uses to exclude political polemic: neither kind of writing, in Bray's view, gives us reliable information about social reality. Basing his case on court records and moral trea-

tises—literal evidence that can be taken at literal face value—
Bray admits no literary evidence except verse satire, which he
likewise takes at literal face value. Even Christopher Marlowe,
who figures prominently as a biographical personage in Bray's
book, is allowed to speak through only one poem, not through
any of his plays. Shakespeare's plays and sonnets figure not at
all. Moral treatises and verse satires may seem to speak directly
and unambiguously about sexual experience, but they speak
about it from the outside. Poems, plays, and fiction speak from
the inside: they give us imaginative access to sexuality that may
be oblique but all the more true for that.

At quite the opposite extreme from the social historians is a
second group of writers who treat literary texts primarily as psychological documents. In *The Homosexual Literary Tradition: An
Interpretation*, Rictor Norton attempts to reduce homosexuality
in all of European and American literature to a single archetype:
Hercules' loss of his minion Hylas, as recounted in Apollo-
dorus's *Argonautica*. As with all such criticism, every text turns
out to be saying the same thing. Such unlikely works as
Spenser's *The Shepheardes Calender*, Sidney's *Arcadia*, and Andrew Marvell's "The Garden" become, in Norton's view, enact-
ments of a "violent primitive initiation ritual, in which a sacred
king would abduct and rape a boy-surrogate in order to be an-
nually reborn or rejuvenated."[40] More narrowly focused and
hence far more substantial and convincing is Joseph Pequigney's
Such Is My Love: A Study of Shakespeare's Sonnets. Pequigney has
brought psychoanalytic theory to bear on close readings of
Shakespeare's sonnets, individually and in groups, to argue that
the poems chart the course of a sexually consummated love affair between the speaker and the male friend to whom the first
126 sonnets are addressed. The key to Pequigney's readings is
provided, not by social history or by biographical information,
but by the theories of Sigmund Freud: "The psychological dynamics of the poet's relations with the friend," Pequigney argues, "comply in large measure with those expounded in
Freud's authoritative discussions of homosexuality."[41] In the
standoff between essentialists and social constructionists Freud
figures as the most important and influential essentialist of them
all. He assumes that the human psyche has an existence outside
history and that human sexual development follows the same
pattern in all times and in all places. Within the limitations of
these assumptions, Pequigney does a masterful job of analyzing
Shakespeare's poems. What I have undertaken here should be

read as a complement to Pequigney's work, an approach to the same subject from the other side of the theoretical divide.

A third critical stance takes literary texts primarily as biographical documents. Nineteenth-century assumptions about the artist as hero and about the private, personal nature of poetry make this approach very hard to resist. If, however, Foucault and Bray are right that concepts of sexuality change and that "homosexual" did not exist as a category of self-definition in the Renaissance, we are asking of texts something totally anachronistic when we expect them to tell us about a particular writer's personal experience. All sorts of anomalies obstruct such a simple view of how art is related to life. Every known fact about Richard Barnfield's relatively well documented life suggests a thoroughly conventional existence of married domesticity, yet his sonnets include some of the most blatantly homoerotic imagery in all of English literature. Francis Bacon's liaisons with his male servants were unapologetically public, yet homosexuality figures not at all in Bacon's *Essays or Counsels, Civil and Moral*. Shakespeare's sonnets convince a homosexual reader that they were written by someone who knew homosexual desire from the inside, yet not a single external fact connects Shakespeare with any particular fair young man. When biographical criticism moves out of texts rather than into them, it ends up all too easily as highbrow gossip like A. L. Rowse's *Homosexuals in History*.[42] Robert K. Martin's conclusion in *The Homosexual Tradition in American Poetry* rings true: if we invoke our contemporary sense of homosexuality as a category of self-definition we have to wait until Walt Whitman for a poet who defined his own nature primarily in sexual terms and saw it

> as the source of his art, the center of his book, and the foundation of his political theory. Prior to Whitman there were homosexual acts but no homosexuals. Whitman coincides with and defines a radical change in historical consciousness: the self-conscious awareness of homosexuality as an identity. "Calamus" is the heart of *Leaves of Grass*, as well as the root; it is Whitman's book of self-proclamation and self-definition.[43]

To label even Whitman the first "gay" poet is perhaps to speak too soon. Whitman did, after all, bowdlerize his own poems in later editions, excising whole passages, making the gender of his subjects ambiguous, putting poeticized fig leaves over graphic images of homosexual acts. Perhaps it is not until very recently indeed, until Allen Ginsberg and Thom Gunn, that we find poets whose verse unapologetically portrays the writer as gay.

To ask of English poetic texts of the sixteenth and seventeenth centuries what they can tell us about homosexuality in early modern England is, in a way, to play the role of an anthropologist putting the same question to the inhabitants of a remote Pacific island. In both cases we need to remind ourselves that it is we, not our subjects, who are doing the asking and that, inescapably, we have our own agenda, our own reasons for posing these particular questions and not others. *We* are imbedded in a social historical moment no less than our sixteenth- and seventeenth-century subjects were: we are historical subjects writing and reading about historical subjects, and we need to acknowledge that fact.[44] Let us stop, then, and clarify why I have written this book and, perhaps, why you are reading it. *Homosexual Desire in Shakespeare's England* is literary criticism. It is social history. It is a political tract. As a piece of literary criticism, this book incorporates ways of reading, teaching, and writing about literature that were current—fashionable might be a better word—in American universities at the time it was written. To that extent it might be seen as an exercise in the New Historicism.[45] As an essay in social history, this book takes its place among several recent studies of human sexuality in particular times and particular places.[46] But *Homosexual Desire in Shakespeare's England* also has a political purpose: it is an attempt to consolidate gay identity in the last decade of the twentieth century, to help men whose sexual desire is turned toward other men realize that they have not only a present community but a past history. In pursuing these three purposes I have not so much followed a particular literary theory as attempted to *find* one.

The task of improvising a theory that answers the needs of literary criticism, social history, and a political program is just the intellectual challenge that feminist critics have been struggling with for the past twenty years. The questions I am posing here would be, quite literally, unthinkable without their example. It is all the more ironic, then, that sexual desire of women for women is absent from these pages. There are three reasons why. Factual documents about male homosexuality in Renaissance England are few enough; documents about female homosexuality are virtually nonexistent. With a few notable exceptions like "Sapho to Philaenis," sometimes ascribed to Donne, and the cavorting nymphs in Spenser's Bower of Bliss, the literary evidence, too, is almost totally concerned with men. That is not surprising when we consider the third reason why lesbians seem invisible to historical scrutiny: the fact that "Elizabethan" England was a male-dominated culture. Even the epithet "Virgin Queen" shows us how women in the sixteenth century were compelled to find their identity, at least their social and literary identity, only vis-à-vis men. However brilliant Elizabeth may have been in turning her virginity into political capital, female virginity had cachet in the first place only because men made it a token of exchange among themselves, a validation of their status among other men.[47] With astonishingly few exceptions the literature of Renaissance England is a series of books written by men to men about men. If, in these texts, female sexuality in general has only a peripheral place, lesbianism seems almost beyond notice.[48] In the Renaissance view, shortsighted as it was in this respect, the subject of human sexuality was by and large the subject of male sexuality. Sexuality was so totally defined in male terms that males could not imagine sexual activity that excluded them. As one anonymous poet put it,

> Were kisses all the joyes in bed,
> One Woman would another wed.[49]

A history of lesbian desire in Renaissance England would be very different from what is described in this book, since women lived in such a different relationship to the ideology and the power structure of Elizabethan and Jacobean society.

In sharp contrast to the feminist concern with rewriting literary history and revising the list of "great books," studying literary discourse about male homosexuality does not entail searching out texts that were obscure at the time they were written or that have been neglected by readers since then. With very few exceptions, the texts I shall be discussing were, in social terms, "privileged" texts in their own time and have remained so, in critical terms, for the past four hundred years. Most of them were, and have remained, "canonical." The story that we shall be following is not, then, a political fable about an autocratic central authority that kept books about homosexual desire safe on the cultural margin or cast them onto the public bonfire. Quite the contrary. Most of the texts I shall be studying were popular books. They were central to Elizabethan and Jacobean society's self-definition.

My three concerns, literary, historical, and political, will, I imagine, speak to three different audiences: to literary scholars, to social historians, and to gay readers. Let me plead with these three kinds of readers to be patient with one another's interests and needs. Literary scholars, for instance, may sometimes find more than they need here in the way of straightforward description of texts little read nowadays by anybody but scholars. Readers interested mainly in social history may find themselves being asked to give literary evidence more weight than they usually do. Gay readers may encounter moments when questions of theory and interpretation seem more important than politics. I hope that these three kinds of readers are not mutually exclusive and that, after reading *Homosexual Desire in Shakespeare's England*, they might have learned something from each other and about each other. In every chapter I have tried to do three things: (1) to connect my own ideas with as much existing theory, factual research, and literary criticism as possible; (2) to explain this theory, research, and criticism in terms that readers who are not academic specialists can understand; and (3) on points of controversy, to survey the full range of arguments and explanations that have been offered, without necessarily accepting one as definitive. In that way, I hope, readers may be in a position to make up their own minds.

You have in hand here, then, a new subject, but a fundamentally old-fashioned book. I assume that people read literature of the past to enhance their lives in the present, not just to exercise their intellects in a particular literary or historical or political theory. I have attempted to open up the texts I discuss to some of the interests of our own age while keeping constantly aware how different our circumstances are from the people who wrote those texts and the people who read them when they were new. To emphasize the dissimilarities between early modern writers and readers and our postmodern selves is not to deny the significance of the ways of experiencing sexual desire that await us in English Renaissance literature. It warns us, however, to heed Ovid's tale of Narcissus when we approach this particular rivulet of Hippocrene. Let us delight in what we find not so much because it reflects our own self-image as because it invites us to look at that image in new ways. We should come away, like the Elizabethan voyagers, possessed of a wider world in which imagination can play.

CHAPTER TWO

COMBATANTS AND COMRADES

Touching the friendshippe betwixt Pirithous and [Theseus], it is sayed it beganne thus. The renowne of [Theseus's] valliancy was marvelously blowen abroade through all Grece, and Pirithous desirous to knowe it by experience, went even of purpose to invade his countrye, and brought awaye a certaine bootie of oxen of his taken out of the countrye of Marathon. Theseus being advertised therof, armed straight, and went to the rescue. Pirithous hearing of his comming, fled not at all, but returned backe sodainly to mete him. And so sone as they came to see one another, they both wondred at eche others beawtie and corage, and so had they no desire to fight. But Pirithous reaching out his hande first to Theseus, sayed unto him. ["]I make your selfe judge of the damage you have susteined by my invasion, and with all my harte I will make suche satisfaction, as it shall please you to assesse it at.["] Theseus then dyd not only release him, of all the damages he had done, but also requested him he would become his friend, and brother in armes. Here upon they were presently sworne brethren in the field.[1]

The twelfth Joye of maryage for to say
Is whan a yonge man by many a day
In suche a maner comen hath and gone
That he in to the lepe hath founde anone
The streyght entre/and also ferthermore
He hath her founde whome he demaunded fore
And he some other myght percas haue had
But for no thynge he wolde/and he is glad
Or this/for as hym semeth he,hath sete
His loue so wele/that no man coude do bete
And that he was so happy her to fynde
Whiche so good is/and mete bnto his mynde
And peraduenture suche a man is he

The Twelfth "Joy" of Marriage
from Antoine de La Sale, *The fyftene Joyes of Maryage*
(London: Wynkyn de Worde, 1509)

The question confronting a young man at sexual maturity in Shakespeare's day was not, am I heterosexual or am I homosexual, but where do my greater emotional loyalties lie, with other men or with women.

Plutarch's story about how a pair of arch enemies became fast friends reconciles two conflicting traits that anthropologists have observed among human males in cultures all over the world: the tendency of human males to be aggressive toward other males and, at the same time, to form strong bonds with them. The "corage" that has made Theseus and Pirithous rivals is the very thing that makes them friends. Plutarch's own word is *he tolma*, "daring," "nerve," "boldness" that shades into a pejorative suggestion of "*over* boldness," even "recklessness." What Theseus and Pirithous admire in each other is physical aggressiveness, not passive fortitude. For 99 percent of its history as a species, *homo sapiens* has been directly involved in hunting for sustenance; for 100 percent of its history, *homo sapiens* has been forming itself into social groups, marking off territory, and defending that group-space from other members of the species. Superior physical strength equips males for these two basic activities, and carrying them out together, with other males, is more effective than carrying them out alone. Whether or not we go as far as Lionel Tiger and see male bonding as a biological given, as a "genetically programmed behavioral predisposition," homosociality as a cultural phenomenon is universal. All-male clubs are the functional equivalent in modern societies of hunting and defense in primitive societies. Sports teams and fraternities are only the most obvious instances of male exclusiveness that embraced, until very recently, military units, political assemblies, educational institutions, and business and professional organizations.[2] It is not only each other's "corage" that Pirithous and Theseus admire, moreover, but each other's "beawtie." *To kallos*, whatever metaphorical suggestion it may have, is first and foremost beauty of the body, and Sir Thomas North, Plutarch's sixteenth-century translator, has not labored to find an English word with a less erotic charge. Plutarch, quite literally, "valorizes" the male body.

Plutarch's scene of reconciliation is restaged, in the same erotic terms, in Shakespeare's *Coriolanus*. The Rome of *Coriolanus* is a fiercely masculine world. Only four female characters have speaking parts in the play. Of these four, only Volumnia makes any impression whatsoever, and she behaves with a thoroughly man-like directness that, on the political front at least, contrasts sharply with the vacillation of her son.[3] War and politics: these two manifestations of male aggression are, indeed, the whole subject of the last of Shakespeare's Roman plays. When Caius

Marcius, fighting the battle with the Cariolans that earns him his cognomen, intercepts the consul Cominius in retreat, he uses the rhetoric of sexual consummation to describe male combat:

> O, let me clip ye
> In arms as sound as when I wooed, in heart
> As merry as when our nuptial day was done,
> And tapers burnt to bedward!

"Flower of warriors!" Cominius exclaims.[4] Fired by Marcius's rhetoric, the consul and his troops rejoin the battle and fight on to a Roman victory.

We remember this passionate moment later in the play when Coriolanus, his political career in shambles, goes over to the enemy camp in disguise and finds his way to his archenemy, Aufidius. Throwing off his beggar's garb, Coriolanus offers himself and his services to the very man he so often has tried to kill. The two of them reenact Plutarch's story of Theseus reconciled with Pirithous. Astounded, Aufidius does more than extend a hand to his sometime enemy; he opens his arms.

> Let me twine
> Mine arms about that body whereagainst
> My grainèd ash an hundred times hath broke,
> And scarred the moon with splinters.
> (*He embraces Coriolanus*)
> Here I clip
> The anvil of my sword, and do contest
> As hotly and as nobly with thy love
> As ever in ambitious strength I did
> Contend against thy valour.

The transformation of brutal aggression into bonded love is expressed in a sexual metaphor that distinctly recalls Coriolanus's exhortation to Cominius in act 1:

> Know thou first,
> I loved the maid I married; never man
> Sighed truer breath. But that I see thee here,
> Thou noble thing, more dances my rapt heart
> Than when I first my wedded mistress saw
> Bestride my threshold.

Our sense of where metaphor leaves off and where reality begins is confused when Aufidius goes on to confess to Coriolanus that he has often dreamed about him:

> Why, thou Mars, I tell thee
> We have a power on foot; and I had purpose

Once more to hew thy target from thy brawn,
Or lose mine arm for't. Thou hast beat me out
Twelve several times, and I have nightly since
Dreamt of encounters 'twixt thyself and me—

These "encounters," one supposes, have been combative, but the imagery Aufidius chooses is charged with sexual power:

We have been down together in my sleep,
Unbuckling helms, fisting each other's throat—
And waked half dead with nothing.

(4.5.110-127)

Plutarch's life of Coriolanus, though suggestively set in parallel with with the life of Socrates' protégé Alcibiades, is altogether innocent of the homoerotic images in which Shakespeare has bodied forth the Roman hero's military career. In Plutarch's account, Coriolanus's speech to Aufidius is one simple sentence:

Stande up, O Martius, and bee of good chere, for in profering thy selfe unto us, thou dost us great honour: and by this meanes thou mayest hope also of greater things, at all the Volsces['] handes.

(2.170)

No embracement, no declaration of love, no dream, no struggle. Possibly the emotional complications of the enemies' pact could have been suggested by Plutarch's life of Alcibiades: the Grecian's good looks, the sexual fascination he aroused in men, and the devotion he inspired in Socrates figure prominently in Plutarch's account.[5] Nowhere in these parallel lives, however, is there any suggestion of the volatile connection Shakespeare makes between male aggression and male sexual desire. To talk about male bonds in erotic terms may be understandable for a Hellenistic writer like Plutarch, but for an early modern writer like Shakespeare it is surprising, for two reasons. In moral discourse, Renaissance writers ordinarily *contrasted*, not likened, the friendly ties between man and man with the sexual ties between man and woman. And in legal discourse, sodomy was a capital offense. Let us consider these two modes of discourse in turn.

To contrast the strength of male friendship with the weakness of erotic love between male and female was a standard *topos* in Renaissance moral philosophy. In the *Nicomachean Ethics* Aristotle argues that true friendship is possible only between equals, between "men who are good, and alike in virtue." Otherwise, there can be no real mutuality, and one "friend" is merely using the other to gratify some need. This is the criterion Aristotle uses to distinguish *philia*, true friendship, from *eros*, sexual desire. *Philia* is rational; it respects the integrity of the other person. *Eros* is "a sort of excess of feeling"; it seeks to overwhelm the other person and possess him.[6] Aristotle's ideas found a wide Renaissance readership in Cicero's dialogue *De Amicitia*. Friendship, Cicero's spokesmen conclude, is a higher, more perfect form of love. Here is Laelius's peroration as translated by John Harington (1550):

> I saie vertue, O C. Fannius and Q. Mutius, both getteth and keepeth freendes. For in it is all agrement, all stedfastnesse, and all constancie: Whiche when she advaunceth her self, and sheweth out hir light, and bothe seeth and knoweth the same in another, she geveth her selfe to that to, and takes likewyse that she findeth in a nother. Whereupon love and lovyng frendship toward eche other, is enkendled. For both these two woordes [*amor* and *amicitia*] have their names of this woord, to love [*amare*]. But to love is nothyng elles, but to beare good wil toward hym, whom you love, not for anie neede or profite that is sought, Whiche profite florisheth yet of freendshippe, although you the lesse nothyng follow it.[7]

Sexual passion, needless to say, always involves the fulfilling of a "neede." True friendship, by contrast, is perfectly symmetrical: because each is already possessed of virtue, neither friend really needs the other, but for that very reason "profite florisheth yet of freendshippe."

Given the nature of Greek and Roman society, the friends that Aristotle and Cicero have in mind are men. Neither writer has anything to say about women. Most Renaissance readers—most male readers, at least—seem not to have considered that a serious omission. As usual, Montaigne is different. Could a friendship like that described by Aristotle and Cicero happen between a man and a woman? Montaigne considers the possibility in his essay "Of Friendship." Ideally, Montaigne says, we might hope that intimate friendship and heterosexual love would coincide; experience teaches us the contrary.

> Seeing (to speake truly) that the ordinary sufficiency of women, cannot answer this conference and communication, the nurse of this sacred bond: nor seeme their mindes strong enough to endure the pulling of a knot so hard, so fast, and durable. And truly, if without that, such a genuine and voluntarie acquaintance might be contracted, where not only mindes had this en-

tire jovissance, but also bodies, a share of the alliance, and where a man might wholy be engaged: It is certaine, that friendship would thereby be more compleat and full: But this sex could never yet by any example attaine unto it, and is by ancient schooles rejected thence.[8]

There was another line of thought about these matters that also went back to classical antiquity, but almost unanimously early modern writers felt compelled to condemn it. This other way of reading the relationship between male bonding and sexual desire started, not with Aristotle, but with Plato and his depiction of male-male love in the *Symposium*, *Phaedrus*, and *Lysis*. In Plato's account, male friendship and sexual attraction, far from being opposites, are two aspects of the same bond. This very different way of looking at the matter reached Renaissance readers, not via Rome, but via Hellenistic Greece. Plato's Hellenistic successors Plutarch and Lucian were in fact better known to Renaissance readers than Plato himself was. The fictional ground of Plutarch's dialogue "Of Love" (*Moralia* 767) is just such a contest between marriage and male companionship as Montaigne addresses in his essay "Of Friendship." What for Plato and other fourth-century Greek writers had been a question of how to distinguish false love from true has become for Plutarch the altogether simpler question of which is better, the love of boys or the love of women.[9] A fair young man named Bacchon is about to be wed to a rich old widow when his male friends, jealous of losing him, stage a debate over which is his better course of action, to get married or to stay single. The trouble, for Christian readers, is that Plutarch gives all the strong arguments for friendship to older men whose interest in Bacchon is quite clearly sexual. What Plutarch does, of course, is simply to reflect the polymorphous sexuality that characterized Hellenistic society.

Protogenes is Plutarch's principal defender of homosexual friendship. "Gynerastice" does have its uses, he will admit.

> This bond in trueth of wedlocke (quoth *Protogenes*) as it is necessary for generation, is by good right praised by Polititians and law-givers, who recommend the same highly unto the people and common multitude: but to speake of true love indeed, there is no jot or part therof in the societie and felowship of women: neither doe I thinke that you and such as yourselves, whose affections stand to wives or maidens, do love them no more than a flie loveth milke, or a bee the hony combe; as caters and cookes who keepe foules in mue, and feed calves and other

such beasts fatte in darke places, and yet for all that they love them not.

The difference between heterosexuality and homosexuality, in Protogenes' view, is Aristotle's difference between excess and moderation. Lust toward a woman overpowers a man and leaves him finally unsatisfied. It ends in "the fruition and enjoying of youth and a beautifull body, and that is all." Love between a man and a boy, by contrast, "endeth by amity in vertue." Effeminate lust is debilitating; masculine love inspires virtuous action:

> The true and naturall love is that of yoong boies, which sparkleth not with the ardent heat of concupiscence, as *Anacreon* saith the other of maidens and virgins doeth: it is not besmered with sweet ointments, nor tricked up and trimmed, but plaine and simple alwaies a man shall see it, without any intising allurements[,] in the Philosophers schooles, or about publicke parks of exercise and wrestling places, where it hunteth kindly and with a very quicke and piercing eie after none but yoong striplings and springals, exciting and encouraging earnestly unto vertue, as many as are meet and woorthy to have paines taken with them: whereas the other delicate and effeminate love, that keepeth home and stirreth not out of dores, but keepeth continually in womens laps, under canapies or within curtaines in womens beds and soft pallets, seeking alwaies after daintie delights, and pampered up with unmanly pleasures, wherein there is no reciprocal amitie, not heavenly ravishment of the spirit, is worthy to be rejected and chased farre away.

Thus Solon, in setting up laws for his commonwealth, forbade slaves to love boys, although he did not bother to keep slaves away from the company of women. In sum: "amitie is an honest, civill and laudable thing: but fleshly pleasure, base, vile, and illiberal."[10]

While Protogenes' misogyny would have been perfectly acceptable to most male readers of Holland's translation, his all-male alternative certainly was not. The objections likely to be in a Renaissance reader's mind are in fact voiced in Plutarch's dialogue. Daphnaeus interrupts Protogenes and protests that love between men "is against kinde," while love toward women "is according to nature." But he goes on to make the unsettling observation that "if we will consider better, & looke nerer into the truth, the passion of Love (o *Protogenes*) be it in one sex or another, is all one & the same" (fol. 1134). Both viewpoints, heterosexual and homosexual, get an ample hearing in Plutarch's dialogue. And neither side really wins: Bacchon's friends are still talking away when a messenger arrives to invite them to Bacchon's wedding, already in progress. Social inevitability carries the day. But the essential point remains clear: in bonds between men there can be a *continuity* between "spiritual" and "sexual," not a distinction.

An even more vigorous defense of sexual love between men was to be found in Lucian's dialogue *"Erotes"*—or rather, in the fourth-century dialogue by that name printed as Lucian's in Renaissance editions of the great humorist's works. Though *"Erotes,"* like most of Lucian's genuine dialogues and poems, was not translated into English until the late seventeenth century, it was handily accessible to readers from the early sixteenth century in an anonymous Latin translation. Like Plutarch, pseudo-Lucian has some surprises in store for modern readers when it comes to ideas about "real men." When Lycinus, the narrator of the dialogue, breaks a sea journey at Cnidus, he chances to run into two old friends who have a long-standing rivalry about matters sexual. Charicles, a Corinthian, loves women; Callicratidas, an Athenian, loves boys. It is Charicles, the defender of heterosexuality, who strikes the narrator as the more effeminate of the two—"a not at all bad-looking young man, not a little given to adorning his body and painting himself up in hopes (I think) that his figure and his taste will be commended by women." Callicratidas is, by contrast, "more straightforward [*simplicorem*] in manner and dress."[11] The three friends decide to see the Temple of Aphrodite that is Cnidus's great claim to fame. When they pass inside and catch sight of the goddess carved in Parian marble, Charicles launches into a loving appreciation of the statue's front; Callicratidas waxes eloquent about its backside. And so the debate begins. The three friends retire to the requisite grove. The narrator Lycinus offers to act as judge.

To Charicles' rehearsal of all the standard objections—we don't see animals lusting after their own sex; a boy's beauty is fleeting in comparison with a woman's; pederasty gives pleasure only to the man who is taking the active role—Callicratidas gives reasoned responses: lions may not know this kind of love but neither do they known anything about philosophy; male bears may not desire other male bears but neither do they enjoy friendship with one another. With the question of friendship Callicratidas comes into his own. He extends the definition of homosexual love beyond the man-boy love that is Plutarch's subject. To Charicles' claim that only the older, active male derives pleasure from sexual relations Callicratidas counters with an encomium of male friendship right out of Aristotle and Cicero—but with this difference: it ends in sexual love. Instancing the friendship of Orestes and Pylades, Callicratidas sees physical affection as the natural end of friendship between equals:

> When that worthy and earnest love, nourished even from boyhood, is strengthened at the age when, mature in mind, one can join together [*colligere*] with others, then he who once was loved gives back a mutual, interchanging love in return. At that point it is hard to know which is the lover of which, since the loving image of kindheartedness is reflected back just as in a mirror. Why, then, do you attack as a foreign debauchery this thing that is part and parcel of our life, laid out in divine laws, and passed down to us as an inheritance?[12]

In effect, the Athenian counters Aristotle's arguments about friendship in Aristotle's own terms. For the narrator at least, Callicratidas is absolutely convincing. Conjugal love may be the *de facto* winner in Plutarch, but in pseudo-Lucian male love carries the day. "Only manly love," Lycinus concludes, "is a thing partaking of both virtue and pleasure."[13] When we consider how Callicratidas has managed to reconcile sexual desire with friendship, *masculus amor* seems a precisely chosen alternative to *paederastia*.

Renaissance writers may have been aware of this other line of thinking about male friendship and male sexuality, but by and large they condemned it. "This Dialogue is more dangerous to be read by yoong men than any other Treatise of *Plutarch*," warns Philemon Holland in his translation of 1603, "for that there be certeine glaunces heere and there against honest marriage, to upholde indirectly and underhand, the cursed and detestable filthinesse covertly couched under the name of the Love of yoong boyes." Let a young man read Plutarch without any warning and he might discover not only that Plutarch's spokesmen were bisexual in their behavior but that none of them saw anything wrong with their sexual proclivities and that some of them actually preferred men to women. In the prefatory "Summarie" before the dialogue, Holland makes sure that his young readers get sufficient warning and so can read the dialogue with "minds guarded and armed with true chastitie and the feare of God" (fol. 1130). Only Montaigne gives Plutarch's ideas anything like a fair hearing. In Aristotle and Cicero the question of sexual attraction between male friends is never raised. Montaigne, unwilling to leave any idea unexamined, addresses the question head-on in his essay "Of Friendship." Sexual relations between men and boys—"this other Greeke licence" as he calls it—is to be condemned not simply because "our customes" prohibit it but because, like relations between men and women, it is not a meeting of equals. In his immaturity, a boy simply cannot possess spiritual qualities that are worthy of devotion. Whatever apologists like Plato may have *said,*

> the first furie, enspired by the son of *Venus* in the lovers hart, upon the object of tender youths-flower, to which they allow all insolent and passionate violences, an immoderate heat may produce, was simply grounded upon an externall beauty; a false image of corporall generation: for in the spirit it had no power, the sight whereof was yet concealed, which was but in his infancie, and before the age of budding.

> (1:232-233)

Like pseudo-Lucian, however, Montaigne does not entirely rule out the possibility that homosexual passion might end in friendship:

> To conclude, all that can be alleaged in favour of the Academy, is to say, that it was a love ending in friendship, a thing which hath no bad reference unto the Stoical definition of love: . . .*That love is an endevour of making friendship, by the shew of beautie.*

> (p. 234)

Montaigne's grounds for distrusting the love described by Plato have less to do with Christian dogma than with Aristotelian ideals of friendship. The fact that Montaigne turns immediately from this disquisition on "Greek license" to a celebration of his friendship with Étienne La Boétie has prompted some twentieth-century readers to see an incautious if not unconscious connection where Montaigne himself, quite in keeping with his sixteenth-century peers, insists on a distinction.

For moral niceties like Montaigne's the lawgivers left no room at all. The letter of the law, in England as in Renaissance Europe generally, was unambiguous: sodomy was an offense punishable by death. In matters of deviant sexual behavior the reign of the Tudor monarchs ranks with the third century A.D., the thirteenth century, and the early nineteenth century as one of the four most intolerant periods in all of European history.[14] From our distant vantagepoint, the laws against homosexual activity that existed in the past can appear to be tablets carved in stone, massive and monolithic, until they began to be attacked in the nineteenth century and, in England at least, were finally dismantled within recent memory. But that is not the case. As John Boswell and James A. Brundage have shown, homosexuality has stood in a constantly changing relationship to the law during the past fifteen hundred years. The general picture is clear: tolerance for homosexuality in late antiquity and the earlier Middle Ages yielded to mounting homophobia from the thirteenth century onward, reaching a climax in the sixteenth century, when homosexual relations between men were made a capital offense under the civil law all over Europe.[15] And that was that—or so it might seem. While noting the greater or lesser severity with which these laws were enforced, Alan Bray, Guido Ruggiero, and other historians of sexual behavior in early modern Europe have assumed that sixteenth-century laws against homosexuality were simply repetitions of the same basic moral position, that they were the culmination of a process that started in the thirteenth century.[16] Legal discourse about homosexuality did not end, however, once the first laws had been proclaimed, printed, and published. In England at least, the legal status of homosexuality was subjected to refinement and redefinition throughout the sixteenth century.

Under the law, sexual crimes are never something *sui generis*: in the definition of what constitutes an offense, in the nature of the evidence required, in the punishments prescribed, deviant sexual acts are grouped, implicitly if not explicitly, with certain other kinds of criminal acts and are dealt with accordingly. From the Middle Ages to the Renaissance and within the Renaissance itself there were shifts in the legal category to which homosexual acts belonged. In the Middle Ages sodomy was a species of heresy. As such it figures in the earliest compendia of English common law, gathered under Edward I in the late thirteenth century—just at the date that Boswell and Brundage tell us intolerance was setting in. Here, for example, is how homosexuality figures in the law-book ascribed to "Fleta":

> Apostate Christians, sorcerers and the like should be drawn and burnt. Those who have connexion with Jews and Jewesses or are guilty of bestiality or sodomy shall be buried alive in the ground, provided they be taken in the act and convicted by lawful and open testimony.[17]

Heretics, magicians, consorters with Jews, sodomites: all four sorts of people are alike in the nature of their crime, in their godlessness, and hence they should be tried and punished in the same way. The lawbook called *The Mirror of Justices* makes the interconnections among these crimes even more explicit by categorizing them among the sins *laesa majestas*, "against the king." Assassination, treason, and rape of the queen or the eldest princess are crimes against the earthly king; heresy, apostasy, and sodomy are crimes against the king of heaven.[18] The punishment most usually demanded in the thirteenth-century laws is not death by being buried alive but death by fire. The lawbook attributed to "Britton," for example, treats sodomy under the heading of "Arson":

> Let inquiry also be made of those who feloniously in time of peace have burnt others' corn or houses, and those who are attainted thereof shall be burnt, so that they may be punished in like manner as they have offended. The same sentence shall be passed upon sorcerers, sorceresses, renegades, sodomites, and heretics publicly convicted.[19]

The link in this case is not the nature of the crime but the nature of the punishment. For arsonists, death by fire is literal justice; for men who have sex with other men, it is figurative justice— "poetic justice," in the phrase of a more prosaic century. "Brimstone, and fire from the Lord out of heaven" is to be visited upon latter-day sodomites as it was upon the biblical city of Sodom.[20]

The fact that some of this religious rhetoric is invoked in sixteenth-century civil statutes against sodomy has led Bray, among others, to assume that medieval ways of categorizing sexual behavior remained unchanged. Heresy, sorcery, and witchcraft, however, are conspicuously absent from the wording of the Parliamentary statute in which sodomy for the first time was made a felony. 25 Henry VIII, chapter 6, treats sodomy as a form of heresy, to be sure, but in a much more specific way than in the common laws codified under Edward I. By acting against sodomy the Reformation Parliament was taking action against the Catholic Church. "An act for the punishment of the vice of buggerie" was passed by Parliament in 1533-34, in the session just after the one in which the Act in Restraint of Appeals paved the way for Henry's divorce and for an eventual break with Rome. 25 Henry VIII, c. 6, was not an isolated piece of legislation but part of a whole battery of laws initiated by the Crown with the single purpose of undermining the political power of the Roman church. While they were considering whether to make sodomy a felony the Lords and the Commons were also preparing bills depriving the Italian bishops of Salisbury and

Worcester of their sees and establishing open trials for accused heretics. In the journal of the House of Lords, the sodomy law is entered as one in a whole list of bills having to do with ecclesiastical abuses.[21] Sodomy had been considered a specifically clerical vice since it first began to be mentioned in ecclesiastical law in the thirteenth century.[22] Making sodomy, along with sorcery and heresy, a felony under the civil law would give Henry's agents the legal power they needed to make answerless accusations during the impending visitation of the monasteries.

Henry's purposes are patent in the memorandum of a letter he sent to the regent of Scotland ten years later, encouraging the regent to fatten his treasury by carrying out in Scotland the same kind of cross-examination of monks and appropriation of their property that Henry's agents had carried out in England in 1535-36:

> . . . for the extirpation of the state of monks and friars, the enterprise whereof requireth politic handling, it shall be first necessary that the governor send substantial and faithful commissioners, as it were to put good order in the same. . . . Which commissioners must have secret commission most secretly and groundly to examine all the religious of their conversion and behavior in their livings, whereby if it be well handled, he shall get knowledge of all their abominations.[23]

Lest there be any question about the "abominations" that Henry's agents had in mind—or their devious methods in bringing them to light—let us consider the letter that one of the commissioners, Richard Layton, sent to Cromwell from Leicester:

> this mornyng I will objecte against divers of them bugrie and adulteries, *et sic specialiter discendere* [i.e., and thus go down the scale], wiche [accusations] I have lernede of other[s], but not of them; what I shall fynde I cannot tell.[24]

The statute 25 Henry VIII, c. 6, is carefully worded so as to exclude "benefit of clergy," an ability to read Latin, as a means of escaping punishment.

The quite specific aims of King Henry's law may be indicated, too, by its temporary jurisdiction. As originally passed, it was not a permanent law but was intended to last only till the end of the next Parliament. Three renewals—28 Henry VIII, c. 6 (1536), 31 Henry VIII, c. 7 (1539), and 32 Henry VIII, c. 3 (1540)—were necessary to keep the law on the books through the remainder of Henry's reign. Only in the third renewal was the law against sodomy made perpetual. Even then, the statute making sodomy a felony was grouped with other statutes that served Henry's campaign against the ecclesiastical establishment by depriving priests of their benefit of clergy. The final purpose of 32 Henry VIII, c. 3, as of all the earlier statutes, was to assure that "such as be within holie orders, should from thensefoorth stand and be under the same paines & dangers for the offenses conteined in anie the said statutes, and be used and ordered to all intents and purposes, as other persons not being within holie orders."[25] All in all, making sodomy a felony seems to have been a convenient way for Henry VIII to get rid of one category of political enemies, priests who were loyal to Rome, and thus consolidate his personal power.

As a political weapon, Henry's sodomy law was capable of inflicting total destruction. It deprived the convicted felon not only of his life but of his "goods, chattels, debts, lands, tenementes, and hereditaments, as felons beene accustomed to doo according to the order of the common lawes of this realme"—in effect, taking away the social status and economic means of the convicted man's entire family and all of his heirs. Since sodomites were now felons like any other felons, death was to be inflicted by hanging. Henry's law thus took away the traditional biblical punishment of death by fire—and in that gesture sealed the transfer of sodomy from one legal category to another. What had been a *religious* offense was now a secular *political* offense. Burning remained the usual punishment for sodomy on the continent—but most countries there, after all, were Catholic. The essentially political nature of sodomy under the laws of Henry VIII is indicated quite clearly by what happened when Queen Mary restored the old faith in 1553. The sodomy law, along with all the rest of Henry's laws on treason and sedition, was repealed. "The love and favor of the subject toward their sovereigne ruler, & governor," says the preamble to 1 Mary, chapter 1, better assure the ruler's state than do "the dread and feare of lawes made with rigorous pains, and extreeme punishment."[26]

In the meantime, however, Henry's sodomy law had undergone subtle but significant revisions when it was reenacted under Edward VI. Like the Reformation Parliament that had passed the original act in 1533-34, the parliament that convened in the first year of Edward's reign (1548) was concerned mainly with religious affairs. In 2 & 3 Edward VI, chapter 29, the same parliament that had passed acts allowing the clergy to marry and establishing the Book of Common Prayer devised a new sodomy law. While incorporating most of the wording of 25 Henry VIII, c. 6, the law added five new provisos: persons convicted of sodomy would henceforth lose only their lives and not their goods and lands; the convicted felon's wife, children, and heirs would enjoy the same claims on his property as if he had died a natural death; there would be no taint or corruption of blood to the convicted felon's heirs; no one could be indicted for sodomy more than six months after the alleged offense; no one could be admitted as a witness who might stand to gain by the defendant's death.[27] Here is more than power politics. The law of Edward VI takes what had been, for all intents and purposes, a political crime under Henry VIII and *personalizes* it. The new provision concerning corruption of blood was an accommodation for aristocratic offenders. Blood, as Foucault observes, was the part of the body most important to the nobility. It was the symbol of their past, present, and future power and the currency in which their alliances were valued.[28] In effect, 2 & 3 Edward VI, c. 29, distinguishes the genitals from the blood, the offending individual from the family to which he belongs. The 1548 statute also reifies the criminal act itself. It could no longer, as under Henry VIII, be a vague accusation that masked some other grievance against the accused (the fact that he was a Catholic friar whose highest loyalty lay to the pope) but was now given specificity in time (accusation had to be made within six months of the alleged act) and in social context (since witnesses were not supposed to gain from a conviction, their interest in the crime was presumed to be moral, not political or economic). The law was becoming ever more exact in putting homosexuality into discourse.

After it had been repealed under Mary, the second Parliament of Elizabeth reinstated the sodomy law—specifically, the original, harsher version of 25 Henry VIII, c. 6—to "stande, remaine, and be in full force, strength and effecte for ever."[29] In its rhetoric at least, 5 Elizabeth, chapter 17 (1562-63), would seem to return to the earlier religious and political ways of conceptualizing sodomy: it invokes, for the first time in the sixteenth-century statutes, the image of divine wrath, and it sets back into place the larger social and economic penalties that were part of Henry's political designs. The parliamentary history of the bill suggests, however, that the personalizing of the act of sodomy begun in the Edwardian law was carried several steps further by the Elizabethan lawmakers. The new sodomy law started out in Elizabeth's first parliament (1559) as a private, not an official, bill—a piece of legislation not initiated by the Crown but by members of Parliament themselves. The wording of the statute conjures up, not a powerful politician sharpening a weapon, but a group of morally indignant individuals reacting to the morally abhorrent behavior of other individuals in their midst. Since Queen Mary's repeal of Henry's statute, says the preamble, "divers evill disposed persons have been the more bolde to commit the said most horrible and detestable vice of buggerie aforesaid, to the high displeasure of almightie God." Religious dogma explains why the proposers in Elizabeth's first Parliament had lumped sodomy with conjurations, sorcery, and witchcraft in an omnibus bill to reinstate the felonies that the Catholic queen had abolished. The fact that the bill did not pass Parliament in this form suggests, however, that writers of legal discourse were no longer totally comfortable with the traditional medieval way of categorizing sodomy. When the bill was reintroduced in Elizabeth's second Parliament three years later, the House of Lords detached conjurations, sorceries, and witchcraft and divided the bill into two parts, one dealing with sodomy, the other with black magic. It was the only time in Elizabeth's long reign when a miscellaneous bill was split up into separate parts.[30] This may seem a small matter, perhaps, but it implies a great deal: however solemn the religious rhetoric in the bill's preamble, sodomy was clearly being thought about, in legal terms at least, as something other than a form of religious heresy.

As an attempt to regulate the sex lives of a sovereign's subjects, 5 Elizabeth, c. 17, is far from unique. All over Europe in the sixteenth century there were attempts to bring, not just homosexuality, but concubinage, consensual unions, and prenuptial cohabitation under legal control. In part, these laws reflect the increasing power of the states that governed people's lives politically; in part, they reflect the changing criteria that governed people's lives morally. "The motor force behind the repression of the sixteenth century," Lawrence Stone proposes, "seems to have been new concepts of virtue and honor, now closely identified with marriage and the family."[31] When we look at the changing legal context within which homosexuality was understood in the sixteenth century, we can detect, then, a gradual narrowing of focus: from the cosmos of God's creation in the legal codes of Edward I, to the secular state in the statutes of Henry VIII, to the family in the revised laws of Edward VI and Elizabeth I. These three contexts are not, of course, mutually exclusive. On the contrary, they include each other like three concentric circles, each smaller than the one before, around the same central point. Across historical time their effect is cumulative, not sequential. Whether we see sodomy as a matter of religion, or politics, or personal morality depends on how broadly we cast our vision. In legal discourse, if not in moral discourse, that frame of reference was getting more and more circumscribed in the course of the sixteenth century.

Lest we attach too much importance to the practical effects of this revolution in legal thinking, let us note how the sodomy legislation of 1562-63 seemed to Sir Simonds D'Ewes when he edited the records of the House of Commons sixty years or so later. For Thursday, 11 February 1562/63, he notes:

> Three Bills of no great moment, had each of them one reading; of which the last being the Bill for Servants robbing their Masters, Buggery, Invocation of evil Spirits, Inchantments, &c. to be Felony, was read the third time, and passed the House.[32]

A bill "of no great moment": Simonds's judgment is confirmed when we investigate how 5 Elizabeth, c. 17, had been enforced during the sixty years since its passage. By and large, it wasn't. Records for the court of assizes in the Home Counties during Elizabeth's reign are fairly complete and representative. In the thousands of cases heard in the assize courts in Essex, Hertfordshire, Sussex, Surrey, and Kent between 1553 and 1602, sodomy indictments are so few as to be less than significant statistically. In Kent, for example, they amount to just two indictments out of some three thousand on record—about .07 percent. During the forty-five years of Elizabeth's reign and the twenty-three years of James I's reign only six men are recorded as having been indicted for sodomy in the Home County assizes. The record on convictions is even more astonishing. During the same sixty-eight-year period there was but one conviction for sodomy. One. In July 1569 Roland Dyer of Margate was found guilty and ordered to be hanged for commiting sodomy with Barnaby Wright. Barnaby was five years old.[33] The low rate of indictments and even lower rate for convictions for sodomy does, to be sure, conform to the relatively small number of indictments and convictions generally in the local courts of early modern England. The reason has less to do with inefficiencies in the sixteenth-century system of justice than with differences from the twentieth century in how people viewed the law. Of the two kinds of legal ideology—one abstract and rule-dominated, the other realistic and grounded in social process—it was the second that governed English society in the sixteenth and early seventeenth centuries. Local authorities had tremendous discretionary powers in applying the law, and securing an indictment, much less a conviction, required a degree of communal will and communal cooperation that was not easy to come by.[34]

Even taking these circumstances into account, the conviction rate for sodomy is signficantly lower than the rate for other categories of crime. Between 1553 and 1602 indictments for bestiality in the Home Counties assizes outnumber indictments for sodomy six to one. Once indicted for bestiality, a person was three times likelier to be convicted and executed than a person indicted for sodomy. When we examine the court record closely, the category of case to which sodomy seems most similar is not bestiality, as we might expect, but rape. Indictments for rape, like indictments for sodomy, usually involve youthful victims (at least half of the rape victims on record were children under 12) and the use of force. What is more, indictments for rape, like indictments for sodomy, had a rather small chance of ending in a conviction (30 percent in the case of rape, less than 20 percent in the case of sodomy), even if more than one witness could be produced. This pragmatic connection between sodomy and rape is confirmed when we look at the advice that legal commentators gave to justices of the peace who were charged with enforcing the statute, to clerks who were studying the law, and to practicing attorneys who wanted to secure a conviction.

On sodomy such advice was not easy to find. Among manuals written for justices of the peace only two, those put together by Anthony Fitzherbert and William Lambarde, make any mention of sodomy whatsoever. Each of them gives it very short shrift, doing little more than naming the crime and categorizing it as a felony.[35] Even scholarly law students could find out little more. Out of the dozens of commentaries and court reports that a student might study, only one makes any mention of homosexuality. Croke, Dyer, Hawarde, Hobart, Noy, Plowden, Yelverton—all of the recognized English legal authorities of the late sixteenth and early seventeenth centuries are, with the exception of Sir Edward Coke, completely silent on the subject of sodomy. For a law student or a practicing attorney the implication is clear: sodomy is not the kind of case one can expect often, or ever, to encounter. Furthermore, Coke's treatment of the subject in his *Institutes*, part 3 (published 1644), is unusual in making only passing allusion to a specific precedent case. Instead, Coke offers a phrase-by-phrase exposition of 25 Henry VIII, c. 6. Three hundred years of British legal history are digested into two folio pages. "Fleta," "Britton," and *The Mirror of Justices*—antedated to the times of King Arthur—are dutifully cited. So are Leviticus, I Timothy, Ezekiel, Genesis, Deuteronomy, Isaiah, Jeremiah, Luke, II Peter, Jude, Romans, Proverbs, and I Corinthians. The religious rhetoric of the thirteenth-century common law is amplified as only someone educated in the Renaissance could manage:

> Buggery is a destable and abominable sin, amongst Christians not to be named, committed by carnal knowledge against the ordinance of the Creator and order of nature, by mankind with mankind, or with brute beast, or by womankind with brute beast.[36]

(The combination of womankind with womankind seems not to have occurred even to this most systematic of thinkers.) Coke's treatment of sodomy represents an extreme instance of the scholastic bias that characterizes legal scholarship in Renaissance England generally. Coke's polemical purpose in this and other entries in his *Institutes* is less to rationalize practice than to demonstrate the reasonableness, the changelessness, and the naturalness of English common law.[37]

When Coke does get down to business, when he turns from the spirit of the law to the letter of the law, he turns out to be talking about something much less cosmic than his preamble would suggest. In effect, Coke treats sodomy as a species of rape. To secure an indictment, one has, first of all, to demonstrate that there was anal penetration:

> The words of the Indictment be, *Contra ordinationem Creatoris & naturae ordinem, rem habuit veneream, dictumque puerum carnaliter cognovit*, &c. [Against the ordinance of the Creator and the order of nature, he had sexual intercourse, and knew the said boy carnally, etc.]. So as there must be *penetratio*, that is, *res in re* [the thing in the thing], either with mankind or with beast, but the least penetration maketh it carnall knowledge.

Ejaculation alone does not constitute proof for indictment:

> *Emissio seminis* maketh it not Buggery, but is an evidence in case of Buggery of penetration: and so in Rape the words be also *carnaliter cognovit*, and therefore there must be penetration: and *emissio seminis* without penetration maketh no Rape.

In addition to limiting sodomy to one kind of act, Coke seems also to be limiting it to one kind of victim. Although he singles out *"Paederastes"* as "a *Species* of Buggery," as one kind of sodomitical act among many, he in effect treats the forcible rape of an underaged boy as the only kind of act in which the law takes an interest. In his formula for indictment Coke includes the phrase *puerum carnaliter cognovit,* and as a precedent he cites the case of a certain H. Stafford, who was indicted, attainted, and executed by the Court of King's Bench in 1607-08 for having anal intercourse with a sixteen-year-old boy. In Coke's earlier *A Booke of Entries: Containing Perfect and approved Presidents* ... (1614), Stafford's case figures in the section on "Indictments" as a carefully worded model for a kind of case in which securing an indictment might be tricky. One has to demonstrate, as for rape, not only penetration but the use of force. Stafford,

> led astray by diabolical instigation, on the twelfth day of May last gone by, in the parish of St. Andrew in High Holborn in the County of Middlesex aforesaid, namely in the dwelling-house of a certain M— in the same place, by force and arms [*vi et armis*] leaped upon [*insultum fecit*] a certain K— B—, a male boy [*puerum masculum*] about sixteen years old, and with the same K— B— did then and there evilly, diabolically, feloniously, and unnaturally have sexual intercourse [*rem veneream habuit*], and did then and there have carnal knowledge [*carnaliter cognovit*] of the same K— B—, and did then and there evilly, diabolically, feloniously, and unnaturally commmit and perpetrate the detestable and abhominable sin of Sodom, called in English "Buggarie" (that ought not to be named among Christians), a thing displeasing to Almighty God and a crime to all mankind, against the peace of the said My Lord the King, his crown, and dignity, and against the form of the law set forth and provided for a case of this kind . . . .[38]

Vi et armis was a standard formula, to be used in indictments for all kinds of felonies, but *insultum fecit* leaves little doubt that in this particular case it was to be taken literally as well. If sixteen seems to be an equivocal age at which to describe someone as a "boy," the record of other court cases bears out Coke's choice of words. With the exception of one case in which only the victim's name is given, all six recorded indictments for sodomy in the Home County assizes between 1559 and 1602 involve victims described as boys. The ages specified are 5, 8, and 10. Use of force, penetration, an underaged victim: Coke's account of sodomy accords not only with the statutes against rape but with actual trials for rape in the Home County assizes during the reigns of Elizabeth and James.

It did not, however, establish an invariable rule of law. When the Earl of Castlehaven was brought to trial in 1631 on three charges—committing sodomy with two of his male servants, and inciting one of those servants to the rape of Lady Castlehaven—the accused nobleman specifically raised the issue of penetration. His servants wisely denied anything more than intercrural masturbation. The Lord Chief Justice declared, however, that *emissio semenis* constituted sufficient proof and with that advice narrowly secured convictions on the two counts of sodomy. On the other indictment, abetting the rape of his own wife, Castlehaven was convicted unanimously by his jury of peers; on the two indictments for sodomy the vote was split, fifteen to twelve. Unlike the trials of Roland Dyer and H. Stafford, the trial of the Earl of Castlehaven was a *cause célèbre*. What was on trial in this case was not a single act but an aggregate of acts, and sodomy was not the most important. The most heinous deed, in the eyes of Castlehaven's peers, was his self-confessed attempt to produce a bastard heir by forcing his wife to bed with one of his male favorites. What angered the lords most was not the *sexual* crimes that Castlehaven committed against the persons of his wife and servants but the *political* crime he attempted against the social order of which the lords were a part and over which they presided. To add to that, he was a prevaricator in religion.[39] Political considerations likewise figure in the other sodomy trial of a public figure in the seventeenth century, that of John Atherton, Anglican Bishop of Waterford and Lismore. Though accused of having committed sodomy with his proctor, John Childe, Atherton's real crime was his political allegiance to the Earl of Strafford, who had forced the Earl of Cork and other leading landowners to surrender portions of their estates in Ireland.[40] As late as 1640, therefore, the crime of sodomy still provided the convenient political weapon that Henry VIII had forged a century earlier. Sodomy in the cases of Castlehaven and Atherton was not at all the same thing as sodomy in the cases of Roland Dyer and H. Stafford. Nor can any of these four cases be taken as typical of homosexual activity in early modern England. Then, as now, getting caught more likely indicates that the accused individual was in some way *not* typical of others who practiced the same behavior.[41] To get into the legal record a sixteenth- or seventeenth-century Englishman would need to have raped an underaged boy or to have fallen afoul of the state politically. Apart from these two extreme circumstances, legal discourse about homosexuality in early modern England tells us little.

What it does tell us seems to have a double plot. Two things seem to be going on as we read the laws, investigate the court record, and study the legal commentators. First, we can follow a shift in ideology, a progression from religious to political to personal ways of thinking about sodomy. As the cases of Castlehaven and Atherton remind us, these changes in legal categories represent less a sequence of meanings than an *accumulation* of meanings: the political entails the religious, the personal entails them both. There is a second development, as well: an increasing exactitude about just what homosexual acts *are*—or, rather, which particular homosexual acts are indictable. No one was, or apparently could be, brought to trial in the late sixteenth and early seventeenth centuries for "being a homosexual." Unless one were famous and had powerful enemies, one could be indicted for sodomy only by forcing another male (more likely than not a minor) to be the passive partner in anal sex. In the way it was applied, 5 Elizabeth, c. 17, was no different from the laws still on the books in England and in most other European countries that have legalized homosexual relations between consenting adults. Whatever the spirit of the law may have been, the letter of the law was not concerned with mutual masturbation between two males ("*Emissio seminis* maketh it not Buggery") or, apparently, with sexual relations of *any* kind between two males when both were adults ("The words of the Indictment be . . . *puerum carnaliter cognovit*") and when one was not forcing the other (Stafford "by force and arms leaped upon a certain K— B—"). This distinction between spirit and letter is crucial. English Renaissance law has nothing to say about homosexual desire; its purview extends only to homosexual acts—and only to acts of one particular kind.[42] By and large, what the legal discourse addresses is the narrow case of forcible rape of an underaged boy by an adult male. On the larger matter of mutual desire between men as equals the law remains tactfully silent. Pirithous could reach out his hand to Theseus without necessarily attracting the attention of Sir Edward Coke.

The verbal embrace in which Aufidius welcomes Coriolanus, even if it does not transgress the letter of Renaissance law, would seem to confuse two categories of feeling that Renaissance moral philosophy takes pains to set apart. The rhetoric of erotic desire is applied to a category of experience to which moral philosophy says it does not belong. Why should emotions win out over moral reason? In particular, why should erotic passion, a way of relating to other people that moral philosophy brands as suspect, be confused with friendship, with a way of relating that moral philosophy privileges? Why should something deemed inferior be used as a name for something deemed superior? In a word, what does it *mean* when an writer like Shakespeare uses erotic imagery to talk about male bonding? All or nothing, depending on which twentieth-century writer is assuming authority. An extreme example of taking "platonic" sentiments to be Platonic sensuality is Martin Green's decoding of sexual puns in *The Labyrinth of Shakespeare's Sonnets.*[43] The traditional academic line insists on just the opposite. Aufidius's rhetoric of erotic desire is "only a metaphor"—with an emphasis on the "only." Renaissance writers used erotic images to describe male friendship, so this line of reasoning goes, only because they wanted an especially powerful metaphor.[44] All or nothing: both explanations make two distinctly twentieth-century assumptions about how sex is put into discourse. According to Freudian psychology, there can be only two kinds of speakers, heterosexual and homosexual. Those two kinds of people can make two kinds of statements, conscious and unconscious. In the case of Aufidius we have, according to this logic, either a heterosexual male consciously deploying a figure of speech, or a homosexual male unconsciously revealing a repressed desire. There is no room for ambiguity.

Seeing the issue in these post-Freudian terms forces a distinction at just the juncture that Renaissance rhetoric labors to obscure. "But that I see thee here,/Thou noble thing, more dances my rapt heart/Than when I first my wedded mistress saw/Bestride my threshold": what we hear and see in speeches like this is not a *logical* proposition, after all, but a *metaphor*. As ways of constructing meaning with words, logic and metaphor are quite different operations. Where logic marks distinctions, metaphor insinuates connections. Where logic insists on clarity, metaphor entertains ambiguities. Where logic thinks, metaphor intuits. Where logic says "this *is*," metaphor says "this is *as if*." Logic directs the arguments of moral discourse and legal discourse; metaphor inspires the musings of poetic discourse.

Looking at metaphor with his customary logic, Aristotle may be more helpful than Freud in helping us understand just what Shakespeare is suggesting when he has Aufidius compare feelings for a sometime enemy with feelings for a "wedded mistress." Taking metaphor to be "the application of the name of one thing to something else," Aristotle gives the term a broader application than we usually assume today. In its playful detaching of names from things, metaphor as Aristotle conceives it is capable of making four kinds of comparisons: genus to species, species to genus, and species to species, as well as unlike to unlike by "proportion" with like to like. Aristotle's idea of metaphor thus includes not only analogy (giving the name of one thing to another thing on the basis of some similarity between them) but synecdoche (comparing species to genus, naming the part for the whole), metonomy (comparing genus to species and species to genus, naming the container for the contained, the effect for the cause, the modifier for the modified, the symbol for the symbolized), and catachresis (comparing species to species, giving a thing which lacks a name the name that belongs to something else).[45]

Which aspect of metaphor do we have in Shakespeare's use of sexual images as metaphors for male bonding? Sixteenth-century moral philosophy would suggest Aristotle's third possibility, a comparison of species to species, the appropriation of the name of one thing (erotic desire) for another thing (male bonding)—two distinct species of emotions within the genus of human affections. Twentieth-century academic discourse would insist on Aristotle's fourth possibility, a strictly figurative analogy between two logically unlike things. What I believe we have in Aufidius's rhetoric is Aristotle's second possibility, a comparison of species to genus. That is to say, erotic desire is the genus of which the feelings attached to male bonding are a species. Instead of demarcating two separate categories of desire, distinguished according to gender, Aufidius's speech intimates only one. What Shakespeare invites us to see, at least for the space of the metaphor, is a *continuum* of erotic desire that embraces both male and female objects, both arch rival and new bride. The rhetorical focus is on the speaker, on Aufidius as the desiring subject, and not as Freudian psychology would have it on the anatomies of the object-bodies he desires. If gender figures here at all, it booms out in the male swagger Aufidius assumes when he speaks about sexual desire.

What can we conclude, then, about the relationship between male bonding and erotic desire in *Coriolanus*? Aufidius's metaphor says that male bonding and erotic desire are *like* each other.

No more than that. But no less than that, either. In Masters and Johnson's terms, the "phase" of human sexual response that is engaged here is only the first: "excitement." Whatever power Aufidius's metaphor had for Shakespeare's audience was generated by the way it fuses two highly charged feelings into one. Aufidius does not pretend to be making a logically consistent statement. He speaks passionately. He speaks poetically. It is in just this respect, in its challenge to logic, that poetic discourse can reflect much more accurately than moral discourse or legal discourse the inconsistencies and conflicts that are a fact of human social life. From our distant vantage point it is all too easy to assume that attitudes and behavior in the historical past constituted a coherent whole. "The Renaissance was a time when . . . ," "Renaissance thought held . . . ," "Renaissance man believed . . . ": formulations like these overlook the *competing* ideas and *competing* discourses that distinguish the untidy facts of day-to-day life from the neat formulations in history books. Metaphor, like logic, can address these inconsistencies by setting them side by side. But metaphor, unlike logic, does not have to decide between them. Only poetic discourse can capture, in Wolfgang Iser's phrase, "the simultaneity of the mutually exclusive."[46] To see the whole truth about sexual desire in early modern England, I believe, we need to pay as much attention to the emotional interconnections suggested by poetic discourse as we do to the logical distinctions marked out by moral and legal discourse.

Competition among these modes of discourse was sharp. Concerning power, they tell a story of conflict between negative and positive "energies," between laws that prohibited acts of sodomy and social arrangements that encouraged the erotic potential in male bonding. The all-male power structure of sixteenth- and seventeenth-century society fostered male bonds above all other emotional ties. Feminist historians and feminist critics have made it impossible for us to ignore that fact.[47] For most sixteenth-century readers the very act of reading North's translation of Plutarch was an exercise in homosociality. Lord North may have dedicated his translation to Queen Elizabeth in her capacity as "an highe and mightie Princesse," but the reader he addresses in his prefatory letter is assumed to be male. And it is not a solitary male reader that North envisions, despite his use of the singular noun, but a *community* of male readers. "All other learning is private," North says in defense of Plutarch, "whereas stories are fit for every place, reache to all persons, serve for all tymes, teache the living, revive the dead, so farre excelling all other bookes, as it is better to see learning in noble mens lives, than to reade it in Philosophers writings" (1.7).

Noble men's lives are the *subject* of North's book, in more ways than one. Inspiring his readers to emulate "the speciall actes of the best persons, of the famosest nations of the world" (1.3) is North's very purpose in publishing *The Lives of the Noble Grecians and Romanes Compared Together*. All of those "best persons" are men. And so, by all accounts, were most of North's readers. Even in a population in which women were almost as likely to be literate as men (one fifth of the female population as opposed to one quarter of the male population if David Cressy's figures are correct), authors assumed that most readers of most books would be men—and, like North, usually addressed them as such.[48] Plutarch's account of the friendship of Pirithous and Theseus was a text written by a man, translated by a man, addressed to a man, who was constantly being reminded that most other readers of the text were also men. In North's Plutarch we have men talking to men about men's affairs. In early modern England the very act of reading a book was a way of affirming male group identity and male political power.

As a sourcebook on what it meant to be male in classical antiquity, Plutarch's *Lives of the Noble Grecians and Romans* offered Renaissance readers a model of male bonding that closely matched the ways in which men related to men in their own society. Plutarch supplied Shakespeare not only with the biographical facts he needed for *Julius Caesar, Antony and Cleopatra,* and *Coriolanus* but with a dramatic universe in which the male protagonists find their identities, not in romantic love or in philosophical ideals, but in their relationships with each other. Plutarch's heroes move in a world defined totally in terms of political bonds. In this intensely masculine world emotional ties are a function of political ties. Only Antony dares to be different. He defies his male peers and for his daring pays the price, the tragic price, of ostracism and death. This, too, is the world of Shakespeare's history plays. However different they may be as individuals, Richard II, Henry IV, Henry V, Henry VI, and Richard III play out their varied careers in the same imaginative universe, an aggressively masculine, staunchly patriarchal society in which women have only a peripheral place. Hotspur's cavalier ways with Kate, Henry Bolingbroke's brusque wooing of Katherine, and Richard III's brutal mastery of Prince Edward's widow are typical of the tension these plays set up between martial devotion and marital duty.[49]

In a series of plays focused on soldier-heroes, Shakespeare portrays the structures of power and ideology that gave males in early modern England their social authority—and their self-identity. In the process he exposes sexual feelings that elude less careful observers of Elizabethan and Jacobean social life. Taken together, this particular way of putting sex into discourse constitutes the most public and pervasive myth of homosexual desire in early modern England, the Myth of Combatants and Comrades. It owes its hold on Renaissance imagination to the way it expresses, in specifically sexual terms, the ambivalences of feeling that are involved in male bonding generally. "Friend" and "brother in arms": the two phrases that Theseus uses to describe his relationship with Pirithous describe also the special balance of power in male bonding. Though all human beings seem to need some sense of opposition to form a self-identity—some sense of psychic "otherness" against which they can play off the individual self and give it definition—opposition seems to be especially crucial for human males. "Adversativeness" is Walter J. Ong's attempt at a less pejorative term than aggression for this basic fact about how human beings, human males in particular, behave toward one another. In *Fighting for Life: Contest, Sexuality, and Consciousness*, Ong gathers abundant evidence from biologists and psychologists to illustrate the special struggle that males face in differentiating themselves from the female environment in which they are born and nurtured. Boys are constantly being challenged to "prove" their masculinity in ways that girls are never challenged to prove their femininity. One very important way in which males prove their masculinity is by bonding with other males—but at the same time keeping other males at an emotionally safe distance.

> It is particularly obvious among human males that the support from the other achieved by distancing him (that is, in effect, distancing or standing off oneself) can be enhanced by grouping. The bonding pattern in male groups is well known: it consists of closeness and distancing simultaneously. It includes banter, "ribbing," constant psychological pushing, shoving, swatting (among young males, the pushing, shoving, swatting are physical as well). Thus each assures himself that everybody is a friend though at the same time everybody is on his own

and keeping everybody else at arm's length—an admiring arm's length, in a kind of diffuse communal narcissism.

In sum: "Male bonding groups are associations of loners."[50] It is just such a "communal narcissism" that draws together Theseus and Pirithous, and all their counterparts in Shakespeare's plays. Two conflicting imperatives govern the actions of all these paired heroes: "fight this man" and "love this man." That conflict of impulses helps explain why the violent and the erotic so often coincide in Shakespeare's plays about soldiering.

A particularly striking example marks the battle sequence in *Henry V*. As the Duke of Exeter recounts the event to Henry V, the battlefield deaths of Suffolk and York seal a mystical marriage. After kissing his friend's wounds and bidding his soul tarry so that the two of them may "fly abreast" to heaven, York smiled up at Exeter and commended himself to the king.

So did he turn, and over Suffolk's neck
He threw his wounded arm, and kissed his lips,
And so espoused to death, with blood he sealed
A testament of noble-ending love.

(4.5.17, 24-27)

No less astonishing than the tenderness of this scene is the brutal violence it immediately inspires in the English army. When an *alarum* signals the arrival of French reinforcements, Henry, still caught up in the emotion of Exeter's tale, orders the English soldiers to kill their prisoners. Male affection and male aggression are allies, just as they are in Plutarch's story of Theseus and Pirithous. Though present to one degree or another in the history plays, the concatenation of aggression, male bonding, and homoerotic desire is perhaps tightest in *Coriolanus, Troilus and Cressida, Othello*, and *Romeo and Juliet*.

Divisions in *Troilus and Cressida* run deep. The Greek camp, taking its identity from Homer, is an all-male world dominated by an ethic of honor and combat; the Trojan camp, inspired by Chaucer and other romance writers, is a courtly world devoted to an ethic of chivalric love. This geographical division, which almost suggests a gender distinction between male/Greek and female/Trojan, effects a curious dislocation of rhetoric: imagery of battle shapes the experience of love in the Trojan camp; imagery of love and courtship colors the depiction of combat and male rivalry in the Greek camp. When Aeneas brings a challenge from Hector, seeking a Grecian

That loves his mistress more than in confession
With truant vows to her own lips he loves,
And dare avow her beauty and her worth
In other arms than hers . . .   (1.3.266-269),

it is Ajax, the most martial, least venereal of the Greeks, who
first steps forward. Achilles, heretofore the most venereal, least
martial, expresses fierce contempt, particularly since the combat
will be only halfhearted sparring between kinsmen. "This Ajax
is half made of Hector's blood," Aeneas explains to Achilles, "In
love whereof half Hector stays at home." "A *maiden* battle then?"
scoffs Achilles (4.6.83-85). A "maiden knight" was a common
epithet in the early seventeenth century for an untried soldier,
but already Achilles has cast a clearly sexual light on the combat
when he has arranged to have Hector invited to his tent. "I have
a woman's longing," he declares to Patroclus,

> An appetite that I am sick withal,
> To see great Hector in his weeds of peace,
> To talk with him and to behold his visage
> Even to my full of view.

> (3.3.230-234)

When Hector is being greeted by the other Grecians, Achilles
satisfies his "woman's longing" with brazen directness: he si-
lently "feeds his eyes" while the others speak, and when Ulysses
almost preempts his invitation to feast the Trojan, Achilles
shoves the commander aside.

> ACHILLES
>   I shall forestall thee, Lord Ulysses. Thou!
>   Now, Hector, I have fed mine eyes on thee.
>   I have with exact view perused thee, Hector,
>   And quoted joint by joint.
> HECTOR   Is this Achilles?
> ACHILLES   I am Achilles.
> HECTOR
>   Stand fair, I pray thee, let me look on thee.

"Behold thy fill," responds Achilles, reintroducing the metaphor
of "appetite" that he has used already in conjunction with "a
woman's longing."

> HECTOR   Nay, I have done already.
> ACHILLES
>   Thou art too brief. I will the second time,
>   As I would buy thee, view thee limb by limb.
>   (4.7.114-122)

Chapter Two

And so he does. What we see as Achilles stalks Hector, what we hear as he speaks, is a violent parody of a lover's blazon. In Shakespeare's source for this scene John Lydgate specifies that Achilles was glad to see Hector "naked," not armed as he was on the battlefield, but absent entirely from Lydgate's account is the imagery of "appetite" and "a woman's longing" with which Achilles has prepared us to view the encounter.[51] The Trojans themselves come to the combat, in Aeneas's words, "with a bridegroom's fresh alacrity" (4.5.145). "A maiden battle" it turns out to be indeed: "Let me embrace thee, Ajax," declares "half Hector" as he leaves off fighting.

> By him that thunders, thou hast lusty arms.
> Hector would have them fall upon him thus.

$$(4.7.19-21)$$

And with that "thus" he embraces the man he hoped to kill. The sexual tension in Achilles' stalking of Hector presses for release. Seen in the terms that Achilles himself provides, the slaughter of Hector becomes an act of sexual consummation, a homosexual gang rape that Achilles and his Myrmidons carry out on their unarmed victim. The fall of night, the abrupt close of the play, and the satisfaction of his desire prevent Achilles from carrying the slaughter further. Putting away his phallic sword, he puts this smug end to the imagery of "appetite":

> My half-supped sword, that frankly would have fed,
> Pleased with this dainty bait, thus goes to bed.

$$(5.9.19-20)$$

Ardent combatant and ardent comrade: the two roles converge in Iago. Latent homosexuality has become virtually a cliché in how twentieth-century actors interpret the part.[52] Instructed by Freud, directors, actors, and critics have looked at Iago from an essentially twentieth-century point of view and discovered "repressed" sexual desire. What, indeed, should we think when Iago tells Othello that he recently shared a bed with Cassio (a common enough happenstance in the sixteenth century) and

> In sleep I heard him say "Sweet Desdemona,
> Let us be wary, let us hide our loves,"
> And then, sir, would he grip and wring my hand,
> Cry "O, sweet creature!", and then kiss me hard,
> As if he plucked up kisses by the roots,
> That grew upon my lips, lay his leg o'er my thigh,

And sigh, and kiss, and then cry "Cursèd fate,
That gave thee to the Moor!"

"O, monstrous, monstrous!" Othello rages. Iago responds, "Nay, this was but his dream" (3.3.423-432). Cassio's dream? Or Iago's?

The dream may have as much to do, however, with Iago's conscious image of himself as it does with any "unconscious" desires. If we turn to Aristotle's *Ethics* and look at Iago from a sixteenth-century point of view, what we discover is not Iago's "sublimated" homosexuality but his militant maleness and his virulent contempt for women.[53] About both traits Iago is unfailingly direct. Consider, for example, how Iago describes Cassio to Roderigo in the opening lines of the play. For his lieutenant Othello has chosen, not an experienced soldier like Iago, but

> Forsooth, a great arithmetician,
> One Michael Cassio, a Florentine,
> A fellow almost damned in a fair wife,
> That never set a squadron in the field
> Nor the division of a battle knows
> More than a spinster . . . .

(1.1.18-23)

In Iago's view, three things make Cassio an outsider: he is a contemplative theoretician, not an active soldier; he is a Florentine, not a Venetian; and he is a lover of women, not a man's man. On all three counts he is damnable. "A fellow almost damned in a fair wife" is a famous editorial crux: Cassio is not, in fact, married. Is he about to take the self-damning step that Othello has taken already? Whatever else it may mean, the phrase reveals, only two minutes into the play, what strong feelings the very thought of male-female sexual relations touches off in Iago. In his famous "Put money into thy purse" speech Iago reveals just what a puritan he is about sex with women. "If the beam of our lives had not one scale of reason to peise another of sensuality," he tells Roderigo,

> the blood and baseness of our natures would conduct us to most preposterous conclusions. But we have reason to cool our raging motions, our carnal stings, our unbitted lusts; whereof I take this that you call love to be a sect or scion.

About such things as "love" he himself knows nothing. Get hold of yourself, he orders Roderigo. "Come, be a man!" (1.3.326-332, 335). The mark of manhood, in Iago's view, is to make "will" control "lust." It is not only, then, Cassio's mathematical skills that prompt the comparison with a "spinster."

Othello's marriage with Desdemona shapes up in Iago's view as a power struggle between male and female in which the general has relinquished command to a woman. "Our general's wife is now the general," he complains to Cassio (2.3.307-308). For his own wife Iago has nothing but contempt: "filth" he calls her when she tries to intervene in the play's last scene (5.2.238). Iago's substitution of wordplay for sex play is at its peak in the witty slanders of women with which he entertains Desdemona and her ladies when they arrive in Cyprus. When Desdemona protests Iago's audaciousness, Cassio consoles her in remarks that sum up Iago perfectly: "He speaks home, madam. You may relish him more in the soldier than in the scholar" (2.1.168-169).

Above all else, Iago is a *soldier*. He belongs to an all-male world in which women have no place. They destroy the bonds that men form with men. Iago defines himself totally in terms of that world, and when the newly married general passes over him and names as his lieutenant a man who is almost damned in a fair wife, Iago's very identity is shaken. Like York, like Achilles, like Coriolanus, like Aufidius, Iago preempts the rhetoric of courtship to describe the all-male world of the army. Before they quarreled and crossed swords, Cassio and Montano were, Iago tells Othello, "in terms like bride and groom/Devesting them for bed" (2.3.173-174). An attentive listener recalls these terms when he watches Othello finally succumb to Iago's insinuations, repudiate Desdemona, and pledge his fealty to Iago. First the general kneels to pronounce his "sacred vow" (3.3.464). Then the new lieutenant, at last possessed of the military office he desires more than the "office" of husband, kneels to give up his "wit, hands, heart" to Othello's service (3.3.469). After this parody of a marriage rite, the pair rise and greet one another in terms more proper for a bride and groom. "Now art thou my lieutenant," Othello affirms. Vows Iago: "I am your own for ever" (3.3.481-482). The parody is all the more grotesque because Iago will use Othello's trust to destroy him. In this physical enactment of the play's verbal images we witness, not Iago's repressed homosexuality, but his male bondedness. Whatever homoerotic feeling he manifests arises, not out of any "repressed" desires that set him apart from other men, but out of his self-definition as a man among men, as a soldier among soldiers.

In this respect, Iago can be seen as an older, more sinister recasting of Mercutio. Several feminist critics have noted the violence that marks male camaraderie in Verona—violence that Romeo grows out of when he falls in love with Juliet. When Romeo and his friends act out their "adversativeness," when they banter, rib, push, shove, and swat, one of the butts of their violence is sex. What most critics have *not* noticed is the specific object of Mercutio's sexual and verbal interest. It is not Juliet's pudenda that Mercutio jokes about but Romeo's. "O Romeo, that she were, O that she were/An open-arse, and thou a popp'rin' pear" (2.1.37-38): Mercutio's lewdest verbal jab, the immediate foil to Romeo's "But soft, what light through yonder window breaks?" (2.1.44), is an image of anal sex, and it climaxes a whole series of earlier jokes to which Romeo's member supplies the point. "If love be rough with you," Mercutio has advised, "be rough with love./ Prick love for pricking, and you beat love down" (1.4.27-28). When verbal sparring about phalluses turns into physical sparring with swords, Mercutio is killed. An exemplar of male violence and misogyny? A martyr to male friendship? A victim of sexual desire that he cannot, will not, or must not acknowledge directly? Mercutio is all three.[54]

Mercutio may die, but only bad timing keeps *Romeo and Juliet* from reaching the comic conclusion of married love. In this respect the play is an anomaly. Generally speaking, the tragic convulsion of male violence and homoerotic desire that we witness in *Coriolanus*, *Troilus and Cressida*, and *Othello* is tempered into comedy when female characters step onto the stage and are given something like an equal voice in what goes on. Male friendship or matrimony: the debate in Plutarch's dialogue "Of Love" is restaged often in Shakespeare's comedies and tragicomedies. Through scripts focused on wooing, courtship, and marriage, Shakespeare plays out the sexual conflict that the Myth of Combatants and Comrades poses for that other Renaissance ideal of human relations, the Myth of Companionate Marriage.[55] "Myth" is, perhaps, too insubstantial a word for the solid political and economic realities of marriage in sixteenth- and seventeenth-century English society. For the aristocracy marriage was a political necessity; for everyone else it was an economic necessity. People who were possessed of lands and a title had no other way of passing those things on to their heirs. People who had to earn a living could not afford to establish a new household without a helpmate. Until a man married he was defined as part of someone else's household. Except for the very wealthy, living alone was virtually unheard of. Indeed, the wealthier one was, the larger one's household was expected to be. In his treatise on

Honor Military, and Civill (1602) William Segar takes pains to point out that "Men married are ever to precede men unmaried, *in pari dignitate* [i.e., other things being equal]."[56]

The full weight of these considerations is felt in that new moral criterion—the family—that Stone detects in sixteenth-century attempts to regulate sexual behavior, homosexuality included, by law. It is the social, and *moral*, importance of the family that explains why the Archbishop of Canterbury and the Bishop of London should have included a new edition of Antoine de La Sale's droll rehearsal of *The fyftene Joyes of maryage* (first English edition 1507) among the books of satire they ordered to be burned in 1599. After bankruptcy, screaming children, and pesky in-laws, a wife's separation of her husband from his friends is the twelfth "joy" that a man can look forward to in marriage. Say that a young man has wedded the woman he wooed and "hath sete/His love so wele/that no man coude do bete"—or so "hym semeth." What happens next?

> ... peradventure suche a man is he
> As by her councell wyll well ruled be
> So that whan ony wyght hath for to do
> With hym/ he sayth[,] ["]I shall go speke unto
> The good wyfe of our house/ and yf she wyll
> It shall be doone/ and yf so be she nyll
> In no wyse shall the mater take effecte.["]

And if the king should call the young man to war?

> Then yf the wyfe it wyll forthe shall he go
> And yf she do replye/ he shall not so.[57]

To read such things in 1509 was amusing; to read them in 1599 was, or so the Archbishop thought, dangerous. What had changed during those ninety years was the moral importance attached to marriage. Young men of a certain age in Renaissance England had, then, to reconcile two conflicting demands: the emotional intensity of male bonds as they were fostered by Renaissance patriarchy and the necessity of marrying to acquire full status within that patriarchy. The question confronting a young man at sexual maturity in Shakespeare's day was not, am I heterosexual or am I homosexual, but where do my greater emotional loyalties lie, with other men or with women. The conflict these young men faced is played out to a variety of ends in Shakespeare's plays.

All the games with disguise and games with words in *Love's Labors Lost*, for example, derive from the French lords' attempt to sequester themselves from women for the space of three years. In proposing the pact, Navarre appeals to his friends' masculine "adversativeness," to the drives that, turned inward, make men want to club with men. "Brave conquerors," he hails them—

> for so you are,
> That war against your own affections
> And the huge army of the world's desires.

(1.1.8-10)

Navarre seems to have taken St. Paul's advice to heart: "It were good for a man not to touche a woman."[58] Be that as it may, Navarre's vision of his friends' all-male life together sounds remarkably like an Oxford or Cambridge college: "Our court shall be a little academe,/Still and contemplative in living art" (1.1.13-14). Longaville and Dumaine are dubious; Berowne is downright rebellious:

> Necessity will make us all forsworn
> Three thousand times within this three years' space;
> For every man with his affects is born,
> Not by might mastered, but by special grace.

(1.1.147-150)

And so Necessity does. The unexpected arrival of the Princess of France and her three ladies sends Navarre's all-male "academe" into a tizzy. Navarre's all-male utopia is made to seem just the silly, adolescent idea that Berowne made it out to be in the beginning. Bravely conquering other males in real wars has nothing to do, it turns out, with metaphorically conquering one's own "affects." For that one needs the "special grace," the divine dispensation that let the bachelor apostle boast, "I wolde that all men were even as I my self am . . . ." Otherwise, "it is better to marie then to burne" (I Corinithians 7:7, 9). When all has been said and done, Berowne makes this confession to the Princess:

> We to ourselves prove false
> By being once false for ever to be true
> To those that make us both—fair ladies, you.

(5.2.765-767)

To be truly happy, the play implies, a man needs a woman. "Necessity" is a powerful word.

The scenario of two male friends set at odds by a woman

clearly fascinated Shakespeare: he returns to it again and again in his plays, setting the dilemma up in different circumstances, changing the character of the friends and the woman, playing the plot out to different conclusions. Several feminist and psychoanalytic critics have discerned this particular figure in Shakespeare's carpet and have interpreted it variously: Leslie Fiedler and Janet Adelman, as a biographical fact about Shakespeare's "personal mythology," Peter Erickson and Catherine Belsey as a social fact about the relations of men and women in sixteenth- and seventeenth-century English society, Coppélia Kahn and W. Thomas MacCary as a psychological fact about how males develop a sense of self and learn to fall in love with females.[59] We find the pattern most often in the comedies Shakespeare wrote at the beginning of his career and in the tragicomedies he wrote toward the end, but it figures also in several of his tragedies: Proteus-Silvia-Valentine, Romeo-Juliet-Mercutio, Bassanio-Portia-Antonio, Sebastian-Olivia-Antonio, Hamlet-Ophelia-Horatio, Bertram-Helena-Parolles, Othello-Desdemona-Iago, Macbeth-Lady Macbeth-Banquo, Antony-Cleopatra-Caesar, Polixines-Hermione-Leontes all play out Shakespeare's idiosyncratic version of the Myth of Combatants and Comrades. The degree of sexual feeling between these pairs of male friends varies from the passionless political understanding between Antony and Caesar to the blind infatuation that makes Antonio of Illyria devote himself so selflessly to Sebastian. Adelman calls Antonio's unrequited love in *Twelfth Night* "the strongest and most direct expression of homoerotic feeling in Shakespeare's plays."[60]

The most pathetic of these severed friends, however, is Shakespeare's more famous Antonio, the merchant of Venice who hazards everything for his friend—and loses him to a woman. The strange melancholy that possesses Antonio when his friend Bassanio starts wooing Portia is an unsettled, and unsettling, mystery from beginning to end. "Such a want-wit sadness makes of me," Antonio confesses in the play's first speech, "That I have much ado to know myself" (1.1.6-7). It must be worry over business, Solanio proposes. No? Perhaps Antonio is in love. "Fie, fie!" (1.1.46). Why then, Antonio must be one of those naturally dour people who never smile at anything. The way the men communicate with each other in act 1, scene 1 of *The Merchant of Venice* leaves no room for talk about feelings. Money and commerce are the topics they toss about in their verbal games of male comradery. Especially after Graziano arrives, no one is ever at a loss for words. No one, that is, but Antonio. When all the other men have gone and Antonio is left alone with his friend, the easy banter continues for a moment. Then comes an awkward pause, signaled by Antonio's ruminative "Well . . . " and his shift away from Bassanio's familiar prose back to the calculated verse that the men as a group were speaking before:

> BASSANIO.
> Graziano speaks an infinite deal of nothing, more than any
> man in all Venice. His reasons are as two grains of wheat hid in
> two bushels of chaff: you shall seek all day ere you find them,
> and when you have them they are not worth the search.
> ANTONIO.
> Well, tell me now what lady is the same
> To whom you swore a secret pilgrimage,
> That you today promised to tell me of.

(1.1.114-121)

The implied silence between these two speeches speaks volumes. We realize all the more what is *not* being said when we shift in scene 2 from Venice to Belmont, from city to country, from an all-male world to an all-female world, and hear the play's two heroines talk to one another about love in a direct, easy way the men cannot manage. Even in language, affairs of the heart prove very different from affairs of the mart. By saving the day in court, by tricking their lovers out of the rings they gave them, by beating the men at their own game, Portia and Nerissa teach Bassanio and Graziano truths about men loving women and women loving men that the two male friends so clearly do not know in act 1, scene 1. Clutching the letter that informs him of his argosies' safe return, the merchant of Venice stands amid the romantic couplings of act 5 as odd man out.

How typical is Antonio's fate? Who wins in Shakespeare's versions of Plutarch's debate? How critics answer that question depends largely on how they read the issues in the conflict between male bonding and matrimony. In charting the development of Shakespeare's "personal mythology," Fiedler sees a move toward melancholy and even guilt about sexual ties between men. Shakespeare's strategy for dealing with the "womanly" aspects of himself, Fiedler proposes, is to project them onto unnatural witches like Lady Macbeth and to play them out in women temporarily disguised as boys, in characters like Rosalind, Portia, and Viola. As a master magician who can effect such transformations at will Prospero represents the ultimate triumph of the male principle.

Most of the other critics, however, find the greater power in the Myth of Companionate Marriage, in the ideal of husbands loving wives. In his essentially social view of male bonding in Shakespeare's plays, Erickson traces a gradual accommodation with women, a move from serious commitment to male bonding in *Henry V* to ambivalence in *Othello* to a decisive break in *Antony and Cleopatra* to a recapitulation of the whole process in *The Winter's Tale*. In pursuing the protagonists' quest for male identity, Kahn and MacCary also see a gradual opening up to the "otherness" of women. Between the militant maleness that Fiedler finds and the accommodation between the sexes that Erickson, Kahn, and MacCary perceive, Adelman and Belsey make out, in different ways, a middle course. The improbable, magical circumstances that allow friendship to be reconciled with marriage in early plays like *The Two Gentlemen of Verona* give way, Adelman suggests, to the defeat of friendship in *The Merchant of Venice* and to tragic consequences for all concerned in *Othello* and *Hamlet*, but Shakespeare returns in *The Winter's Tale* to his earlier "fantasy of sexual simultaneity," a dubious vision of experience in which heterosexual and homosexual desires can be satisfied in one relationship. Just as Valentine announces at the end of *The Two Gentlemen of Verona* that he and his friend, once married, can share "one feast, one house, one mutual happiness" (5.4.171), so Leontes at the end of *The Winter's Tale* is restored, quite against his deserving, to both wife and friend.[61] Belsey is likewise sceptical of a really viable "solution" to the dilemma: by playing male bonding off against matrimony Shakespeare calls traditional gender roles into question without offering any permanent redefinitions. The net effect, Belsey proposes, is an existential "gap" in which "we are able to glimpse a possible meaning, an image of a mode of being, which is not a-sexual, nor bisexual, but which disrupts the system of differences on which sexual stereotyping depends."[62]

If we accept Shakespeare and not John Fletcher as the controlling presence behind *The Two Noble Kinsmen*, it is much harder to see an ultimate reconciliation between the conflicting demands of friendship and matrimony.[63] One of Shakespeare and Fletcher's sources was Plutarch's Life of Theseus, and the image of male bonding they found there seems to have guided them as they adapted the main story of the play from Chaucer's Knight's Tale. The very last thing Shakespeare wrote for the stage, *The Two Noble Kinsmen* reenacts the plot of *The Two Gentlemen of Verona*, but with a much sharper sense of the sexual and emotional complexities that are entangled in the earlier comedy's simplicities. Palamon and Arcite are no less devoted to one another than Valentine and Proteus; Arcite is no less precipitous than Proteus in conceiving a passion for the lady his friend has loved first; male friendship is no less severely tested by romantic passion. This time, however, the two friends' speeches pulse with sexual innuendo—innuendo of which they themselves seem blithely unaware until they both fall in love with Emilia. Until that moment they delight in presenting themselves as complete sexual innocents. In the discrepancy between what they say and what the audience sees resides much of the comedy in this otherwise tragic play.

The two friends' decamping from Thebes to Athens is, in Arcite's view, not so much a flight from Creon's despotism as a flight from sexual experience:

> Dear Palamon, dearer in love than blood,
> And our prime cousin, yet unhardened in
> The crimes of nature, let us leave the city,
> Thebes, and the temptings in't, before we further
> Sully our gloss of youth.
> And here to keep in abstinence we shame
> As in incontinence.

(1.2.1-7)

That phrase "the crimes of nature" has a most curious ring. Just what *are* such acts? Crimes to which the whole sublunary world is susceptible? Crimes of *human* nature in particular? Crimes that spring from "natural" urges? Or does Arcite have in the back of his mind crimes "against" nature? One thing is certain: Arcite imagines the "nature" of these crimes as sexual. They are "temptings" from which the two noble youths stand back in "abstinence," lest they "sully" their "gloss" of innocence. Arcite makes Thebes sound for all the world like Sodom and Gomorrah.

Arrived in Athens and thrown into prison, the cousins take comfort in their self-sufficiency as friends. Once again Arcite is the speaker, and once again his language is full of sexual suggestion. Prison becomes a "holy sanctuary," protecting the young kinsmen from the "corruption" of worse men and "the poison of pure spirits." And this "poison," this threat to "purity," Arcite identifies specifically with women. Turned inward, the two friends' sexual desires find their object, metaphorically at least, in each other: "We are one another's wife," Arcite declares, "ever begetting/New births of love." Along with business, quarrels, envy, and death, Arcite includes "a wife" among the things he fears might part friend from friend outside prison. Locked up together, "we shall live long and loving" (2.1.71-94). During these passionate denials of passion Palamon maintains a certain reticence. Once Palamon has spied Emilia and promptly fallen in love, the two friends' roles are reversed: Palamon becomes the eager leader, Arcite the reluctant follower. Catechized by his friend, Arcite confesses his own passion for Emilia. Even so, he would love her with less abandon than Palamon—and he would love her *along with* Palamon:

> I will not, as you do, to worship her
> As she is heavenly and a blessèd goddess!
> I love her as a woman, to enjoy her—
> So both may love.

> (2.1.165-168)

A witty quibble? Or a desperate ploy not to be left behind? Only when Palamon tells him point-blank, "You shall not love at all," does Arcite become defiant and proclaim himself the enemy of his friend. To the end Arcite maintains his contemptuous view of Emilia as merely a body to be enjoyed—and dies a martyr to male friendship when Palamon kills him in the tournament.

What we are invited to feel for Arcite, as for Antonio in *The Merchant of Venice* and Antonio in *Twelfth Night*, is not the contempt we usually feel for blocking figures, but pity. "I was false,/Yet never treacherous. Forgive me, cousin" (5.4.91-92) are Arcite's dying words. On first hearing, the distinction sounds strange. "False"? In what sense is "false" the opposite of "treacherous"? Throughout the play "false" has been alliterated with "friend" and "friendship." If Arcite pretends to love Emilia, Palamon protests, he is

> a fellow
> False as thy title to her. Friendship, blood,
> And all the ties between us I disclaim,
> If thou once think upon her.

> (2.2.174-177)

When Arcite perseveres, Palamon tells him how he wishes "thy false self and thy friend" were out of prison and could take up swords (2.2.211). Crossing paths with Arcite in the forest, Palamon addresses him as "falsest cousin" (3.1.38). And when Theseus interrupts their fight in act 3, scene 6, Palamon reveals Arcite's identity to the duke in two contemptuous fricatives: "A falser ne'er seemed friend" (3.6.142). In his dying words Arcite attempts to answer these accusations. He dies true to the cause of male friendship. What we see in *The Two Noble Kinsmen*, as in many of Shakespeare's earlier comedies, is the social and psychological "necessity" of marriage that Berowne points out in *Love's Labors Lost* but, at the same time, the emotional weight of necessity's yoke on men who will not, or cannot, marry. On the issue of male bonding versus marriage Shakespeare finished his career, not with one of the reconciliations that are the common theme of his other late plays, but with a fresh recognition of the impasse between the two.

In Shakespeare's comedies and tragicomedies marital love's labor is always won. However diverse these plays may be in circumstance and character, however different they may be in emotional effect, however strong the demands of male bonding may be, all of Shakespeare's comedies and tragicomedies end with male friendship yielding place to heterosexual love. What varies are the feelings that attend this inevitable event. Shakespeare's plays, early and late, simply reproduce what happened to most young men when they left the all-male social groups in which they had come to maturity. Most students martriculated at Oxford and Cambridge when they were 16, 17, or 18; almost none took up residence after the age of 20. Most young men admitted to the inns of court fell in the same age range.[64] In both institutions men who had lived together as members of all-male households throughout their youth were spending their last years together as members of closed all-male societies before they married, set up their own households, and assumed their duties as fully responsible members of Elizabethan society.

We come away from Shakespeare's plays, then, with a strong sense of the erotic force behind both male traits, a disposition toward aggression and a disposition to form strong bonds with other males. At the same time, we are forced to confront the problematic place of homosexuality in sixteenth- and seventeenth-century English society—and in sixteenth- and seventeenth-century English literature. To a degree perhaps greater than today, structures of power in early modern England fostered the homosexual potentiality in male bonding, yet society gave official sanction only to matrimony. Likewise with structures of ideology. Plutarch's Life of Theseus articulates an ideal of male friendship that plumbs its sexual undercurrents, yet the Myth of Combatants and Comrades works at cross-purposes to the Myth of Companionate Marriage celebrated in romantic comedy.

Which, then, *was* the case? Was early modern England, as Coke and the moralists suggest, homophobic, or was it, in some less outspoken way, homophilic? By attending to the arguments of the moralists and the laws of the jurists, Alan Bray concludes the former.[65] By attending to the laxity with which these arguments and laws were enforced, B. R. Burg describes a society that was at least tolerant of homosexual behavior if not positively disposed toward it.[66] Surely the truth lies somewhere in between. Patriarchy, Eve Sedgwick argues, always founds its power by harnassing the energies of homosexuality—or by stifling them:

> in any-male dominated society, there is a special relationship between male homosocial (*including* homosexual) desire and the structures for maintaining and transmitting patriarchal power: a relationship founded on an inherent and potentially active structural congruence. For historical reasons, this special relationship may take the form of ideological homophobia, ideological homosexuality, or some highly conflicted but intensively structured combination of the two.[67]

If fifth- and fourth-century Athens exemplifies "ideological homosexuality," if our own society exemplifies "ideological homophobia," the society of Shakespeare's England quite clearly exemplifies conflict. Since our own patriarchal culture subscribes to the first of Sedgwick's ideological possibilities, homosexuality is popularly regarded today as a rejection of masculine identity. That was no more the case in Shakespeare's day than it was in Plutarch's. However loudly the moral and the legal discourse of Renaissance England may insist on the first of these three relationships, the poetic discourse of the age intimates the third.

The result is an indeterminacy that keeps homosexuality hidden and elusive but at the same time makes it provocative to the imagination of a perspicacious playwright like Shakespeare. Several writers on homosexuality in early modern England have attempted to get at this ambiguity. It was the *vagueness* with which homosexuality was defined, Alan Bray proposes, that allowed men to dissociate the personal fact of homosexuality from the social sanctions against it. The fact that there were so few prosecutions between 1550 and 1650 does not reflect an enlightened tolerance, Bray argues;

> it was rather a reluctance to recognise homosexual behavior, a sluggishness in accepting that what was being seen was indeed the fearful sin of sodomy. It was this that made it possible for the individual to avoid the psychological problems of a homosexual relationship or a homosexual encounter, by keeping the experience merely casual and undefined: readily expressed and widely shared though the prevalent attitude to homosexuality was, it was kept at a distance from the great bulk of homosexual behavior by an unwillingness to link the two.[68]

Vagueness about the "sin" of sodomy is a feature of moral discourse about homosexuality. The legal discourse, with its limited, absolutely precise terms and conditions, provided just the opposite reason for not seeing homosexuality in situations where a twentieth-century observer would. Looking, not at legal and moral discourse, but at poetry and painting, Philippe Ariès discerns a curious ambivalence about sexual desire and gender identity:

> I think that in certain cultures, e.g., the Italian Quattrocento and Elizabethan England, there developed, out of an apparently asexual form of sentiment, a particular kind of manly love that verged on homosexuality; but it was a homosexuality that was undeclared and unadmitted, that remained a mystery, less through fear of prohibition than from a distaste for labelling oneself in the eyes of contemporary society as non-sexual or sexual. One hovered in a mixed zone that belonged to neither.[69]

Jonathan Goldberg's phrase for the same situation is an "open secret"—with an emphasis on "open": homosexuality in early modern England was something that existed, something that everyone knew existed, but something that had no name of its own.[70]

To ask, as some social historians have done, whether any homosexual subcultures existed in early modern Europe is to miss the point.[71] Moral and legal ideology about homosexuality in early modern England may sound much like the moral and legal ideology of contemporary Europe and America, but in its disposition of power the culture of early modern England situated homosexuality in a more ambiguous and complicated way. Far from being the rallying point for a subculture that served to isolate one category of males from another, homosexuality was one of many symbolic ways in which males could enact and affirm the patriarchal power that dominated the entire culture. However rigorously English law may have proscribed acts of genital contact between men, English society encouraged the feelings that could lead to such acts. In a post-Freudian view, Shakespeare's plays seem to reveal a "repressed" sexuality. But such a view is anachronistic, the result of drawing the lines of sexual distinction very differently from the way they were drawn in Shakespeare's own culture. Behavior that we would label homosexual, and hence a rejection of maleness, was for them an *aspect* of maleness. Seen in this light, homoerotic power play at the court of James I may not be a strange aberration from the court of his predecessor but a manifestation of forces that had been covertly at work throughout the reign of Elizabeth I. The erotic charge to politics at the court of James I may be more a sign of how power circulated in the society at large than an accident of how a single man happened to distribute political favors. In terms of the male power structure of English Renaissance society, James's homosexuality may be the equivalent of Elizabeth's virginity: the erotic seal of men's political transactions with one another. It may be more than coincidence that Shakespeare's three main plays about soldiering date from the very year of James's coronation (*Troilus and Cressida* was entered in the Stationers Register in 1603) and the years immediately following (*Othello* has been dated to 1604 and *Coriolanus* to 1607-08).

The general fact of gender segregation and patriarchy in Elizabethan and Jacobean society, the imagery in Shakespeare's plays about military heroes, Coke's specification that pederasty is but one species of sodomy, the fact that Castlehaven's servants were considered adults and were later tried and executed for complying with their master's desires, even the beard that identifies John Childe as a mature adult in the woodcut that illustrates *The Shamefull Ende, of Bishop Atherton, and his Proctor John Childe*: all of this evidence suggests that one received idea about homosexuality in the Renaissance needs to be reexamined. Adapting a typology first proposed by Geoffrey Gorer, Stephen O. Murray has attempted to connect *Social Theory, Homosexual Realities* by isolating three "social organizations of homosexuality"—age-graded, gender-marked, and egalitarian—to account for all the culture-specific and time-specific evidence that has been collected by anthropologists and social historians.[72] Among social historians a consensus seems to have emerged that age-graded sexual relations—men taking their pleasure with younger boys—characterized Renaissance Europe just as it had fifth-century Athens. It was not until the eighteenth century, so Murray, Randolph Trumbach, Alan Bray, Gert Hekma, David F. Greenberg, and others have argued, that gender entered the ontological picture and males who enjoyed sex with other males, the passive partners at least, began to speak, act, and sometimes dress like women. Only in the twentieth century, so the argument goes, has there emerged an egalitarian subculture in which age or stereotyped gender roles are not decisive factors in how males who have sexual relations with other males perceive themselves, if not in how they are perceived by others. Pedophilia precedes androphilia.[73] Much of the legal discourse about homosexuality in sixteenth- and seventeenth-century England would suggest that this is true. Poetic discourse is another matter. We come closer to the lived experience of being male in early modern England, I believe, if we recognize a *potential* for erotic feeling in male relationships of all kinds. Age-graded homosexuality, gender-marked homosexuality, egalitarian homosexuality: all three were possible ways of enacting male bonds among Shakespeare and his contemporaries.

In the progressions we shall be following in this book, the Myth of Combatants and Comrades is both the starting point and, in a sense, the whole. All the other myths are but particular ways of acting out the universal fact of male bonding in human society. All the other myths take this one as a subtext. In anthropological terms, then, we have here the broadest, most inclusive myth of all. In chronological terms, it is a myth that remained current throughout the period. In social terms, it represents a licit, public way of acting on homoerotic desire. Since all men in Elizabethan and Jacobean society participated in patriarchy, the Myth of Combatants and Comrades incorporated them all, high and low, literate and illiterate alike. That social inclusiveness was strengthened, in psychological terms, by the way the Myth of Combatants and Comrades leaves homosexual desire so diffuse and undefined, making it possible to deny any connection between desire and deed, between *masculus amor* and the precisely defined crime of sodomy. In artistic terms, finally, Shakespeare's plays about soldiering and about courtship pursue safe, well charted courses through the treacherous waters of sexual desire. In both kinds of plays homosexuality remains only an implicit subject. Both kinds of plays celebrate social orthodoxy: Theseus may grasp Pirithous's hand, but he also weds Hippolyta.

CHAPTER THREE

THE PASSIONATE SHEPHERD

The shepherd *Corydon* loved sore *Alexis* faire that youth
His lords delight, and yet he had not that which he did hope,
He came full oft the beeches thicke unto with shadie tops,
There all alone he cast unto the mounteins and the woods
These words rude and disordered with labour spent in vaine,
["]O cruell *Alex* for my songs thou doost not care a straw
Of us thou doost no pitie take, yea more, thou mak'st me die.["][1]

ASC.

ROXIMA formosum) Secundæ Eclogæ quæ in scribitur Alexis, argumentum tale est: Corydó pastor impatienter amans Alexim, formosissimum puerum, ipsumque per auia, & inaccessa, quæritans, omnia ferè quæ ad conciliandū amorem facere possent, commemorat, quibus cum
nihil proficeret prope suadet, stulto amori modum impone re. Huius Eclogæ scribendæ, ratio potuit esse, Vt Theocriti Eclogam tertiam, cui similli ma est imitaretur, sed illic Amaryllis, vt hic Alexis, amatur. Siue, vt pueri a se, licet honestè dilecti, quem ab Asinio Pollione dono acceperat amicabiliter meminisse posset, Siue, vt Pollioni blandiatur, nam (vt Donat. dicit) eũ maxime amauit Maro, & ab eo magna munera tulit, quip pe qui inuitatus ad coenam captus pulchritudine, & diligentia, seu indulgentia Alexandri, Pollionis pueri, eum dono accepit. Quam rem videtur Horatius tangere. 1. epistolaṛ, dicens: Non

ancilla tuũ iecur vlceret vlla, puer ue Inter marmoreum vene randi limen amici, Ne dominus pueri pulchri, earũ ue puellæ, Munere te paruo beet, aut incommodus angat. Hæc ibi. Quàm rem Virgilio vsu venisse dicunt, sed neque illud Horaṛ, Maronem exprimit, neque hic aliud ad id, quod Donatus asserit, magis alludit, quàm quòd dicit eum Delicias amasse domini. Verum cum in fine dicat, se eo non potuis, aliomque quæsiturus, non videatur semper de Alexandro loqui, quo Donatus fuerat. De hac re autem plenius dicam ibi, Mille mea sicula, &c. Lege etiam Macrobium. Ordo versiculorum.

ASC.

ARGVMENTVM ASCENSIANVM
IN ALEXIM VIRGILII.

Prima forsum Corydon qua lustrat Alexim .
Si nequeat flecti , discedere suadet amori .

nostrorum est : Proxima, scilicet a prima, hoc est secunda Eclo ga. qua, id est in qua, Corydon pastor ille amatus, lustrat, id est quærit Alexim puerum illum, formosum. spectiosum, & formæ plenum suadet, scilicet in fine carmina, discedere amori. id a more, si nequeat flecti . Dicit enim, Inuenies alium si re hic fastidit Alexis. Et hæc de argumento in generali.

SERV.

ORMOsum Pastor Corydon) Virgilius in persona Corydonis intelligitur, & Cæsar in persona Alexis inducitur. [Corydon) Fictum nomen est ab aue, quæ corydalus dicitur. [Ardebat Alexim) Impatienter diligebat. [Alexim) Quem dicunt Alexandrum, fuit seruus Asinij Pollionis, quem Virgilius rogatus ad prandium, cum vidisset in ministerio omnium pulcherrimum, dilexit, eumq. dono accepit. Cæsarem quidam acceperant formosum in operibus & gloria. Alij puerum Cæsaris, quem si quis laudasset, gratam rem Cæsari feciset. Nam Virgilius dicitur in pueros habuisse amorem, nec enim turpiter eos diligebat. Alij Corydonem Asinij Pollionis puerum adamasse a Virgilio ferunt, eumq. à domino ipsi datum, Corydonem a Virgilio ficto nomine nuncupari ex eo genere auis quæ corydalus dicitur , dulce carnem . Alexim vero puerum, quasi sine responsione ac super bum . hunc autem dilectum fuisse Pollionis, & Virgilium gratum se futurum existimasse, si eum laudaret, cuius formæ Pollio delectabatur , qui eo tempore Transpadanam Italiæ partem tenebat, & agris præerat diuidendis. [Delicias domini) Hoc est qui suo domini Cæsari, vel Pollioni in delicijs erat. [Nec, quid speraret) à nec spem potiundi habebat. [Tantum) Tantummodo [Assidue) a sæpius. [Incondita) Incomposita, subito dicta, agrestia, vel insanæ mentis dicta verba. vel incondita .i. inconcinna, vt Salustius in Iugurthino. At illi quibus res incognita erat, ruere, cuncti ad portas , incondita tenere . [Montibus) Qui amorem ei præibant, [iactabat) .i. fundebat incassum . [inani) Præ amore nihil sibi procurans, sed in absentem iuuenem lo quebatur.

ORYDON Pastor impatienter amans Alexim puerum formosissimum, omnia fe rè, quæ ad conciliandum amorem facere possent , commemorat : quibus cum nihil profi ceret, quod maximum est in amore reme dium . ad neglectam rerum domesticarum curam animum sibi esse conuertendum censet, iuxta illud, Otia si tollas, perie re Cupidinis artes.

ALEXIS.
ECLOGA SECVNDA.

ORMOSVM Pastor Corydon
ardebat Alexim ,
Delicias domini, nec, quid speraret, habebat.
Tantum inter densas vmbrosa cacumina fagos
Assidue veniebat. ibi hæc incondita solus
Montibus, & siluis studio iactabat inani.

ORMOSVM ASC
Pastor Corydon ardebat, &c.)Corydon inquit pastor, pastor quidam vehementer amabat Alexim formosum puerum , quem in debcijs suis, dominus eius habuerat, vnde nulla eius potuundi spes Corydoni erat , nec tamen minus amauit, vnde assidue veniebat ad solitudinem nemorum , vbi cantilenam de amato poterat inaniter repetebat. hoc dicit Seruius, per Corydona, Virgilium, & per Alexim , Alexandrem Pollionis puerum intelligit, ad quod di cendum , dixi, non cogit interpretem, quia si ex communi pastorum æteruo, persona de promptus dixerit, non minus consequeretur, quod præteditt poeta amoris .i. impatientis fruitntiam exponere, & remedium dare, verum quia (vt di xit Mancinellus) Apul. manifestè prædicat per Corydona, Virgilium intelligi; dicamus id verum esse, sic tñ vt non omnia ei quadrent, q artificio se facit, ne historiam contexisse dicatur, nec Augustum per Alexim significatse, vllo modo dicendum est. Ordo est. Corydon pastor. formosum, ardebat .i. impatienter amabat, ac depe ribat Alexim, puerũ illum formosam. formæ, & species ple num, appositorie, delicias domini. i. patroni sui, nec, supple Corydon habebat quid speraret .i. vnde eius potiundi spem haberet, tñ .i. tantummodo, sup. hoc spei habere videbatur, q assidue veniebat inter densas fagos, appositorie, cacumina vmbrosa .i. summitates montium, aut arborum, vmbris arboris rectas, & ipse solus iactabat .i. incassum fundebat, inani studio .i. stulto conatu in montibus, & siluis, hæc incondi a. i. rudia, & incomposita, quæ sequuntur carmina. [Formosus) Dicitur à for ma, & forma (tñ Donatum) à formo, seu foruo, q ̃ od est calidõ fm eundem, quia sanguinei, & ferè iuniores omnes, q ̃ ibus sanguis adhuc calidus est, formosi esse solent potius q ̃ pui hri. [Co
Virg.

b

Virgil, Eclogue 2

from *Universum Poema* (Venice: Giovanni Maria Bonelli, 1558)

The introductions and line-by-line commentaries that literally frame Virgil's text in sixteenth- and seventeenth-century printings of the *Bucolica* offered Renaissance readers a morally comfortable point of view on what might otherwise seem to be a scandalous text.

Τhe scenario of Virgil's second eclogue is all the more beguiling for seeming so guileless. What could be more inviting than this landscape of mountains and woods, of "beeches thicke . . . with shadie tops"? What could be more disarming than this simple shepherd who pours out his heart's desire? All the other senses—sight, smell, taste, touch—are fused with the seductive sounds of Corydon's verse as he woos Alexis with promises of pleasure:

> O faire well favoured youth come heere, behold the nymphs
>   doo bring
> Lillies for thee by baskets full . . . .
> . . . .
> My selfe will gather peaches gray, with tender cotton cotes
> And chestnuts too, which *Amaryll* my sweet hart loved well,
> And I will put plums unto these[,] plums red and soft as wax.

Corydon's monologue conjures up an irresistible vision of how the world *ought* to be, a place where mountains, trees, flowers, animals, indeed every feature of the landscape is suffused with human feeling.

In the imaginations of poets and painters the landscape of Virgil's eclogues suggested what the world was like in the Golden Age, before greed and war had turned the world into a place of work and turmoil. Ovid gives that primeval time its classic description in book 1 of the *Metamorphoses*:

> The Springtime lasted all the yeare, and Zephyr with his milde
> And gentle blast did cherish things that grew of owne accorde,
> The ground untilde, all kinde of fruits did plenteously afforde.
> No mucke nor tillage was bestowed on leane and barren land,
> To make the corne of better head, and ranker for to stand.
> Then streames ran milke, then streames ran wine, and yellow
>   honny flowde
> From ech greene tree whereon the rayes of firie Phebus
>   glowde.[2]

For Renaissance readers at least, this was the setting for the ensuing episodes in Ovid's vision of boundless passion, a place where desire was unconstrained, forever changing, never sated. Encountering it again and again in classical, medieval, and Renaissance literature, philologists have given this local habitation of heart's desire a name: the *locus amoenus*.[3] To the Elizabethan imagination it was a place charged with erotic feeling, a place where being in love and composing eclogues about being in love are mankind's only concerns.

For English readers, the *locus amoenus* took shape not only as shepherds' fields but as a forest, the setting for Whitsuntide revelry presided over by a local young man dressed up as Robin Hood. Arcadia and Arden, the golden world and the greenwood, are fused when Charles in *As You Like It* tells Oliver that the exiled duke

> is already in the Forest of Ardenne, and a many merry men with him; and there they live like the old Robin Hood of England. They say many young gentlemen flock to him every day, and fleet the time carelessly, as they did in the golden world.[4]

In these lines Charles indicates another feature of Virgil's eclogues that is transferred to Arden: the exclusion of women. Nymphs like Nais and Amaryll may be glimpsed in the distance, but Virgil's spokesmen are without exception male. Arcadia is a society in which men do all the feeling and all the talking. Charles's description of Arden, home to Robin Hood and his merry men, also makes explicit what is implicit in Arcadia: the equality of its inhabitants. By leaving behind the world of the court, Duke Senior and his retinue escape not only political strife but the distinctions between men that are the cause of that strife. In Arden, all men are foresters; in Arcadia, shepherds. What we discover in these visions of "the golden world" is male bonding in its purest form, unadulterated by women, uncomplicated by social hierarchy, uncompromised by disguise.

As such, the pastoral scenario presents a perfect homolog to the all-male social institutions that nurtured sixteenth- and seventeenth-century males from boyhood to manhood. For the sons of gentlemen and for the sons of ambitious gentry and merchants those rites of passage were carried out away from home and family, in someone else's household or, increasingly in the sixteenth century, in residence at Oxford, Cambridge, or London. At the beginning of the century most boys were educated by private tutors; by the end most were attending a grammar school. To finish his education a young man at the beginning of the century customarily undertook service in an aristocratic household; by 1600 he was more likely to enroll in an educational institution like Oxford or Cambridge or in one of the London inns of court that were home to aspiring lawyers. It was during the sixteenth century that most students at Oxford and Cambridge moved out of dispersed lodgings into organized colleges. At the same time the social range of the young men who went up to Oxford and Cambridge broadened, so that sons of merchants and artificers were brought into contact with sons of the nobility and the gentry.[5] The increasing size and importance of London in the sixteenth century brought new prominence to the inns of court. The effect of all these changes in educational institutions was, as Keith Wrightson points out, to create a sense of homogeneous national culture among the English ruling class.[6] And part of that homogeneity was its maleness.

An Elizabethan schoolboy learned his masculine identity while he was learning his letters. As Walter J. Ong observes, the whole social premise of education from antiquity well into our own century was competitiveness. It was not until the late 1960s, when coeducation finally conquered the last bastions of male exclusivity in British and American colleges and universities, that teachers dropped the role of friendly adversary for the role of friend, that physical punishments and dormitory regulations disappeared, that competitive debates gave way to political rallies celebrating partisan unity, that handshakes after the "defense" of a dissertation were replaced by a receipt from the dean for the completed typescript—and that Latin was dropped as a required subject.[7] The history of Latin education is, in Ong's view, the history of all-male education. In the Renaissance, Latin functioned as a code-language that initiated boys into manhood:

> Puberty rites are *rites de passage,* transition rites. They are didactic, for in them the initiates are given understanding of more or less secret tribal lore. They involve calculated hardship: often the boys are snatched with violence or mock violence from the arms of their mothers and established in an all-male extrafamilial environment where they undergo various trials and often physical torture. They emerge with an *esprit de corps,* a feeling that they have gone through rough times together, which helps to establish the typically male "bonding pattern" . . . . By the Renaissance—and indeed for centuries before—Learned Latin was eminently qualified as an instrument for a puberty rite of this sort.[8]

In effect, Latin was the tribal language of educated men. As a male code, Latin in the Renaissance was the language of law, diplomacy, and international trade. It was also the language of sexual knowledge.[9] As long as Martial, Horace, Catullus, and Ovid remained in Latin, the frank picture they offered of sexual license in pagan antiquity posed no particular cause for alarm. It could be put into Christian perspective by the teacher. But when Christopher Marlowe translated Ovid's salacious elegies into English, the moralists burned his book. To translate such texts into English was not only to cast pearls before monolingual swine; it was to divulge male secrets to women. Something of that same exclusivity attaches to Virgil's second eclogue, even in English translation. On the surface, the poem seems to be about the elegantly expressed passion of a shepherd; read *in situ*, in the social context of a school, college, or one of the inns of court, its reference could be construed as something much more personal and immediate. For Renaissance schoolboys like Marlowe and Shakespeare, Latin was the public language of male power and the private language of male sexual desire—of homosexual desire in particular.

Schools, colleges, and the inns of court were *households* in both the literal and the figurative senses of the word: young men studied together, played together, ate together, and, like everybody else in the sixteenth century, slept together two to a bed. Existence for an Elizabethan boy who was set by his parents on an ambitious course in life was very different from what it would be today. He was removed from his mother and home at an early age to an all-male environment; he came to maturity in an all-male household that had a sharp sense of its own identity, its own traditions, even its own language; he married at what, for us, would be a late age, a full ten to fifteen years after sexual maturity; and he had extremely limited sexual access to women of his own age and social class because of the high premium placed on female virginity. If an anthropologist were to tell us these things about a society in the Antipodes, what conclusions would we draw about the sexlife of a youth in that society? Doubtless something very different from the comfortably familiar image we maintain of Renaissance England simply because we speak the same language. Lawrence Stone, for one, finds it remarkable that parents could send their sons away from home with so little anxiety about what might happen to them sexually.[10] About what actually went on in schools, colleges, and the inns of court there is very little direct evidence. Nicholas Udall was fired as headmaster of Eton in the 1540s because he "did commit buggery . . . sundry times" with one or more of his scholars (but went on to become headmaster of Westminster School a short time later).[11] Among his prize pupils Roger Ascham recalls that "John Whitney, a young gentlemen, was my bedfellow, who, willing by good nature and provoked by mine advice, began to learn the Latin tongue" (the text—pre-, sub-, and actual—was *De Amicitia*).[12] And the character of "A young Gentleman of the University" in John Earle's *Micro-cosmographie*

Chapter Three

(1628) includes the detail that he "ha's beene notorious for an Ingle to gold hatbands, whom he admires at first, afterward scornes."[13] But the most telling evidence is indirect: it is to be found in the poetic discourse of pastoral.

For those young men who did not pursue a classical education but who set out to learn a craft or a trade there was an all-male subculture with a similarly sharp sense of its own identity. In the eyes of the city authorities who dreaded Shrove Tuesday and the annual assault on London's whorehouses, in the eyes of playwrights who incorporated characters like Ralph into plays like *The Knight of the Burning Pestle*, above all in their own eyes as up and coming males in their teens and twenties, the apprentices of London constituted a universally recognized category of person. Not only their sense of themselves but the functions they performed for society mark them as the English equivalent of the confraternities and youth-abbeys that social historians have studied in early modern Italy and France. The functions these organizations performed were as much sexual as social and economic. The youth confraternities of fifteenth-century Florence, as Richard C. Trexlar points out, were organized specifically to counteract the demographic fact of late marriage and the consequent temptations to fornication. Their sixteenth-century equivalents in France, Natalie Zemon Davis has argued, served to reinforce the sexual mores and gender stereotypes of the whole society at the same time that it allowed the boys to use up some of their own libidinal energies. The racket-making charivari visitations carried out by French youth-abbeys against adulterers, older women who married younger husbands, and cowardly husbands who let themselves be beaten by their wives were not only fun; they were socially, and psychologically, functional.[14] London apprentices seem to have had their own version of charivari in their ritual attacks on brothels—places of business at which they themselves were probably regular customers. Be that as it may, "fraternal affection" is the most prominent feature that Steven R. Smith finds in his study of the apprentices' subculture.[15]

In different ways, then, each of these social institutions for young males—schools, colleges, the inns of court, apprenticeship—incorporated a sexual agenda. If social historians have had difficulty discerning that fact, the blame must be laid in part on those historians of *mentalité* who have assured us that in early modern Europe there was no such thing as adolescence and hence no such thing as a specifically adolescent sexuality. Before the eighteenth century, Philippe Ariès has argued, people may have thought about youth as having its own activities, both in work and in leisure, but they did not think about it as constituting, as it does for us, a separate, noncommunicating world apart from adults: "Although adolescents had their own special jobs to do, there was no separate category of adolescence, and so hardly any stereotype of adolescent. There were exceptions. For instance, in fifteenth-century Italy and in Elizabethan literature, adolescence does seem to be personified in a slim, elegant youthfulness, with a faintly ambivalent touch of homosexuality."[16]

What Ariès discerns about physical appearance from painting and poetry is confirmed in body chemistry by the medical discourse of the sixteenth and seventeenth centuries. If psychological states are controlled by the four basic body fluids, if those humors vary according to a person's age, then it is possible to chart the stages of a man's life not according to his social activities but according to what is going on in his body. Seven stages make up the life of man in Lemnius's *The Touchstone of Complexions: Expedient and profitable for all such as been desirous and carefull of their bodily health* . . . (first English edition, 1576). The sixth, between the ages of 15 and 25, is "wilfull and slippery Adolescency"; the seventh, between 25 and 35, "Youth or flourishing Age." During both periods the body is dominated by blood, which makes for health problems that are specifically sexual:

> Thus doe they incite and egge those that abound with blood, and bee sanguine complexioned, to riot, wantonnesse, drunkennesse, wastfulnesse, prodigality, filthy and detestable loves, horrible lusts, incest, and buggery.[17]

In the social scheme of things the major difference between being 15 to 25 and 25 to 35 in early modern England was the fact of marriage. Though not himself an Englishman, Lemnius draws the line between adolescence and youth at precisely the age when most young men in England had accumulated the money that would allow them to marry and set up a household of their own. How they managed the excesses of blood before that age is open to investigation. About students in Oxford and Cambridge colleges and at the inns of court, as well as about apprentices in London, there is plenty of contemporary testimony as to riot, wantonness, drunkenness, wastefulness, and prodigality. Testimony as to "filthy and detestable loves, horrible lusts, incest, and buggery" is understandably harder to come by.

Chapter Three

The sexual difficulties faced by English adolescents are explicitly addressed in Thomas Coghan's *The Haven of Health. Chiefly gathered for the comfort of Students . . .*, a popular manual that went through seven editions between 1584 and 1636. In the last chapter, "Of Venus," Coghan takes up directly the question of what a young man is to do with sexual desire while he remains a student. In this case, the "comfort" promised in Coghan's title is pretty cold. Basically, there are three things one can do: follow St. Paul's advice and pray for relief, keep away from women, and stay hard at work. Any other ideas the reader may have in mind are anticipated—and pointedly disallowed:

> marriage is the onely lawfull meanes to remedy this infirmity of Nature, and all other meanes are abominable in the sight of GOD; as Fornication, Adultery, Buggerie, incest, and that practise of *Diogenes* mentioned of *Galen, Genitalia contrectando semen ejicere*.[18]

Masturbation, despite the recommendation that Galen gives it in his treatise *On the Affected Parts*, is, for Coghan at least, in the same category of abominations as fornication, incest, and sodomy. Not all Renaissance medical authorities agreed. Against the Judeo-Christian abhorence of any kind of sexual activity that was not procreative stood the argument of no less an authority than Aristotle that denial of sexual release could actually be dangerous. The question is raised and answered in the chapter "Of carnall copulation" in Aristotle's *Problems*. Why is moderate sexual activity good?

> bicause it doth expell the fume of the seed from the braine, and it doth expell the matter of impostume. And therefore sometimes, through the intermitting of this act, the darkenes of the sight doth issue, and a giddines in the head. And therefore the seed of a man retained above a due time, is converted into some infectious humour.[19]

Hence the advice by Follopius (a specialist in the tubes of both sexes) and certain other Renaissance medical authorities that masturbation is healthy.[20] And hence the possibility that Thomas Coghan knows precisely whereof he speaks when he raises and condemns masturbation and buggery, along with fornication and incest, as ways that an adolescent male might cope with the excess of blood that is, for the time being, his physiological lot in life. The erotically charged atmosphere that Coghan implies in Renaissance schools and colleges is caught in some of the surviving manuscript collections of pornographic verse known to have been owned by students at Oxford and Cambridge and by young gentlemen at the inns of court. One such manunscript, compiled in the 1630s by Tobias Alston while he was a teenager, contains several homoerotic poems of a satirical bent, as well as some in which the tone is a little harder to get. On the wish list he is making for Fortune the speaker of one such poem includes

> A house that is convenient
> For a lord of ample rent
>   With a posterne door
> In to convay each implement,
> And people to my pleasure lent.

Since in the very next lines he also asks for "A well borne & a pleasing dame/ / . . . able to appease my flame," it is tempting to see anatomical references in that postern door and the lord's ample rent. The bawdy of the satirical poems that struck Alston's fancy would suggest as much.[21]

Having situated sixteenth-century adolescents both institutionally and medically, we can begin to understand why pastoral poetry, seemingly so innocent, could be invested with erotic significance. Pastoral poetry was ideally suited for negotiating the pulls and pushes, the conflicts of positive and negative power, that Foucault sees as the essence of putting sex into discourse. In Arcadia a poet and his readers could escape the prohibitions against desire; they could also, if they chose, confront them in a simpler, more manageable form. Behind the hundreds of pastoral poems, plays, and paintings produced in the sixteenth and seventeenth centuries there were, in fact, two fundamentally different versions of pastoral: "soft" and "hard." The soft version, essentially escapist in spirit, celebrates the pleasures of the *locus amoenus*. Guided by the poet, we find ourselves on the verge of a landscape that delights our eyes and enchants our senses. It beckons us to step beyond the verge of reality where we stand and wander into the dreamworld spread out before us. Modeled ultimately on the idylls that Theocriticus wrote in rustic Doric Greek in the third century B.C., the soft version of pastoral has found a twentieth-century critical apologist in Thomas Rosenmeyer.[22] In the hard version of pastoral the poet has his real sights set on concerns beyond the boundaries of the shepherds' fields. We encounter a landscape of ideas that engages the intellect just as insistently as the landscape of images enchants the senses. It asks us, in effect, to step back from the prospect in front of us and get our bearings in the world we stand in, the world of social and political realities. As George Puttenham puts it in *The Arte of English Poesie* (1589),

> the poet devised the Eglogue . . . not of purpose to counterfeit or represent the rustical manner of loves and communication; but under the vail of homely persons, and in rude speeches to insinuate and glance at greater matters, and such as perchance had not been safe to have disclosed in any other sort.[23]

Modeled ultimately on Virgil's eclogues, this hard version of pastoral has proved the more attractive of the two to twentieth-century academics and has found a particularly eloquent guide in Louis Montrose.[24]

In the specific case of Virgil's second eclogue, these two approaches reveal two rather different poems. What appears, in the soft version of pastoral, to be self-indulgence in homoerotic fantasy can also be seen as a hard look at all the realities—physical, social, and psychological—that keep Corydon from realizing his desires. Or so the Renaissance commentators insist. The introductions and line-by-line commentaries that literally frame Virgil's text in sixteenth- and seventeenth-century printings of the *Bucolica* offered Renaissance readers a morally comfortable point of view on what might otherwise seem to be a scandalous text.

Virgil's persona remembers, first of all, the everyday realities that make sexual passion only a sometime thing:

> Ah *Corydon* ah *Corydon* what madnesse hath thee caught?
> Thou hast a vine halfe cut and lopt growing upon an elme
> All full of leaves; why doost thou not yet rather now at last
> Some wicker worke of ivie rods, or else of rushes soft?
> Thou shalt find out another if this *Alex* thee disdaine.

There are bullocks to be yoked, fields to be plowed, vines to be lopped, baskets to be made. This is the *Argumentum ab utili* that Melanchthon finds in the poem. Next to Corydon's words "what measure can there be for love?" Melanchthon places a marginal tag that turns the whole poem into a negative example of passion's power to corrupt.[25] That is just what Abraham Fleming saw when he translated the poem into English in 1575. Here is "The Argument" Fleming places at the start:

> *Corydon* a shepheard unreasonably in love with a passing faire youth named *Alexis*, and seeking him up and downe in waylesse woods and places void of passage, rehearseth all things which might or could obtaine love and liking; wherewithall when he saw he could doo no good, nor any whit

prevaile, at length he falleth to persuasion, giving himself coun-
sell and advise to keepe a measure in love, least it grow into
foolish outrage.

A second constraint on Corydon's desire is social. Erasmus
singles out the second eclogue for special attention in *De ratione
studii* (1511 et seq.), his how-to manual for Renaissance schoolmasters, and recommends that the eclogue be taught as an illustration of failed friendship. Alexis's disdain seems to turn on
Corydon's lowly status as a shepherd:

> O *Alex* I am scornd of thee, ne ask'st thou what I am,
> How rich in cattell white as snow, how greatly stord
> with milke,
> A thousand lambs of mine doo stray upon *Sicilia* hilles,
> New milke in summer failes me not, ne yet in winter time[.]

Taking this detail at social face value, Erasmus sees Alexis as a
high-born lord. Cordyon the countryman and Alexis the courtier
lack the likenesses that have bound together history's great
friends.[26] *Delicias domini*: what *does* that mean? *Is* Alexis a lord?
Or is he so good-looking that he is worthy only of a "lord's
delight"? Erasmus's speculations may be third-person extrapola-
tions on a first-person poem, but they indicate how Renaissance
readers could never quite forget the social distinctions of their
own world—distinctions that made Arcadia all the more appealing to read about. In the hard version of pastoral, the social
order of the world beyond the shepherds' fields casts shadows
on the landscape of desire. Read as an escapist fantasy, Virgil's
second eclogue might seem to be a Renaissance version of Tobias
Schneebaum's *Keep the River on Your Right*, a celebration of
(homo-)sexual freedom among the natives. Read as allegory, it
becomes a way of talking about real historical personages, real
events, real political conflicts.

A third power that shapes Corydon's passion is time. The
setting sun and "th'increasing shades" prompt the persona to
measure out how far he still remains from realizing his desires.
To Platonizing readers like Christoforo Landino this consciousness of time was a reminder of the decay that ultimately over-
takes all things corporeal. Landino seizes on the philosophical
implications of the eclogue's first two words: *formosum pastor*
leads Landino to a distinction between *forma* and *materia* and to
a lecture on the true source of beauty in form or idea, not in
body or substance.[27] *Forma* is forever, *materia* for just a day.

Above all else, however, Corydon has to face up to the disdainful distance his beloved keeps. As a strategem of seduction, Corydon's verses are, at bottom, a power ploy, an attempt to have his will with Alexis. Corydon is the would-be active giver; Alexis, the passive receiver. That is not how things turn out: Corydon has everything to give, but he cannot compel Alexis to accept his gifts. Virgil's second eclogue may be a plea for communion, but we come away with a sense of the persona's ultimate aloneness. After promising Alexis a shepherds' bounty, Corydon's enthusiasm suddenly fails. He leaves off conjuring images of delight and turns back to his lonely self, addressing himself in the third person:

> O *Corydon* thou art a clowne, *Alex* regards no gifts,
> Ne if by gifts thou strive and straine, may *Iol* give thee place.
> Alacke what might I doo unto my selfe poore sillie man?
> Lost and undone; I have let in southwinds among the floures,
> And bores into the watrie springs[;] my pleasures I have spoild.

For all its fervor, the Myth of the Passionate Shepherd is only a fantasy. Corydon's monologue remains a poem of wooing; it stops short of sexual consummation. In Masters and Johnson's "cycle" of human sexual response, the Myth of the Passionate Shepherd is focused on "excitement" and "plateau." Any orgasm happens only in the speaker's imagination, and only in prospect.

An indulgence of homosexual desire? Or a denial of homosexual desire? Virgil's second eclogue could be, and can be, read as both. Much of the appeal of Renaissance pastoral poetry lies in the shadowy interplay between the "soft" version of what the poem says and the "hard" version of what it seems to imply. Seldom do we find ourselves in a strictly either/or situation. Instead, the mind and the senses are both engaged, producing a sort of "sensuous cerebration" that is distinctive to Renaissance aesthetics. We can see that effect visually by examining the page on which eclogue 2 begins in Giovanni Maria Bonelli's *Universum Poema*, a complete edition of Virgil's works published at Venice in 1558. The folio itself is pleasant to touch and take in hand; a woodcut sinuously expressive of Corydon's passion arrests our eyes; Virgil's verses, elegantly printed in large type, keep the eyes delighted as imagination takes possession of the poem's sensual images of sight, smell, hearing, taste, and touch; read aloud, the clean, clear tones of Virgil's Latin sound in our ears; the frame of commentary challenges our intellect—and makes an appeal to our moral judgment. A Renaissance reader's experience of homosexual desire in Virgil's second eclogue was all these things. The conflict between soft versions of pastoral and hard, between delight and denial, is played out in a variety of ways, but to one end, in works by Christopher Marlowe, Edmund Spenser, William Shakespeare, and Richard Barnfield. They give voice to Corydon's passion; they confront in their own culture the constraints that hedge his passion in.

Only when we have read Virgil's second eclogue do we realize, with a start, that one of the most famous lyric poems of the English Renaissance is implicitly set in Virgil's landscape, is spoken by a persona like Corydon, and may well be addressed to a lovely lad like Alexis. What is Christopher Marlowe's "Come live with mee, and be my love" but a recital of the country pleasures with which Corydon tries to woo Alexis? Marlowe's shepherd is far more seductive than Virgil's, however—and far more witty. Corydon promises lilies, violets, poppies, fleurs-de-lys, fennel-blossoms, sweet-smelling herbs, marigolds. Marlowe's shepherd turns these things to see and smell into things to wear:

> And I will make thee beds of Roses,
> And a thousand fragrant posies,
> A cap of flowers, and a kirtle,
> Imbroydred all with leaves of Mirtle.[28]

Though *kirtle* in its original sense as a tunic or cloak for a man seems to have passed out of usage after 1500, the word survived in the sixteenth century primarily as a term for a robe of state (OED 1, where both of the sixteenth-century examples concern men) and only secondarily as a term for a woman's gown (OED 2). The way Marlowe's shepherd turns Corydon's images of sight and smell into images of touch is altogether typical of the persona's kinaesthetic assault on his beloved's senses. Nor do we find ourselves any less susceptible when we read the poem aloud. We not only see those "shallow Rivers, to whose falls,/Melodious byrds sing Madrigalls"; we hear them, and we feel them as reverberant, rotund sounds in the mouth. Considering Corydon's loving description of the fruits he will bring to Alexis, it is surprising that Marlowe's shepherd attempts to seduce every other sense but taste. That, presumably, must wait until the beloved says yes.

At first glance Marlowe's persona seems totally ingenuous. What could there be in this vision of delight to indicate any differences in status between wooer and wooed? If nothing else, there is the vision of delight itself. As a poem of seduction "Come live with me and be my love" turns words into weapons: the persona seeks to overwhelm his beloved with images of sensuous pleasure, to make the beloved's will bend to his own. After his appeals to sight, hearing, smell, and touch, Marlowe's shepherd concludes,

> If these delights thy minde may move;
> Then live with mee, and be my love.

If not in legal terms, this is nonetheless ravishment. "Come live with me and be my love" is an exercise in soft pastoral. It attempts to seduce the beloved—and us as readers—with promises of a homoerotic idyll beyond the exigencies of time and place that enclose the heroes' desires in the Myth of Combatants and Comrades. Marlowe approaches the pastoral landscape via Ovid's vision of the Golden Age, via the pass that leads into the valley of heart's desire. It was left to Sir Walter Raleigh in his famous "Nymph's Reply to the Shepherd" to approach from the opposite direction: to tarnish Marlowe's golden vision with reason, to point out time's destructiveness, to doubt that there is "truth in every shepherd's tongue."[29] Raleigh does for Marlowe's "Come live with me and be my love" what, as we shall see, George Chapman does for Marlowe's "Hero and Leander."

Raleigh could count on having the last word not only because men everywhere feel the conflict between passion and reason but because Renaissance readers looked upon pastoral as a particularly youthful kind of poetry subject to re-vision from the wiser perspective of middle age. Virgil, they knew, began his writing career with the lowly style and humble subject matter of the *Bucolica*, moved on to the "higher" style and broader range of the *Georgica*, and finished his career with the larger-than-life heroes and epic amplitude of the *Aeneid*. This hierarchy of pastoral-georgic-epic was seen by Renaissance writers as a matter not only of style and breadth of vision but of maturity—the poet's and his readers'. Just as Renaissance writers, following Virgil's example, were expected to start out with pastoral verse and then move on to greater things, so Renaissance schoolboys were set to work on the *Bucolica* before they were allowed to read the *Aeneid*. Abraham Fleming explains this educational program in "The maine argument" prefaced to his translation of Virgil's eclogues:

Now, forsomuch as there bee three kinds of writing or speaking by art (according to *Tullie*) the first homelie and base, the second meane and indifferent, the third stately and aloft; the poet [Virgil] therefore very aptly doubtlesse hath used these three kinds of art: for his Pastoralls are written in a base, his ruralls [the *Georgica*] in a meane, and his Martialls [the *Aeneid*] in a loftie style. Wherefore such as meane to be acquainted with poetrie, let them begin with these Pastoralls, as the *Italians* doo, whose youths or Grammar boyes doo learne these said Pastoralls perfectly, and thereby proove learned yoongmen, wittie and rare poets, deintie in devise, abounding in matter, near in words, and curious in order. . . . For these Pastoralls (the beginning of poetrie) being understood and learned, the entrance and proceeding in greater matters will have the lesse hardnesse.

(sigs. A4-A4ᵛ)

Pastoral verse, then, offered an aspiring young writer a way to try his wings. He could use it as a kind of artistic manifesto, a gathering in of his accumulated experience, a preparation for the "epic" work that lay ahead. It could function, like James Joyce's story of his Dublin upbringing, as *A Portrait of the Artist as a Young Man*. That is just the use to which Edmund Spenser puts the pastoral scenario in *The Shepheardes Calender* (1579) and Richard Barnfield in his three pastoral monologues (1594, 1595). For both writers, the homosexual stirrings of Virgil's second eclogue are a part of youthful experience—and ultimately must be abandoned for "higher" things.

Against the cycle of the twelve months *The Shepheardes Calender* traces the career of Spenser's alter ego, Colin Cloute, as a fledgling poet. As early as "Januarye" we see Colin being deflected from his high calling by the low promptings of sexual passion. The source of these distractions is Rosalind, a girl from the town neighboring the fields in which Colin pursues his poetic labors. It is bad enough that Rosalind keeps Colin from the literary tasks at hand, but she causes him to neglect also his friend Hobbinol:

> It is not *Hobbinol*, wherefore I plaine,
> Albee my love he seeke with dayly suit:
> His clownish gifts and curtsies I disdaine,
> His kiddes, his cracknelles, and his early fruit.
> Ah foolish *Hobbinol*, thy gyfts bene vayne:
> *Colin* them gives to *Rosalind* againe.[30]

The shift in perspective from Virgil is typical of the multiple viewpoints that Spenser gives us on Colin's career. Hobbinol is the Corydon-figure; Colin, the Alexis-figure. The character who was the speaker in Virgil has become a secondary character in Spenser; Virgil's secondary character has become Spenser's speaker. "Alexis" gets to answer "Corydon" just as Raleigh's "nymph" gets to answer Marlowe's "passionate shepherd." We hear a variety of shepherds speak in Spenser's twelve eclogues, but through all the cross talk the one loud voice that booms out over the others is that of "E.K.," the pedantic commentator who supplies for *The Shepheardes Calender* the same kind of learned marginalia that Servius, Landino, Erasmus, and Melanchthon provided for Virgil's *Bucolica*. And E.K. insistently raises the question of homosexual desire on the part of Colin's wooer:

> Hobbinol) is a fained country name, whereby, it being so commune and usuall, seemeth to be hidden the person of some of his very speciall and most familiar freend, whom he entirely and extraordinarily beloved, as peradventure shall be more largely declared hereafter. In thys place seemeth to be some savour of disorderly love, which the learned call paederastice: but it is gathered beside his meaning. For who that hath red Plato his dialogue called Alcybiades, Xenophon and Maximus Tyrius of Socrates opinions, may easily perceive, that such love is muche to be alowed and liked of, specially so meant, as Socrates used it: who sayth, that in deede he loved Alcybiades extremely, yet not Alcybiades person, but hys soule, which is Alcybiades owne selfe. And so is paederastice much to be preferred before gynerastice, that is the love whiche enflameth men with lust toward woman kind. But yet let no man thinke, that herein I stand with Lucian or hys develish disciple Unico Aretino, in defence of execrable and horrible sinnes of forbidden and unlawful fleshlinesse. Whose abominable errour is fully confuted of Perionius, and others.

(p. 18)

Hard as it may be to take this as anything but intellectual over-kill, E.K. does set up here a distinction between spiritual "paederastice" and bodily "gynerastice" that is important to Spenser's view of his youthful self.

Rivalry between a man and a woman for the poet's affections has its origins, perhaps, in the shepherdesses that Virgil's Corydon casually mentions in his suit to Alexis. So disdainful is Alexis that Corydon wonders whether he should not have kept his affections settled on Amaryllis instead:

<blockquote>
had it not better beene
T'avoid the heavie anger and the proud disdaine and spite
Of Amaryll that wench? and had it not far better beene
T'abide Menalca, blacke though he and lovely white were she?
</blockquote>

Later Corydon promises to bring Alexis the fruits that were favorites of Amaryll "my sweet hart." Absent entirely from Virgil, however, is any sense of moral or psychological conflict, any suggestion that Amaryll appeals to Corydon's fleshly side and Alexis to his spiritual side. What Spenser has done in "Januarye" is to raise the great debating point about love that figures so prominently in the Myth of Combatants and Comrades. Male friendship is a higher, nobler thing than love between the sexes. Perfect friendship, even in the view of so free a thinker as Montaigne, is possible only between men. E.K. doesn't even entertain the possibility of friendship between men and women: for him "paederastice" and "gynerastice" constitute totally separate areas of emotional experience.

In setting up this contrast between "paederastice" and "gynerastice" E.K. helps us to see the tragedy in Colin Clout's career. In effect, Spenser turns Virgil's second eclogue into a kind of morality play in which Colin is Everyman, Hobbinol is The Good Angel, and Rosalind is The Bad Angel. Colin, alas, listens to the wrong voice. Instead of listening to his older, wiser friend Hobbinol, he fritters away his talent and his time writing love poems to Rosalind. By the time "December" arrives, Colin has failed to live up to his poetic promise, a victim of sexual passion. Spenser takes his leave of The Shepheardes Calender in a first-person Envoy that distances himself from Colin. He is no longer Colin but the creator of Colin—and of the whole book in which Colin is only a character:

<blockquote>
Loe I have made a Calender for every yeare,
That steele in strength, and time in durance shall outweare:
And if I marked well the starres revolution,
It shall continewe till the worlds dissolution.
</blockquote>

(p. 120)

I've risen beyond being a pastoral love-poet, Spenser implies, and now I'm ready to begin work on my epic. The Shepheardes Calender was published in 1579; the first three books of The Faerie Queene followed eleven years later. One of the ways in which Spenser prepared himself for his epic task was by coming to terms with sexual passion. In that symbolic action, Jonathan

Goldberg has argued, Spenser may also have been coming to terms with his mentor Gabriel Harvey.[31]

Spenser's final view of the relationship between male friendship and heterosexual love forms one of the great set pieces in book 4 of *The Faerie Queene*. As an exemplum of friendship, book 4 ostensibly tells the story of Cambel and Triamond, two fast friends from Chaucer's unfinished *Squire's Tale*. Most of the book, however, follows the fortunes and misfortunes of the male and female lovers whose stories spill over from book 3, an exemplum of chastity. Scudamour, the principal among these lovers, casts his account of falling in love as a journey through a *locus amoenus* at the center of which stands the Temple of Venus. All about him in this garden of delights stroll thousands of pairs of lovers:

> All these together by themselves did sport
>> Their spotlesse pleasures, and sweet loves content.

In a place apart he discovers "another sort of lovers," some famous pairs of friends. They are distinguished from their male and female counterparts not only by where they are but by what they are. Just as Aristotle, Cicero, Plutarch, and Montaigne describe them, these friends consort with one another as equals:

> But farre away from these, another sort
> Of lovers lincked in true harts consent;
> Which loved not as these, for like intent,
> But on chast vertue grounded their desire,
> Farre from all fraud, or fayned blandishment;
> Which in their spirits kindling zealous fire,
>> Brave thoughts and noble deeds did evermore aspire.

Hercules and Hylas, Jonathan and David, Theseus and Pirithous, Pylades and Orestes, Titus and Gesippus, Damon and Pythias catch Scudamour's attention in turn. Leaving these male friends behind, Scudamour presses on to the very center of the garden and the Temple of Venus. Passing through the porch, he penetrates to the temple's innermost part and discovers there a statue of Hermaphroditus, the son of Hermes and Aphrodite, covered with a veil to hide from profane eyes the mystery that "she hath both kinds in one,/Both male female, both under one name."[32] A suppliant standing by sings a hymn to Venus, a paean that sweeps the diapason of all creation, seas and winds, fruitful plants, birds, and savage beasts, into one great burst of generative pleasure. Amid the women attendant on the statue

Scudamour spies the lady Amoret, falls in love with her, woos her, and takes her with him. A garden of delight with the Temple of Venus at its center, the physical topography of Spenser's landscape is graphically anatomical. It is also transparently moral. The central mystery about human love, Spenser implies, is the attraction of opposites, the fusion of male and female into one hermaphroditic whole. Where does male friendship stand in relation to that mystery? Spenser's topography is ambiguous. At the very least, male friendship is set apart from married love. The fact that Scudamour sees the famous friends of history *before* he reaches the Temple of Venus perhaps implies that male friendship is something to be left behind, something to be given up for the higher truth of heterosexual love. With or without sexual desire, the love of Corydon for Alexis must yield to the generative love of man for woman.

It is this sense of pastoral not only as a place in the mind but as a time in life that explains why Polixines in *The Winter's Tale* should think of a landscape like Virgil's when he tells Hermione about his boyhood friendship with Leontes. Polixines' pastoral memories take him back not only to a pleasurable Golden Age but to an innocent Garden of Eden. Until tempted by their wives-to-be, the two friends lived in an all-male paradise, free from the original sin visited upon them by heterosexual desire:

> We were as twinned lambs that did frisk i'th'sun,
> And bleat the one at th'other. What we changed
> Was innocence for innocence. We knew not
> The doctrine of ill-doing, nor dreamed
> That any did. Had we pursued that life,
> And our weak spirits ne'er been higher reared
> With stronger blood, we should have answered heaven
> Boldly, "Not guilty," the imposition cleared
> Hereditary ours.
> HERMIONE.   By this we gather
> You have tripped since.
> POLIXINES.   O my most sacred lady,
> Temptations have since then been born to's; for
> In those unfledged days was my wife a girl.
> Your precious self had then not crossed the eyes
> Of my young playfellow.
> HERMIONE.   Grace to boot!
> Of this make no conclusion, lest you say
> Your queen and I are devils.

> (1.2.69-84)

Chapter Three

Ironically it is just this "innocent" exchange that throws Leontes into the jealous suspicion of wife and friend that sets *The Winter's Tale* on its tragic course toward comedy.

In their very different but equally hard versions of pastoral Spenser and Shakespeare both testify to the connection between adolescence and homosexual desire that Ariès perceives in Elizabethan ways of imagining youth. The Elizabethan writer who most fully exploits the myth, however, is Richard Barnfield. *The Affectionate Shepheard* (published anonymously in 1594) is a miscellany of three pastoral eclogues, one sonnet, "The Complaint of Chastitie. Briefly touching the cause of the death of *Matilda Fitzwalters* an English Ladie; sometime loved of King *John*, after poysoned," and "Hellens Rape. Or a light Lanthorne for light Ladies." It was successful enough for Barnfield to publish a second miscellany the next year and to lay claim to the earlier volume. In the course of his preface to *Cynthia. With Certaine Sonnets* he calls *The Affectionate Shepheard* "a little toy of mine" and cites its source in "*Virgill*, in the second Eglogue of *Alexis.*" In eglogue-with-a-*g*, the eccentric spelling that E.K. insists upon at such length in *The Shepheardes Calender*, Barnfield identitifes the poems' more immediate source in Spenser.[33] Sir Philip Sidney was also in his mind. Though published with no author's name on the title page, *The Affectionate Shepheard* is dedicated to no less a personage than Penelope, Lady Rich, the "Stella" of Sidney's *Astrophel and Stella*, first printed three years earlier. In the third eclogue Barnfield's persona catalogues some of Love's victims and includes among them "great *Collin*" and "sweet *Astrophel*."[34] Like Spenser with *The Shepheardes Calender* and Sidney with *Astrophel and Stella*, Barnfield sees himself as launching his poetic career with *The Affectionate Shepheard*. Like Spenser and Sidney, he finds his identity as a poet by coming to terms with sexual passion. Unlike Spenser and Sidney, he can only stumble, not soar, along the *gradus ad Parnassum*.

Passion in *The Affectionate Shepheard* is of a rather different sort than passion in *The Shepheardes Calender*. From the opening lines of the first eclogue, "The teares of an affectionate shepheard sicke for love," we find ourselves reading the most explicitly homosexual poems of the entire English Renaissance:

> Scarce had the morning Starre hid from the light
> Heavens crimson Canopie with stars bespangled,
> But I began to rue th'unhappy sight
> Of that faire Boy that had my hart intangled;

Cursing the Time, the Place, the sense, the sin;
I came, I saw, I viewd, I slipped in.
If it be sinne to love a sweet-fac'd Boy,
(Whose amber locks trust up in golden tramels
Dangle adowne his lovely cheekes with joy,
When pearle and flowers his faire haire enamels)
If it be sinne to love a lovely Lad;
Oh then sinne I, for whom my soule is sad.

(I-II, p. 7)

The lovely lad's name is Ganymede. Coy indeed is the counterpoint here between Caesar's boast (*veni, vidi, vici*) and St. Paul's contrition ("If we say that we have no sinne, we deceive our selves, and trueth is not in us").[35] Just how sorry *is* the persona? He may curse the time when he came, the place where he saw, and the senses through which he viewed, but he "slips into sin" with the alacrity of a lover slipping into his beloved's arms—or into another part of his anatomy. Although the gifts that he promises Ganymede are borrowed from Virgil and Marlowe, Barnfield's persona offers them up with a wink and a smirk that are all his own:

O would to God (so I might have my fee)
My lips were honey, and thy mouth a Bee.

Then shouldst thou sucke my sweete and my faire flower
That now is ripe, and full of honey-berries:
Then would I leade thee to my pleasant Bower
Fild full of Grapes, of Mulberries, and Cherries;
Then shouldst thou be my Waspe and else my Bee,
I would thy hive, and thou my honey bee.
I would put amber Bracelets on thy wrests,
Crownets of Pearle about thy naked Armes:
And when thou sitst at swilling *Bacchus* feasts
My lips with charmes should save thee from all harmes:
And when in sleepe thou tookst thy chiefest Pleasure,
Mine eyes should gaze upon thine eye-lids Treasure.

(XVI-XVIII.p 11)

No mere decorative details, these, but parts in a precisely imagined sexual fantasy. What we have here, in Simon and Gagnon's terms, is Barnfield's quite distinctive "interpersonal script" for homosexual lovemaking.[36] In the usual Petrarchan conceit the lady's lips are the honey that attracts the male persona as bee; here the persona casts himself in the female role, as the honey awaiting its ravisher. Just what might be going on "at swilling

Bacchus feasts" from which Ganymede should need protecting? Are there rivals to be fended off? Is there a suggestion of manacles in those "amber Bracelets" and "Crownets of Pearle" that the persona would wind about his lover's arms? Daphnis delights to imagine the sense of full possession that would come with having Ganymede all to himself, the secret pleasure that would come with watching him sleep. The dawning day would find bard and boy bedded down together: "My Coote thy Chamber, my bosome thy Bed/Shall be appointed for thy sleepy head" (XIX, p. 12).

The animals that course through Virgil's landscape as metaphors of desire—"the sterne and lowring lion she dooth follow in chase the woolfe,/The woolfe dooth follow in chase the gote, the wanton gote likewise/Doth covet after *cythisus*"—reappear in Barnfield's plaints as metaphors of sexual conquest. Bird hunting, in particular, serves Daphnis's seductive turn. In "The second dayes lamentation of the *Affectionate Shepheard*" he promises Ganymede other disports besides keeping sheep:

> Or if thou wilt goe shoote at little Birds,
> With bow and boult (the Thrustle-cocke and Sparrow),
> Such as our Countrey hedges can afford's;
> I have a fine bowe, and an yvorie arrow:
>   And if thou misse, yet meate thou shalt [not] lacke,
>   Ile hang a bag and bottle at thy backe.

> (VIII, p. 19)

The bow and arrow is one of the oldest anatomical puns in English; "Thrustle-cocke" shows us the male organ in action; and sparrows, in Eric Patridge's glossary of Elizabethan bawdry, "are often taken as symbolic of feathered lechery, as monkeys and goats are of animal lustfulness." After these merry word games there is no mistaking what the persona really has in mind when he promises to supply Ganymede with "meate" by hanging a "bag and bottle" at his back. ("Away, you mouldy rogue, away!" cries Doll Tearsheet to Pistol in *Henry IV, Part Two*, "I am meat for your master," and Leontes in *The Winter's Tale* imagines his wife's infidelity in graphically physical terms: "Be it concluded,/No barricado for a belly; know't;/It will let in and out the enemy/With bag and baggage.")[37] The birding blandishments come to a climax when Daphnis promises Ganymede "a pleasant noted Nightingale/(That sings as sweetly as the silver Swan)." Kept in "a Cage of bone" that sounds very much like a codpiece, this "noted" bird was won "with singing of *Philemon*" (whatever happened to female Philomel?) and is "as white as Whale." All these things will be Ganymede's, "If thou wilt be my Boy, or els my Bride" (XIII, p. 20).

The sexual innuendo was not lost, apparently, on Barnfield's sixteenth-century readers. In the preface to his second collection of poems Barnfield pointedly disavows any double meanings in the first, but he does so with the very disingenuousness with which he avowed those double meanings in the first place:

> Some there were, that did interpret *The affectionate Shepheard*, otherwise then (in truth) I meant, touching the subject thereof, to wit, the love of a Shepheard to a boy; a fault, the which I will not excuse, because I never made. Onely this, I will unshaddow my conceit: being nothing else, but an imitation of *Virgill*, in the second Eglogue of *Alexis*.

> (p. 63)

We might take these remarks to imply that Barnfield was not altogether sure of his audience. Quite the contrary. Barnfield's epistle "To the curteous Gentlemen Readers" is addressed to one group of gentlemen in particular, the gentlemen of the inns of court. In Barnfield's own phrase *The Affectionate Shepheard* came out, not during the last calendar year, but during "the last Terme" of the legal season. After taking his B.A. at Brasenose, Oxford, in 1592, Barnfield apparently took the route to the future that sons of gentry and would-be gentry had been taking for the last fifty years of the sixteenth century: he took up residence at one of the inns of court in London. The records of Gray's Inn do not in fact record his entry, but tradition connects him with that house.[38] All of Barnfield's readers, then, were male. At least half of them had just come down from Oxford or Cambridge. Most of them were in their late teens or twenties. Many of them were at the crucial transition point in their lives where ties of male friendship were yielding to married love.[39]

Like the apprentices who were their working-class counterparts, the gentlemen of the inns of court constituted a distinct social group in early modern London: well educated, witty, licentious, poised between youth and manhood. In the quarter century from 1550 to 1575 the inns of court had been the literary center of England, and in Barnfield's day they still were home to writers like John Donne (Lincoln's Inn, 1591-1594, 1616-1622), John Marston (Middle Temple, c. 1594-1606), and Francis Bacon (Gray's Inn, 1576-1626). Bacon would, in fact, have been a contemporary of Barnfield at Gray's Inn. Across these fifty years the literature produced by inns-of-court gentlemen had been characterized by two things: its commerce with the Greek and Roman classics and its political engagement. In the earlier half of those fifty years inns-of-court writers had been almost single-handedly responsible for translating the classics into English, at a time when Oxford and Cambridge dons jealously wanted to keep them in Greek and Latin. And because the inns of court were the vital place where the world of political power and the world of academic learning touched orbits, the ancient classics were frequently made to serve a modern political program, as, for example, in *Gorboduc*, mounted by the Inner Temple before Queen Elizabeth in 1562. Queen and courtiers, benchers and barristers, may have been watching the first classical tragedy in English, but more immediately impressive must have been the play's plea that the queen settle her succession. Serious in these respects, life and letters at the inns of court could be self-ironic, as well. In their revelry, as in the literature they produced, the inns-of-court gentlemen defined themselves through paradoxes: learning offset by license, scholastic seriousness offset by playful parody, orthodox ideals and ambitions offset by licientiousness, youthful idealism offset by cynical sophistication.[40] The opening stroke of John Webster's character of "A Fantasticke Innes of Court man" catches these ironies exactly: "He is distinguished from a Scholler by a paire of silke stockings, and a Beaver Hatte . . . ."[41] Inns-of-court gentlemen were as paradoxical about love and sex as they were about dress. In the poems they wrote themselves and in the poems by others that they collected in manuscript, these boys on their way to manhood cultivated two very disparate modes, the courtly love-lyrics of Petrarch and the sexy elegies of Ovid. The first spoke the language of the court to which they aspired; the second spoke the language they used among themselves. It was when he was in his early twenties, while he was resident in Lincoln's Inn, that John Donne likely wrote most of his paradoxes, satires, and elegies, as well as many of the poems of seduction and postcoital delight that were published after his death as *Songs and Sonnets*.[42]

Richard Barnfield's *Affectionate Shepheard* is addressed to this coterie readership. Barnfield may have written monologues, but the impulse behind his book is partly social. It is not only his own individual identity that Barnfield is affirming in these poems but the group identity of his inns-of-court readers. *The Affectionate Shepheard* is calculated to appeal to the gentlemen-readers' classical erudition, to their scorn for conventional morality, to their sense of themselves as an all-male in-group, and to their anxieties as young men uncertain of their future. Erudition, first of all, is required to appreciate the ingenuity of these poems—and the more recently one has had to suffer through boring academic lectures, the easier it is to laugh at it all. Barnfield knows that Latin is a male code-language—and revels in it. Only readers sophisticated enough to know all about pastoral poetry—its origins in Virgil, its artificial conventions, its capacity for allegory—can appreciate just how outrageous Barnfield is when he takes those conventions and makes sport with them. Servius and all his learned successors may have found all sorts of cerebral subtleties in Virgil's second eclogue; Barnfield dares to take Virgil, homoeroticism and all, at sensuous face value. Here, indeed, are matters "such as perchance had not been safe to have disclosed in any other sort." Against pedants like E.K., who turns *The Shepheardes Calender* into an occasion for philological exegesis, Barnfield plays the naughty schoolboy. Percolating through all his eclogues is a spirit of spoof and parody. He manages to catch exactly the "mixture of disorderly conduct, mock solemnity, and a serious miming of dignified roles" that one modern critic finds in inns-of-court revelry.[43]

Barnfield also appeals to his readers' self-identity as a closed society that is exclusively male. Women, as we have seen, have only a peripheral place in Virgil's eclogues. In Spenser's *Calender* one woman in particular, Rosalind, emerges out of this group of supernumeraries to stand forth as a rival against Hobbinol for the poet's affections. Conflict between "paederastice" and "gynerastice" may merit only a footnote in *The Shepheardes Calender*, but in Barnfield's eclogues it figures as a major theme. The rival woman becomes a sexual aggressor who threatens to destroy the persona's all-male idyll. Crossing the scenario of Virgil's second eclogue with the plot of a pastoral romance like Lodge's *Rosalynde*, Barnfield sets up a love triangle in *The Affectionate Shepheard*. Not only does the poet have to try all his wiles to turn Ganymede's disdain into mutual desire; he also has to compete with "the faire Queene *Guendolen*." What was the merest suggestion of male-female rivalry in Virgil and only a passing note in Spenser becomes a major conflict in Barnfield. So beautiful is Ganymede that all the shepherdesses have attempted to woo him:

> Upon a time the Nymphs bestird them-selves
> To trie who could his beautie soonest win:

But he accounted them all as Elves,
Except it were the faire Queene *Guendolen,*
      Her he embrac'd, of her was beloved,
      With plaints he proved, and with teares he moved.

(IV, p. 8)

Since pastoral romances would hardly be so much fun with only one triangle, Barnfield obligingly complicates matters by giving Ganymede a comic rival for Guendolen's favors: a gray-bearded Old Man. It was quite by accident that January came to fall in love with May. Cupid and Death, it seems, got drunk together "at swilling *Bacchus* house" and mistakenly exchanged arrows. Thinking he was aiming one of his steel-tipped darts, Death wounded the Old Man with one of Cupid's gold-tipped arrows instead. The steel-tipped dart, shot off by unwitting Cupid, found its fatal mark, not in the Old Man, but in a "faire and beautifull young-man" with whom Guendolen was already in love (XIV, p. 10). Thus Daphnis loves Ganymede, who loves Guendolen, who loves a dead swain—and is beloved in turn by a ridiculous Old Man. Does a real-life story lurk in Barnfield's lines? The Virgilian half of Barnfield's inspiration, if not the pastoral romance half, would make us think so. But Barnfield has, alas, no Servius, no E.K. to tell us for sure. Perhaps part of the fun for Barnfield's coterie readers was knowing the real identities masked by the fiction.

Plot complications of this order might have challenged even Shakespeare's ingenuity. To Barnfield they serve chiefly as occasion for contrasting Daphnis's own pure passion with the sordid fact of Guendolen's sexual allure:

Oh would shee would forsake my *Ganimede,*
Whose sugred love is full of sweete delight,
Upon whose fore-head you may plainely reade
Loves pleasure, grav'd in yvorie Tables bright:
      In whose faire eye-balls you may clearely see
      Base Love still staind with foule indignitie.

(XV, p. 11)

Ganymede's ivory forehead and crystaline eyes present pages of adolescent innocence on which the persona reads texts of heterosexual experience—and recoils in disgust. In the contrasts between pure ivory and "Base Love," between "faire" eyes and "foule indignitie," we can discern the same conflict between male friendship and heterosexual passion that we encounter in Plutarch's dialogue "Of Love" and in *The Shepheardes Calender.*

Barnfield sets up that conflict in decidedly Platonic terms—or pretends to. He loves Ganymede for his spiritual perfections; Guendolen loves him for his body:

Compare the love of faire Queene *Guendolin*
With mine, and thou shalt [s]ee how she doth love thee:
I love thee for thy qualities divine,
But shee doth love another Swaine above thee:
    I love thee for thy gifts, She for hir pleasure;
    I for thy Vertue, She for Beauties treasure.

(XXXV, p. 16)

How are we to square these high claims with Daphnis's low puns about his "bag and bottle"? That is no clearer here than it is with Protogenes' similarly chaste protestations in Plutarch's dialogue "Of Love."

Uncertainties about the future loom large on the horizon of Barnfield's pastoral landscape. There is, first of all, that ever-present sense of Time as destroyer that casts such cold shadows over quick bright things in all Elizabethan verse. Barnfield's claim that he loves Ganymede for his "Vertue" is made the stronger by reminding the young shepherd that the "Beauties treasure" so doted on by Guendolen is subject to decay. After cataloging all the country pleasures he and Ganymede will enjoy together, Daphnis closes the first eclogue with this ominous thought:

Insteed of Beautie (when thy Blossom's past)
Thy face will be deformed, full of wrinckles:
    Then She that lov'd thee for thy Beauties sake,
    When Age drawes on, thy love will soone forsake.

The "gifts divine" that Barnfield esteems will, by contrast, abide forever (XXXVI-XXXVII, p. 16). The withering of beauty might seem to be only a distant eventuality. But Time refuses to remain so comfortably remote in Barnfield's poems. The rising of the sun in "The second Dayes Lamentation of the *Affectionate Shepheard*" reminds the persona, not of Ganymede's mortality, but of his own. For the first time he alludes to the age gap that separates him from youthful Ganymede and betrays a sharp sense that Time's chariot is overtaking him:

O glorious Sunne quoth I (viewing the Sunne),
That lightenst everie thing but me alone:
Why is my Summer season almost done?

My Spring-time past, and Ages Autumne gone?
    My Harvest's come, and yet I reapt no corne:
    My love is great, and yet I am forlorne.

(II, p. 17)

By the end of the eclogue he is casting himself as an old man with a head of gray hair, a face full of furrows—and a heart empty of passion. Weightier matters now occupy his mind than the "birding" jokes of before. Barnfield takes on, then, the older identity of Virgil's Corydon, of Marlowe's Passionate Shepherd, of Spenser's Hobbinol and carries that identity to its logical, moral, disillusioning end. He shifts from the sensuous perspective on pastoral to the cerebral. In that shift from immediate delights to the distant view Daphnis prepares to take leave of the pastoral scenario. Pastoral must yield to epic, youthful pleasures must give place to manly action, the cloistered student world of the inns of court must open out into adult life.

To wild young Ganymede, Daphnis becomes the wise old counselor—just the role that an elder bencher might take toward a young outer-barrister in the hierarchical society of Gray's Inn. This shift in role is, at bottom, more of a political move than a moral one. It shows us the would-be seducer returning from the field with an empty seed sack: his wild oats are all sown. He is ready to accommodate himself and his desires to the conventional structures of power in Elizabethan society. A conflict between individual desire and the social order may have been in the speaker's mind all along—however coy the tone, "sin" does figure in the poems' very first stanza—but Barnfield makes sure that we experience these things in chronological order: first desire, then constraint. If Daphnis sounds in the first eclogue like a doting Passionate Shepherd, he finishes the second eclogue sounding for all the world like a dotty Polonius:

Sweare no vaine oathes; heare much, but little say;
Speake ill of no man, tend thine owne affaires,
Bridle thy wrath, thine angrie mood delay;
(So shall thy minde be seldome cloyd with cares:)
    Be milde and gentle in thy speech to all,
    Refuse no honest gaine when it doth fall.

(LVI, p. 31)

He in fact goes so far as to advise Ganymede to *marry*. The kind of wife Ganymede should choose and how he should behave toward her are part of Daphnis's sober lecture. Even in these speeches, however, we detect a fear of female sexuality. Ganymede is counseled not to take "a flattring woman to thy wife/ . . . /whose lust will end thy life"; rather, one who "shines in Truth and Vertue pure" (LXV, p. 33). "Embrace thy Wife," he is enjoined, but "live not in lecherie" (LXVII, p. 34).

The persona takes his leave of the second eclogue just as Colin Clout finishes his career as a poet in *The Shepheardes Calendar*: all passion spent, he has become a disillusioned old man. The night that descends on "The second Dayes Lamentation" suggests rather more than the easing of passion that comes with the setting sun in Virgil. Here we see sexual passion in the context of an entire life:

> By this, the Night, (with darknes over-spred),
> Had drawne the curtaines of her cole-blacke bed;
> And *Cynthia*, muffling her face with a clowd,
> (Lest all the world of her should be too prowd)
>   Had taken *conge* of the sable Night,
>   (That wanting her cannot be halfe so bright).
>
> When I poore forlorn man and outcast creature,
> (Despairing of my Love, despisde of Beautie)
> Grew male-content, scorning his lovely feature,
> That had disdaind my ever zealous dutie:
>   I hy'd me homeward by the Moone-shine light;
>   Forswearing Love, and all his fond delight.

(LXXIII-LXXIV, p. 35)

The moral frame that Barnfield here sets in place is even starker in "The shepherds content, or The happines of a harmless life." This third and final eclogue closes with an image of that ultimate Shepherd whose love transcends human love and to whose bosom we turn in death,

> He that can make the most unhappie blest:
>   In whose sweete lap Ile lay me downe to sleepe,
>   And never wake till Marble-stones shall weepe.

(XLIII, p. 50)

The effect of these renunciations is to make the Myth of the Passionate Shepherd seem a distinctly adolescent vision of sexuality: something to be enjoyed in youth but to be given up when one becomes an adult. One can hear the echo of St. Paul in I Corinthians 13:11: "When I was a childe, I spake as a childe, I understode as a childe, I thoght as a childe: but when I became a man, I put away childish things." Here is age-graded homosexuality with a vengeance.

At first glance the "certaine Sonnets" that Barnfield appended to *Cynthia* (1595) seem simply to continue the homoerotic games of his eclogues. The context, however, is surprising: *Cynthia*, a 180-line celebration of Queen Elizabeth in one of her many mythical guises, is the "epic" work for which Barnfield's Daphnis gave up pastoral dalliance at the end of *The Affectionate Shepheard*. From the epic heights of *Cynthia*, such as they are, Barnfield cannot help sliding back into the pastoral valley of desire—a milieu in which he is much more at home as a poet. In his sonnets we encounter the same cast of characters (libidinous Daphnis in pursuit of languid Ganymede), the same pastoral setting, the same playful tone of passion edged with parody. What Barnfield has done is to take the conventions of sonnet sequences like Sidney's *Astrophel and Stella* and Spenser's *Amoretti* and adapt them to the scenario of Virgil's second eclogue. The effect is sensual and yet self-ironic. Sonnet 11, perhaps the best of the lot, illustrates how the entire sequence is calculated to startle and amuse his gentlemen readers. Barnfield takes the ordinary conventions of courtly love poets and applies them, rather mischievously, to his own extraordinary circumstances. Instructed by Barnfield, Petrarch is made to speak the language of Ovid:

> Sighing, and sadly sitting by my love,
> > He askt the cause of my hearts sorrowing,
> > Conjuring me by heavens eternall King,
> To tell the cause which me so much did move.
> Compell'd: (quoth I) to thee will I confesse,
> > Love is the cause; and only love it is
> > That doth deprive me of my heavenly blisse,
> Love is the paine that doth my heart oppresse.
> And what is she (quoth he) whom thou do'st love?
> > Looke in this glasse (quoth I) there shalt thou see
> > The perfect forme of my felicitie.
> When, thinking that it would strange Magique prove,
> > He open'd it: and taking off the cover
> > He straight perceav'd himselfe to be my Lover.

(XI, p. 87)

Clearly, the reader is supposed to be no less surprised by this witty and audacious device than Ganymede himself.

For all the similarities to his eclogues, Barnfield's sonnets represent a widening of dramatic possibilities. As in his eclogues,

Barnfield gives us poems of wooing (numbers 5, 19, 20), but he also takes us through all the conventional poses and situations of the Petrarchan lover. There is a psychomachia in which the persona tells us how he came to fall in love (1); there are blazons of the beloved's beauty (4, 8, 9, 10); an echo poem (13); a lament during the beloved's absence (16); a gloating triumph over jealous rivals (18). Barnfield goes on, however, to give us poems for which there are no Petrarchan precedents, poems that seem specific to his homosexual subject. Sonnet 7, for example, returns us to the love triangle of the eclogues, in which Daphnis has to fend off female rivals as well as male. We encounter the same fear of female sexuality that Daphnis betrayed before when he was praising the purity of his passion and counseling Ganymede on how to manage a wife in bed. After describing his "fairest faire," his "silver Swan," swimming in the Thames, Daphnis reflects that it is not the sea-god he has to worry about but the sea-goddess, the mother of Achilles. The whole conceit of this sonnet, as well as its conclusion, suggests that Barnfield had read and relished Marlowe's *Hero and Leander*:

> Neptune, I feare not thee, nor yet thine eie,
>   And yet (alas) *Apollo* lov'd a boy,
>   And *Cyparissus* was *Silvanus* joy.
> No, no, I feare none but faire *Thetis*, I,
>   For if she spie my Love (alas), aie me,
>   My mirth is turn'd to extreame miserie.

(VII, p. 83)

It is not, finally, this fear of female rivalry that disheartens Daphnis but a sense of his impotence as a poet. To so challenging a subject he can never do justice. After cataloging in sonnet 12 all the famous fair youths of classical poetry—Ganymede, Adonis, Narcissus—the persona turns to his own beloved and concludes,

> They were (perhaps) lesse faire then Poets write,
> But he is fairer then I can endite.

(XII, p. 88)

That much is a Petrarchan cliché. But it is the note on which Barnfield decides to conclude the entire sequence of twenty sonnets. His leave-taking here has the same finality as his leave-taking in the eclogues—and the same wistful reference to Spenser as a role model:

But now my Muse toyld with continuall care,
    Begins to faint, and slacke her former pace,
    Expecting favour from that heavenly grace,
That maie (in time) her feeble strength repaire.
Till when (sweete youth) th'essence of my soule,
    (Thou that dost sit and sing at my hearts griefe,
    Thou that dost send thy shepheard no reliefe:)
Beholde, these lines; the sonnes of Teares and Dole.
Ah had great *Colin* chiefe of sheepheards all,
    Or gentle *Rowland*, my professed friend,
    Had they thy beautie, or my pennance pend,
Greater had beene thy fame, and lesse my fall:
    But since that everie one cannot be wittie,
    Pardon I crave of them, and of thee, pitty.

(XX, p. 96)

And there it all ends. The sentiments are commonplace; the timing is not. Barnfield concludes his sequence of "certaine Sonnets" by making us see his success as a wooer and his success as a poet as two aspects of the same thing. In the last line he glances in two directions: on the one hand toward Ganymede but on the other toward fellow poets. At issue here is a question of power—over the beloved, certainly, but also over the medium of verse. Barnfield's sonnets stop short of sexual union, just as his eclogues do, but the cause this time is not so much moral or political as aesthetic: we witness, not a renunciation of the will, but a failure of the imagination. "Everie one cannot be wittie"— few poets, wittingly or unwittingly, have described themselves so well. Considering Barnfield's limitations, we should probably be grateful that Ganymede never said yes. What would poor Daphnis have done? Barnfield's imagination is simply not equipped to address the complexities that wait on the far side of the *locus amoenus*. He can go no farther than the conventions of the eclogue and the sonnet take him.

However maturely he manages the ending of *The Affectionate Shepheard*, however wisely modest he may be about his poetic powers in the "certaine Sonnets" he appended to *Cynthia*, Barnfield writes poems that are "adolescent" in more ways than one. Compared to Lord North addressing the whole community of male readers in his translation of Plutarch's *Lives*, Barnfield's appeal to "the curteous Gentlemen Readers" of the inns of court comes across as the silly secrecy of a boys' club. For the manner that John Webster calls "Fantasticke" the twentieth century has its own word: "campy." In their rhetorical teasing and relentless sexual punning there is something pornographic about Barnfield's poems. They are completely self-absorbed. They never get beyond sexual desire. They are, in effect, poems of masturbation. Until he takes his leave with epic solemnity Barnfield is apparently interested only in the soft side of pastoral poetry, in sensual self-indulgence. And yet he never really manages to escape the cultural prohibitions at which he so delights to thumb his nose. In the last analysis, Barnfield's poems *do* figure as versions of hard pastoral, as ways of coming to terms with the conflict between escapist desires and social constraints. Barnfield accepts those traditional values explicitly in his third eclogue. But he has done so already in the very act of *trying* to be scandalous—and trying to get away with it by being secret.

These same qualities characterize a manuscript (formerly among the manuscripts owned by Sir Charles Isham; now MS V.a.161 in the Folger Shakespeare Library) that has come to be known as "Barnfield's commonplace book." In a statement that has been accepted as authoritative, Alan Bray siezes on the "robustly pornographic and entirely heterosexual" character of this manuscript to declare that *The Affectionate Shepheard* is not about homosexuality at all but about friendship, "a Platonic meeting of minds."[44] Several problems with Bray's claim have not been examined. One of them concerns the manuscript's authorship and provenance. Among the twelve pieces in verse and prose that have been entered into the little manuscript booklet, only one can be ascribed to Barnfield on external evidence—the dedicatory poem for *Lady Pecunia*, the collection of satirical poems Barnfield published in 1598—and in the manuscript that one poem is indeed followed by Barnfield's name. (The manuscript also includes, without attributions, six Latin lines on the rape of Lucrece adapted from Ovid's *Fasti* (2.771-774), Ben Jonson's epitaph on the boy-actor Salomon Pavy, and Chidiock Tichbourne's elegy "My prime of youth is but a frost of cares," as well as one poem labeled *"INCERTI AUTHORIS"* ["by an unknown author"].) Since no other specimen of Barnfield's handwriting survives (his will in the Litchfield Joint Record Office is signed with a monogram), it is impossible to be certain that the Folger manuscript is in Barnfield's hand or, indeed, that it ever had any personal connection with Barnfield at all. There may, in fact, be two different hands represented in the manuscript. The first item and the last are written in a different, darker ink from the rest and in a hand that lacks the emphatic horizontal strokes that distinguish the main writer's lowercase *d*'s. The other problem concerns the manuscript's contents. In fact, only one item, a prose sketch titled "The Shepherdes Confession," is overtly pornographic. Heterosexual it certainly is, and robust, not to mention amusing. But the interlineation of words, phrases, and whole lines suggests that it was copied from somewhere else, and none too carefully, rather than written out for the first time on these pages. The interlineated items do not represent additions or revisions but words and phrases that are necessary for the passage to make basic grammatical sense. In one case (fol. 5, line 12), the writer has had to insert a whole line that he evidently overlooked in copying the text. In another case (fol. 5, line 18), he has cancelled the "how" that he first saw and has gone on to write the "her" that his copy-text apparently contained. Neither mistake is the sort one is likely to make with one's own work, even in making a copy. Whether the Folger manuscript is Barnfield's commonplace book is, then, doubtful.[45]

That said, one has to admit that the manuscript does catch Barnfield's arch tone, or something remarkably like it. "The Shepherdes Confession" plies Phillis with the same smirky innuendo that Daphnis brings to Ganymede, the poem inscribed "Incerti Authoris" ("Thus [W] w[i]th I, w[i]th f, w[i]th E:/Brings nothinge els but miserie") strikes the same mysogynistic tone as Daphnis's snide remarks on Guendolen, and a prose piece giving regulations for Knights of "The Order of the Snuff" reads very much like the mock-regulations drawn up for the "Prince of Purpoole" in the Gray's Inn Christmas revels of 1594.[46] Knowing the compiler's penchant for sexual puns, one wonders if all his talk about candles and sockets isn't really about thrustlecocks and sparrows:

> Every knight of [th]e order of [th]e Snuffe shall be well provided in tearmes concerninge [th]e candle, as havinge occasio[n] to bid one light [th]e candle he shall say ["]incense [th]e candle,["] for puttinge him in to [th]e candle sticke, ["]advance him into his throwne,["] for snuffing of [th]e candle he shall say ["]reforme [th]e candle,["] for takeinge away [th]e theefe, ["]assiste [th]e candle,["], for fastninge him into [th]e socket ["]establish [th]e candle,["] for stickinge of flowers ["]adorne [th]e candle["]; and if he be taken a way by ratts or mice, he shall say, ["]he is taken prisoner,["] if he be gnawne he shall say ["]he is indented.["][47]

The true commonplace in "Barnfield's commonplace book,"

even if not by Barnfield himself, is sixteenth-century adolescence.

As a way of articulating homosexual desire the pastoral scenario has enjoyed remarkable staying power. Byrne R. S. Fone finds a continuous track through Arcadia not only in the homoerotic literature of the seventeenth, eighteenth, and nineteenth centuries but even in novels as recent as Gore Vidal's *The City and the Pillar*. The reasons for this imaginative vitality, Fone proposes, are three.[48] Arcadia offers, first of all, an escape, "a place where it is safe to be gay"—even, we should add, in a culture in which "gay" did not exist as a term of self-definition. Virgil's second eclogue creates a fantasy-world of sexual pleasure. All other concerns have been pushed to the periphery: social distinctions, gender distinctions, political distinctions. All of these concerns seem distant and unsubstantial in comparison with the bodily *physicality* of the speaker's desire.

Arcadia is, furthermore, a *secret* place: it is not necessary there to talk about homosexual desire explicitly. The inhabitants all speak the same language, known only among themselves. The collaborative agreement between the pastoral poet and his readers illustrates perfectly what Foucault has to say about the positive effects of negative power. One result of prohibition is to turn secretiveness into a form of pleasure:

> Discourses are not once and for all subservient to power or raised up against it, any more than silences are. We must make allowance for the complex and unstable process whereby discourse can be both an instrument and an effect of power, but also a hindrance, a stumbling-block, a point of resistance and a starting-point for an opposing strategy. Discourse transmits and produces power; it reinforces it, but also undermines and exposes it, renders it fragile and makes it possible to thwart it. In like manner, silence and secrecy are a shelter for power, anchoring its prohibitions; but they also loosen its holds and provide for relatively obscure areas of tolerance.

As an instance Foucault singles out the position of sodomy in the eighteenth century and earlier: reticence in talking about sodomy publicly made it possible, on the one hand, to prescribe severe punishments but, on the other, to tolerate homosexuality to a degree not possible once that reticence had been broken.[49] In Renaissance poems inspired by Virgil's second eclogue we have just such a "starting-point for an opposing strategy" to moral and legal prohibitions. As Barnfield's endings remind us, we have also an instance of how "silence and secrecy" can serve not only to "loosen the holds" of power but also to "anchor" it.

Barnfield and his sixteenth-century readers were prepared to abandon Arcadia for more adventurous places.

Finally, Arcadia offers "a metaphor for certain spiritual values and myths." In sixteenth- and seventeenth-century versions of pastoral, those myths and values are the ideals of male friendship articulated by Aristotle, Cicero, Plutarch, pseudo-Lucian, and Montaigne, and the realities of male political power instituted in Elizabethan and Jacobean society. A sojourn in Arcadia prepared Renaissance young men for adult lives of public action. In this respect the Myth of the Passionate Shepherd seems to enact in symbolic terms the actual retreat to the wilderness that typifies adolescent rites of passage in many traditional kinship societies. Important in both cases, the symbolic and the actual, is some form of homosexual initiation into manhood, a physical passing along of adult secrets.[50] The sexual license that adolescent boys enjoyed once in Arcadia could, as we shall discover, be relived on certain occasions in the English greenwood.

CHAPTER FOUR

THE SHIPWRECKED YOUTH

The haven being left, we began to sayle foorth a prosperous journy; the lande did seeme to go backe from the shippe, as if that it did saile it selfe; . . . there was by chance in the same ship a yoong man sitting by us, which because it was now dinner time, very curteously invited us, that we also would eate with him: wherefore when *Satyrus had made readie that which hee provided for us, we did eate togither in common, making our selves both partakers of our dinner and talke also; when I began thus: ["]I pray you sir what country-man are you, and what is your name?["] Then answered he,* ["]I am an *Aegyptian* borne, my name is *Menelaus*: but by your leave, may I demaund the same of you?["] Then quoth I, ["]my name is *Clitiphon*, his *Clinias*: both *Phoenicians* by birth. And if it please you sir, first to declare unto us the cause of this your travaile, we also will recompence you with the like.["] Then said *Menelaus*, ["]the summe of this my navigation, is ungrateful love, and an unfortunate hunting; from which, although I did divers times earnestly exhort him, yet I could not prevaile.["][1]

Die boeren verhlyen hun in sulken feesten_ Te danfen fpringhen en_ dronckendrincken als feesten_ Bier
Sy moeten die Kermiffen onderbouwen_ Al fouwen fy vaften en fteruen van Kauwen_ . de numpere

"The Village Fair of Hoboken" (1559)
After Pieter Brueghel the Elder (*above*)

The liminal festivities of Renaissance England, like fraternity hazing in our
own day, exorcised homosexual desire by turning it into a game.

(The National Gallery of Art, Washington, Rosenwald Collection)

"The Village Fair of Hoboken"
(detail, *top right*)

"Than, these goodly pageants being done, every mate sorts to his mate, every
one brings another homeward of their way verye freendly, and in their secret
conclaves (covertly) they play *the Sodomits*, or worse. And these be the fruits
of Playes and Enterluds for the most part."

"The Village Fair of Hoboken"
(detail, *bottom right*)

When we read a twelve-year-old apprentice's testimony before the Somerset
quarter sessions that his bedfellow Meredith Davy customarily masturbated
against him "on Sunday and Holy day nights when he had been a drinking,"
we are in a position to understand why it was just on those nights, and just in
that drunken condition, that Davy could act on his desires.

And so Menelaus begins the tale of the beautiful boy he loved, of the boy's passion for hunting, of the misdirected spear that brought their love to the same violent end as Apollo's love for Hyacinth in book 10 of Ovid's *Metamorphoses*. Clinias, for one, has reason to hear Menelaus's story with sympathy. He has undertaken the present voyage in part to escape his grief over the young man *he* loved, killed when the horse he had given him raged out of control. For Clitiphon, on the other hand, it is a voyage toward living happily ever after. On board is Leucippe, the beautiful maiden who has claimed his heart; together they are fleeing their peremptory parents, whose authority recedes with the shoreline of Tyre. Between love at first sight and bedded bliss, however, stretches the sensational sequence of shipwrecks, abductions by brigands, sacrifices of virgins, fallings into madness, curings of madness, attempted rapes, feigned decapitations, lockings into prison, escapes from prison, and unlooked-for reunions that make up Achilles Tatius's *Clitophon and Leucippe*. Within minutes, the congenial dinner of Menelaus, Clinias, and Clitiphon is interrupted by shipwreck, and the lovers are cast ashore. They make their way toward Alexandria—and straight into the snares of thieves.

Clitiphon and Leucippe, like the anonymous *Apollonius of Tyre*, Heliodorus's *Aethiopica*, and Longus's *Daphnis and Chloe*, is a testament to the staying power of good storytelling. Classical scholars may have never forgiven Heliodorus, Longus, and Achilles Tatius for not being Homer, but the stories they wrote in Greek prose during the third century A.D. have enjoyed a popularity that stretches down to our own day, when *Daphnis and Chloe* at least has inspired a famous ballet and still earns profits for publishers of elegant pornography.[2] During the seventeen hundred years of their popularity the Greek romances have never been more widely read or more influential than they were during the sixteenth century. Translated into Latin and into vernacular languages, belatedly edited as Greek texts, they were printed literally hundreds of times in the fifteenth and sixteenth centuries. Heliodorus, Longus, and Achilles Tatius had all been translated into English before 1600.[3] The reason for such popularity is not hard to seek: these tales transport us into a realm of the imagination where anything is possible, where desires, fears, and aggressions of all sorts are given full play, untrammeled by the exigencies of everyday life. Dropping out of sight as the ship sails away from the coast of Tyre are not only the autocratic powers of Clitiphon and Leucippe's parents but all the constraints that make day-to-day existence so humdrum. Ahead lie the mysteries of Egypt, dangers out of nightmares, escapes out of daydreams. It is a time and a place apart. During such a time, in such a place, free reign can be given to desires that normally are held in check. Fathers falling in love with daughters, girls falling in love with girls, men falling in love with boys—such things can happen in the world of romance. Fleeing its dubious place in sixteenth- and seventeenth-century England, homosexual desire found a safe haven on the shores of Egypt.

Voyaging out to sea, Menelaus and Clinias can speak of their love for boys with a license that, for sixteenth-century readers at least, the two men could never assume onshore. Clinias, when he finds out that his lover Charicles is to be married off to a rich old crone, seizes the occasion, as Plutarch's spokesman Protogenes does in the *Moralia*, and launches into a tirade against women. "[D]o not," Clinias pleads, "I pray thee (good *Charicles*) do not, I say, undoo thy selfe: and let so deformed a Gardener croppe so fayre and sweete a Rose" (chap. 1, p. 10). Charicles' death in a riding accident makes the issue moot—and sends Clinias off on his voyage. When Clinas and Clitiphon sit down to dinner aboard ship, they hear from Menelaus a remarkably similar tale of homosexual love brought to a tragic end. Seeing how sad Clinias and Menelaus are, Clitiphon tries to cheer them up by starting up a little debate of the sort found in Plutarch's dialogue "Of Love" and pseudo-Lucian's "*Erotes*":

> turning my self to them, I smiled, ["]*Clinias* (said I) for the most part in argument overcometh me, and even now (for he desireth to inveigh against women, as his maner is) he may do it the better, because hee hath found a like companion of his love: what is the cause why so many are in love with boyes? surely I my selfe cannot tell, neither see any cause why?["]

That is all the cue Menelaus needs. Boys are better looking than women. And because making love with boys is only a sometime pleasure, it never gives satiety. Jupiter never carried a *woman* off to heaven, as he did Ganymede. Whenever he wanted a woman, the king of the gods came down to earth and, after taking his pleasure, left her behind. Clitiphon voices objections, but Menelaus has the last word. Women are full of wiles. Their beauty consists of nothing but "painting, colouring, and curling their haire." Take that away, and you are left with a bird plucked of its feathers, but the bewtie of boyes is not besmeared with the counterfeyt of painting, neither spunged up with borrowed perfumes: the very sweate of the browes of a boy, doth excell all the sweete savours of Muske and Civet about a woman: and a man may openly talke and play with them and never bee ashamed: neither is there any tendernesse of flesh which is like to them: their kisses do not savour of womens curiositie: neither beguile with a foolish error: the kisses of them are sweete and delightfull, not proceeding of art, but of nature: and the very image and picture of their kisses are so sweete and pleasant, that you might very wel thinke, that heavenly Nectar to bee between your lippes.

(chap. 2, pp. 43-46)

And there the debate ends.

Compared with Plutarch's story of Theseus and Pirithous, *Clitiphon and Leucippe* portrays homoerotic desire with undisguised directness. Desire that is potential, indirect, repressed in the Myth of Combatants and Comrades is actual, immediate, openly talked about in the Myth of the Shipwrecked Youth. Desire that is there diffuse, one strand among the intertwined emotions that connect one man with another, is here focused on a specific sexual object: an adolescent boy. In this particular kind of discourse, in romance, the physical fact of sexual feeling is more insistent than it is in Renaissance discourses about friendship—and far more dangerous. "The bewtie of boyes," the object of desire so passionately praised by Menelaus, was the very thing that English Renaissance law singled out for surveillance and control. To act on Menelaus's desires, especially if it involved force, was to risk hanging.

In some ways, the Myth of the Shipwrecked Youth would seem to be a retelling of the Myth of the Passionate Shepherd—but with a difference in point of view and a difference in timing. Arcadia is a place that stands for a time: its sensuous delights and youthful protagonists compose a metaphor for the sexual desires of adolescence. Achilles Tatius's Egypt is presented to us from a specifically adult perspective. And its time frame is not generational, but seasonal. Confronted with the passage we have just read, nineteenth- and early twentieth-century translators of *Clitiphon and Leucippe* take refuge in the male code-language of Latin, yet in 1597 William Burton, brother of the author of *The Anatomy of Melancholy*, can give the passage all its salacious due, for a simple reason.[4] Renaissance readers approached texts like this one obliquely, from a special vantage point. Romance, by definition, was not real life. It was a place apart. It was time out. When the reader closed the book, he settled back into the mundane realities and the moral rules he had temporarily left behind.

While gentlemen were reading about such things in their libraries, villagers were acting them out. If pastoral provides an homology in verse for sixteenth- and seventeenth-century schooling, romance narratives provide an homology for sixteenth- and seventeenth-century festival making. For example: when Queen Elizabeth was entertained by the Earl of Leicester at Kenilworth in 1575, one of the things she saw, in addition to scenes out of King Arthur—a romance remote in time if not in space—was some local countrymen putting on "a lively morisdauns, according to the ancient manner: six dauncerz, mawd-marion and the fool."[5] Skipping and leaping and giving each other rhythmic thwacks with swords or sticks, Elizabethan "Moorish" dancers were reenacting medieval battles between Christians and Moors. As Gerald the pedantic schoolmaster explains to Duke Theseus when introducing the village morris dancers in *The Two Noble Kinsmen*,

> look right and straight
> Upon this mighty "Moor"—of mickle weight—
> "Ice" now comes in, which, being glued together,
> Makes "morris," and the cause that we came hither.[6]

The bumptious morris dancers who burst in on the noble wedding-celebration in *The Two Noble Kinsmen* are six male-female couples: a May Lord and a May Lady, a servingman and a chambermaid, a shepherd and a country wench, the host and the hostess of an alehouse, a "He-babion" and a "She-babion," and a "He-fool" and a "She-fool." The he-baboon has pointedly been warned by the schoolmaster to "carry your tale without offence/Or scandal to the ladies" (3.5.34-35). Other sixteenth- and seventeenth-century witnesses suggest that more often the dancers of the morris were all male—as in fact they were in performances of *The Two Noble Kinsmen* by the King's Men. Enacted by the men of a single village as a badge of their group identity, the stylized combat of morris dancing was a choreographed, proletarian version of the Myth of Combatants and Comrades. But this version of the myth, like Achilles Tatius's romance, was apparently more daring than the Myth of Combatants and Comrades in the sport it made with gender roles—and with sexual desire.

As a "language" with its own vocabulary, grammar, and syntax, dance is capable of encoding all kinds of cultural messages, but it is particularly adept at encoding messages about gender and sex. Dance and sex, after all, use the same instrument, the human body. In her study of the interconnections among *Dance, Sex and Gender: Signs of Identity, Dominance, Defiance, and Desire*, Judith Lynne Hanna lists seven ways in which dance and sex have been associated in cultures all over the world: (1) dance as courtship for marriage, (2) as allure for sexual relations outside marriage, (3) as sacred aphrodisiac, (4) as a means of controlling natural forces, (5) as sex-role scripting, (6) as a way of exerting power over partners of the opposite gender, (7) as a form of sexual sublimation. In one way or another, all seven sexual functions of dance seem relevant to morris dancing and to the social occasions of which it was a part.[7] Sexual flirtation is as much a part of the "script" as stylized combat. Amid the fighting Moors in sixteenth-century versions of the morris tripped the figure of Maid Marion. Contemporary witnesses leave little doubt that this female figure was customarily played by a boy. Maid Marian "trimly dressed up in a cast gown and a kercher of Dame Lawson's, his face handsomely muffled with a diaper-napkin to cover his beard, and a great nosegay in his hands" is how Thomas Nashe describes the figure in one of his contributions to the Martin Marprelate controversy.[8] Martin's ill-disguised beard may be part of Nashe's parody. "I have a beard coming," Flute pleads when his fellow rude mechanicals assign him the part of Thisbe in their play-within-the-play in *A Midsummer Night's Dream* (1.2.43-44). Are we to gather that among tradesmen putting on a play, as well as among professional actors, it was a boy's smooth face in addition to his high-pitched voice that suited him to take on the female part? Long before Elizabethan morris dancers invited Robin Hood and Maid Marion into the dance, the outlaw and his female counterpart were lending their identities to the young men and maids crowned as kings and queens of Whitsuntide festivals all over southern England. Morris dancing being a rite of male bonding, however, Maid Marion had to undergo a change of sex to take part in the dancing. Hence she took on the identity of the Fool's consort and emerged as the transvestite burlesque figure that inspired Nashe's description of Martin Marprelate and survives in twentieth-century morris dancing as the balloon-breasted "Old Bess" who tries his best to trip up the other dancers. That, presumably, is the farcical business Richard Harvey has in mind when he tells about a stranger who came to the edge of an Elizabethan town and saw "a quintessence (beside the fool and the Maid Marian) of all the picked youth, strained out of an whole Endship, footing the morris about a may-pole."[9] As buffoons, the Fool and Maid Marian were not part of the "quintessence" of local youth. It is, surely, just such an image of a man dressed up as a woman that Falstaff conjures up when he taunts the Hostess in *Henry IV, Part One*,

> There's no more faith in thee than in a stewed prune, nor no more truth in thee than in a drawn fox; and, for womanhood, Maid Marian may be the deputy's wife of the ward to thee. Go, you thing, go!

> (3.3.112-115)

A stewed prune has no faith, a drawn fox no truth—and Maid Marian no womanhood. Neither male nor female, she is a "thing" indeed. Knowing the use to which the Hostess seems to have put her female capacities with Falstaff, we can appreciate how low his insult hits.

Amid the high spirits of folk festivity, playing about with gender roles could easily turn into playing about with sexual roles. Take, for example, the "wooing-ceremony," the oldest and most primitive of the three types of traditional mummers' plays. A boy dressed up as a Lady receives various suitors, rejects the wealthy and powerful among them, and ends up marrying the Fool. Traditionally acted in January, on the first Monday after Twelfth Night, the play enacts a sacred marriage intended to stimulate the fertility of man, beast, and plant in the coming season.[10] It elevates the two least powerful members of the social group, the woman and the fool, to temporary superiority. And it lets the homoerotic energy in male bonding find release. The oldest mummers' play text we have, an amalgam of all three types performed at Revesby Abbey, Lincolnshire, in 1779, is full of speeches inviting sexual byplay between the men playing the roles. The Fool leaves no doubt about his descent from the phallus-bearing *kalogheros* of Greek fertility rites. When Pickle Herring boasts of his dancing prowess, the Fool rushes in:

> A fool, a fool, a fool,
>   A fool I heard thou say,
>   But more the other way,
> For here I have a tool
>   Will make a maid to play,
> Although in Cupid's school.
>   Come all away![11]

When Pickle Herring tries to woo the man dressed up as the Lady (here called Cicely) the Fool is ready with more sexual squibs:

PICKLE HERRING.
>   Nay, then, sweet Ciss, ne'er trust me more,
>   For I never loved lass before like the[e].
>   *Enter Fool.*
FOOL. No, nor behind, neither.

(p. 118)

The boy playing Cicely gives as good as he gets from the Fool. Blue Britches's attempts to persuade Cicely to marry the rich old man earn this rejoinder:

> Yes, sir, but you are not in the right.
>   Stand back and do not council me!
> For I love a lad that will make me laugh
>   In a secret place, to pleasure me.

To which the Fool cries out, "Good wench!" (p. 119). What have we here? A parody of gender roles? Or an excuse for a man to flirt with a boy? The conflicted relationship between patriarchy and homosexuality in English Renaissance society suggests that we have both. To the degree that the patriarchy was confident of its (hetero-)sexual identity, having a boy "dress up" as a woman was a way of "dressing down" women, a way of making fun of women's wiles. To the degree that the patriarchy was *not* confident of its sexual identity, to the degree that it was troubled by homosexual desire, disguise became a way of saying what otherwise could not be said, of doing what otherwise could not be done. In the privileged time and place of the mummers' wooing rite, a male could flirt with another male, "Cicely" could play the coquette with her suitors, because at day's end the costumes would be packed away for another year. So, too, would sexual horseplay among men.

With respect to sexual license, then, romances like *Clitophon and Leucippe* simply translated to the printed page what Renaissance Englishmen experienced firsthand in the traditional festivities that celebrated the cycle of seasons. The rites that marked the natural turning points in the Renaissance year were a licensed time when chaos could reign; when society's usual rules were relaxed; when people on the bottom swapped places with people on the top. In villages and towns, in schools, colleges, and the inns of court, Christmas was presided over by a Lord of Misrule. "Topsyturvydom" is Robert Weimann's term for the state of mind over which this king-for-the-nonce ruled. In *Rabelais and His World* Mikhail Bakhtin has turned "Carnival" into a stylistic and structural principle, not only in social and political life but in literature. At Whitsuntide, when the year turns from winter to spring, the presiding ruler was, in many places in England, Robin Hood. As a denizen of the forest, he stood forth as the Greenman, the incarnation of spring; as a celebrated outlaw, he thumbed his nose at authority and social hierarchy. *Stealing* the maypole and boughs of hawthorne from some local lord's demesne, sometimes with the lord's connivance, was an essential part of the game.[12]

A popular print (1559) after Pieter Brueghel the Elder's painting "The Village Fair of Hoboken" shows us such goings-on in all their gregarity. "These peasants rejoice in holding village fairs like this," says the caption. "They love dancing, jumping, and getting drunk like animals. They must have these fairs and they must pay for them, even if they must fast and die with cold." The Flemish word for fairs of this sort is *kermesse* (literally, "church mass"), but the religious procession shown entering the church in the center is probably the *last* thing a viewer notices amid the riot of movement that swirls around it. There are other things a viewer might not at first notice, either. In addition to dancing, jumping, and getting drunk, these peasants also love huddling up with members of their own sex. As the dancers to the left rush in a giddy circle and draw our gaze away, two women sit embraced on the harness-pole of the wagon just below. Their male counterparts sit a few feet to the left. As the archer in the lower right hesitates before shooting, one of the two men hunched together near the target takes advantage of everyone's distraction and extends his hand towards his companion's waist—a little too high to be only after his purse. The position of these two men amid their frolicking neighbors is a perfect image of the position of homosexuality in Renaissance society: obvious but hidden, seen but unseen. Equally remarkable in Brueghel's social topography is the marginal place of the stage where a play is in progress.

As ways of putting sex into discourse, folk-plays and romance narratives share similar structures of power and ideology. The balance they strike between positive and negative controls is the same. Both, for a season, "valorize" polymorphous passion. Both, in the end, take that value away. Whatever occasion folk customs gave for turning society upside down, whatever invitation they offered for parodying gender roles, whatever license they gave for homosexual shenanigans, such moments were totally contained by the power structure of Elizabethan society. Whitsunday was the threshold across which a village or town danced its way from winter to spring. Whatever might happen on that special Sunday, the normal rules of society obtained on Saturday and Monday. It is this quality of being in between two orders of existence that Arnold Van Gennep has termed "liminality." As a *limen* is, literally, the threshold between two physical spaces, so in traditional societies rituals are "liminal" occasions that mark the passage between two seasons, between birth and life, between two stages in a person's life, between life and death. In this period of transition, in the temporal and psychological space between two different orders of existence, society's usual rules and regulations are suspended. In that open space, presided over by Robin Hood or another Lord of Misrule, a community experiences Saturnalian release.[13] The effect of liminal excesses, paradoxically, is not to undermine the social order but to reinforce it. Aristotle seems to be thinking along similar lines when he describes the "cathartic" effect of experiencing pity and fear in tragedy. Get such violent feelings out of an audience's system, he implies, and the citizens of Athens will be able to go about their daily lives more calmly and collectedly. In Freud's terms, the festivities of Christmas and Whitsuntide give release to the energy that is normally invested in maintaining inhibitions, so that those inhibitions can be reimposed more comfortably when the season of revelry comes to an end.[14] For male-male sexual desire, as for other outlawed forms of behavior, the effect is the same: impulses that run counter to social rules are allowed expression, but they must be played out within carefully prescribed boundaries. In the process they lose their threatening power. They are rendered safe. The liminal festivities of Renaissance England, like fraternity hazing in our own day, exorcise homosexual desire by turning it into a game.

The structures of thought linking folk festivities and romance narratives are perhaps harder to see than structures of power, but they are no less decisive in the way they stimulate, but ultimately stifle, sexual desire. The ideology that informs most sixteenth-century versions of Achilles Tatius is the code of chivalry. Chivalric romance is, perhaps, *the* distinctive mode of Elizabethan high culture. In the books they read, in the great countryhouses they built, in the way they had their portraits painted, in the plays they watched at court between Christmas and Lent, in the entertainments they staged to celebrate the queen's Accession Day and her progresses over the realm, Elizabethan Englishmen delighted in imagining themselves as the heirs to Aeneas, the crusadors, and the knights of King Arthur.[15] On the annual anniversary of her accession to the throne, Elizabeth's courtiers staged a tournament in which they dressed up and performed as knights of romance. The physical arrangements on these occasions catch precisely the gender distinctions that are acted out in romantic fantasy: the queen *observed* the deeds of derring-do, the men *performed* them. Chivalry, especially as it was adapted to the changed economic and political conditions of early modern Europe, engages all the dynamics of male bonding that make the Myth of Combatants and Comrades a universal feature of human society. It is particularly well suited to negotiating the balance between aggression and affiliation.[16] On the one hand, chivalry inspires a man to individual action, to the achievement of personal glory; on the other, it enjoins his loyalty to other members of his order of knighthood. To William Segar, writing in 1602, chivalry seemed to be one of two major ways that a man in his society could situate himself vis-à-vis other men. Segar's *Honor Military, and Civill* is, among other things, a kind of manual on how to be a hero. A distinction that Segar gets around to drawing in book 4 between two spheres of male action, business and arms, is stated straightaway in the preface contributed by one T— B—:

> There are but two arenas of action for men, business and honor: The principall markes whereat every mans endevour in this life aimeth, are either Profit, or Honor, Th'one proper to vulgar people, and men of inferior Fortune; The other due to persons of better birth, and generous disposition. For as the former by paines, and parsimony do onely labour to become rich; so th'other by Military skil, or knowledge in Civill government, aspire to Honor, and humane glory.[17]

Since, of the two arenas of action, money has become by far the more important in our own time, it takes an effort of imagination to reconstruct a time when "honor," not money, measured the dominance, and the submission, of one male with respect to one another. "Humane glory" may be one of the goals of chivalry; loyalty to one's fellows is another. Segar's list of "The office and dutie of every Knight and Gentlemen" is eloquent in its priorities. Out of nineteen duties, "the love of friends" yields in importance only to fear of God, charity toward the afflicted, and service to king and country.

In the code of chivalry sexual desire occupies a highly volatile place. Segar would keep it under rigorous control, making adultery a military as well as a civil crime.[18] The scope of action opened up in romance narratives, however, works against such strictures—as the quests of Lancelot, Tristan, and Gawain so forcefully illustrate. A quest is a means of escaping all the things that ordinarily constrain individual action—for the reader no less than for the hero. And among those constraints are controls over sexual desire. As a translation of the Myth of Combatants and Comrades into an imaginary realm where anything is possible, Renaissance versions of romance enlarge the range of passion in medieval romance to include, not only the sexual desire that men feel for other men's wives, but the sexual desire that men feel for each other.

To speak of chivalry among artisans and farmers would seem, to Segar at least, ridiculous. However streightened by their "inferior Fortune," these men nonetheless exercised their imaginations—indeed, their very selves—in the same fictions as their social betters. "Moorish" dancers acted out their stylized combat in the same fictional locale as Achilles Tatius's heroes. Being unable to read a romance, they, for a limited season, lived one. Like morris dancing, Saint George plays, the most widely distributed of the three types of mummers' plays, belong to the distant Mediterranean world of *Clitophon and Leucippe*. Traditionally acted at Christmastime, Saint George plays pit the hero-saint of Cappadocia against a "Turkish Knight." In most versions Saint George loses, only to be resurrected (along with the vegetation in the months ahead) through the magical ministrations of a "Doctor." In putting on their plays and in dancing the morris, artisans and farmers were after the same freedom of action—specifically the same freedom of sexual action—as "persons of better birth, and generous disposition," and they sought it in the same fictional corner of the globe. St. George plays illustrate perfectly what Roger Chartier calls "cultural appropriation." In a hierarchical society like early modern England, in which way does cultural influence work? Do the elite impose their ideology, and their fictions, on their inferiors? Or do the inferiors supply the elite with forms of dance, song, speech, and story that are taken up, rationalized, and made part of the official culture? The influence, Chartier claims, works *both* ways, each social group appropriating images and ideas from the other and putting those images and ideas to their own cultural uses.[19] In the case of chivalry, one of those uses seems to be the same in both elite culture and popular culture. Chivalric romance pro-

vided a ready way of negotiating the conflicts in power that ener-
gized homosexual desire.

It was, in part at least, the sexual freedom associated with
romance in popular imagination that helped destroy some real-
life exemplars of the chivalric ideal. The Order of Knights Templars excited envy because of their rich holdings and suspicion
because of their secrecy. As Segar tells the story, Philip IV's brutal suppression of the order in the thirteenth century had as
much to do with property as impropriety. Still, the charges
against them read as if the latter-day Templars were suspected
of having taken on the vices of the very enemy their order had
been founded to defeat. "The Articles produced against them,"
says Segar, "were these."

> First, that by practise of their predecessors the holy land was
> lost, and left to Infidels.
> Secondly, that in election of their great Master, they secretly
> used certaine superstitious and Pagan ceremonies.
> Thirdly, that they were heretikes in holding some opinions con-
> trary to the Christian faith.
> Fourthly, that they made profession of their faith before an
> Image apparelled in a mans skinne.
> Fifthly, that making their confession, they dranke mans blood,
> & tooke a secret oth, one to aid another in defence of that impi-
> ous custome.
> Lastly, that they used the sinne against nature.[20]

(p. 92)

The interlinking here of the Middle East, "Pagan ceremonies,"
heresy, idolatry, male bonding, and sodomy sounds no different
from most moral discourse about homosexuality in early modern Europe. In fact, it sounds remarkably like the charges that
Henry VIII's visitors brought against another all-male subculture, the men in British monasteries, in 1535-36. The charges
against the Knights Templars show us the chivalric code *in extre-
mis*. The fate of these knights, once the conquerors of Jerusalem,
stands as a warning of what can happen when the license of
romance is translated too literally into political and social reality.
In romance the true peril lies not in distant lands but on the
voyage home.

The problem of closure, of how it all ends and what happens
afterwards, is a crucial concern in all three genres in which Renaissance readers, watchers, and listeners could indulge in homoerotic romanticizing. Verse narratives modeled on Ovid's
Metamorphoses, prose narratives modeled on the likes of Achilles

Tatius, and romantic comedies on the public stage all end in similarly ambivalent moments of leave taking. Only in Christopher Marlowe's "Hero and Leander" does that moment never arrive: Marlowe's exercise in out-Oviding Ovid conveniently lacks an ending.

The *epyllia* that Renaissance poets wrote in imitation of episodes from Ovid's *Metamorphoses* are romantic, not because they concern the deeds of chivalric heroes, but because they stimulate the sexual fantasy that is so often a part of chivalric narratives. Ovidian *epyllia*, chivalric narratives, and romantic comedies are alike in the appeal they make to the imagination. Sexual desire in these verses, stories, and plays is not limited to what the protagonists feel for each other. The real *subject* of desire in these fictions is the reader; the protagonists become objects of his fantasy. Like Moors flirting with Maid Marion, like the Fool wooing Cicely, the reader is invited, for a limited season, to give free play to desires that must ordinarily be held in check. Marlowe's "Hero and Leander" illustrates the appeal that these fictions had for Renaissance readers. The sentimentalist's tears invited by the story of two young lovers separated from their happiness by the dark waters of the Hellespont is offset in Marlowe's version, just as it would be in Ovid, sometimes by the lecher's licked lips and then again by the satirist's amused smirks. From the start Marlowe makes it clear just which parts of the poem will be treated with ironic detachment and which with sensual abandon. After a forty-line description of Hero's clothes ("*Hero* the faire,/Whom young *Apollo* courted for her haire"), Marlowe's narrator launches into a loving description of Leander's delectable boyish beauty: "His bodie was as straight as *Circes* wand,/*Jove* might have sipt out *Nectar* from his hand."[21]

The shadow of Ganymede in this description becomes in short order a fleshy presence. Where earlier the narrator cataloged Hero's sleeves, kirtle, veil, jewelry, and shoes, he here offers a blazon of Leander's neck ("Even as delicious meat is to the tast,/So was his necke in touching"), his hairless breast, white belly, and "That heavenly path, with many a curious dint,/That runs along his backe" (1.63-64, 68-69). Marlowe's narrator is content merely to look at Hero, but Leander he tastes and touches:

> Some swore he was a maid in mans attire,
> For in his lookes were all that men desire,
> A pleasant smiling cheeke, a speaking eye,
> A brow for Love to banquet roiallye,
> And such as knew he was a man would say,

Chapter Four

Leander, thou art made for amorous play:
Why art thou not in love, and lov'd of all?
Though thou be faire, yet be not thine owne thrall.

(1.81-90)

Neptune can be forgiven, then, for thinking that Ganymede himself has fallen out of heaven when Leander leaps into the sea and swims the straits to Hero. In a wonderful metaphor of what it is like to be overwhelmed by sexual desire Neptune pulls Leander to the bottom of the sea. Pearls strewn on the ground, mermaids singing in "low corrall groves" (2.161), heaps of gold, an azure palace—all these sensuous details swirl past in the erotic undertow. Only when Leander gasps out his protests does Neptune realize that he has a drowning mortal, not Jupiter's page, in his watery embrace. Neptune lets Leander go but cannot forebear indulging in some amorous play:

He clapt his plumpe cheekes, with his tresses playd,
And smiling wantonly, his love bewrayed.
He watcht his armes, and as they opend wide,
At every stroke, betwixt them would he slide,
And steale a kisse, and then run out a daunce,
And as he turnd, cast many a lustfull glaunce,
And throw him gawdie toies to please his eie,
And dive into the water, and there prie
Upon his brest, his thighs, and everie lim,
And up againe, and close beside him swim,
And talke of love . . . .

Just as we ourselves begin to drown in pleasure, Marlowe's narrator backs away with a characteristic smile on his face:

> *Leander* made replie,
> You are deceav'd, I am no woman I.

(2.181-192)

In such quick manouevers Marlowe manages to outdo his mentor. It is not Ovid, however, who is the likely inspiration for this particular passage, but Suetonius, whose tales about Nero's boy-bride make for some very salacious reading. Tiberius's debauches on the Isle of Capri include some of the same aquatic sports we see in "Hero and Leander":

He incurred yet the infamie of greater and more shamefull filthinesse, such as may not be well named or heard, and much lesse beleeved: to wit, that hee should traine up and teach fine boyes the tenderest and daintiest that might be had (whom he called his little fishes) to converse and play betweene his thighes as he was swimming, and pretily with tongue and teeth seeme to make unto his secret parts, and there to nibble . . . .[22]

Compared to these sybaritic delights, the heterosexual lovemaking of Hero and Leander is the farcical fumbling of two adolescents. In describing Leander's attempts at seduction Marlowe's narrator seems remarkably like Longus in *Daphnis and Chloe*: we as readers revel in our worldliness while we watch two innocents discover desire. What was graphic and passionate with Neptune and Leander becomes figurative and ridiculous with Leander and Hero. Neptune pulls Leander down to the splendors of the sea-bottom; out of bed and on the floor is where Hero lands.

It is just at this point, after Hero and Leander's first night of bliss, that Marlowe leaves off his narrative. "*Desunt nonnulla,*" says the first quarto printing: "Nothing else has come down." Did Marlowe lose interest because there were no more opportunities for homoerotic titillation? Did he despair of how he might reconcile his comic tone with the tragic facts of Leander's drowning? How, indeed, *would* he have portrayed Leander's death? The Renaissance Ovid was expected to combine merriment with morality. With this subject at least, Marlowe could manage only merriment. Morality had to wait until George Chapman supplied a continuation of Marlowe's poem, published in 1598. There Hero and Leander are punished for having offended the goddess Ceremony with the rashness of their lovemaking. Such a thought seems remote indeed from the salacious imagination of Marlowe's narrator. Perhaps Marlowe left off where he did precisely because he could *not* make the punishment fit the crime. Structures of prohibiting power, questions about the social limits of desire, never obtrude to spoil our pleasure in the poem's homoerotic fantasy.

The most usual ending to Ovidian narrative poems, the most usual way of negotiating the inevitable clash between sexual fantasy and social reality, is the death of one or both of the amorous protagonists, followed by metamorphosis into some transhuman form of being, a plant or a star, whose beauty will last forever. That, for example, is the fate of Adonis, "Stain to all nymphs, more lovely than a man," in Shakespeare's "Venus and Adonis" (1593).[23] But the merging of male and female into a single body in Francis Beaumont's "Salmacis and Hermaphroditus" (1602) satisfies even more graphically the ambiguous sexual desire that is both the literal subject of these poems

Chapter Four

and the experience of male subjects as they read them. Beaumont leaves no doubt that the reader he imagines is male—and that the effect of reading the poem will be to make sport with contemporary society's rigid ways of separating male from female: "I hope my Poeme is so lively writ,/That thou wilt turne halfe-mayd with reading it."[24] Which, of course, is just what happens to Hermaphroditus in the course of the poem.

"Salmacis and Hermaphroditus," unlike "Hero and Leander," displays no distinction between male bodies and female bodies in the detail and lusciousness of description lavished upon them. In pursuing her unwilling beloved, Salmacis chances to catch him stripping off his clothes and preparing to bathe in a stream. Her hiding place gives her license to look—and the male reader of the poem license to take delight along with her in what she sees:

> . . . he did begin
> To strip his soft clothes from his tender skin,
> When strait the scorching Sun wept teares of brine,
> Because he durst not touch him with his shine,
> For feare of spoyling that same Iv'ry skin,
> Whose whitenesse he so much delighted in;
> And when the Moone, mother of mortall ease,
> Would fayne have come from the *Antipodes*,
> To have beheld him naked as he stood,
> Ready to leape into the silver flood;
> But might not: for the lawes of heaven deny,
> To shew mens secrets to a womans eye:
> And therefore was her sad and gloomy light
> Confin'd unto the secret-keeping night.

(ll. 838-850)

What the laws of heaven deny to women Beaumont obligingly unveils for the male readers of his book. What they see cannot, however, outlast the limits of the poem—unless they can find in fact the miracle-working stream described in the fiction's last lines: "since that time who in that fountaine swimmes,/A mayden smoothnesse seyzeth halfe his limmes" (ll. 921-922).

Failing the fountain, a man can always read the poem again. For all the titillating foreplay they offer, Marlowe's "Hero and Leander," Shakespeare's "Venus and Adonis," and Beaumont's "Salmacis and Hermaphroditus" all stop short of sexual consummation. They are, in fact, poems not about the consummation of sexual desire but about desire's frustration. In these poems, as in other versions of the Myth of the Shipwrecked

Youth, we never get to see sexual activity in the fiction itself. Sexual arousal in these poems is as much the reader's as the protagonists'. Perhaps, indeed, it is more the reader's. Robert P. Merrix is quite right in studying "Venus and Adonis" and "Salamacis and Hermaphroditus" as species of "soft-core pornography."[25]

Marlowe's "Hero and Leander," Shakespeare's "Venus and Adonis," and Beaumont's "Salmacis and Hermaphroditus" are alike in placing the erotic focus not just on a male youth but on a male youth who is innocent of both sexual experience and gender identity. Why that combination of youthfulness, innocence, and androgyny should have such visceral appeal cannot be explained simply; otherwise, we would not so often encounter such figures in Ovidian verse, romance narratives, and comedies for the public stage. In all these figures we discover an erotic allure far stronger than that of heroes and heroines whose gender is certain. Why should that be so? Aside from the physical beauty of a body and a face in their prime, the youthfulness of these figures illustrates how male bonding operates "vertically" as well as "horizontally." Leander, Adonis, Hermaphroditus, and their counterparts in chivalric romances inspire in other men, especially in older men, a desire to initiate the youths into maleness, to *incorporate* them, physically, into the male power structure. The appeal of their innocence is paradoxical, just as it would be if they were in fact girls: by possessing the boy physically a man could both violate the boy's innocence and repossess the innocence he himself once had. Poems like "Hero and Leander," "Venus and Adonis," and "Salmacis and Hermaphroditus" allowed male readers to repossess the Arcadia they once knew. In their androgyny, finally, figures like Leander, Adonis, and Hermaphroditus embody, quite literally, the ambiguities of sexual desire in English Renaissance culture and the ambivalences of homosexual desire in particular. They represent, not an exclusive sexual taste, but an *inclusive* one. To use the categories of our own day, these poems are bisexual fantasies. The temporary freedom they grant to sexual desire allows it to flow out in all directions, toward all the sexual objects that beckon in the romantic landscape.

Chivalric narratives in the manner of *Clitophon and Leucippe* offer the same imaginary pleasures, and the same temporal constraints. Chief among the latter-day adventurers who followed in the wake of Heliodorus, Longus, and Achilles Tatius were Robert Greene, Sir Philip Sidney, and Thomas Lodge. Robert

Greene's *Menaphon* (1589) is a veritable anthology of forbidden lusts. Most famous today for having called the fledgling Shakespeare an "upstart crow," Greene manages to find opportunities for titillation at every turn. And of turns *Menaphon* has plenty. The shepherd who is the tale's titular hero is out tending his flocks and drinking in the beauty of the Arcadian landscape when he chances to spy three shipwrecked figures on the beach: an old man, a young woman, and a child. Samela, as the woman calls herself, is of course as beautiful as can be. Menaphon promptly falls in love. So, too, do all the other shepherds round about, particularly a shepherd named Melicertus, who is conspicuously better than everybody else at improvising eclogues, the principal occupation in Arcadia after tending sheep. Samela and her son settle in with the shepherds, and, as things go in Arcadia, none of the shepherds' infatuation abates with the passing years. In the meantime, Pleusidippus, the son, grows into a "beauteous boy" who easily assumes presidency over a society for whom everyday is Whitsuntide. Pleusidippus

> began to shew himselfe among the shepheards['] children, with whom he had no sooner contracted familiar acquaintance, but straight he was chosen Lord of the May game, king of their sports, and ringleader of their revils.[26]

The lad's good looks prove to be his undoing, however, when a Thessalian pirate sees him gathering seashells on the shore. It is lust at first sight:

> gazing on his face, as wanton *Jove* gazed on *Phrygian Ganimede* in the fields of *Ida,* hee exhaled into his eyes such deepe impression of his perfection, as that his thought never thirsted so much after any pray, as this pretie *Pleusidippus* ['] possession.

(p. 91)

First the pirate tries sweet talk. When that fails, he resorts to brute force, carries Pleusidippus off to Thessaly, and presents him, attired in "choyce silks and *Tyrian* purple," to the king (p. 93). As so easily can happen in romances, the moment of Pleusidippus's arrival finds the King of Thessaly and his wife doing something thematically appropriate, walking in the garden and talking about hyacinths and anemones, flowers that were once beautiful boys. The King of Thessaly is struck as forcibly with Pleusidippus's charms as the pirate was: "What ever may deserve the name of faire have I seen before, beautie have I beheld in his brightest orb, but never set eye on immortalitie before this houre" (p. 96). Even the queen appreciates his androgynous beauty. Pleusidippus, she complains, makes the women of Thessaly look plain.

Confronted with youthful androgynous innocence in the person of Pleusidippus, there is nothing for the King of Thessaly—"such a courteous Foster-father" (p. 97)—to do but to marry him off to his daughter and make him heir to the throne. But not too soon to spoil a good story. Eleven years go by, and Pleusidippus hears about the beautiful shepherdess of Arcadia. He voyages to Arcadia, seeks out Samela, fails to recognize her as his mother, falls in love, does some assiduous wooing, and is prevented from marrying his own mother only by the timely appearance of an aged prophetess who tells everyone who is who. To a reader seated among the mundane realities of everyday life, Greene's *Menaphon* offers passage to an imaginary world that is liminal in two dimensions. Arcadia is a place apart, but it is also a time apart, during which personal identities are not fixed and desire is free to wander. The story's conclusion, however, shoves us firmly back into mundane reality. Poor Menaphon is left out of the happy ending. All these glamorous people, his beloved "Samela" included, embrace one another and leave his homely fields as abruptly as they arrived sixteen years before. The sad resignation in the last words of Greene's story define our own reluctance as readers to return to a world where time weighs more heavily than it does in Arcadia and where sexual desire, unlawful sexual desire in particular, cannot always enjoy its object. Menaphon, "seeing his passions were too aspiring, and that with the *Syrian* wolves, he barkt against the Moone, he left, such lettice as were too fine for his lips, and courted his old love *Pesana*, to whom shortly after he was married" (p. 45). In Greene's *Menaphon*, as in other Renaissance romances, homosexual desire barks against the moon.

For all our reluctance as readers, Greene's ending comes as no surprise. All along, Greene has supplied enough clues to let us know who each of the exiled characters really is, even when the other characters remain in ignorance. The result, as in Shakespeare's comedies, is a kind of double perspective that lets us sympathize with the characters' feelings at the same time that we remain omnisciently and bemusedly detached. As far as sexual desire is concerned, this double perspective makes the tale all the more titillating. *We* know that it is a son soliciting his mother when *they* do not. At the same time, our omniscience lets us anticipate the ending in a way that the characters cannot. We know that true identities will be revealved and that Arcadia will be left behind. In that knowledge there is a certain moral security: we can enjoy the *prospect* of forbidden desires without actually seeing them consummated.

Sir Philip Sidney is a rather more coy storyteller. Consider this description of a shipwreck near the beginning of book 1 of *The Countesse of Pembroke's Arcadia* (published 1593):

> But a little way off they saw the mast whose proud height now lay along, like a widow having lost her make, of whom she held her honour; but upon the mast they saw a young man (at least, if he were a man) bearing show of about eighteen years of age, who sate as on horseback, having nothing upon him but his shirt which, being wrought with blue silk and gold, had a kind of resemblance to the sea on which the sun then near his western home did shoot some of his beams. His hair, which the young men of Greece used to wear very long, was stirred up and down with the wind, which seemed to have a sport to play with it, as the sea had to kiss his feet; himself full of admirable beauty set forth by the strangeness both of his seat and gesture, for, holding his head up full of unmoved majesty, he held a sword aloft with his fair arm which often he waved about his crown as though he would threaten the world in that extremity.[27]

This almost nude figure, sported with by the wind and the waves, radiates an androgynous fascination that the narrator emphasizes all the more by anticipating the reader's first thought that long hair belongs to women. Attracting the flirtations of Aeolus and Neptune, the figure on the mast languishes like a woman; brandishing his sword, he fights back like a man. The would-be rescuers of the young man, "if he were a man," react much as Greene's characters do when they first see Pleusidippus. His beauty amazes them.

Who *is* this captivating figure? We as readers know no more than the fishermen do until suddenly another survivor of the wreck leaps up, snatches the rope out of the fishermen's hands, and shouts across the waves to his friend. The young man in the fishing boat is Musidorus, the young man on the mast is Pyrocles, and Sidney's *Arcadia* is the story of their adventures. The friends' reunion is, of course, not yet to be. The fishermen's boat is cut off by the galley of a pirate "who hunted not only for goods but for bodies of men, which he employed either to be his galley-slaves or to sell at the best market." The distinctly sexual edge to this whole episode is continued in Musidorus's thoughts as he watches helplessly while the pirates snatch his friend aboard their galley:

> "And alas," said he to himself, "dear Pyrocles, shall that body of thine be enchained? Shall those victorious hands of thine be commanded to base offices? Shall virtue become a slave to those that be slaves to viciousness?"

> (1.1.8-9)

Conventional enough phrases, to be sure, but in the distinctly sexual atmosphere that Sidney gives to the opening scene of *Arcadia* it is hard not to think of those phrases in graphically physical, provocatively sadistic terms.

As heroes of romance are wont to do, Pyrocles survives the pirates. Reunited with Musidorus when the two of them, both in disguise, meet, challenge one another, and cross swords, Pyrocles goes home with Musidorus to the house of the shepherd Kalander, where Musidorus has taken refuge. The real shepherds and the king, queen, and princesses living nearby in pastoral exile find in Pyrocles the same androgynous fascination that the King and Queen of Thessaly do in Greene's Pleusidippus. Pyrocles combines feminine bashfulness with male valor "as if nature had mistaken her work to have a Mars' heart in a Cupid's body" (1.6.42). Among Pyrocles' admirers in Arcadia none is more ardent, however, than Musidorus himself. When Pyrocles falls in love with one of the exiled king's daughters, Musidorus is as devastated as Valentine in *The Two Gentlemen of Verona*, Antonio in *The Merchant of Venice*, Leontes in *The Winter's Tale*, and Arcite in *The Two Noble Kinsmen*. Pyrocles and Musidorus play out their own version of the friendship/marriage debate that figures so prominently in the Myth of Combatants and Comrades. Pyrocles broaches the fact of his love obliquely: he praises the beauty of Arcadia and the delights of solitude. It must be that some goddess inhabits the region, he says, looking at Musidorus in hope of pity. Musidorus marks his friend's words "with no less loving attention." What can be coming? "Kindly embracing" his friend, Musidorus gives Pyrocles leave to defend solitude so long as *he* can share it with him. When the straight truth comes out at last, Musidorus is indignant:

> "Now the eternal Gods forbid," mainly cried out Musidorus, "that ever my ear should be poisoned with so evil news of you!

Oh, let me never know that any base affection should get any lordship in your thoughts."

(1.9.51-53)

Soon afterwards Pyrocles disappears from the shepherds' demesne, and Musidorus goes after him, "arming him self in a black armour as either a badge or prognostication of his mind" (1.10.56).

What he encounters in his quest is an Amazon warrior whose arms take the accoutrements of a male fighter and feminize them. The Amazon's ample hair is drawn up into a golden net that imitates a helmet. Her satin doublet, covered with "plates" of gold "nailed" with precious stones, is a feminine mock-up of a knight's armor. Beneath it all Musidorus gets tantalizing glimpses of flesh:

> The nether part of her garment was so full of stuff and cut after such a fashion that, though the length of it reached to the ankles, yet in her going one might sometimes discern the small of her leg, which with the foot was dressed in a short pair of crimson velvet buskins, in some places open (as the ancient manner was) to show the fairness of the skin.

(1.12.68-69)

A lascivious reader has ancient custom to thank once again. All the androgynous details here are focused in a rich jewel the Amazon wears about her neck: on it is incised Hercules in women's clothes, Omphale's distaff in hand, together with the inscription "Never more valiant" (1.12.76). Only when Musidorus hears the Amazon sing does he—and the reader—realize that the Amazon is none other than Pyrocles in feminine disguise. The long hair, the naked leg, the fair skin—we have seen those enticements before.

In Sidney's original version of book 1 the sexual allure of Pyrocles in the guise of an Amazon is made even more explicit. As Sidney first wrote the story, Musidorus actually helps Pyrocles put on the disguise. He finds his newly transformed friend quite irresistible:

> But Musidorus, that had helped to dress his friend, could not satisfy himself with looking upon him, so did he find his excellent beauty set out with his new change, like a diamond set in a more advantageous sort. Insomuch that he could not choose, but smiling said unto him:
> "Well," said he, "sweet cousin, since you are framed of such a

loving mettle, I pray you, take heed of looking yourself in a glass lest Narcissus's fortune fall unto you. For my part, I promise you, if I were not fully resolved never to submit my heart to these fancies, I were like enough while I dressed you to become a young Pygmalion."[28]

Afterwards the narrator of the original version delights in finding occasion to refer to Pyrocles as Musidorus's "dear he-she friend" (1.41).

By withholding the Amazon's identity from the reader in the revised version, Sidney not only shows what a delightful tease he is as a storyteller; he forces us to see full-face the androgyny that has only been hinted at before. Grief-stricken to see what love has done to his friend, Musidorus launches into a full-scale tirade against women that is worthy of Plutarch's Protogenes. Pyrocles responds with all the Platonic arguments about love out of Castiglione's *The Courtier*, and little by little Musidorus is won over. Musidorus does not give in, however, until he has exacted three promises from Pyrocles: that he not increase his "evil" with "further griefs," that he love his lady "with all the powers of your mind," and that he command his friend to do whatever he can to help him attain his desires. Pyrocles lays on Musidorus only one command in return:

"that you continue to love me, and look upon my imperfections with more affection than judgement."

"Love you!" said he. "Alas, how can my heart be separated from the true embracing of it, without it burst, by being too full of it?"

(1.12.77)

As the symmetries of the plot demand, Musidorus goes on to fall in love with the king's other daughter, and many adventurous pages later the two friends marry the sisters—but not before Sidney has played Pyrocles' transvestite disguise for all it is worth. First the King, taking the disguise at face value, falls passionately in love with Pyrocles; then the Queen, seeing through the disguise, follows suit; finally the king's daughter, charmingly naive about sexual desire, returns her disguised suitor's love but can't quite figure out what to feel or do since "Zelmane," as Pyrocles calls himself, is a woman. Sidney helps the fun along by always referring to Pyrocles in drag as "she."

However delightful the confusions may be, however true the story may be to the way human beings do in fact arrive at sexual self-definition, Sidney's *Arcadia* ends with the lovers casting off disguise and taking on their "real" identities. As in Greene's *Menaphon*, Topsyturvydom has plenty of room for homosexual flirtation—but only till the Lord of Misrule abdicates. From the friends' separation from the real world in the shipwreck, through their sexual flirtation with one another in Arcadia, to their separate marriages at the end, Sidney follows Musidorus and Pyrocles through a rite of passage from boyhood to manhood. Much more than Greene, however, Sidney lets us experience liminality from the inside. In such narrative tricks as not telling us who is tied to the mast or who the Amazon is, Sidney makes us share the confused feelings Musidorus has as he works his way from infatuation with his friend toward connubial love for the king's elder daughter. At the same time, however, Sidney never loses his characteristic light touch. He carries the whole thing off with *sprezzatura*. Compared with Greene, Sidney has a great deal more of what we now would call psychological insight, but ultimately he treats homosexual desire exactly as Greene does: as a kind of game. At the story's end we leave the sexual freedom of Arcadia and return to the strictures of Elizabethan society. It is these strictures, after all, that make romance romantic.

In addition to the interiority he gives his characters, Sidney is unusual in directing his story to a woman. If we take Sidney's prefatory letter at face value, he dashed off the sheets of the romance for the amusement of his sister and her friends, the "fair ladies" who are constantly addressed in the original version. What particularly female pleasures might have been stimulated by the fantasy of dressing a male up in women's clothes? However much this female audience may have been in Sidney's mind as he wrote the original version of *Arcadia*, it was a man, Sidney's friend and biographer Fulke Greville, who took the manuscripts in hand after Sidney's death and had printed the first edition of the two revised books of *Arcadia* that Sidney had managed to complete. Only after that edition was in circulation did the Countess of Pembroke—whether to meet popular demand or to assume authority over the text is not clear—take up the job of editor and paste together the two revised books with the three books that Sidney had left unrevised to make up the version of *Arcadia* that bears her name. Greene is more typical of Renaissance writers of romance in imagining an all-male readership. Greene's *Menaphon* may be dedicated to Lady Hales, in her capacity as *"wife to the late* deceased Sir James Hales," but the work is prefaced with two direct addresses of the author to his readers: a short one "To the Gentlemen Readers" generally and a longer one "To the Gentlemen Students *of both Universities*" (pp. 5, 7-8, 9-28). Greene appeals not only to his readers' self-esteem as individuals but to the group identity they have as students in Oxford and Cambridge colleges. Like Barnfield addressing his inns-of-court colleagues in his pastoral eclogues, Greene asks his readers to take the romance in hand as a kind of all-male in-joke. Greene's *Menaphon* is an exercise in male bonding—the equivalent for a printed text of what illiterate men did when they put on a folk-play or danced the morris.

That, too, is Thomas Lodge's tactic in *Rosalynde: Euphues Golden Legacie* (1590). Among the "Gentlemen Readers" Lodge addresses in his opening epistle was, it turned out, William Shakespeare, who used *Rosalynde* as the source for *As You Like It* eight years or so later. Before reading Lodge's story of a disguised princess who dons a male disguise and woos her lover, Shakespeare would have encountered this aggressively masculine apologia:

> Heere you may perhaps find som leaves of *Venus* mirtle, but heawen down by a souldier with his curtleaxe, not bought with the allurement of a filed tongue. To be briefe Gentlemen, roome for a souldier, & a sailer, that gives you the fruits of his labors that he wrought in the *Ocean*, when everie line was wet with a surge, & everie humorous passion countercheckt with a storme.[29]

Lodge is explaining how he came to write the work on a voyage back from the Canary Islands, but in effect he is also asking his readers to read the text as *men*. If Sidney casts himself as a writer of letters to his sister, Lodge imagines himself as a sailor elbowing his way into a tavern with a tale to tell. The main focus of the story, sure enough, is not on the love of Rosalynde, but on the quarrel of the Orlando-figure with his elder brother. The moral that Lodge draws at the end is concerned exclusively with relations between older brothers and younger brothers, between fathers and sons, between nature and nurture in the education of a gentleman:

> Heere Gentlemen may you see in *Euphues Golden Legacie*, that such as neglect their fathers precepts, incurre much prejudice; that division in Nature as it is a blemish in nurture, so tis a breach of good fortunes; that vertue is not measured by birth but by action; that younger brethren though inferiour in yeares, yet may be superior to honours; that concord is the sweetest

conclusion, and amitie betwixt brothers more foreceable than fortune.

(p. 256)

In this summary romantic love figures not at all.

That same masculine perspective colors Lodge's presentation of Rosalynde in disguise as Ganymede. Like Greene and Sidney, Lodge plays up the disguised figure's androgynous appeal to the other characters. A "pretie swayne" she appears to the Orlando-figure when he first sees her in the forest (p. 206). For the love-struck shepherdess Phoebe, Rosalynde as Ganymede calls to mind all the other famous boys who were pursued by lusting gods and goddesses: Adonis (p. 232), Endymion, Paris (p. 247). To Lodge himself Rosalynde in disguise is an "amorous Girleboye" (p. 233) whom he sometimes refers to as "he" (e.g., pp. 180, 232) but more often as "she." Lodge, straight-talking soldier that he is, shuns the kind of narrative coyness we find in Sidney. We are never tempted to forget that Rosalynde is a woman; the Orlando-figure never takes her for anything but a man. All of Lodge's sexual jokes turn, in fact, on keeping that distinction clear. When "Ganymede" starts making flirtatious allusions to Rosalynde right in front of her lover, the Celia-figure begins to get nervous. She has nothing to worry about; listening to Ganymede's prattle, the Orlando-figure "took him flat for a shepheards Swayne" (p. 208).

All the easier, then, for Rosalynde and the Orlando-figure to carry on their mock-wooing and mock-marriage. In Lodge the wooing rite is a stylized eclogue in which Rosalynde, already in disguise as Ganymede, assumes a second disguise as a shepherdess out of Montano or Sannazarro, and the Orlando-figure, already in disguise as a forester, takes on a second disguise as a shepherd. They sing, not speak, to one another about love, and they do so through personae that are even further removed from their real identities. After this "courting Eclogue" is over, it is the bemused Celia-figure, not an over-eager Rosalynde, who proposes a mock-marriage. No wonder, then, that the Orlando-figure is able to walk away believing that the whole thing has only been a game and that satisfaction for his desires is as remote as ever.

None of this certainty about who is male and who is female marks Shakespeare's treatment of the same episode. Quite the opposite. Not in disguises twice removed from their real identities, not as singers of an eclogue, do Rosalind and Orlando woo

each other, but face to face, in prose, in words that come peril-
ously close to peeling off the one thin layer of disguise that
separates the lovers from their desires. Instead of stylized verses
we hear some audaciously direct talk about sex. "Come, woo
me, woo me," Rosalind commands; "for I am in a holiday humour, and like enough to consent." Orlando teases: "I would kiss
before I spoke." "Nay, you were better speak first . . . " (4.1.64-
65, 68). However Rosalind manages that rejoinder—nervously,
brashly, or flirtatiously—we see in these exchanges not how little fantasy has to do with reality but how much. One *double
entendre* after another keeps the sexual tension high. When they
have run out of something to say, good orators, says Rosalind,
will spit; "for lovers, lacking—God warn us!—matter, the clean-
liest shift is to kiss." What lover could possibly be out of something to say when standing before his mistress, Orlando
protests.

> ROSALIND. Marry, that should you, if I were your mistress,
>   or I should think my honesty ranker than my wit.
> ORLANDO. What, of my suit?
> ROSALIND. Not out of your apparel, and yet out of your suit.

(4.1.81-83)

Clothed or naked, Orlando is invited to woo Rosalind while
she puts herself "in a more coming-on disposition." "Ask me
what you will," she invites, "I will grant it." After all this seductive game-playing there is, almost certainly, a sudden shift to
seriousness in Orlando's simple reply: "Then love me, Rosalind." But the woman playing a man remains cavalier to the end:
"Yes, faith, will I, Fridays and Saturdays and all." Undaunted,
Orlando keeps up the romance: "And *wilt* thou have me?" Rosalind would put the emphasis on "have": "Ay, and twenty such"
(4.1.105-111, emphasis added). In keeping with her aggressive
role in the game of seduction, it is Rosalind, not Celia, who
proposes the mock-marriage in *As You Like It*. In two respects,
then, Shakespeare goes far beyond Lodge in making sport with
gender roles. First, he lets the woman play the role of sexual
aggressor. But the confusion of sexual identities runs deeper
than that. Orlando, unless he breaches all the rules of romantic
comedy and sees through Rosalind's disguise, plays along with
the game far more eagerly than his counterpart in Lodge and
trades come-hither dares with someone he thinks is a boy. There
is something about this scene not unlike Cicely and the Fool in
the Revesby play.

At the Globe, of course, Shakespeare's alterations to Lodge would have been all the racier: the audience would have seen, not a man falling in love with a woman dressed as a boy, but a man falling in love with a boy actor dressed as a woman dressed as a boy. They would have not just read about the androgynously alluring adolescent; they would have seen him. In the dalliance of "Orlando" and "Rosalind" they would have witnessed in literal fact what Orlando and Rosalind were playing out in fiction: a man and a boy flirting with abandon and getting away with it. What did Shakespeare's audience make of such things? Everything or nothing, if we believe the extreme answers suggested by observers then and argued by scholars now. On the one hand, boys playing women's parts was one of the things about stage plays that Puritans objected to most. Did not Deuteronomy forbid men to wear women's clothes?

> The woman shal not weare that which perteineth unto the man, nether shal a man put on womans raiment: for all that do so, *are* abominacion unto the Lord thy God.[30]

In his polemical book advocating *Th'Overthrow of Stage-Playes* (1599), John Rainolds leaves no doubt about the ultimate reason for this prohibition: cross-dressing leads to homosexual acts. We must consider, Rainolds insists,

> what sparkles of lust to that vice the putting of wemens attire on men may kindle in uncleane affections, as *Nero* shewed in *Sporus*, *Heliogabalus* in himselfe; yea certaine, who grew not to such excesse of impudencie, yet arguing the same in causing their boyes to weare long heare like wemen . . . .[31]

The connection between cross-dressing and homosexuality would not have been lost on readers of the Geneva Bible of 1560, where a marginal note to Deuteronomy 22:5 explains that for a man to dress up as a woman "were to alter the ordre of nature, & to despite God." In questioning "Why Did the English Stage Take Boys for Women?" Stephen Orgel has taken Rainolds and his kind at face value and has teased out three assumptions about the stage that seem to lie behind their attacks: (1) the basic form of response to the theater is erotic, (2) the theater is uncontrollably exciting, and (3) an essential form of erotic excitement for men is homosexual. Since plays written for the public stage betray no anxiety about these matters (anxiety seems to be focused instead on disobedient children and unfaithful wives), Orgel concludes that Rainolds was apparently making a valid point.[32] Several feminist critics have taken the same line and suggested that homosexual titillation was *always* a factor in a society in which men were writing and acting plays primarily for other men. Boy-actors dressed as women become, in this view, a licensed way of arousing and satisfying homosexual desire.[33] Often implicit in such arguments about homosexual desire in early modern England is the distinctly modern idea that homosexuality is all about men wanting to be like women.

On the other hand, we have the testimony of sixteenth- and seventeenth-century playgoers like Thomas Platter, George Sandys, Thomas Coryate, and Lady Mary Wroth to suggest that audiences simply accepted boys in women's clothes as a stage convention. On a visit to London in 1599 Thomas Platter, a student from Basle, saw a performance of *Julius Caesar* at one of the South Bank theaters: "When the play was over, they danced very marvellously and gracefully together as is their wont, two dressed as men and two as women."[34] That, Platter implies, is simply how they do it.

George Sandys and Thomas Coryate, two Englishmen who traveled abroad and saw firsthand that there were other ways of portraying women onstage, speak about English practice in just such conventional terms. When he saw actresses performing in a comedy at Venice in 1608, Coryate was surprised at how *good* they were:

> I was at one of their Play-houses where I saw a Comedie acted. The house is very beggarly and base in comparison of our stately Play-houses in England: neyther can their Actors compare with us for apparrell, shewes and musicke. Here I observed certaine things that I never saw before. For I saw women acte, a thing that I never saw before, though I have heard that it hathe beene sometimes used in London, and they performed it with as good a grace, gesture, and whatsoever convenient for a Player, as ever I saw any masculine Actor.[35]

(Just where in London women performed in plays in Coryate's time is not at all clear. Does he have in mind amateur performances in schools or in certain noble households?) Coryate was far more interested in the sumptuously dressed and mysteriously masked courtesans who were present in the audience than he was in the actresses onstage. Like Coryate, Sandys was surprised at seeing actresses onstage in Italy; unlike his fellow countryman, he didn't much like what he saw. Returning home by ship from a trip to the Middle East in 1610, Sandys stopped at Messina in Sicily, where he took in a play. The play itself was not remarkable enough to record, but the way it was acted stirred Sandys to pointed comment. Along the strand between the city wall and the harbor, Sandys says,

> is to be seene the pride and beauties of the Citie. There have they their play-houses, where the parts of women are acted by women, and too naturally passionated; which they forbeare not to frequent upon Sundayes.[36]

Too "naturally" performed: the implied antithesis to natural is "artificial," in the nonpejorative Renaissance sense of the word. Sandys sees boys acting women's parts not as a moral issue but as a dramatic convention, and he prefers it because it allows for greater artistry. Sandys' interest is not in the boy beneath the costume but in the female illusion the boy creates. Artistry is likewise what Lady Mary Wroth implies about boy-actors when she twice finds occasion in her prose romance *Urania* to compare a "real" woman with women as played by boys on the stage. The would-be lover to whom one of Lady Mary's heroines plies her charms "was no further wrought, then if he had seene a delicate play-boy acte a loving womans part, and knowing him a Boy, lik'd onely his action."[37] Until feminist critics reopened the question, twentieth-century students of Renaissance drama who bothered to think about the matter at all tended to assume that Rainolds was a crank and that witnesses like Platter, Coryate, Sandys, and Wroth are more representative of how Elizabethan spectators actually looked at boys acting women's parts.[38] We are left, then, with two extreme views: whatever erotic allure the boy actors exuded must have been, according to this dichotomy, *either* as the women they were pretending to be (the heterosexual appeal implied by Platter, Coryate, Sandys, and Wroth) *or* as the boys they were in fact (the homosexual appeal attacked by Rainolds).

We can never know, of course, what went on inside the heads of people who have been dead for four hundred years, or even if everyone thought and felt the same. As Michael Shapiro argues, interplay between the theatrical "surface" of boys playing women and the theatrical "depth" of the women they were protraying must have varied from moment to moment in the course of a play. The few firsthand witnesses whose responses we can read suggest that theatergoers in early modern England remained conscious of *both* things, of the actor and of the illusion he created.[39] Any erotic element in boys' impersonations of women must surely have varied from actor to actor, from author to author, from play to play.[40] This much is certain, however: whenever a character's fictional gender is changed by disguise, whenever a boy actor dressed up as a girl dresses up as a boy, Shakespeare seizes the chance to play up the artifice of acting and the sexual ambiguity of the actor. The effect is exactly that of a play-within-the-play. *Hamlet* seems natural; *The Murder of Gonzago*, self-consciously artificial. Before London's public theaters were closed by Puritan edict in 1642, "play-boys" disguised as girls disguised as boys appeared in at least seventy-five plays by nearly forty different playwrights. Incarnations of the Shipwrecked Youth in scripts by John Fletcher, Phillip Massinger, Thomas Middleton, Thomas Heywood, and other playwrights represent, according to Michael Shapiro, exploitation of ideas originally put on the stage by Shakespeare.[41]

The bawdiest such scene in Shakespeare is probably also the earliest: the Induction to *The Taming of the Shrew* (c. 1593). For the Lord who takes drunken Christopher Sly in hand and turns him into a nobleman, a big part of the joke is dressing up his page boy, Bartholomew, and sending him to Sly in the guise of a wife. Tell Bartholomew to speak to Sly "with soft low tongue and lowly courtesy," the Lord orders. If the page lacks "a woman's gift/To rain a shower of commanded tears," let him try an onion concealed in a handkerchief when he welcomes his "husband" back to health after seven years' insanity (Ind. 1.112, 122-126). Bartholomew does only too good a job. The seven years of insanity recommended by the lord get stretched to fifteen. To the poor "wife" it seems like even more:

> . . . the time seems thirty unto me,
> Being all this time *abandoned from your bed.*

Sly rises to the lure.

> . . . Servants, leave me and her alone.
> Madam, undress you and come now to bed.

Oh, no, that would drive his lordship back into madness: "I hope this reason stands for my excuse." Quips Sly, "Ay, it *stands* so that I may hardly tarry so long . . . ." And by "it" Sly does not mean matters in general. Bartholomew has given Sly plenty of provocation even before that. The lines he speaks are humble, certainly; they can also be heard as sexual invitations, which is exactly how Sly takes them. "Where is my wife?" Sly demands at the beginning of the scene. "Here, noble lord, what is thy *will* with her?", the page pipes, with a vaginal pun out of Shakespeare's sonnets. Antimetabole gives the boy a chance for yet more special emphases:

> My husband and my lord, my *lord* and *husband*;
> I am your wife *in all obedience.*

(Ind. 2.100-101, 104-105, 111-114, 121-122, emphasis added)

After this, one wonders if the boy doesn't gesture to his crotch and wink at the audience when he delivers his retort "I hope *this* reason stands for my excuse." In sixteenth-century pronunciation, *rez'n* for "reason" could sound alot like *rezin* for "raising." Exaggerated play with gender identity in the Induction to *The Taming of the Shrew* sets us up for all the liminal role-reversals in the play proper: servants who swap places with their masters, a wandering scholar who poses as a father, and a woman (played by a boy) who dares to behave with the swagger of a man. Julia in *The Two Gentlemen of Verona* (1594) and Portia and Nerissa in *The Merchant of Venice* (1597) give us the same kind of bawdy banter when they assume disguises as men—and go off to turn catastrophe into comedy.

The bawdy part-songs we hear in *The Taming of the Shrew, The Two Gentlemen of Verona*, and *The Merchant of Venice* are transmuted into complex polyphony in *As You Like It* (1598) and *Twelfth Night* (1600). In these two plays, the ripest of Shakespeare's romance comedies, we do not simply hear teasing jokes about androgyny; we see men appear to fall in love with boys. If Orlando's mooning over "Ganymede" has still something of Whitsuntide revelry about it, Orsino's fascination with Viola/Cesario is, like everything else about Orsino, in a lyric mode. The love messages Orsino sends to Olivia will, he believes, have a greater effect because of the youthfulness of the "little Caesar" who carries them to her. As indeed they do, when Olivia falls in love with Orsino's page. When Viola/Cesario protests what Orsino says, he counters with first-hand observation:

> Dear lad, believe it;
> For they shall yet belie thy happy years
> That say thou art a man.

The traits he goes on to describe compose an image of androgynous beauty that is as appropriate to "Cesario"—and to the actual boy who is playing the role—as it is to "Viola":

> Diana's lip
> Is not more smooth and rubious; thy small pipe

Is as the maiden's organ, shrill and sound,
And all is semblative a woman's part.

(1.4.29-34)

Fortunately for Orlando, circumstance changes a lover of the same sex into one of the opposite.

When Shakespeare returned to these comic themes toward the end of his career, he did so with a much sharper sense of how powerfully sexual energies motivate human actions. All of the violent and dishonest acts that impel *Cymbeline* (1609) toward tragedy—Cymbeline's desire to please his wife, Cloten's brutality, Iachimo's treachery, Posthumus's gullibility—erupt out of sexual desire. As in Shakespeare's earlier romances, however, the comic outcome in *Cymbeline* depends on a female character assuming control in the guise of a man. The result, as critics have liked to point out, is a strange combination of realism and fantasy. In his disguise as "Fidele," the boy actor playing Imogen works the same erotic magic on the exiles in Wales as Greene's Pleusidippus and Sidney's Pyrocles do in Arcadia. Helping Imogen choose her disguise, Pisanio advises her to change timidity for "a waggish courage," to be "ready in jibes, quick-answered, saucy, and/As quarrelous as the weasel" (3.4.158-160)—just the traits we see in Portia's lawyer, Rosalind's "Ganymede," and Viola's "Cesario." When "Fidele" first shows up in Wales, the old royal retainer Belarius is as thunder-struck as Greene's King of Thessaly or Sidney's Kalander. "By Jupiter, an angel," he first exclaims, and then decides to grant the figure sex.

or, if not,
An earthly paragon. Behold divineness
No elder than a boy.

(3.6.42-44)

The king's estranged sons, having never seen a woman before, don't know what to make of "Fidele." Guiderius almost believes him to be a maid—

Were you a woman, youth,
I should woo hard but be your groom in honesty,
Ay, bid for you as I'd buy.

Arviragus is willing to accept him as a boy: "He is a man, I'll love him as my brother" (3.6.66-69). For all that, the two princes and their foster-father treat "Fidele" as if he were a girl. "Pray be not sick," Berlarius pleads, "For you must be our housewife" (4.2.43-44). As in Shakespeare's earlier plays, the magic that

turns tragedy into comedy involves retreat to a liminal landscape where social identities, and sexual identities, dissolve in
the half-light. This general feature, as well as several specific
details like Cloten's beheading, links *Cymbeline* with *Clitiphon
and Leucippe*.[42]

Why should cross-dressing work the marvelous alchemy it
does in Shakespeare's comedies and tragicomedies? To that complex question critics have given a variety of partial answers,
each of them in its own way true. In political terms, it is tempting to hail Shakespeare as an incipient feminist. Responding,
apparently, to the relative powerlessness of women in
Elizabethan society, Shakespeare lets his heroines, during the liminal time of the play at least, enjoy a man's latitude of action.[43]
In philosophical terms, we may also be seeing in these plays an
enactment of the Renaissance assumption, ultimately derived
from Aristotle's *Metaphysics*, that the male is more "perfect" than
the female. As part of its idealized vision of experience, romantic
comedy includes the perfectability of womankind by letting
women, temporarily at least, become men.[44] Certainly the one
occasion in Shakespeare, in *The Merry Wives of Windsor*, when we
see the reverse situation of a male character dressing up as a
woman suggests that the magic works in one direction only.
Falstaff's in Mistress Page's clothes: what more can one say? A
woman disguised as a man is full of suggestive power; a man
disguised as a woman is ridiculous.[45] In psychological terms, the
convention of boy actors dressing up as women dressing up as
boys has such power because it recapitulates the process by
which men do in fact come to love women. Drawing on Freud's
theories of psychic development, W. Thomas MacCary has
traced in Shakespeare's comedies a pattern in which men first
fall in love with other men, with mirror images of themselves,
before they learn to love the non-masculine traits in women.[46]
Their tutor in this process is often a figure like Rosalind, enough
of a man to meet them on equal terms but enough of a woman to
seduce them. In anthropological terms, then, each comedy enacts a rite of passage, a romantic hero's transition from homosexual adolescence to heterosexual manhood.

The truth of Shakespeare's comedies is more, however, than
the sum of these political, philosophical, psychological, and anthropological parts. Shakespeare sees in cross-dressing just what
his Puritan detractors did: a particularly volatile symbol of
liminality, a relaxation of the social rules that hold man's animal
passions in check.[47] In the specific matter of gender identity, as

in more general ways, Shakespeare's romantic comedies loosen up the rigidities that separate society as a whole from nature, people from one another, and individuals from their true selves. "Ganymede"/Rosalind, Bartholomew/Sly's wife, "Cesario"/Viola, and "Fidele"/Imogen engage in us the same desires as the innocent, androgynous youths of prose romance, but because they are dramatic characters, physical presences in front of us, they challenge us in a direct way that Pleusidippus, Pyrocles, and Rosalynde do not. In the last analysis, cross-dressing is a challenge to audiences in exercising a habit of mind that Shakespeare himself possessed to an extraordinary degree, what Keats called "negative capability." Getting outside oneself, experiencing the world through somebody else's eyes, is central to Shakespeare's comic vision. Giving up our pat assumptions about sexual identity is perhaps the greatest challenge of all.

Once we have seen how many mysteries lurk in the shadows of Arcadia, we can see how perilous is the journey home. How can the experience of liminality be reconciled with the exigencies of everyday life? As far as sexual desire is concerned, particularly prohibited sexual desire, it would seem that romance reconciles all the disparities in power and ideology—the conflict between positive and negative controls and the ambiguous place of sexual desire in the chivalric code—by keeping those disparities separate. In Arcadia desire can assume all sorts of fantastic forms, but at the story's end the protagonists return to court, and the reader closes the book. Desire has its holiday in the forest, but at nightfall Custom locks the city gates behind us. Romance functions as a way of indulging homosexual desire and yet not indulging homosexual desire. For the participant in the folk-play, for the reader of the book, for the watcher of events enacted onstage, the conventional endings serve as ways of *separating* himself from the fantasies in which he has reveled. By stepping back into social reality, by objectifying the desire he has felt and distancing himself from it, the sexual subject can keep himself free of any suspicions of sodomy. It was not "I" who felt these things and did these things, but "he." The conventional ending is, in effect, an "escape clause" in the reader's contract with the narrator, in the audience's contract with the actors.

Puritan attackers of the stage were smart enough to know that not everyone who set out for Arcadia was willing to make the trip back home. The true ending to stage-plays, Phillip Stubbes complains, is played out in bed:

marke the flocking and running to Theaters and curtens, daylie and hourely, night and daye, tyme and tyde, to see Playes and Enterludes; where such wanton gestures, such bawdie speaches, such laughing and fleering, such kissing and bussing, such clipping and culling, Suche winckinge and glancinge of wanton eyes, and the like, is used, as is wonderfull to behold. Than, these goodly pageants being done, every mate sorts to his mate, every one bringes another homeward of their way verye freendly, and in their secret conclaves (covertly) they play *the Sodomits*, or worse. And these be the fruits of Playes and Enterluds for the most part.[48]

The ultimate enormity is not what the characters say and do in the play but what the watchers and listeners say and do when they leave the theater. With Shakespeare's plays Stubbes and his kind may have good reason for their suspicions. Take, for example, Rosalind's epilogue. Having just taken off his disguise as Ganymede, the actor starts out in the person of Rosalind: "It is not the fashion to see the lady the epilogue . . . " (Epi. 1-2). But he completes the step-by-step stripping away of disguise by finishing the epilogue in his own person as a boy. With his curt, pert little phrases he remains teasingly androgynous to the end:

If I were a woman I would kiss as many of you as had beards that pleased me, complexions that liked me, and breaths that I defied not. And I am sure, as many as have good beards, or good faces, or sweet breaths will for my kind offer, when I make curtsy, bid me farewell.

(Epi. 16-21)

One can see Stubbes start to squirm. The purpose of an epilogue, ostensibly, is to close the play, to give the actor a chance to take off his disguise, to usher the audience back into the mundane concerns that await them outside the theater. The effect of Rosalind's epilogue is quite the opposite: the boy actor may first take off his garb as Ganymede and then his costume as Rosalind and gradually start speaking in his own person, but his pose as androgynous flirt invites us to take with us as we leave the theater some of the liminal freedom we allowed ourselves during the play. That, after all, is what the characters in the play itself have done: they have been changed by their experiences in the forest of Arden and have become better lovers, brothers, and rulers as a result. And so, Shakespeare implies, can we.

As You Like It leaves us in an altogether different place than if we were exhausted morris dancers taking our rest, or mummers packing away our costumes, or gentlemen-readers turning the last page of Greene's *Menaphon*. If we have undergone a rite of passage, it is a journey toward another country, not a return trip to the shores we left behind. In artistic terms, Shakespeare challenges the ancient ways in which romance puts homosexual desire into discourse. The Myth of the Shipwrecked Youth ordinarily engages desire only to deny it. In psychological terms, it indulges *libido* but under rigidly policed conditions. That must be so, since in anthropological terms it addresses not just the diffuse homoeroticism of male bonding generally but the particular subject of legal discourse in Renaissance England: the dangerous fact of sexual desire between a man and an adolescent boy. In chronological terms, as well, the Myth of the Shipwrecked Youth is quite specific. As the broadest, most basic myth of all, the Myth of Combatants and Comrades articulates a way of experiencing homosexual desire that characterizes the entire English Renaissance. The Myth of the Shipwrecked Youth is preeminently a myth of one part of that period, the last decades of the sixteenth century. For the writers and the readers who made and consumed the elite culture of Renaissance England, romance was the distinctive mode of Elizabeth's reign. For the commonality of Englishmen, for the men and women who made and consumed popular culture, the "romance" of morris dancing and mummers' plays was ever more militantly beleaguered by Puritan enemies as the sixteenth century drew to a close. In many places maypoles were pulled down and mummers' plays were suppressed—until James I intervened in 1618 with a royal proclamation specifying that the "having of May-Games, Whitson Ales, and Morris-dances, and the setting up of May-poles" were all perfectly "lawful recreations" after divine services were over on Sundays. Charles I's reissue of the proclamation in 1633—with the requirement that all preachers read it from their pulpits—was one of the politically false steps that led out the window of the Whitehall Banqueting House and onto the executioner's scaffold that had been built outside.[49]

The interplay of elite and popular culture in the Myth of the Shipwrecked Youth marks the end, in social terms, of what we can know about homosexual desire among the 75 percent of the men in early modern England who did not, because they could not, read and write books. As sodomites, they figure in the court record. But as men experiencing homosexual desire, their story ends here. About such men there probably is no more *to* find out. For the illiterate majority of Renaissance Englishmen the controlling myths of sexual desire, the ways of speaking about it to oneself and to others, are all embodied, not in written documents, but in popular custom, popular belief, and popular tales. That is just what we see in morris dancing and the mummers' plays. When we read a twelve-year-old apprentice's testimony before the Somerset quarter sessions that his bedfellow Meredith Davy customarily masturbated against him "on Sunday and Holy day nights when he had been a drinking," we are in a position to understand why it was just on those nights, and just in that drunken condition, that Davy could act on his desires.[50] What is different about the oral fictions that Davy knew, as opposed to fictions that were written down, is not their narrative content (after all, Shakespeare's comedies draw much of their imaginative energy from the motifs they share with folk drama) but the fact that they are so severely delimited in time. The Revesby wooing-rite was something that happened only on Plough Monday. *As You Like It* could happen whenever the Lord Chamberlain's Men chose to turn Shakespeare's script into speeches and action. In the public theater we still encounter, however, the public, communal circumstances that characterize the Myth of the Shipwrecked Youth in village festivals. At the Globe, or at the market-cross, dramatized romance sets men talking to each other, face to face, man to man, about their mutual experience of sexual desire. For readers of Greene, Sidney, and Lodge that sense of community is only figurative. Writing and reading do two things, therefore, for sexual feeling: they free it up in time, and they privatize it. Text in hand, a reader can take a discourse of sexual desire and make it part of his own imaginative world, a world that he inhabits alone.[51] That possibility poses political questions that romance is simply not equipped to mediate. Conflict between group values and individual experience is an increasingly important theme in the pages that follow. For a start, it fuels the fury of satire.

CHAPTER FIVE

KNIGHTS IN SHIFTS

No trust to faces. For what street but fills
With reverend vices? thou rebuk'st our ills,
When thou thy selfe art knowne to be so right,
So perfect a *Socraticke* Catamite.
Indeed, rough hairy limbs and armes that beare
Such stiffened bristles, promise minds severe.
But from their smooth posteriours when he files
Th'unnaturall tumours off, the Surgion smiles.[1]

Wenceslas Hollar, after Johan Danckerts

Detail from The Second Designe for Juvenal, *Mores Hominum: The Manners of Men*, trans. Sir Robert Stapylton (London: Humphrey Mosley, 1660)

As an exercise of power, satire puts the satirist in peril of getting caught up in the very vices he castigates, it encourages his "victims" to enjoy their vices all the more, and for the reader, what starts out as a homily can easily turn into a piece of pornography.

(Reproduced by permission from a copy in the Folger Shakespeare Library)

When Twelfth Night laughter died away in the Lenten dawn, when the ship came home from Illyria, it was time to lay aside strange costumes and strange desires. Anyone who dared to keep the game going risked the jeers of society and of its moral spokesman, the satirist. English Renaissance satire is not just the social, psychological, and literary sequel to romance but its chronological sequel as well. There had been a continuous tradition of satire in England, gentle in the case of Chaucer, plaintive in the case of Langland, but in the very last years of the sixteenth century there was a burst of satiric energy so virulent that it made Chaucer and Langland seem dated and dull and so popular that it attracted the notice of the Archbishop of Canterbury and the Bishop of London, who in 1599 sent the Stationers Company a list of satirical books to be banned and burned. Greene's *Menaphon* was published in 1589, Lodge's *Rosalynde* in 1590, Sidney's revised *Arcadia* in 1593. *As You Like It* and *Twelfth Night* were probably first acted between 1599 and 1600. The sexual freedom celebrated in these romances was vigorously attacked in John Donne's satires (written and presumably circulated in manuscript 1593-98), John Marston's *Certaine Satires* and *The Scourge of Villanie* (both 1598), and Ben Jonson's *Epicoene* (1609) and *Epigrammes* (c. 1612), as well as in anonymous poems about James I (crowned 1603) and his favorites that understandably were never put in print. All of these turn-of-the-century satirists single out sodomy as an explicit target for attack. If plays about soldiering are homologs to male friendship and male political power, if pastoral poems are homologs to schooling and adolescence, if romances are homologs to carnival, satires are homologs to institutionalized morality.

For a voice to bait men who take sexual pleasure with other men, Elizabethan and Jacobean satirists listened not to the plainspeaking of Piers Plowman or the gentle joking of Chaucer's persona but to the invective of Juvenal, Horace, and Martial.[2] The great Roman satirists gave Renaissance writers everything they needed to keep their countrymen in line: a dramatic scenario, a choice of styles, and a set of standards for passing moral judgment. Juvenal startles us with his dramatic immediacy. *Sermones*, "speeches," is what Horace calls his own exercises in verse satire. The scenario of Juvenal's second satire is typical of Horace and Juvenal alike in bringing the indignant persona and his undignified subjects face to face. "*Thou thy selfe* art knowne to be so right,/So perfect a Socraticke Catamite," the persona taunts the first in a parade of perverts that cross his imaginary path. In the persona's perambulation through the sexual byways of Roman life the reader tags along as a listening friend. We are assumed to share, of course, the speaker's prejudices. Compared with romances and with celebrations of male friendship, satire is much more explicit about who the speaker is and whence he speaks. In all its various guises satire is a highly *political* form of discourse. As watchers of satiric comedy in the theater, we are invited to feel moral solidarity with the people to our left and right, laughing along with us at the ridiculous things we are seeing onstage. Implicitly, the same thing happens when we read verse satire: we take sides with the speaker, who smugly distinguishes *us* from *them*. Even in the form of epigrams satire keeps its public, social character. English cultivators of the form like John Donne and Ben Jonson may be more prolix than Martial, but they never quite lose the sense that epigrams are *inscribed* poems, the kind of thing that might be written on a tomb, scratched on a wall, or written on a piece of paper and tacked up in a public place. At bottom, satire is a nasty business. It denies that there is any other way of looking at the persons being singled out for attack. Its object is to make the world a better place, possibly by reforming its victims, but better still by destroying them, by burying them under an avalanche of epithets. Satire is funny only if we side with the satirist, only if we are not the object of attack. The satirist does not invite our imaginative collaboration; he demands it. In this respect he is more like a jurist or a writer of moral polemic than a poet: he speaks from a position of unquestioned, and unquestionable, authority. As a way of putting sex into discourse, satire is less close to other forms of verse than it is to moral treatises and law books.

Close, but not quite the same. Unlike law books, satire takes as its real subject the emotions of the satirist: amused, amazed, infuriated, outraged. Of emotions like these Juvenal has plenty. From Socratic catamites whose manly legs belie the piles on their worn-out asses, Juvenal's persona moves on to a certain judge who dares to sentence female prostitutes who wouldn't be caught dead in what *he* likes to wear:

> But what in others can deform'd appeare?
> When thou, grave *Judge*, dost *mingled sarcenet* weare,
> Nay sitt'st in those thin silks, amazing *Rome*,
> And dost our *Procula's* and *Pollinea's* doome?

The Judge, poor dear, has his excuses:

Chapter Five

["]But *July*'s hot, I sweate["]; then naked go,
For madnesse will not halfe disgrace thee so.

(p. 20)

Confronted with such monstrosities, Juvenal's persona can feel nothing but fuming fury—and his style shows it. Even in Sir Robert Stapylton's polite translation of 1647, Juvenal's spokesman fairly shouts at the statesmen and soldiers in drag. One by one they join in what Stapylton's marginal gloss calls "The progresse and degrees in sinning." As the speaker's anger mounts, the rhetorical questions, the ironic quotations, the exasperated exclamations get shorter and faster, the syntax looser, the rhythm more syncopated. First comes a gaggle of priests with trussed-up hair and bejeweled necks. They claim to be worshipping the Bona Dea, a goddess revered by women, but "Men Only" reads the sign outside *these* rites: "to men they only open lye,/[']You prophane women get you gone,['] they crye" (p. 21). Bodies decked out in blue satin, eyes mascaraed, they swill wine from phallic cups and, like women, swear by Juno. One of them carries a military trophy, the kind of mirror that the "pathick" emperor Otho used for primping himself before battle. Last in the throng of grotesques comes a nobleman of the Gracchus family, leaning on his "husband":

A Piper, or a Trumpeter, had fowr
Hundred sestertia for *Gracchus* Dower:
Deeds were drawn, joy giv'n, a great Supper made,
The *Bride* was in *his* Bridegroome's bosome layd.

To understand such things who needs an official censor or a divining priest?

these *strange sights* exceed
All monsters, though a woman should be damme
Unto a Calfe, or a Cow calve a Lambe.
He who the *sacred shields* th'*Ancilia* bore
By unseen thongs, toyling and sweating sore,
Weares a *fring'd petticote* and flame-colour'd veyle.

There is one consolation, at least: from such prodigies we don't get any progeny.

For Renaissance writers, who believed that *satire* derives from *satyr*, Juvenal's rough rhetoric had an etiological appeal, but it is only one way of responding to the vanities and perversities that throng the city's streets. Horace's regulated reasonableness is another. With Horace, the order and restraint of the poem itself become the poet's defense against chaos, a strategy for containing the ethical anarchy that rages around him. With Juvenal, by contrast, the satirist is always in danger of being swallowed up by the monster that is his subject. Martial manages to have it both ways: passion akin to Juvenal's is restrained by the terseness required in epigrams. "Cool" or "hot," detached or engaged, rational or enraged, Latin satire offered Renaissance writers a polarized choice of feelings that is all the more fascinating when sexual desire is the subject at hand.

As an exercise of power, satire puts the satirist in peril of getting caught up in the very vices he castigates; it encourages his "victims" to enjoy their vices all the more; and for the reader, what starts out as a homily can easily turn into a piece of pornography. Foucault calls attention to this curious effect of power in connection with the medical examinations, psychiatric analyses, pedagogical reports, and family controls that have been set in place to monitor sexuality since the eighteenth century. These attempts to control sexual behavior

> may have the over-all and apparent objective of saying no to all wayward or unproductive sexualities, but the fact is that they function as mechanisms with a double impetus: pleasure and power. The pleasure that comes of exercising a power that questions, monitors, watches, spies, searches out, palpates, brings to light; and on the other hand, the pleasure that kindles at having to evade this power, flee from it, fool it, or travesty it. The power that lets itself be invaded by the pleasure it is pursuing; and opposite it, power asserting itself in the pleasure of showing off, scandalizing, or resisting.[3]

These "perpetual spirals of power and pleasure" are always at work in Renaissance satire. The Archibishop of Canterbury and the Bishop of London did not need Foucault to tell them that when they ordered the Stationers Company to round up all copies of Marston's *The Scourge of Villanie* and Antoine de La Sale's *Fifteen Joys of Marriage*, along with seven other satirical books, and bring them to the Bishop for burning. They knew how easily scourgers could be seduced by their sexual subjects and how easily the seducers could turn into scourgers of moral authority. Such questions of power are very much at issue in the satires of Donne, Marston, and Jonson.

In addition to a dramatic scenario and a choice of styles, Juvenal, Horace, and Martial also supplied Renaissance satirists with standards of moral judgment. At the end of his survey of Rome's sexual freaks, Juvenal turns to address Mars himself. Where can the god of war and founder of Rome be keeping himself?

> Behold a *man*, great both in wealth and birth,
> *Marryes* a *man*; yet *thou* into the Earth
> Runst not thy speare, nor thy plum'd helmet shak'st.
> Not a complaint unto thy *father* mak'st.

(p. 22)

Perhaps the Campus Martius should be dedicated to some more attentive god. Gathered around the Stygian lake, the Romans of older, manlier times must be looking around for sulphur, torches, and laurel branches with which to purify themselves against the effeminate newcomers. Rome may have conquered the world to its farthest reaches, to the Orkney Islands and be-nighted Britain, but the conquerors' own city countenances dis-plays of depravity that the conquered barbarians could not even imagine.

Juvenal invokes here two standards of moral judgment. By comparing a man "marrying" a man to a woman giving birth to a calf or a cow to a lamb, Juvenal implicitly distinguishes "mon-sters" from the natural order of things. His explicit, more impor-tant standard, however, is the *virtus* of Rome's founders—with an emphasis on the *vir*. For Juvenal's readers, Rome's early days were the mythical equivalent of the American frontier. Both of Juvenal's criteria, nature and the virility of the old-time Romans, are, as Foucault would put it, structures of ideology. They are offered up as indisputable truths about the way things are. As such, they provide a standard for judging what is, and is not, acceptable sexual behavior. Latin satire implies a model of or-thodox sexuality, an inter-articulated structure of ideology and power that turns homosexual desire—or, at least, certain modes of homosexual desire—into something disgusting, antisocial, po-litically vulnerable, patently contradictory to reality.

What sixteenth- and seventeenth-century satirists did with this Roman scenario, this Roman choice of styles, and these Roman standards of judgment was not unrelated to what other Renaissance writers were saying about sodomy in legal and moral discourse. How the satirists approached the subject had a great deal to do with the sixteenth-century shift in legal catego-ries from sodomy as a species of heresy to sodomy as a political crime to sodomy as a matter of personal morality; how they de-picted it was much indebted to the legal clarification of sodomy as anal sex between a man and a boy. In the writings of Renaissance satirists, it was the legally defined sodomite who emerged as a recognizable *type*. If romance is focused on the boy as an object of desire, satire is focused on the man who is subject to that desire. In this respect, the satirist seconds the lawgiver. Despite Coke's insistence that "both the agent and consentient are felons," the law is concerned mainly with the man who *acts* on desire, not with his "victim."[4] In the eyes of the law there are no sexual partners, only "agents" and "consentients." And so in the eyes of the satirists.

In Coke's *Institutes* the satirists could even find out what a legally defined sodomite looked like. Before getting down to the business of how to secure an indictment, Coke offers a general disquisition on "Buggery or Sodomy" that includes not only the detail that it was first brought into England by a Lombard but an explanation of what inspired the vice in the first place: "The Sodomites came to this abomination by four means, *viz.* by pride, excess of diet, idlenesse, and contempt of the poor. *Otiosus nihil cogitat, nisi de ventre & venere* [the lazy man thinks of nothing but his belly and sex]."[5] Sodomites, Coke implies, are haughty, fat, lazy, and snobbish—and they are apt to be caught up by foreign fashions. It is remarkable how often Renaissance satirists depict their victims in just these terms. Equally often they pick up on the social distinction that Coke's caricature implies: sodomy is an aristocratic vice, a temptation especially appealing to men who have nothing better to do.

Since the Middle Ages the cliché had been current that sodomy was a vice peculiar to three sorts of people: the clerical, the wealthy, and the urban.[6] The Protestant Reformation made the first of these three groups a more obvious target than ever. Out of all the lusty clerics with vows to the Roman church, anti-Catholic polemicists loved to single out two in particular: Pope Julius III, notorious (among these writers at least) for having preferred only his own catamites to ecclesiastical honors, and Archbishop Giovanni Della Casa, reputed to be the author of a book (not a single copy has ever come to light) in praise of sodomy. At least one Counter-Reformation propagandist returned the favor: Kaspar Schoppe wrote several pieces attacking James I, head of the Anglican Church, in just the sodomitical terms that Protestants had used in attacking the Pope.[7] Priests, rich people, city-dwellers: often two or more of these categories overlapped, but never more powerfully than in the case of the urban and the wealthy. In a linkage between sodomy and urban capitalism David F. Greenberg finds the political engine that has both generated repression against homosexual acts and stimulated the formation of homosexual subcultures. The beginnings of legal discourse about homosexuality in the thirteenth century, Greenberg argues, had as much to do with wealthy merchants and their appropriation of aristocratic ways as it did with new ideas about nature in the philosophy of Thomas Acquinas. "A class defines itself in opposition to other classes culturally by turning its own traits and standards into universal values," Greenberg observes. With their recently acquired riches the capitalist venturers of thirteenth-century Lombardy and Tuscany upset traditional social distinctions and traditional social values and thus alienated the artisans and shopkeepers who saw themselves as defenders of that traditional order:

> The *popoli minuti* castigated the aristocracy, and the *popoli grassi* who mimicked them, for their profligate life-styles and vulgar ostentation. In essence, they were attacking those vices that their own class position did not allow them to indulge: adultery, prostitution, gambling, and sodomy (by which they meant all nonprocreative sexual activity, hetereosexual or homosexual).[8]

The logical, temporal, economic, and political result of this class rivalry is the hegemony of middle-class morality since the eighteenth century. Part of the received myth about sodomy in Elizabethan and Jacobean England was that it had first been brought into the country in the thirteenth century by Italian merchants, men who were not only foreign and Catholic—but rich.[9]

The ancient and modern ideas rehearsed in moral discourse about sodomy in the Renaissance reinforced these legal distinctions regarding power and responsibility. From the Christian Middle Ages the moral spokesmen of the sixteenth century inherited rationalizations for condemning homosexual acts which were different from the rationalizations of Greek and Roman antiquity but which ultimately reinforced them. Taken together, the three sets of criteria constitute a moral case against homosexual acts that is very much with us still. From the Greeks to the Romans to the early Middle Ages to the later Middle Ages to the Renaissance we can trace the development of the moralists' case: the physiological way in which the Greeks thought about human appetite in general and sexual desire in particular was transformed by the Romans into something social and by St. Paul into something theological. The basis of this increasingly elaborate argument is simple enough. Behind the objections of

Horace, Juvenal, Martial, and the other Roman satirists is the idea, ultimately Greek, that sexual activity, like everything else, ought to be governed by moderation. Essentially that is a physiological way of looking at sexual desire: it starts with the human body and goes on to consider what is and is not good for it. In this view homosexual acts are not wrong in and of themselves, but only when carried to extremes. That, essentially, is the message of Horace's second satire in book 1, in which sexual mavericks of all sorts are linked with young noblemen who can't manage their estates. Profligates with money and profligates with sexual desire both go to extremes. Here, in Thomas Drant's translation of 1566, Horace conjures up a procession of transvestite dandies as provocative—and provoking—as Juvenal's:

> *Malkin* to make him singuler, a fashion freshe hath founde,
> He swings and swoupes from streete to streete, with gowne
>   that sweepes the grounde,
> And thincke you *Malkin* wants his mates? no fye, that were a
>   misse[.]
> An other pleasaunte[-]headed chylde, in no sauce lyketh this.
> To prove himselfe a pretye man, and quaynte in his devyse,
> He maks his garmente to be shapde, not of so large a syse:
> For wote you what? he coortails it, it hardlye hydes his rumpe,
> *Rufillus*, he is perfumde with muske[;] *Gorgomi*, smelles
>   o[']th[']pumpe.

In such behavior Horace sees, not unnaturalness, but a lack of moderation:

> Meane, hath no mantion in this flocke, they kepe no steedy stay
> In matter, and in novell shape, they varye every day.[10]

Moderation, avoiding extremes, is the key to Horace's own response as a satirist. It provides his standard of moral judgment, it informs his urbane style, it invites a like response from his readers.

How one decides what constitutes extremes is, of course, another matter. Physiological issues quickly turn into social issues. The Greeks and the Romans alike were conscious of power play in homosexual relations, but they drew distinctions in power in characteristically different ways. The Greeks eroticized power distinctions according to age: an older man of the citizen class might initiate an adolescent boy of the same class into manhood not only by overseeing his education but by forming a sexual liaison. Both participants in the transaction were assumed to be of the same social class; the erotic power was generated by their

Chapter Five

difference in age. To continue to enjoy the passive role when one's years forbade it was to invite contempt, even legal action.[11] The Romans, by contrast, judged power differences not so much by age as by gender and social class. As the master of his slaves, a man might take his pleasure with the boys in his retinue just as he might with his wife or his mistress, but Roman parents of the ruling class were careful to protect their sons from pederastic schoolmasters. A man could take his pleasure as he would, so long as it did not challenge the power structure that positioned men over women and masters over slaves.[12] Juvenal's most biting argument against catamites is not concerned with social class but gender: homosexual desire is emasculating. It makes men act like women. In fifth-century Athens sexual communion between men and boys served to strengthen, not challenge, the male power structure. For Horace, Juvenal, and Martial alike, the relationship between homosexual activity and masculinity is more problematic.

The Roman satirists' insistence on a rigid code of male behavior has several implications, each progressively more serious than the other. At the most superficial level, men who refuse to act like other men are simply funny. They furnish the stuff of comedy. Take, for example, Ovid's advice to men in *The Art of Love*:

> Thy legs with eating pumice do not weare,
> Use not hot irons to crispe and curle thy haire,
> No spruce starch fashions should on lovers waite,
> Men best become a meere neglected gate.
> Blunt *Theseus* came with no perfumes to *Creete*
> And yet great *Minos*['] daughter thought him sweete.
> *Phaedra* did love *Hippollitus*, yet he,
> Had on his back no Courtly bravery.
> *Adonis* like a woodman still was clad,
> Yet *Venus* doated on the lovely lad:
> Go neate and handsome, comelines best pleases
> And the desire of women, soonest ceases.

Later Ovid advises women to beware of men who "starch their haire" and "smell of Civit": they promise more than they can deliver![13] In Juvenal we encounter the more ominous idea that playing about with gender roles is decadent. Men who refuse to act like men signify the decline of civilization, a falling away from the moral innocence of Rome's founders. Precisely because they saw themselves as the pinnacle of civilization, the Romans were fascinated with the idea that they might end up in the ignominious position of the peoples they had conquered, particularly the "Socratick Catamites" across the Adriatic. Stapylton amplifies this imperialistic fear in his note on the transvestite judge of Juvenal's second satire:

> The old *Romans*, whose richest apparell was their wounds, their strongest fortifications the Mountaines, and their healthfullest exercise the Plough; with what indignation would they have beheld the more then strumpet-like impudence of these sarsenet Judges.

> (p. 28)

The logical consequence of this social and political way of looking at gender is to turn homosexual behavior into a threat to the very order that makes society possible. That threat looms large in Suetonius's lives of the Roman emperors. So dissolute was Nero, for example, that he had himself wedded to a boy. In his English translation of 1606, Philemon Holland reluctantly tells the story in all its salacious detail:

> A boy there was named SPORUS, whose Genitories he cut out, & assayed therby to transforme him into the nature of a woman. Him he caused to be brought unto him as a bride, with a dowry, in a fine (yellow) veile, after the solemne maner of mariage: not without a frequent and goodly traine attending upon him: whom he maintained as his wife.

Such debaucheries began, appropriately enough, in Greece, but Nero and his "bride" found their way to Rome itself:

> This SPORUS trimly set out with the jewels, decked with the ornaments of the Empresses, and caried in a licter, hee accompanied all about the shire-townes of great resort and market burroughes of Greece: yea and afterwardes at *Rome*, up and downe the street *Sigillaria*, manie a time sweetly kissing him by the way.[14]

So far, so bad. What is a reader to think, then, when Nero gets bored with the boy, has a go at a rather imaginative form of bestiality, and finally (outrage of outrages) casts *himself* in the woman's role?

> As for his owne body, CERTES, he forfeited the honour thereof, prostituting it to bee abused so farreforth, as having defiled in manner all the parts of it, at the last, he devised a kind (as it were) of sport and game: that being covered all over in a wilde beastes skin, hee should be let loose forth of a cage and then give the assault upon the privities of men and women both as they stood tyed fast to a stake: and when he had shewed his

rage to the full, be killed by DORIPHORUS his freed man, unto whom himselfe also was wedded like as SPORUS unto him: insomuch as hee counterfeited the noise and cries of maidens, when they bee forced and suffer devirgination.

(p. 192)

As the ultimate in self-degrading passivity, fellatio is the only specific sexual act singled out by the Romans for moral condemnation.[15] For a woman to take a man's genitals into her mouth was disgusting. For a man to do so was almost unthinkable. For an emperor to do so was nothing short of annihilating.

Because Roman homophobia so closely matches the homophobia of our own culture, it is easy to let this equation of homosexual activity and effeminacy pass without question. As Sedgwick reminds us, however, homophobia is only one way in which homosexuality can be related to patriarchy. The two can also reinforce one another, as they did in fifth- and fourth-century Athens. Or they can coexist in "some highly conflicted but intensively structured combination."[16] If in early modern England it was the third possibility that related homosexuality to patriarchy, we cannot be so sure that all sodomites were perceived to be men who acted like women. Nicholas Breton's character of "An Effeminate Fool" suggests just the opposite. At first Breton's caricature in prose seems to match perfectly the modern stereotype of a faggot:

> An Effeminate foole is the figure of a Baby; he loves nothing but gay, to look in a Glasse, to keepe among Wenches, and, to play with trifles: to feed on sweet meats, and to be daunced in Laps, to be imbraced in Armes, and to be kissed on the Cheeke: To talke Idlely, to looke demurely, to goe Nicely, and to Laugh continually . . . .[17]

But when Breton tells us that the effeminate fool keeps a mistress and that he is a "Womans man," we realize that Breton's ideas about effeminacy are no different from those of Plutarch's Protogenes. Homosexual desire in Protogenes' view is not a matter of men wanting to be like women. Quite the contrary. It is too great a sexual interest in women that makes a man become like them. Homosexuality is a matter of men desiring other men. The first evidence we have of homosexual acts being associated with *our* sense of effeminacy does not occur until the eighteenth century.[18] Even then, however, patriarchy and homosexuality were still equated in the minds of certain outsiders who ought to have known whereof they spoke—and acted. During the late eighteenth-century wave of homophobia in England, it was the *women* in the crowd who were the most angry and the most abusive when sodomites were pilloried.[19] Why such outrage? Was it their identity as women that was threatened? Or their prerogatives? Did they suspect that a conspiracy of men was cheating them of sexual satisfactions that ought to be theirs alone?

In Christian moral discourse about homosexual activity another, more philosophical argument far outweighs the Roman obsession with gender roles. Juvenal, as we have seen, thought it "monstrous" for a man to "marry" a man, but it was the prospect of social decline that horrified him more. The structure of ideology that Christian moralists brought to bear on the case reverses the classical priorities: for men to have sex with other men is reprehensible first and foremost because it is "against" nature. This is the crucial shift that distinguishes how the ancients conceptualized same-sex sexuality from how, until very recently, we have. The Romans' fundamentally *social* standard of judgment becomes a *theological* standard.

In his study of *Christianity, Social Tolerance, and Homosexuality,* John Boswell has charted the emergence of this "nature" argument in the thirteenth century.[20] In the earlier Middle Ages the benign tolerance of homosexual behavior that was characteristic of the ancient world lingered on, whatever St. Paul may have advised to the contrary. In the later Middle Ages, Thomistic philosophy elevated Nature to the status of an ethical criterion— and cast men who make love with men out of the scheme of creation. The scriptural basis for this position was to be found in Romans, chapter 1. When men turned their backs on God, writes Paul, God in turn "gave them up to their hearts lustes, to unclennes, to defile their owne bodies betwene themselves." Among these "vile affections" were homosexual acts:

> the men left the natural use of the woman, and burned in their luste one towarde another, and man with man wroght filthines, & received in themselves suche recompense of their errour, as was mete. For as thei regarded not to knowe God, *even so* God delivered them up unto a reprobat minde, to do those things which are not convenient.[21]

"Convenient" carries here the literal Latin sense of "coming together," of being suitable or appropriate. And Paul's standard of appropriateness, clearly enough, is nature. Since taking hold in western thought, this particular "truth" has had amazing tenacity.

The medieval and Renaissance idea of Nature is bound up, of course, with a symmetrical, hierarchical view of the universe in which mankind occupies a central, divinely ordained position. Homosexuality, as Alan Bray points out, simply had no place in that scheme:

> It was not part of the chain of being, or the harmony of the created world or its universal dance. It was not part of the Kingdom of Heaven or its counterpart in the Kingdom of Hell (although that could unwittingly release it). It was none of these things because it was not conceived of as part of the created order at all; it was part of its dissolution. And as such it was not a sexuality in its own right, but existed as a potential for confusion and disorder in one undivided sexuality.[22]

Hence that damning preposition: not just "outside" nature but "against" nature. As a threat to the divine order of things, homosexual desire was lumped with all the other things that threatened the stability of the Renaissance cosmos: heresy, witchcraft, treason. In the first Epistle to Timothy, Paul distinguishes Old Testament law from New Testament love. "The Law is not given unto a righteous man," Paul says—and goes on to provide a handy list of the ethical company that "buggerers" keep:

> but unto the lawles and disobedient, to the ungodlie, and to sinners, to the unholie, and to the prophane, to murtherers of fathers and mothers, to manslayers, to whoremongers, to buggerers, to men stealers, to liers, to the perjured, & if there be anie other thing, that is contrarie to wholsome doctrine, *which is* according to the glorious Gospel of the blessed God, which is committed unto me.

(I Timothy 1:9-11)

A formidable list, to say the least.

After he had been stabbed to death—in the head—Christopher Marlowe was accused of heresy as well as sodomy. Marlowe was said to have said not only "that all they that love not Tobacco & Boies were fooles" but also "that St. John the Evangelist was bedfellow to Christ and leaned alwaies in his bosome, that he used him as the sinners of Sodoma." A memorandum of Marlowe's remarks was sent to the queen. His murderers were not prosecuted.[23] Taken all together, these classical and Christian arguments against homosexual acts constituted a stiff case. Giving expression to homosexual desire showed a lack of moderation, it was ridiculous, it was a symbol of social decay, it was against nature, it threatened political order. English Renaissance satirists took up all of these arguments, and added a few new ones of their own.

The verse satires of John Donne had not yet been published in 1599, but they would have given the Archbishop of Canterbury and the Bishop of London less cause for concern than the satires of Marston. As a spokesman for the moral arguments against sodomy, Donne remains confidently in control of his medium. The cosmic context in which the Renaissance viewed homosexual behavior is wittily sketched in John Donne's fragmentary "Metempsychosis, or The Progresse of the Soule" (1601; pub. 1633). Part parody of Pythagorean philosophy and part beast fable, Donne's poem traces the metamorphosis of a soul from Eve's apple to mandrake plant to sparrow to fish to whale to wolf to ape to the fifth daughter of Adam and Eve and, along the way, exposes human vanities and absurdities in the guise of animals—and (leave it to Donne to think of such a thing) plants. Even the mandrake root participates in a cycle of lust not altogether unlike Arthur Schnitzler's *La Ronde*. The "toyfull" ape, penultimate creature in this lecherous chain of being, is distinguished by the dumb intensity of his desires. In making a pass at Adam's daughter the ape may have been the first in the chain to care about having one particular female over another, but since he is unable to speak he has to woo her with looks alone—which prompts Donne's persona to this moral reflection:

> Sinnes against kinde
> They easily doe, that can let feed their minde
> With outward beauty; beauty they in boyes and beasts do finde.

"Boys" and "beasts": that alliterative pairing shows just where homosexual acts rank in the cosmic hierarchy. To act on homosexual desire is to lower one's status in the great chain of being, as Donne's persona makes explicit in the succeeding stanza:

> By this misled, too low things men have prov'd,
> And too high; beasts and angels have beene lov'd.[24]

Like bestiality, homosexual lust abandons language for looks, reason for passion, the "higher" endowments man shares with angels for the "lower" urges he shares with animals. Donne's subject in "Metempsychosis" may be human lust in general, but the place he finds for acts of lust between men is at one further remove from Godhead than acts of lust between man and woman.

It is this cosmic context, this Christian cosmic context, that Donne has in mind whenever homosexual behavior comes up in the verse satires he modeled on Horace and Juvenal. The persona Donne adopts in his first satire is a scholarly, reclusive relative of Horace. "Away thou fondling motley humorist," the speaker cries to the visitor who wants him to leave his paneled library and go out for a walk through London's streets,

> Leave mee, and in this standing woodden chest,
> Consorted with these few bookes, let me lye
> In prison, and here be coffin'd, when I dye.

The persona's preferred companions are his books. They teach him about the principles of things; they give him his standards of moral judgment:

> Here are Gods conduits, grave Divines; and here
> Natures Secretary, the Philosopher;
> And jolly Statesmen, which teach us how to tie
> The sinewes of a cities mistique bodie;
> Here gathering Chroniclers, and by them stand
> Giddie fantastique Poets of each land.
> Shall I leave this constant company,
> And follow headlong, wild uncertaine thee?

(1.1-12)

Well-read in theology, philosophy, political theory, history, and poetry, the satirist is everything the importunate visitor is not: rational (not "fondling"), whole (not "motley"), stable (not a "humorist" given to every passing whim). The humorist's appetite is voracious; his tastes capricious. When he meets anyone, his inquiring eyes first appraise his new companion's silk and gold—an obsession not without its irony, considering his sexual predilections:

> Why should'st thou (that dost not onely approve,
> But in ranke ichie lust, desire, and love
> The nakednesse and barenesse to enjoy,
> Of thy plumpe muddy whore, or prostitute boy)
> Hate vertue, though shee be naked, and bare?
> At birth, and death, our bodies naked are;
> And till our Soules be unapparrelled
> Of bodies, they from blisse are banished.

(1.37-44)

Reluctantly agreeing to go along, Donne's persona follows the humorist out into the city streets. The guide's way with the people he meets has a distinctly sexual edge. He allures them "with amorous smiles" (1.73), he points out a certain "well-favour'd youth" who "dances so divinely" (1.84-85); he finally abandons the persona when he spies "his Love" in a window. But he comes back with hanging head:

> Many were there, he could command no more;
> He quarrell'd, fought, bled; and turn'd out of dore.

(1.109-110)

The gender of the vision in the window is left unspecified, not so much because it may be a boy as because it focuses *all* the things after which the humorist lusts: fashion, money, and position, as well as sexual pleasure.

Further outrages await the persona of satire 4 when he ventures to court. The courtier who takes him around, "A thing more strange than on Nile[']s slime, the Sunne/ E'r bred" (4.18-19), knows everything about everybody.

> Who wasts in meat, in clothes, in horse, he notes;
> Who loves Whores, who boyes, and who goats.

(4.127-128)

Whores, boys, goats: Donne's order is eloquent. It traces a classical decline of civilization, a Christian slippage down the chain of being.

The horrors that Donne conjured up in these verses of the 1590s were, to some observors at least, more than matched by the court of James I ten years later. The diary that Sir Simonds D'Ewes kept between 1622 and 1624, while he was reading law in the Temple, contains more than one passage of gossip about the king. Sequestered in his chamber one afternoon in August 1622, Simonds exchanged these private words with an old friend from Cambridge:

> Of things I discoursed with him that weere secrett as of the sinne of sodomye, how frequente it was in this wicked cittye, and if God did not provide some wonderfull blessing against it, wee could not but expect some horrible punishment for it; especially it being as wee had probable cause to feare, a sinne in the prince as well as the people, which God is for the most part the chastiser of himselfe, because noe man else indeed dare reprove or tell them of ther faults.

To add substance to his suspicions Simonds goes on to give an example:

I told him a true storye which was a great presu[m]ption to this, of an usher in a schoole, a Frenchman, whoe had buggered a knights sonne and was brought into the Guild Hall, when Been was recorder and had surelye receaved his just punishment, but that [Sir Henry] Mountague then cheife justice, was sent to save him and by the king, as twas thought. Nay, besides Dr Hearne, one of the kings phisitians offred to have the usher kelled privatelye, soe they would suffer it to passe over in darkenes; and that the childs uncle rann at him with a rapier, after his acquittance, and had slaine him, but that hee was stopped by the people saiing that, though hee had scaped the justice of man, hee could not the judgement of God.

About the truth to this part of Simonds's conversation we have no collaborating proof, but we do know all about the fall of Robert Carr, once a page in James's Scottish court and now Earl of Somerset, who was being replaced in the king's affections by George Villiers, Marquis of Buckingham, soon to be raised to Duke of Buckingham, despite what Simonds had heard about the king's boredom with him:

Besides, wee resolved that the King was wearye enough of the Marquess, but for shame would not putt him away. I tolde him of the letter in Sommersetts caskett, found by my Lord Cooke, for which since the King never loved him and finallye that, in other cuntryes, men talked familiarly of it.

Sodomy remained a subject right to the end in this sharing of secrets between friends: "After which and some other matters passed over (where I tolde him that boyes weere growen to the height of wickednes to paint), wee parted."[25]

What was contained in the letter that Sir Edward Coke found hidden away in Somerset's "caskett"? Two of the three surviving letters that James wrote to Carr would have been cause for public outrage on James's part, if not private embarrassment, especially if it was the letter in which the king tries to temper Somerset's jealous rebelliousness by making bold threats but also by vowing, "I must ingenuously confess you have deserved more trust and confidence of me than ever man did—in secrecy above all flesh, in feeling and impartial respect, as well to my honour in every degree as to my profit." In the same letter James goes on to scold Somerset for "long creeping back and withdrawing yourself from lying in my chamber, notwithstanding my many hundred times earnest soliciting you to the contrary."[26]

Most of the homoerotic verses in Tobias Alston's manuscript of 1637-39 are satiric poems directed at James, at Francis Bacon, at George Villiers, and at all the other courtiers, female as well as male, who had mastered the arts of sexual politics. The political career of Villiers, elevated from royal cupbearer to the only duke not of the royal blood, illustrates that blood may be thicker than water but that other fluids are thicker still. Typical of the satirical poems in Alston's manuscript is this diatribe on the politic marriage of one of Buckingham's kindred, Sir Anthony Ashley:

> Old Abbott Anthony
>   I thinke hath well done,
> Since hee left Sodomy,
>   To marry Sheldon.
> Shee hath a buttocke plumpe,
>   Keepe but thy tarse whole,
> And sheele hold up her rumpe,
>   With her black arse hole.[27]

In the context, it is easy to picture what is meant by the slang-word "tarse."

The speaker in this particular tour about the court of James I takes gleeful delight in what it falls his moral task to describe. Donne's persona is more cautious in his tour of the court of Elizabeth. Fearful that he himself will be sucked into the corruption he sees, the speaker in Donne's fourth satire returns home to his "wholesome solitarinesse" (4.155) and reflects on the visit to court as a descent into Hell. "Wholesome" is an advised choice of words: it suggests not only "salutary" and "salubrious," but *whole*ness, completeness, being all of a piece. Characters like the fondling motley humorist and the hangers-on at court lack this essential integrity. In place of the persona's "wholesome solitarinesse" they live lives of empty gregariousness. Along with vanity in dress, calculation in making friends, and hunger after power, homosexual debauchery is part of that vacuous existence.

John Marston shares Donne's horror at the inner emptiness of his subjects. The "dapper, rare, compleat, sweet nittie youth" in the third of Marston's *Certaine Satyres* (1598) is like the hat he wears: all huge showy brim, and tiny crown. His clothes crisscrossed with lace, his body perfumed, his face clean-shaven, his cheeks "glazed," the young man drags the ultimate mark of his depravity along behind him:

But ho, what *Ganimede* is that doth grace
The gallant[']s heeles. One, *who for two daies space*
Is closely hyred. Now who dare not call
This *AEsops* crow, fond, mad, fantasticall.
Why so he is, his clothes doe sympathize,
And with his inward spirit humorize.
An open Asse, that is not yet so wise
As his derided fondnes to disguise.[28]

As in Donne, homosexual lust shapes up in Marston as a passion for externals: *"Faire outward show, and little wit within"* (*CS*, 3.24), as the persona remarks apropos the nitty youth's hat. The young gallant exemplifies perfectly the general subject of satire 3, *Quedam et sunt, et videntur*, "Those who are [detestable]—and look it." Toward the end of the poem, Marston's persona manages to contain his explosive wit in two epigrammatic lines that sum up his standard of judgment. To a fool named Duceus (an echo here of *deuce*, bad luck, mischief, the devil?) the persona complains, "The world too much, thy selfe too little know'st/Thy private selfe. Why then should *Duceus* boast?" (*CS*, 3.91-92). Why indeed? The fools in Marston, like those in Donne, *have* no private selves.

Marston plays Juvenal to Donne's Horace. "My rough-heu'd rime" is how Marston describes his own style in the third of the *Certaine Satyres*. Unlike Donne's mild-mannered persona, Marston's spokesman was notorious at the time for being fiery and foulmouthed, in dangerously close touch with the passion he castigates. Especially in his second collection of verse satires, *The Scourge of Villanie* (also 1598), Marston gives us a titillating, up-close view of Renaissance debauchery in which the pleasure is as much the poet's and the reader's as the subjects'. Leaving his wife to make do with her porcelain dildo and her monkey, one Luscus (we can hear in his name both "lust" and "loose") has moved on to new objects of desire:

Alack, alack, what peece of lustfull flesh
Hath *Luscus* left, his *Priape* to redresse?
Grieve not good soule, he hath his *Ganimede*,
His perfum'd shee-goate, smooth kembd & high fed.
At Hogsdon now his monstrous lust he feasts,
For there he keepes a baudy-house of beasts.

(*SV*, 3.37-42)

Once again, boys and beasts, Ganymede and goats, allure in al-literative alliance. Once again, we make a graduated descent down the great chain of being, leaving behind the angelic for the animalistic. Diogenes the Cynic philosopher once saw a youth going off to dine with some powerful men, nabbed the boy, dragged him home to his friends, and told them to keep strict watch over him.[29] Luscus goes Diogenes one better:

> Fayth, what cares he for faire *Cynedian* boyes?
> Velvet cap'd Goates, duch Mares? tut common toies.
> Detaine them all, on this condition
> He may but use the Cynick friction.

> (*SV*, 3.49-52)

This distinctively Renaissance version of the Descent of Man goes on not just in such notorious places as Hogsdon ("Hogs' den" Ben Jonson once dubbed the London suburb) but in the "male stews" of Catholic seminaries and even in Cambridge colleges (*SV*, 3.53-82).

Universal decay is where it all ends, as Marston proclaims in the "Cynicke Satyre" that concludes *The Scourge of Villanie*. "*A Man, a man, a kingdome for a man*," the persona cries out in a parody of Richard III (*SV*, 7.1). But in the Britain of 1598 a man is not to be found: not the gallant in his sumptuous clothes with the "fayre appendant whore" who "lackyes" him in "Sodom beastlines" (*SV*, 7.21, 22, 25), not the clotheshorse courtier who sleeps secure "in effeminate invention,/In beastly source of all pollution" (*SV*, 7.34-35), not the "effeminate sanguine *Ganimede*" whom men seek out like a beaver-skin blanket to keep them warm in bed (*SV*, 7.158). In Marston's "Cynicke Satyre" we have both senses of "effeminate" side by side: the one that has sur-vived, an attribute of the boys who serve the pleasure of the gallant and the courtier, and the one that dominates early mod-ern usage, an attribute of the gallant and the courtier them-selves. Casting off the manly virtues of self-control, gallant and courtier have imitated women in giving themselves up to plea-sures of all sorts—adulterous, sodomitical, beastial. The one thing that all the myriad creatures of Marston's "Cynicke Satyre" share is emptiness. When Marston complains that no men are to be found, what he sees instead are not women but beasts. Circe has turned all the men into swine. Or, rather,

> the soules of swine
> Do live in men, for that same radiant shine,

That lustre wherewith natures *Nature* decked
Our intellectual part, that glosse is soyled
With stayning spots of vile impietie,
And muddy durt of sensualitie,
These are no men, but *Apparitions,*
Ignes fatui, Glowormes, Fictions,
Meteors, Ratts of Nilus, Fantasies,
Colosses, Pictures, Shades, Resemblances.

(*SV*, 7.7-16)

The most damning thing Donne and Marston can say about men who act on homosexual desire is not that they are immoderate, not that they are effeminate, not that they are decadent, not that they abuse nature, but this: they extinguish the soul that makes man Man.

The spiral of power and pleasure that locks the satirist and the satirized in a furious embrace is especially tight in *Micro-cynicon: Sixe Snarling Satyres* (1599). The anonymous author T— M— owns up himself to the vices he lambastes in others. In satire 5 the vice he confesses is a particularly salacious variety of Cynic friction. With a confessed sinner's zeal the speaker describes the "ingle," the "pale Chequered black *Hermophrodite,*" he picked up on the streets of London. Sometimes Pyander swaggered about like a gentleman; other times, like a wanton courtesan. To tell the truth, "she" was excellent in neither.

Yet *Troynovant*[,] that all admired towne,
Where thousands still do travell up and downe,
Of Bewtie['] s counterfets affords not one,
So like a lovely smiling parragon,
As is *Pyander* in a Nymphes attire,
Whose rowling eye sets gazers harts on fire:
Whose cherry lip, black brow & smiles procure
Lust burning buzzards to the tempting lure.[30]

Among those carrion birds the persona himself was one. What he got, however, was not a single morsel of tasty flesh but an empty purse. The moral that the convert preaches is in one way like the message of Donne and Marston: Pyander was all show and no substance. Because T— M— actually participated in what he writes about, however, the emphasis falls not on the cozener but on the cozened. What we see from that subjective vantage point is a jolting discrepancy between appearance and reality. "Rash[-]headed Cavaleires[,] learne to be wise,/And if you needs will do, do with advise," the speaker concludes.

Tye not affection to each wanton smile,
Least doting Fancie truest love beguile:
Trust not a painted puppet as I have done,
Who far more doted then *Pigmalion*:
The streets are full of jugling parasites,
With true shape of Virgins counterfets.

(sig. C6)

T— M—'s speaker internalizes the experience in a way that Donne and Marston's smugly self-possessed personae cannot. Acting on "doting Fancie," he warns, threatens one's hold on reality.

That, too, is Ben Jonson's word on the matter. Jonson gives the ideological case against sodomy its most sophisticated statement; he also *enacts* the power-pleasure spiral that operates implicitly in the works of other satirists. The confusions of gender that make *Epicoene, or The Silent Woman* (1609) one of Jonson's stage triumphs are set up in the opening moments of the play. When Clerimont asks his Boy what luck he's had in getting received at the mansion of Clerimont's mistress, the Boy replies that he's "the welcom'st thing under a man that comes there."

> CLERIMONT. I thinke, and above a man too, if the truth were rack'd out of you.
> BOY. No faith, I'll confesse before, sir. The gentlewomen play with me, throw me o'the bed; and carry me in to my lady; and shee kisses me with her oil'd face; and puts a perruke o'my head; and askes me an' I will weare her gowne; and I say, no: and then she hits me a blow o'the eare, and calls me innocent, and lets me goe.[31]

Enter Clerimont's friend Truewit, and in his joking greeting we learn how most of the gentry in the London of *Epicoene* spend their time:

> Why, here's the man that can melt away his time, and never feeles it! what, betweene his mistris abroad, and his engle at home, high fare, soft lodging, fine clothes, and his fiddle; hee thinkes the houres ha' no wings, or the day no post-horse.

(1.1.23-27)

What Clerimont's Boy has described is just what we see in the play: women as sexual aggressors in the persons of "the Collegiate Ladies" and a boy dressed up as a woman. Dauphine's trick of disguising a gentleman's son and passing the lad off to his eccentric uncle as a bride is a device for gulling not only all the fools in the play—Morose, looking for a silent woman; the

Collegiate Ladies, looking for a new recruit; LaFoole and Jack Daw, looking for an imaginary conquest to brag about—but *us* as members of the audience. At the play's end we are as astonished as everyone else to discover that Morose has married a boy. Even Clerimont and Truewit, the stage-manager figures who have guided us through the play's maze of fools like the persona in a verse satire, are totally taken by surprise.

All the more beguiling is Jonson's trick when we recall that the play was originally performed by boy-actors, by the Children of the Queen's Revels. Probably because of their entanglement in the Martin Marprelate controversy the all-boy troupes who had kept Elizabeth's court entertained during the 1580s were ordered to stop acting about 1590. When they made their comeback in 1599, they quickly discarded their old repertory of romances like Lyly's *Gallathea* and took up the new genre of satiric comedy that Marston, Jonson, Chapman, and Middleton were establishing on the public stage. By the time they acted *Epicoene* the boy-actors were past masters at figuratively poking their childish limbs into costumes several sizes too large and aping the decadent ways of their elders.[32]

Jonson knew his troupe's strengths: constantly he plays up the lascivious possibilities of boy-actors as women—but as *what* women! In *Epicoene* we encounter, not romantic heroines like Rosalind, Portia, or Viola, but amazons like Madame Haughty, Madame Centaur, and Mistress Dol Mavis, who parcel out Dauphine's locks, eyes, nose, and legs as they vie over which of them will enjoy which part of him first. A boy pretending to be a woman: what we see in the fiction of the play is what we see in fact on the stage. Our willingness to go along with convention is cunningly exploited. Jonson seduces us into taking pleasure, perhaps even sexual pleasure, at the pretense—only to work his power over us in the end. If we can be so easily deceived by appearances in a play, how much more easily might we be deceived by appearances in social life? No trust to faces. *Epicoene* is full of posturing, of gulling, of eavesdropping, of gossiping. Jonson bids us look at society as just such a farce as the play itself. Cross-dressing in Jonson's satires thus points to a very different end from cross-dressing in Shakespeare's romances: in Jonson's hands it is a device not for licensing sexual confusion but for censuring it. Shakespeare lets us take pleasure in boys dressing up as women, and lets us take that pleasure home with us as we leave the theater; Jonson turns the trick on us and snatches our pleasure away. Shakespeare makes us see the liberating possibilities in playing about with gender roles; Jonson makes us see it as a matter of moral—and psychological—disintegration.[33] In women who act like men, in boys who tease men by dressing up like women, there is no center, no inwardness, no reality.

The same point is made from a different angle in Jonson's two epigrams "On Sir Voluptuous Beast." Like Martial, Jonson in his collected *Epigrammes. I Booke* (c. 1612) manages to strike a balance between Juvenal's rage and Horace's restraint. The moralist's fervor is tempered by the chiseled coolness of the poet's lines; poems of attack are offset by poems of praise. Just before the epigram on Beast, for example, comes this epigram "To the Parliament": "There's reason good, that you good lawes should make:/Mens manners ne're were viler, for your sake."[34] Just afterward, in the shape of the chest-tomb on which it might be inscribed, appears an encomium on Jonson's deceased friend Sir John Roe. It is this larger context, this vision of law and virtuous example, that we should hold in mind when we read how Beast turns his own wife into a female cuckold:

> While BEAST instructs his faire, and innocent wife,
>   In the past pleasures of his sensuall life,
> Telling the motions of each petticote,
>   And how his GANIMEDE mov'd, and how his goate,
> And now, her (hourely) her owne cucqueane makes,
>   In varied shapes, which for his lust shee takes:
> What doth he else, but say, leave to be chast,
>   Just wife, and, to change me, make womans hast?

> (XXV)

Implicitly Jonson invokes here all the strictures against homosexual acts that we have heard before: its lack of moderation ("Voluptuous" is Beast's Christian name), its decadence and abuse of nature (once again "Ganymede" and "goat" catchily alliterate), its threat of chaos (Beast's lust demands "varied shapes"). There is also the distinctively Renaissance idea that homosexual activity presents not only a social but a *psychological* threat. By making "woman's haste" Beast's wife will "change" him. Change him how? By assuming sexual freedom herself, exchanging him (OED 1) for someone else, and transforming him (OED 6) into a cuckold as he makes her a cuckquean? By learning to meet him halfway in his desires, giving and taking reciprocally (OED 3)? By playing along with his polymorphous fantasies and metamorphosing him into infinitely "varied shapes"? One thinks here of the obsession that Volpone uses to woo Celia: a vision of lovemaking that exhausts the fables of Ovid and ransacks the costumes of Europe in an endless quest for ever-new shapes,

> Where we may, so, trans-fuse our wandring soules,
> Out at our lippes, and score up summes of pleasures,
>> *That the curious shall not know,*
>> *How to tell them, as they flow;*
>> *And the envious, when they find*
>> *What their number is, be pind.*[35]

To such fantasies, Jonson implies, the only conclusion is annihilation of self. That troubling word "change" in the first epigram on Beast echoes in the second:

> Then his chast wife, though BEAST now know no more,
> He'adulters still: his thoughts lye with a whore.

(XXVI)

Jonson paraphrases in these lines a sentiment from Seneca's *De Constantia*, but with a characteristically Renaissance twist. "*Si quis cum uxore sua tanquam aliena concumbat, adulter erit,*" says Seneca: "If anyone lies with his wife as if she were someone else, he becomes an adulterer."[36] Jonson turns this legalistic scruple into a psychological truth: Seneca's emphasis falls on "*adulter erit*"; Jonson's, on Beast's "thoughts." Jonson sees the power of sexual fantasy to falsify reality, and he backs away in horror.

Against homosexual acts, like all the other "vile affections" proscribed by St. Paul, the Renaissance satirist's ultimate argument was its vacuousness. To act on homosexual desire was to give up one's social and even one's psychological identity. In the satires of Donne, Marston, and Jonson is proof positive, or rather proof negative, of Bray's contention that "homosexual" did not exist in the sixteenth and seventeenth centuries as a way of defining one's self. The satirist stood ready to make sure it never was. Compared to the Myth of Combatants and Comrades and the Myth of the Shipwrecked Youth, the Myth of Knights in Shifts goes further in giving homosexual desire a recognizable body and a distinctive voice, but it does so in terms that are useless to a man who feels that desire himself. Despite the curious anomoly of T— M—, once a pursuer of boys, the satirist stands aloof, a detached observer of other men's behavior. The body he gives to homosexual desire is only what he chooses to see from the outside; the voice he hears is nothing but his own.

What is more, he sees and hears a great deal less than he

thinks he does. Blinded by satiric stereotypes, he can picture no subject of homosexual desire but a fat, lazy lecher. Instructed by the law, he can imagine no object of homosexual desire but a boy. Donne's philosophical frame of reference may be broad, but the specific sexual target he marks out for attack in his satires is as narrowly defined as it is in legal discourse. Sodomy, for Donne as for Coke as for all the satirsts, is a man lusting after a boy. On the sexual potentiality in male bonding, so difficult to see because so pervasive and so undefined, they all remain silent. They respond to the Myth of the Shipwrecked Youth, not to the Myth of Combatants and Comrades. Instructed by their own culture's prejudices about women, they can imagine sodomy only in male-female terms, in terms of "agent" and "consentient." Because Renaissance ideas about sexuality in general were so phallocentric, the symbolic discourse of sexual acts seemed, to most men, to be all about power. In same-sex relations someone *had* to be the weaker partner. For a man to assume that role was to give up his male power—and hence his male identity. Dramatic evidence of those casual assumptions is to be found in the court testimony of a yeomen from Somerset who told the quarter sessions judge that he chanced to be sharing a bed with an innkeeper named Dowdeney when about midnight Dowdeney grabbed him

> by his privy member or secret parts and said . . . : "What? Are they no better? . . . Mine are better than thine!" And with that Dowdeney kissed him . . . about the cheek and culled him about the neck and with violence got up upon the right side of the examinate, albeit . . . [he] resisted him and put him over as well as he could but . . . [he] being weak could not put him off, until . . . Dowdeney had defiled . . . [his] thighs and shirt after a lustful manner . . . Dowdeney saying when he had done, that . . . the said examinant *had done him as much pleasure as if he were a woman*.[37]

Hence the satirsts' insulting term "Ganymede." They apply that epithet, not to sodomites in general, but only to the younger, passive partner who serves another man's pleasure. For the older, active partner there was no similar piece of slang. The satirists had to invent names of their own: Donne's "fondling motley humorist," Marston's "Luscus," Jonson's "Sir Voluptuous Beast."

What does the satirists' specificity about sodomy have to do with the obliquity of homosexual desire? What do "Luscus" and "Ganymede" have to do with Antonio and Bassanio? In most respects, the poems and plays by Juvenal and his Renaissance successors might seem to constitute more a moral indictment or a legal brief than a myth on the order of Combatants and Comrades or The Shipwrecked Youth, but the satirists do in fact define one way of experiencing sexual desire. To a male who feels stirrings of passion for another male the Myth of Knights in Shifts offers a simple alternative: either conform with the rest of society and give up your desires, or become one of the grotesques all reasonable men despise. About so simplisitic a way of dealing with sexual desire Shakespeare has this to say: nothing.

CHAPTER SIX

MASTER AND MINION

O Muse my mother, frame my song of Jove, for every thing
Is subject unto royall Jove. Of Jove the heavenly King
I oft have shewed the glorious power. I erst in graver verse
The Gyants slayne in Phlaegra feeldes with thunder, did reherse.
But now I neede a meelder style to tell of prettie boyes
That were the derlings of the Gods: and of unlawfull joyes
That burned in the brests of Girles, who for theyr wicked lust
According as they did deserve, receyved penance just.
The King of Goddes did burne erewhyle in love of Ganymed
The Phrygian and the thing was found which Jupiter that sted
Had rather bee than that he was. Yit could he not beteeme
The shape of any other Bird than Aegle for to seeme
And so he soring in the ayre with borrowed wings trust up
The Trojane boay who still in heaven even yit doth beare his cup,
And brings him Nectar though against Dame Junos will it bee.[1]

The Execution of Piers Gaveston

from Raphael Holinshed, *The Chronicles of England, Scotland, and Ireland*
(London: Lucas Harrison, 1577)

"Tis something to be pitied of a king": depending on how an actor chooses to
deliver the line, we can see Gaveston, not as the hard-edged politican he pretends to be, but as a man who has let his guard down and betrayed how
desperately he wants to be loved.

(Reproduced by permission from a copy in the Folger Shakespeare Library)

Back from the underworld without Eurydice, Orpheus sits down in a hilltop grove and sings a series of tales that burn with a vehemence, violence, and variety that are remarkable even among the rest of Ovid's *Metamorphoses*. The trees and bushes around him, transformations of ill-fated lovers, bend to his lyre as Orpheus tells how Jupiter turned the shepherd-boy Ganymede into his heavenly cupbearer; how Apollo pursued Hyacinth, stripped and oiled, onto the athletic field where the lad met his death but found immortality as a flower; how the confirmed bachelor Pygmalion fell in love with the image of woman he himself had made and was rewarded for his change of heart when Venus gave the statue life; how Myrrha became a perpetually weeping tree after falling in love with her own fa-ther and staging a bed-trick to enjoy him; how Venus was help-less to save Adonis from the boar's tusks but used her divine powers to transform the lover who was always running away into a flower that returns every year. In the midst of his song Orpheus himself is metamorphosed. The women of Thrace, furi-ous that the poet ignores their sexual lures, even more furious that "He also taught the Thracian folke a stewes of Males to make/ And of the flowring pryme of boayes the pleasure for to take" (10.83-85, p. 251), rip Orpheus apart with their bare hands and send his still-singing head floating down the river and out to sea.

For Renaissance Englishmen, like their counterparts all over Europe, the story of Jupiter and Ganymede was the best known, most widely recognized myth of homoerotic desire.[2] Of that fact the satirists have given us plenty of scurrilous evidence already. But there was, so to speak, another side to the story. If the Gany-mede of satire exposes sodomy's ugly rump, the Ganymede of learned poetry displays homoeroticism's public face. Since late antiquity grammarians, philologists, and Christian apologists had been working their own special metamorphosis on Ovid, turning his handy compendium of pagan myth into an *Ovide Moralisé* full of useful doctrine.[3] In his translation of 1567 Arthur Golding manifests this essentially medieval interest in the poem. "The tenth booke cheefly dooth containe one kynd of argu-ment," Golding declares in his prefatory Epistle, "Reproving most prodigious lusts of such as have bene bent/To incest most unnatural." And by "incest" Golding clearly means what we would now call homosexuality: Orpheus's death "sheweth Gods just vengeance on the vyle/And wicked sort which horribly with incest them defyle" (p. 411). Fewer and fewer readers in the sixteenth century may have been quite so literal, and anachronistically wrong, but even in the self-consciously neoclassical climate of the seventeenth century, readers never gave up the habit of reading Ovid as if he were a philosopher. The full commentary that George Sandys appended to his translation of the *Metamorphoses* in 1632 simply substitutes a more speculative and eclectic kind of philosophizing for what we find in Golding:

> But *Ganimed*, according to Xenophon; was rather assumed into heaven for the beauty of his mind, then that of his body: not so called of banquetting and indulgency, but to expresse the excellency of Wisdome and Counsell. *Ganimed* therefore, or a wise and understanding Soule, uncontaminated with the vices of the flesh, and drawing neerest unto the nature of God, is by him beloved, and rapt into heaven, (as *Enoch*, or *Eliah* in a fiery charriot) and on the wings of an Eagle, in regard of her high-touring and perspicuity. He is fained to fill Nectar for *Jupiter*, in that prudence and innocency is so acceptable to God; whereby we feast him, as it were, with coelestiall viands.[4]

In effect, Golding, Sandys, and their colleagues deconstruct the ancient myth to suit the very different cultural needs of their own time.

Those needs included the very matters that Golding and Sandys take such pains to deny. If the story of Jupiter and Ganymede was the best known myth of homoerotic desire in early modern England, that was so not only because the myth was decorative and decorous but because, for men living in that society at that historical moment, it was a particularly eloquent way of putting homosexual desire into discourse. More explicitly than any other myth, it articulated the social and political dynamics that complicated male-male desire in the cultural context of sixteenth- and seventeenth-century England. In social terms, it spoke to the tensions in power that were at the heart of homoerotic relations between men in early modern England. Power, indeed, is the meta-theme of Ovid's *Metamorphoses*. The power of *eros* to overwhelm anybody and everybody, even the gods, is what Orpheus sings about in book 10. Desire metamorphoses them all into something they formerly were not. Eyeing Ganymede's tender flesh from afar, Jupiter discovers something he "sted/Had rather bee than that he was." His passion takes shape as an eagle that can clutch the shepherd-boy in his talons and whisk him away to his nest on Olympus. In all of Orpheus's tales—in Apollo's transforming the dying Hyacinth into a flower, in Venus's breathing life into Pygmalion's statue, in the gods' answering Myrrha's prayer for oblivion, in Venus's finding consolation in Adonis's yearly rebirth as an anemone—we witness the superior power that the gods, for all their susceptibility to erotic passion, enjoy over mortals. The homosexual couplings in Orpheus's catalog are no exceptions. I sing of "prettie boyes/That were the derlings of the Gods," says Orpheus in Golding's English. [P]ueros . . . canamus dilectos superis, he says in Ovid's more graphic Latin: "I sing about boys desired by those above" (10.152-153). Power and power ploys are at the center of Ovid's vision of love.

The intersection of ancient and modern, of the universal and the culturally specific is so sharp in the Myth of Master and Minion for one reason above all others: as a structure of power, it reinforced the hierarchical relationships in which Renaissance readers defined themselves as individuals, as members of society, and as partners in love. When William Harrison set out in the *Description of England* (1577) to characterize his own society, he distinguished four "sorts" of people: gentlemen; property-holding inhabitants of cities and towns; yeomen farmers with their own holdings; and day laborers, poor husbandmen, artificers, and servants.[5] Harrison not only sees the social structure of which he is a part as a hierarchy; he sees it totally in terms of adult males like himself. In the course of his life an Elizabethan male of the two upper classes in Harrison's scheme, gentlemen and urban property-holders, belonged to a series of social groups—schools, colleges, guilds, political bodies—that were alike in two fundamental ways: they were hierarchical in organization, and they were exclusively male. In both respects they constituted a microcosm of Elizabethan society. It is in just such circumstances of patriarchal power and gender polarization that anthropologists have most often encountered some form of institutionalized homosexuality.[6]

The scenario of "one above" taking his pleasure of a "boy" reflects the mores of medieval Europe and early modern England no less than the mores of ancient Greece and Rome. Alan Bray's survey of sixteenth- and seventeenth-century court records suggests that homosexual activity in early modern England, like illicit sexual activity of all sorts, usually involved a person in a superior position of power exercising his social prerogative over a person in an inferior position: "What determined the shared and recurring features of homosexual relationships was the prevailing distribution of power, economic power and social power, not the fact of homosexuality itself. It is a crucial realization."[7] Schoolmasters being arraigned for abuse of their pupils, masters for abuse of their apprentices, householders for abuse of their servants constitute all the record we have about ordinary people. The nobility have left behind their own record in the persons of James I, Francis Bacon, and the Earl of Castlehaven.[8] That is to say, Renaissance Englishmen, like the ancient Greeks and Romans, eroticized the power distinctions that set one male above another in their society. Sexual desire took shape in the persons of master and minion; sexual energy found release in the power play between them. The subject of the Myth of Master and Minion is, indeed, the very subject of Renaissance legal discourse about sodomy: power-bedeviled sexual relations between a man and a "boy."

How we are to understand "boy" in these circumstances is not so straightforward as it might seem. When Richard Williams (alias Richard Cornish), a ship's master, came before the Council and General Court of the Virginia Colony in 1624-25 on a charge of sodomy, two people were called to witness: the alleged victim William Couse, who was one of Cornish's stewards, and Walter Mathew, who is described in the court records as the boatswain's mate. Couse testified that

> Richard Williams, also [known as] Cornish, master of the said ship called the Ambrose, being then in drink, called to this examinee to lay a clean pair of sheet into his bed, which this examinee did, and the said Williams went into the bed, and would have this examinee come into the bed to him, which this examinee refusing to do, the said Richard Williams went out of the bed and did cut this examinee's cod piece, . . . , and made this examinee unready, and made him go into the bed, and then the said Williams also Cornish went into the bed to him, and there lay upon him, and kissed him and hugged him, saying that he would love this examinee if he would now and then come and lay with him, and so by force he turned this examinee upon his belly, and so did put this examinee to pain in the fundament, and did wet him, and after did call for a napkin which this examinee did bring unto him.

The only other man on board the ship at the time, Mathew testified that "the master called the boy into his bed cabin . . . . But of what it was that the Master did urge him to do he [Mathew] knoweth not, nor heard not the boy cry out for help after this." Richard Williams was found guilty and executed. "Master" and "boy": the court record consistently uses these terms to refer to the parties in question. "A rascally boy" is likewise how a friend of Richard Williams's brother is reported to have described Couse when someone asked why Williams was hanged: "he was put to death through a scurvy boy's means."[9]

As speakers of modern English, we naturally assume that this "rascally boy" must have been a teenager. The court record specifies, however, that Couse was "aged 29 years or thereabouts"— just at the age when most men married.[10] In what sense, then, could Couse be called a "boy"? Early modern English included two senses of the word that are now obsolete. In addition to "boy" as "a male child below the age of puberty" (OED 1) and "boy" as a term "applied playfully, affectionately, or slightingly to a young man, or one treated as such" (OED 2), speakers of English in the early seventeenth century could also use "boy" to refer to a servant or slave (OED 3) and as "a term of contempt," as a synonym for "knave, varlet, rogue, wretch, caitiff" (OED 4).

Despite its obsolete label in the *Oxford English Dictionary*, "boy" in the third sense survived in British colonial societies and in the American South until relatively recently. In which sense, or senses, was William Couse a "boy"? As "master" of the ship, Richard Williams clearly thought of his steward as an OED 3: it is Couse, not Williams, who lays the sheets, endures the pain in his fundament, and even fetches the towel when the whole thing is over. Possibly Williams hoped that Couse might become an OED 2: he does promise to "love" Couse if he will come to bed with him now and again. With OED 2, as with OED 1, the Virginia tribunal was not concerned: the court recorder thinks of Couse only as an OED 3. The friend of Richard Williams's brother, on the other hand, regards him as an OED 4. The criterion for the ship's master and for the court recorder is Couse's social position as a steward; for the friend of Williams's brother it is Couse's despicable behavior. Couse's age has little if anything to do with it. Understanding these multiple possibilities of meaning, we are in a better position to understand why five men, discovered in "wickedness not to be named" during a voyage to New England in 1629, could be described by a fellow passenger as "beastly Sodomiticall boyes."[11] What the fellow passenger is specifying is most likely not the five men's ages but their moral contemptibility. "Servant" and "rogue": the common denominator in these two obsolete senses of "boy" is a distinction in power vis-à-vis a social or a moral superior. When speakers of early modern English wanted to make distinctions among sodomites, they thought about power. "Ganymede"—the commonest epithet in early modern English for a homosexual male—refers to the passive partner, to the male who bends to the other's pleasure. The satirists leave no ambiguity about that. For the active partner, for the man who "takes his pleasure," early modern English offered no cant term, presumably because no such term of opprobrium was needed.

One obvious way for such distinctions in power to be expressed—obvious, at least, to us—is in terms of gender. As the passive partner, does not Ganymede play the "female"? And the active partner—does he not play the "male"? It is in just such gender-marked terms, as we saw in chapter 4, that some contemporary scholars would like to read homosexuality in early modern England. If we take at face value what Stephen Gosson, Phillip Stubbes, and other Puritan attackers of stage-plays have to say, sodomy is the ultimate in a Babylonian school of abuses that also includes—often in this particular order—morris dancing, May games, stage-plays, and cross-dressing. Boy-actors dressed up like women come across in these accounts as a kind of fetish: witness not only the lust that Gosson, Stubbes, *et al.* attribute to theatergoers but the passion about the subject they themselves betray.[12] To play the sodomite is, in the these writers' eyes, to play the female. How do we square that with what Nicholas Breton and the satirists say when they call a man "effeminate" because he likes women only too much? The "Effeminate Fool" described in Breton's character-book may gossip endlessly, look demurely, walk mincingly, and laugh continually, but he also keeps a mistress. He is, in Breton's paradoxical phrase, a "Womans man."[13] With Breton, as with Gosson and Stubbes, "effeminate" has much more force as a metaphor for wanton behavior than it does as a label for sociopsychic identity. What we are dealing with here is, in fact, a different idea of "effeminacy" from our own. We read "female" in terms of Freud; writers like Gosson and Stubbes read it in terms of Aristotle's *Ethics.* Their distinction seems to be, not between male and female as modes of self-identity, or even between male and female as postures in making love, but between sexual moderation and sexual excess. Against those scholars who would equate "sodomy" in early modern England with "effeminacy" as we understand that term today, I would argue that homosexual desire in the Myth of Master and Minion is enacted within, not across, gender lines. The differentials in power that are played out in Renaissance retellings of the story of Jupiter and Ganymede are the differentials that positioned men vis-à-vis one another, not the differentials that positioned men vis-à-vis women. "Female" is but one way among many of signifying one male's subjection to another. The three models of homosexual behavior outlined in chapter 1—age-graded, gender-marked, and egalitarian—may not be quite adequate to the social and political circumstances of early modern England. Just as important as the age-graded distinctions that inspire pictures of Ganymede as an adolescent, just as important as the gender-marked distinctions that render him smooth of face and lithe of body, are the class-ranked distinctions that make him a "boy."

The Myth of Master and Minion, unlike all the other myths described in this book, is not linked to a single literary genre. It can be played out in a variety of genres, to a variety of ends. Ovid may have given the story of Jupiter and Ganymede its most familiar telling, but the myth is not limited to the *epyllia* that Ovid inspired Renaissance poets to write. For poets, as for painters, the *Metamorphoses* was not so much a story in the manner, say, of *Clitophon and Leucippe* as a gallery of sensuous *tableaux*. What, after all, is the *plot* of Ovid's tale of Jupiter and Ganymede? More than a story, it is an image. What kind of ending can an image have? Ganymede supplants Juno, and Orpheus moves on to other heroes and other passions. All the questions that a dramatist, a pastoral poet, a writer of romances, a satirist would have to confront are left unasked and unanswered. Ovid celebrates a series of sensual moments in time. One epiphany of erotic pleasure follows another. What happens when a reader remembers all the constraints imposed on desire by ideology, law, and social custom? Is it enough to follow Golding and Sandys and transpose sexual desire into an allegorical idea? Plotless, open-ended, focused on the nexus of pleasure and power, the Myth of Master and Minion figures in all of the myths we have investigated so far, just as it does in the final myth still to be considered.

Even in the Myth of Combatants and Comrades, with its commemoration of egalitarian maleness, questions of power arise. *Troilus and Cressida,* Shakespeare's quintessential play about the nature of men in groups, is a case in point. Jupiter and Ganymede enter the play in the guises foisted onto them by satire. Throughout the play the satyr/satirist Thersites reviles everyone and everything, but he particularly enjoys baiting Patroclus, who like the other Greeks ends up using physical force to counter Thersites' verbal volleys. "Prithee be silent, boy," Thersites tells him, right in front of Achilles; "I profit not by thy talk. Thou art thought to be Achilles' male varlet."

> PATROCLUS. "Male varlet," you rogue? What's that?
> THERSITES.   Why, his masculine whore.

And to abuse the "boy" further Thersites heaps on him diminutive insults by the fistful. Is Patroclus not taking offense at Thersites' curses?

> No? Why art thou then exasperate? Thou idle immaterial
> skein of sleave-silk, thou green sarsenet flap for a sore eye,
> thou tassel of a prodigal's purse, thou! Ah, how the poor
> world is pestered with such waterflies! Diminutives of nature.
> PATROCLUS. Out, gall!
> THERSITES.   Finch egg![14]

The finch is a very small bird. Such sibilant sneers we have heard and seen before in the verses of Marston and Donne when they found themselves face to face with sodomites in the streets of London. Thersites derides this coupling of two males, not in moral terms, however, but in political terms. He sees it all as a matter of one man's power over another. A "varlet" is primarily a social, not a moral, inferior. Patroclus deserves insults, not because he is morally wrong, but because he willingly accepts an unmanly, passive role: he is Achilles' "masculine whore."

Most producers of *Troilus and Cressida* in recent years have taken Thersites' taunts at face value and portrayed Achilles and Patroclus as lovers.[15] Certainly that helps explain the vehemence of Achilles' revenge when Patroclus is killed by Hector. "Where is this Hector?" Achilles cries when he gets the news. "Come, come, thou brave boy-queller, show thy face . . . " (5.5.46-47). Achilles presents himself as a man revenging the death of a defenseless "boy." If Thersites is to be believed, he is the master revenging the death of his minion. He is also, perhaps, a tragic hero. But the satirist's jibes are hard to forget. Thersites represents one way of making the Myth of Master and Minion fit the moral constraints imposed by Elizabethan society: by detaching ourselves from it and laughing at it. Any possibility of tragic grandeur in Achilles' action is undercut, furthermore, by the sheer brutality of his murder of Hector. The event seems gruesome not so much because Hector is surprised without his weapons, or even because Achilles summons his Myrmidons to turn what could have been a grand gesture of honor into a gruesome murder, but because Shakespeare denies Achilles enough words to give the action any heroic stature whatsoever. "Strike, fellows, strike": only five stark lines accompany the climactic event of the entire play. The play ends, then, as the war itself began, with a sexually inspired act of violence. Nothing has changed; nothing is resolved. This particular playing out of the Myth of Master and Minion ends in the social chaos threatened by satire.

"The shepherd *Corydon* loved sore *Alexis* faire that youth/His lords delight": even in Arcadia male sexual desire validates differences in power. The Myth of the Passionate Shepherd may invite fantasies about a closed-off world where all men are simple shepherds, but that fantasy's appeal has everything to do with the fact that all men are no such thing. The would-be ravisher who speaks Marlowe's "Come live with me and be my love" addresses his beloved in terms not at all inappropriate for Jupiter wooing Ganymede. If, as Jonathan Goldberg has argued, Edmund Spenser's Colin is a stand-in for the youthful poet himself and Hobbinol is an alias for Spenser's Cambridge mentor Gabriel Harvey, *The Shepheardes Calender* can be read as one Renaissance Ganymede's reply to his particular Jupiter.[16] The "Ganymede" addressed so sensually and sagely by Richard Barnfield's *Affectionate Shepheard* much more clearly is cast as the student to the master, as the inns-of-court outer-barrister to the inns-of-court bencher.

When Shakespeare crosses the Myth of Master and Minion with the Myth of Combatants and Comrades, he ends up with satire. When he does the same with the Myth of the Shipwrecked Youth, he arrives at more harmonious conclusions. Sexual politics in *As You Like It* appear all the more revolutionary when we realize that "Ganymede" wields such power not only as a woman but as an ingle, as a "consentient" male. Rosalind as Ganymede is not only a woman; she is a figure out of satire. In both roles, in her actual person and in her disguise, Rosalind ought to be subject to Orlando's control. The happy ending for everyone in the play, for Orlando in particular, turns on the fact that, for a time at least, she is not. The Myth of Master and Minion figures more prominently still in *A Midsummer Night's Dream*, a play directly inspired by Ovid. The world we enter in the woods outside Athens is the topsy-turvy world evoked by Orpheus's song of desire run amok. All the magical metamorphoses that the fairies work on the mortals in *A Midsummer Night's Dream* devolve from a single case of jealousy that has its origins in Ovid's tale of Jupiter and Ganymede: Oberon wants Titania's

"little changeling boy" to be his "henchman," and Titania refuses absolutely (2.1.120-121). As well she might. Oberon has a
sexual appetite to rival Jupiter's. Like Jove, he ranges all over
the world in all sorts of guises to satisfy all sorts of desires.
When Oberon counters Titania's cool welcome by asking, "Am
not I thy lord?", she replies like an aggrieved Juno:

> Then I must be thy lady; but I know
> When thou hast stol'n away from fairyland
> And in the shape of Corin sat all day,
> Playing on pipes of corn, and versing love
> To amorous Phillida.

Even Hippolyta has caught his roving eye:

> Why art thou here
> Come from the farthest step of India,
> But that, forsooth, the bouncing Amazon,
> Your buskined mistress and your warrior love,
> To Theseus must be wedded, and you come
> To give their bed joy and prosperity?

$$(2.1.63-72)$$

In just what capacity, then, might Titania's "changeling boy"
serve as Oberon's page? Whatever he has in mind, Oberon
wants the boy badly enough to visit on Titania the hilarious
indignity of falling in love with Bottom, ass's head and all. The
trick, he hopes, will persuade Titania to relent. "I'll to my
queen," he tells Puck, "and beg her Indian boy;/And then I will
her charmèd eye release/From monster's view, and all things
shall be peace" (3.2.376-378).

So all things are. But the Indian boy is heard about no more.
Instead, Oberon's meeting with Titania is the happy reconciliation of a married couple who have loved each other long enough
to forgive and forget. The Myth of Companionate Marriage triumphs yet again. "Now thou and I are new in amity," exclaims
Oberon, having taken the just-awakened queen by the hand and
initiated a dance that eventually winds its way through the multiple weddings in Duke Theseus's palace (4.1.86). Literally as
well as metaphorically, all the couples in the cast, fairies and
mortals alike, are caught up in this grand dance of nuptial love.
In the bottoms-up world of the forest outside Athens homosexual desire may be unleashed along with other forms of erotic
passion, but A Midsummer Night's Dream, like the other comedies
that play out the clash between male bonds and married love,
ends with the lovers leaving behind the mysteries of forest,

night, and unbridled passion for the certainties of city, daylight, and bridal vows.

As Patroclus and Rosalind remind us, Ganymede never quite loses his identity as a satiric type, however tragic or romantic the dramatic circumstances may be. The Myth of Master and Minion handily furnishes characters and speeches for the Myth of Knights in Shifts. In satiric treatments of Jupiter and Ganymede by Thomas Heywood, John Marston, an anonymous court satirist, and Ben Jonson we can distinguish three degrees of satiric irony. Heywood's is the gentlest. The irony in his translations of two of Lucian's irreverent "Dialogues of the Gods" goes beyond the irony of Lucian's lines; it resides in the incongruity between the obvious delight Heywood takes in homoerotic love-talk and the official disapproval he is careful to register first. In Heywood's *Pleasant Dialogues and Dramma's* (1637), as in most Latin editions of Lucian's collected works, the dialogue between Jupiter and Ganymede and one of Lucian's two dialogues between Jupiter and Juno are paired as if they were installments in the debate set up by Plutarch. In the brief "Argument" prefaced to the dialogue of Jupiter and Juno, Heywood takes the expected Renaissance hard line: "Although this Fable to the gods extends,/Base sordid lust in man it reprehends."[17] Once we actually turn to the witty one-upmanship between jealous wife and profligate husband that scales the gods down to satiric human size, Heywood's moral tag seems more an afterthought than a forethought. So, too, with his claim in the other dialogue that Ganymede represents "a simple Swaine,/Who would leave heaven to live on earth againe" (3536-3537). Ganymede, to be sure, seems astonishingly naive about just why he has been brought up to Olympus, but that makes him all the more desirable. When he warns Jupiter that he will make a restless bedfellow, Jupiter assures him,

In that the greater pleasure I shall take,
Because I love still to be kept awake.
I shall embrace and kisse thee then the ofter,
And by that means my bed seem much the softer.

To which Ganymede makes this ambiguous reply: "but whilst you wake I'le sleepe" (3665-3639). Are we, prompted by the moral "Argument," to interpret Ganymede's part in this poem of seduction as a country bumpkin's stupidity? What Heywood shows us is a none too carefully considered ambivalence. On the one hand, he labels male-male sexuality "base sordid lust." On the other hand, he does nothing to make the dialogue less than the pleasantry promised by the collection's title. Heywood's way with the myth is, in a word, *jovial*.

Marston's irony in *The Scourge of Villanie* is altogether harsher. In high Anglican indignation, Marston's satiric persona orders "falsed, seeming, Patriotes" who study in Catholic seminaries in Flanders and Spain to keep their filthy habits where they found them:

> Returne not with pretence of salving spots,
> When here yee soyle us with impuritie,
> And monstrous filth, of Doway seminary.
> What though *Iberia* yeeld you libertie,
> To snort in source of Sodom vilanie?
> What though the bloomes of young nobilitie,
> Committed to your *Rodons* custodie,
> Yee *Nero* like abuse? yet ne[']re approch,
> Your newe S. *Homers* lewdnes here to broch.
> Tainting our Townes, and hopefull Accademes,
> With your lust-bating most abhorred meanes.

To hear the persona tell it, Cambridge colleges are already full of this "ranck filth." Look to your sons, oh fathers.

> Had I some snout faire brats, they should indure
> The new found *Castilian* callenture:
> Before some pedant-Tutor, in his bed
> Should use my frie, like Phrigian *Ganimede*.[18]

Harsher still is the irony in an anonymous poem beginning "Arm, arm in heaven!" that appears in several seventeenth-century manuscripts but was never printed. The first stanza perhaps reveals why:

> Arm, arm in heaven! There is a faction,
>   And the demigods
> Now are bent for action!
>   They are at odds
> With him that rules the thunder
>   And will destroy
>   His white-fac'd boy
> Or rend the heavens in sunder.[19]

It is not Olympus that is being talked about here but Whitehall. He that rules the thunder is James; his white-faced boy, presumably George Villiers.

> Great Jove (that sways the imperial scepter
>   With his upstart love

That makes him drunk with nectar)
 They will remove.

(ll. 10-13)

When we note that Villiers began his rise to power as James's official cupbearer, it is hard to decide where art leaves off and life begins. The daring of the anonymous author of these verses includes not only talking about a disgruntled court faction who would overthrow the soon to be if not already Duke of Buckingham but intimating in just what way Great Jove transferred political power to his favorite:

 Love's Queen stood disaffected
  To what she had seen
 (Or what suspected),
  As she in spleen
 To Juno hath protested,
  Her servant Mars
  Should scourge his arse,
 Jove's marrow so had wasted.

(ll. 33-40)

The arse in question is presumably the duke's. "I sing about boys desired by those above": the Myth of Master and Minion is here put to quite specific political use. And "boy" is to be understood as much politically as literally. George Villiers was 23 when he came to favor with James, 25 when he was created Duke of Buckingham.[20] He was exactly the age when most aristocratic men married.[21] Even more sharply than in Marston's verse, the Myth of Master and Minion is deployed in this poem for what it reveals about political exchanges among men.

 Though less specific in its objects of attack, Jonson's satiric irony is the most vituperative of all. If Shakespeare in *Troilus and Cressida* portrays the Myth of Master and Minion as tragedy edged with satire, Jonson in *Sejanus* portrays it as satire edged with tragedy. *Sejanus* was performed by the King's Men in 1603, in the same season they may have acted *Troilus and Cressida*. One reason, surely, that *Sejanus* was a popular failure is Jonson's scrupulous attention to Greek and Latin models and to the implication there that the stage is for talk, not action. It is not only murders that we are disappointed not to see in *Sejanus* but Tiberius's debauches. We get to hear about them, however, from Arruntius:

 He is our monster: forfeited to vice
 So far, as no rack'd vertue can redeeme him.

His lothed person fouler than all his crimes:
An Emp'rour, only in his lusts. Retir'd
(From all regard of his owne fame, or *Rome's*)
Into an obscure Iland; where he lives
(Acting his *tragedies* with a *comick* face)
Amid'st his rout of Chaldee's . . . .

Astrology is one of Tiberius's vices, methods of murder another, but more serious than these, to judge from the lines Arruntius devotes to them, are Tiberius's "strange and new commented lusts." He takes a satirist's pleasure in cataloging the very things he castigates:

Thither, too,
He hath his boyes, and beauteous girls tane up,
Out of our noblest houses, the best form'd,
Best nurtur'd, and most modest: what's their good
Serves to provoke his bad. Some are allur'd,
Some threatned; others (by their friends detain'd)
Are ravish'd hence, like captives, and, in sight
Of their most grieved parents, dealt away
Unto his *spintries*, *sellaries*, and slaves,
Masters of strange, and new commented lusts,
For which wise nature hath not left a name.[22]

Arruntius tells all this not so much to expose Tiberius's moral depravity as to explain why the Roman patriots cannot depend on Tiberius for political leadership. Unnoticed by Tiberius, the ambitious minister Sejanus is setting himself up to become emperor. As in *Troilus and Cressida*, the dissolution of sexual roles portends social chaos. Rome ruled by a sexual maverick is vulnerable to an upstart manipulator like Sejanus. In the end, however, the "tragedies" that Tiberius acts out on Capri are not allowed to overwhelm the empire: Arruntius and his cohorts persuade the emperor to withdraw favor from Sejanus, who is pulled limb from limb by the angry Roman mob. The ethical complications involved in using so darkly depraved an emperor for such pristinely patriotic ends are perhaps one reason Tiberius spends so much time offstage and behaves with such surprising decorum when on.

In different ways, then, the Myth of Master and Minion is implicated in the Myth of Combatants and Comrades, the Myth of the Passionate Shepherd, the Myth of the Shipwrecked Youth, and the Myth of Knights in Shifts. As a discourse about pleasure and power, it is not limited to any one genre. It is, however, affiliated in the literature of Renaissance England with one particular writer. Questions about pleasure and power are central concerns in the works of Christopher Marlowe. For Shakespeare, Heywood, Marston, and Jonson, the Myth of Master and Minion is a narrative means to other thematic ends; for Marlowe, it is the very center of his vision of human affairs. He pursues the myth throughout his career as a poet and dramatist, testing it in a variety of genres and finding in it finally the substance of tragedy. Put to explicit use in *Dido Queen of Carthage*, it figures as an implicit image in "Hero and Leander" and in *Tamburlaine*. In *Edward II* it is the pattern that relates the male protagonists to each other as lovers and as political subjects. The comic detachment that marks the appearance of the myth in Marlowe's earlier works darkens into tragic ambivalence in *Edward II*. These differences in vision have to do not only with differences in the genres Marlowe takes in hand but with differences in the audiences he addresses. *Dido*, if the title-page of the 1594 quarto is to be believed, was "played by the Children of her *Majesties Chappell*," presumably at court, in ritual circumstances that dictated not only the classical subject matter of the play and its ingenious style but the political message it delivers.[23] "Hero and Leander," as we have seen already, is a narrative poem calculated for readers who took their Ovid rather less seriously than Golding. *Tamburlaine* and *Edward II* commanded a far wider audience. As scripts for the public stage they enjoyed a fame that can be measured not only in numbers of revivals but in allusions by other playwrights.[24] From *Dido* to "Hero and Leander" to *Tamburlaine* and *Edward II* we can follow, then, a gradual widening of audience from a coterie of courtiers to educated readers to the commonality of Elizabethan Englishmen.

Two revelations open *Dido Queen of Carthage*. The first is visual. "*Here the Curtaines draw*," say the opening stage directions, "*there is discovered* Jupiter *dandling* Ganimed *upon his knee, and* Mercury *lying asleepe*" (1.1.S.D.). When this tableau—possibly posed within a stage mansion—comes to dramatic life, the king of the gods and his little minion toss between them some playfully licentious banter that leaves no doubt that Ovid is lurking behind the scenes. In performance Marlowe's speaking emblem would have been even more licentious—and even more ironic. According to the title page to the quarto, these two notorious male lovers were none other than two pert boy-actors of Queen Elizabeth's Chapel Royal, veterans at acting plays before the queen:

GANYMEDE.

> Sweet *Jupiter*, if ere I pleasde thine eye,
> Or seemed faire walde in with Egles wings,
> Grace my immortal beautie with this boone,
> And I will spend my time in thy bright armes.

JUPITER.

> What ist sweet wagge I should deny thy youth?
> Whose face reflects such pleasure to mine eyes,
> As I exhal'd with thy fire darting beames,
> Have oft driven backe the horses of the night,
> When as they would have hal'd thee from my sight:
> Sit on my knee, and call for thy content,
> Controule proud Fate, and cut the thred of time.
> Why, are not all the Gods at thy commaund,
> And heaven and earth the bounds of thy delight?

(1.1.19-31)

And to prove the point Jupiter reaches over and plucks a feather from the wings of Mercury, still sleeping away as we discovered him at the beginning of the scene. What Ganymede wants, however, is nothing so grandiose as controlling proud Fate:

> I would have a jewell for mine eare,
> And a fine brouch to put in my hand,
> And then Ile hugge with you an hundred times.

(1.1.46-48)

In Lucian's dialogue between Jupiter and Ganymede, which may have been the inspiration for this scene, the shepherd-boy betrays a charming naïveté; Marlowe's Ganymede sweeps onto the stage, trailing the sarsenet and jewels of satire behind him. Marlowe takes up the satirsts' stereotype of the sodomite and plays it for all its comic worth. Or does he? With the actual Ganymede of *Dido*, as with all the figurative "Ganymedes" of his later plays and poems, we can never quite tell whether Marlowe is *playing* the satirist or *taunting* the satirists. One of the effects of the "power-pleasure spiral," we should recall from Foucault, is the pleasure that victims of power can take in "showing off, scandalizing, or resisting."[25]

Jupiter's talk about fate is timely. No sooner has Jupiter, playing the doting master, given Ganymede the very jewels that Juno wore on her marriage day than Venus rushes in to interrupt the amorous dalliance—and to get the narrative of this "tragic" drama on its way at last. Her son Aeneas has set out by ship from ruined Troy, and she needs Jupiter's help in getting him through the storms that Juno has set in his way. Jupiter calms

Chapter Six

Venus by making the second of the two revelations that open Marlowe's play. Venus should be content: "thy *Aeneas['s]* wandring fate is firme" (1.1.83). Through hardships Aeneas is fated to arrive in Italy, to do battle there for three years, and to found a city that will flourish as a new Troy. As his agent in helping Aeneas on his way to that firm fate, Jupiter finally awakes Mercury and sends him off to bid Neptune calm the seas.

These two revelations, one visual and one verbal, sound the two tones heard alternately throughout *Dido Queen of Carthage*: one a tone of Ovidian comic irony, the other a tone of Virgilian solemnity. More important still, the two revelations conjure up two visions of experience whose conflicting demands on Aeneas create the real drama of the tragedy: one a vision of amorous dalliance in the persons of Jupiter and Ganymede, the other a vision of heroic destiny in the person of Mercury. When he meets Dido, Aeneas is caught between these two demands. When Dido tries to persuade her lover to give up his destiny, she invests him with her own crown and scepter—and invests the whole situation with a mythic parallel that is ultimately her undoing:

> Now lookes *Aeneas* like immortall *Jove,*
> But where is *Ganimed* to hold his cup,
> And *Mercury* to flye for what he calles?

> (4.4.45-47)

Here is a restaging, with mortals as performers, of the play's first scene. As Ganymede uses feminine wiles to manipulate Jupiter, so Dido tries to manipulate Aeneas.

Dido, unlike Ganymede, fails. First in a dream, then in person, Mercury appears before Aeneas with pointed reminders of the play's second revelation, the prophecy about Rome. Mercury thus acts as the agent that calls Aeneas to his destiny, and in that action Jupiter's messenger brings the tableau that opened the play—Jupiter dandling Ganymede while Mercury lies aslseep—into sharp thematic focus. When Jupiter woos Ganymede with promises of controlling proud fate, his gesture of plucking the sleeping god's feathers is not without meaning: love-longing Jupiter is, in effect, "grounding" the agent of destiny. In the struggle between sexual desire and imperial destiny, it is destiny, however, that wins out. Dido and Aeneas emerge from Marlowe's play exactly as Renaissance audiences expected to see them: Aeneas as the divinely appointed founder of empire, Dido as the evil temptress who tries to divert him from his destiny.[26]

Jupiter and Ganymede emerge, in turn, as the very types of sexual desire—amusing and seductive, but ultimately pernicious to social duty. The play is a tragedy only for Dido, who gives herself up to passion. The higher claims of epic duty over romantic passion is the trite message of literally dozens of plays acted before Queen Elizabeth after it became clear she would never marry. As Marlowe manages it, however, Virgil's sonority never quite succeeds in drowning out Ovid's laughter.

Sexual passion occupies a more equivocal position vis-à-vis the social order in *Tamburlaine, Part Two*, and in *Edward II*. After rising as master of an empire in part 1 of Marlowe's epic play, Tamburlaine faces two formidable challenges in part 2: how to keep hold of his empire at the same time that he keeps hold of the audience's admiration. Both things have been won against great odds, and on both fronts Tamburlaine's three sons present problems. Two of them follow their father's fierce example to the last bloody detail; the third has other pursuits—and another parent—on his mind. "Be al a scourge and terror to the world," Tamburlaine challenges his sons. "Or els you are not sons of *Tamburlaine*." Calyphas demurs:

> But while my brothers follow armes my lord,
> Let me accompany my gratious mother,
> They are enough to conquer all the world
> And you have won enough for me to keep.

> (1.3.63-68)

This occasions one of Tamburlaine's most brutally consonantal, aggressively polysyllabic, and expansively periodic speeches in the entire play. Can this be *his* son? No sooner does the boys' gracious mother die than Tamburlaine decides the time has come to turn his sons into soldiers. When he sets out to teach the three boys the arts of war, Calyphas is terrified: "My Lord, but this is dangerous to be done,/We may be slaine or wounded ere we learne" (3.2.93-94). As before, Tamburlaine calls his son's paternity into loud question. And when Tamburlaine demonstrates his bravery by wounding himself, Calyphas shrinks back while the other brothers rush forward to be next: "I know not what I should think of it. Me thinks tis a pitifull sight" (3.2.130).

Calyphas's real trial comes in Tamburlaine's war with the Turks. When the two valiant sons try to raise their brother to arms, Calyphas refuses. It is not high-minded objections to war that prompt him but laziness, languor, and addiction to wine and cards. "Take you the honor," he tells his brothers, "I will take my ease" (4.1.49). Calyphas the timid momma's boy emerges as the diminutive dallying Ganymede of *Dido*. Once again Marlowe seems to be taking up the satirists' stereotype of the "consentient" sodomite and playing it for laughs. This time, however, the dramatic situation is not so simple. Calyphas is not an ageless figure in an ageless Olympian myth. He has to confront earth-bound mortal demands about gender, about becoming a man. How old is he? The Ganymede of *Dido* behaves like a spoiled boy—because he *is* one. Calyphas is challenged to act like a man. With Tamburlaine's misfit son Marlowe confronts the question of what happens when Ganymede grows up. However funny the audience finds Calyphas, Tamburlaine is anything but amused. In front of the captive Turks, the irate emperor fetches Calyphas onstage, berates him in one last magnificent barrage of epithets—and stabs him to death. The words that this willing Abraham speaks, weapon poised above his son, call attention not only to Calyphas's cowardice but to the boy-like slightness of his body. Perhaps, indeed, it is Ganymede himself that Tamburlaine has in mind when he prays,

Here *Jove*, receive his fainting soule againe,
A Forme not meet to give that subject essence,
Whose matter is the flesh of *Tamburlain*.

(4.1.111-113)

How is an audience to take *that*? Calyphas could hardly be called a tragic character—amid the bellicose brutalities of the play he is bound to come across as comic—but the emotional effect of his murder is not so easy to "place" as Ganymede's feminine wiles in *Dido*. We can comfortably laugh at Ganymede. But how are we to reconcile our amusement at Calyphas's antics with the sudden horror of his death? He is the butt of the satirists' ridicule and yet a sympathetic figure at the same time. For all its thrilling theatricality, Tamburlaine's symbolic defense of manhood breaches some unmarked barrier of decency. Calphyas's murder marks, in fact, the beginning of the end for Tamburlaine on both fronts. He begins to lose his grasp politically; more disastrously, he begins to lose his hold on the sympathies of his audience. Calyphas the mincing minion may threaten Tamburlaine's mastery of the world, but that mastery itself is called into question. The result is an unsettling ambiguity, emotionally as well as politically.

In *Edward II*, possibly the last play Marlowe wrote, satirical stereotypes of sodomy and sodomites are once again transposed into dramatic situations in which they do not quite fit. Once again, we are made to measure the gap between what satire tells us to see and what the characters onstage invite us to feel. The result, this time, is tragedy. *Edward II*, as should be clear by now, is far from being the only play for the public stage that deals with homosexual desire. But it is, as Stephen Orgel observes, the only play that invests homosexual desire with any of the anxieties that attend other forms of rebellion against orthodoxy, for example, the intransigence of children against their parents, or the unfaithfulness of wives to their husbands or lovers.[27] Among plays written for the public stage, *Edward II* seems to be unique in setting up a homosexual relationship as an explicit subject and—in a term of current critical jargon—"problematizing" it. We should, therefore, pay particularly close attention to how the play states the problem. What we discover is not a moral issue at all, but a political one. As an enactment of the Myth of Master and Minion, *Edward II* engages three separate questions of power: questions having to do with gender, social class, and the autonomy of individuals vis-à-vis the society in which they live.

Brandishing the letter from Edward that has summoned him home from exile, Gaveston opens the play with a soliloquy that is disarming in its frankness, suasive in its rhetoric, and provocative in the mythic parallel it draws:

> What greater blisse can hap to *Gaveston*,
> Then live and be the favorit of a king?
> Sweete prince I come, these these thy amorous lines
> Might have enforst me to have swum from *France*,
> And like *Leander* gaspt upon the sande,
> So thou wouldst smile and take me in thy armes.
>
> (1.1.4-9)

Edward awaits him with a passion equally intense—and with an equally provocative allusion to classical legend. The friends have their reunion, not in private, but in front of all of Edward's court. Yielding to the social circumstances, Gaveston first offers Edward a subject's obeisance. "What *Gaveston*, welcome," exclaims the startled king:

>   kis not my hand,
> Embrace me *Gaveston* as I do thee:
> Why shouldest thou kneele, knowest thou who I am?
> Thy friend, thy selfe, another *Gaveston*.
> Not *Hilas* was more mourned by *Hercules*,
> Then thou hast beene of me since thy exile.
>
> (1.1.140-145)

Hero and Leander, Hercules and Hylas: the roles in which Edward and Gaveston cast themselves are those of master and minion. In Marlowe's imagination at least, Leander is the "maid in mans attire" who enflames Neptune's lust. Hercules, the very exemplar of virility, and Hylas, the beautiful page boy who sailed with the Argonauts, figure among the famous pairs of male lovers cataloged later in the play by the elder Mortimer. Alone among Edward's nobles, the elder Mortimer proposes that the lords humor Edward in his desires. "The mightiest kings have had their minions," he tells his nephew,

Great *Alexander* lovde *Ephestion*,
The conquering *Hercules* for *Hilas* wept,
And for *Patroclus* sterne *Achillis* droopt:
And not kings onelie, but the wisest men,
The Romaine *Tullie* loved *Octavius*,
Grave *Socrates*, wilde *Alcibiades*:
Then let his grace, whose youth is flexible,
And promiseth as much as we can wish,
Freely enjoy that vaine light-headed earle,
For riper yeares will weane him from such toyes.

(1.4.391-401)

Cast in the role of "frantick *Juno*," Edward's neglected wife Isabel has already drawn the inevitable comparison with Jove and Ganymede (1.4.178-181). "Minion," the contemptuous epithet that the lords always use for Gaveston, is on one occasion used even by Edward himself (1.4.30-31).

In the eyes of the other lords, indeed in their own eyes, Edward and Gaveston play out the roles of "master" and "minion," with all the disparities in power that those roles imply: king over commoner, "male" over "female," man over "boy." Certainly it is from the minions of legend that Gaveston fashions his public identity. In his opening soliloquy he portrays himself as just the kind of frivolous but devious female-boy that we have seen in the Ganymede of *Dido* and the Calyphas of *Tamburlaine, Part Two*. When three poor men walk into his soliloquy straight out of a morality play and beg service from him, Gaveston plays the Nice Wanton: he takes on the horseman and the traveler, with their promises of amusement, but rejects the worn-out soldier. "These are not men for me," he confides when they have gone,

I must have wanton Poets, pleasant wits,
Musitians, that with touching of a string

May draw the pliant king which way I please:
Musicke and poetrie is his delight,
Therefore ile have Italian maskes by night,
Sweete speeches, comedies, and pleasing showes . . . .

The divertissements that Gaveston has in mind sound at first like the pageants that actually greeted Queen Elizabeth when she visited the countryhouses of her courtiers:

And in the day when he shall walke abroad,
Like *Sylvian* Nimphes my pages shall be clad,
My men like Satyres grazing on the lawnes,
Shall with their Goate feete daunce an antick hay.

The Princelye pleasures that kept Elizabeth entertained at Kenilworth Castle in 1575 did, indeed, include some of the Earl of Leicester's retainers decked out as nymphs and satyrs.[28] A boy dressed up as Diana was also scheduled to make an appearance on that famous occasion—but hardly, we must imagine, as the androgynous tease that Gaveston conjures up:

Sometime a lovelie boye in *Dians* shape,
With haire that gilds the water as it glides,
Crownets of pearle about his naked armes,
And in his sportfull hands an Olive tree,
To hide those parts which men delight to see,
Shall bathe him in a spring, and there hard by,
One like *Actaeon* peeping through the grove,
Shall by the angrie goddesse be transformde,
And running in the liknes of an Hart,
By yelping hounds puld downe, and seeme to die.
Such things as these best please his majestie,
My lord.

                                                          (1.1.50-73)

Such salacious images have more to do with Tiberius on the Isle of Capri than they do with Elizabeth at Kenilworth. It is not just the details of Gaveston's scenario but the grandiloquent tone in which he describes it all that links Gaveston's dramatic projects for Edward with Suetonius's life of Tiberius: "He devised in the woods also and groves here and there, certaine places for lecherie and venerous Acts: wherein he had within caves and holow rockes youthes of both sexes standing at receit readie prostitute, in habit of *Paniskes* and *Nymphes*" (p. 99). Though we never get to see them onstage, the younger Mortimer bewails "the idle triumphes, maskes, lascivious showes,/And prodigall gifts" that Edward has squandered on Gaveston (2.2.157-158).

"Lascivious" shows? With good reason does Mortimer find something pornographic in Edward's theatrical extravagance.

The plot of this particular playing out of the Myth of Master and Minion moves, like Suetonius narrating the lives of Nero and Tiberius, like Donne's "motley humorist" surveying the streets of London, from one affront to conventional propriety to another. Gaveston plays the minion's part to the hilt, wearing "a lords revenewe on his backe." He and Edward, congratulating themselves on their exquisite good taste, like to look out the window and make fun of how the other lords are dressed. The richness of Gaveston's wardrobe provokes Mortimer to a comparison not only with Midas but with "*Proteus* god of shapes" (1.4.407, 411). The lovers' fascination with dressing up, with role-playing, with acting things out threatens to drain the world of substance and set up instead the infinite regressions of Ovid's *Metamorphoses*. Edward does not wage real wars, only stage-play wars. Mortimer berates him:

> When wert thou in the field with banner spred?
> But once, and then thy souldiers marcht like players,
> With garish robes, nor armor, and thy selfe
> Bedaubd with golde, rode laughing at the rest,
> Nodding and shaking of thy spangled crest,
> Where womens favors hung like labels downe.

> (2.2.182-187)

Mortimer and the other nobles speak as conventional men who find themselves in the midst of a stage-play world created by a pair of men who refuse to play the usual male roles.

For all that, the role of "minion" does not quite fit Gaveston. Both in age and in the political power he wields, he is *not* a boy. Like Robert Carr and George Villiers, he is too old to be a literal Ganymede. And he enjoys tremendous power, politically over other men and psychologically over his supposed "master" Edward. In Holinshed's *Chronicles*, Marlowe's source for the characters, the plot, and much of the imagery of the play, Gaveston is depicted as a formidable personage:

> The malice whiche the Lordes had conceyved agaynst the Earle of Cornewal still encreased, the more in deede through the high bearing of him, being now advanced to honour. For being a goodly gentleman and a stoute, he woulde not once yeelde an ynche to any of them, which worthily procured him great envie amongst the chiefest Peeres of all the realme . . . .[29]

"A goodly gentleman and a stout": here is no Ganymede. In

Edward and Gaveston we have, not a man and a boy, but two men. The power play between them is nothing so simple as a man exerting dominion over a woman or a king over his subject or a master over a boy.

From the beginning of the play Gaveston presents himself to us frankly as the social opportunist he is: "What greater blisse can hap to *Gaveston*/Then live and be the favorit of a king?" Holinshed, too, is absolutely clear about who controls whom. Though "of nature given to lightnes," the newly crowned Edward, says Holinshed, was restrained in the beginning by the wise advice of his counselors. However,

> having revoked again into England, his olde mate, the said Peers de Gaveston, he received him into most high favoure, creating hym Earle of Cornewall, and Lord of Man, his principall secretarie, and Lord Chamberlaine of the Realm, through whose company & societie hee was suddainely so corrupted, that he burst out into most hainous vices, for then using the said Peers as a procurer of his disordred doings, he began to have his nobles in no regarde, to set nothing by theyr instructions, and to take small heede unto the good governement of the commonwealth, so that within a while, he gave himself to wantonnes, passing hys time in voluptuous pleasure, & riottous excesse, & to help them forward in that kinde of life, the foresaid Peers, who (as it may bee thought, he hadde sworne to make the King to forget himself, and the state, to the whiche hee was called) furnished hys court with companies of Jesters, ruffians, flattering parasites, musitions, and other vile and naughty ribaulds, that the King might spend both dais & nights in jesting, playing, banqueting, & in other filthy & dishonorable exercises: and moreover, desirous to advance those that were like to himselfe, he procured for them honorable offices.
>
> (2:847)

Holinshed's term "olde mate" makes it sound as if we have here a fully sexualized enactment of the Myth of Combatants and Comrades. That we do not find the Gaveston of Marlowe's play as utterly contemptible as the Gaveston of Holinshed's history is testimony to Marlowe's powers as a playwright—and his ability to see character from the inside as well as the outside. So ingenuous is Gaveston in his opening soliloquy that we actually sympathize with his efforts. We understand him. Having secured our good favor by baring his breast to us, Gaveston remains well into the play the most captivating speaker we meet. With their obtuse snobbery and equally obtuse language the lords do little to win us over. Marlowe even loads the case against them by playing on Protestant prejudice. Backed by the Archbishop of Canterbury, alias Popery, the lords force Edward to send Gaveston back into exile. The two friends have a tender scene of leave-taking in which they exchange pictures. Edward's grief prompts Gaveston to a memorable one-line speech: "Tis something to be pitied of a king" (1.4.130). Depending on how an actor chooses to deliver the line, we can see Gaveston here, not as the hard-edged politican he pretends to be, but as a man who has let his guard down and betrayed how desperately he wants to be loved.

The dynamics of gender between Edward and Gaveston are not, then, what the satirists would have us believe about master and minion. In fact, they are the obverse of what they seem from the outside: "female" controls "male." So, too, with the dynamics of social class. When the elder Mortimer pleas with the peers to humor the profligate king, his nephew frames a reply that isolates the real issue:

> Unckle, his wanton humor greeves not me,
> But this I scorne, that one so baselie borne,
> Should by his soveraignes favour grow so pert,
> And riote it with the treasure of the realme,
> While souldiers mutinie for want of paie.

> (1.4.402-406)

It is Gaveston's lowly birth, not the sexual relationship between Edward and Gaveston, that truly enrages the lords. "Minion" seldom passes their lips without a qualifying "base." The reunion scene, in which Gaveston first kisses Edward's hand, then is raised by Edward to an embrace, enacts the conflict before our eyes. Whatever else he may be, Gaveston to the hereditary nobles is a "night growne mushrump" (1.4.286). For the lords, the question of Edward's sexual desire is at bottom, then, a question of political power. As Jonathan Goldberg has argued, what we see in the relationship of Edward to Gaveston is "a travesty of class, not gender." In casting off Isabel and taking on Gaveston, Edward substitutes a man for a woman, but not because the man in question is like a woman. Far from it. The misogyny of *Edward II* does not equate homosexuality and effeminacy; it insists on their separation.[30]

For the lords, it is Gaveston's lowly social station that makes him so threatening. For Edward, it is what makes Gaveston so beguiling. In the Myth of Master and Minion we encounter for the first time in these pages an eroticization of class difference. Male bonding is a phenomenon that transcends class distinctions. Romance is likewise concerned with obliterating class differences in pursuit of a fantasy-world of sexual freedom and sexual pleasure. In Greene's *Menaphon*, in Sidney's *Arcadia*, in Shakespeare's *As You Like It*, shepherds and kings happily inhabit the same landscape. Only in satire, with its insistent attention to the social surface of human experience, does social class become important in articulating homoerotic desire—or, rather, in depicting sodomy. Sodomy, for certain of the satirists at least, is an aristocratic vice. In the Myth of Master and Minion the social distinctions implicit in satire become the very source of erotic power. Perhaps we have here yet another illustration of Foucault's "power-pleasure spiral," the delight that a victim of oppression takes in scandalizing and resisting his oppressors. The more the lords condemn Gaveston as "base," the more ardently Edward defends him. What seems to be eroticized in *Edward II* is not likeness, as it is in the myths of friendship and romance, but difference, as it is in satire. In that coupling of king and commoner the lords, like the satirists, perceive a threat to social order itself. In the orthodox hierarchy of Elizabethan society, power was conceived as a force that properly operates in one direction only, from "higher" to "lower"—from god to mortal, from king to subject, from older to younger, from male to female. The framers of the sixteenth-century sodomy laws saw power in similar terms: as a matter of prohibitions that could control the sexual behavior of the queen's "subjects." 5 Elizabeth, chapter 17, is an attempt to bring sexuality "under the law." With politics, as with gender and social class, *Edward II* demonstrates that power works in two directions.

In several ways Holinshed set Marlowe up to see Edward's sexuality primarily as a political issue. Though he never comes right out and calls Edward a sodomite, Holinshed leaves little doubt, as a rhetorician or as a storyteller, about the nature of Edward's "disorderd doings." The "most hainous vices" with which Gaveston "corrupts" the king, the "wantonnes" to which the king surrenders himself, the "voluptuous pleasure, & riottous excesse" in which he passes his time, the "vile and naughty ribaulds" with whom Gaveston furnishes the court, above all the "filthy & dishonorable exercises" in which the king, his "olde mate," and their cohorts spend their days and nights: all of these phrases come straight out of moral polemics against sodomy.

"Filthy," in particular, is a word one seldom sees in connection with any other moral concern. In saying that Gaveston was "desirous to advance those that were like to himselfe" Holinshed may even be implying a conspiracy of sodomites to take over the government. Not only in the words he chooses but in the way he tells the story, Holinshed insinuates the political issue posed by Edward's sexuality. Since it is not the complete story but only what happened in a given year that dictates the format of the *Chronicles*, Holinshed is able to imply a great deal by juxtaposing one event with another as he moves through the record year by year. And the main thing he keeps interleaving with the story of Edward's debauches is the suppression of the Knights Templars. So striking are the parallels that the first four years of Edward's reign read almost like a double-plot Elizabethan play. The subplot concerning the Knights Templars provides a kind of running commentary on the main plot concerning Edward and Gaveston, even though the two are never directly linked. The "hainous vices" and "filthy & dishonorable exercises" to which Gaveston seduces Edward have their counterpart in the "haynous crimes and great enormities" laid to the Knights Templars. Edward's lords meet in the Knights' headquarters, "in the new Temple," to lay plans for Gaveston's banishment to Ireland. Later, their deliberations about Gaveston's moral character and whether it is safe to summon him home come just before the Knights Templars' trial. Since the Knights "confessed the fame, but not the fact of the crymes layde to theyr charge," they are not executed but are sentenced to "perpetuall penance within certaine Monasteries." Then comes an account of how Edward pretends to sentence Gaveston, sending him to Bamburgh Castle and feigning his imprisonment there to protect his lover from the lords' envy. In Holinshed's *Chronicles*, the politics of Edward's reign are, by and large, *sexual* politics.

And so they are in Marlowe's play. In comparison with the contrived ending of *Dido*, the lack of an ending in "Hero and Leander," and the unsettling ending to *Tamburlaine, Part Two*, *Edward II* is relentless in telling the truth. By facing up to the conflict between one man's sexual desires and the moral precepts of his peers Marlowe gives us nowhere to take refuge: not in satiric laughter, not in philosophical detachment, not in a reactionary political message. Instead, we are allowed to see all sides of the situation: Gaveston's calculations, Edward's devotion, the lords' distress, England's needs as a kingdom. The ambiguities in this state of affairs are never sharper than in Edward's desperate attempts in act 1, scene 4, to keep the lords from banishing Gaveston a second time. Let the lords take over the country, he says. Let the Archbishop of Canterbury become Chancellor, let Lancaster become Admiral of the Fleet, let Mortimer and his uncle become earls, let Warwick become President of the North, Pembroke the President of Wales.

> If this content you not,
> Make severall kingdomes of this monarchie,
> And share it equally amongst you all,
> So I may have some nooke or corner left,
> To frolike with my deerest *Gaveston*.
> BISHOP. Nothing shall alter us, wee are resolv'd.
> LANCASTER. Come, come, subscribe.
> MORTIMER. Why should you love him, whome the world
> hates so?
> EDWARD. Because he loves me more then all the world.

> (1.4.69-77)

Marlowe's genius is to let us see the truth of all sides in turn. In the beginning everything conduces to make us sympathize with Gaveston and Edward: the lords' snobbery, the dictatorial power of the Catholic Church, the fact that no one comes near the dazzling rhetoric that flows from the mouths of Gaveston and Edward. Then our sympathies begin to turn against them: lonely without Gaveston, Edward takes on a substitute minion in Spenser Junior, a self-proclaimed hypocrite who lacks Gaveston's rhetorical brilliance to make up for it; Edward squanders the treasury; he wrongly accuses Isabel of adultery with Mortimer; the Earl of Kent, his own brother and the one unimpeachable moral spokesman in the play, deserts Edward for the nobles; the younger Mortimer emerges as an epic hero and begins to speak with the fiery eloquence of a Tamburlaine. Towards the end of the play, however, the emotional tide shifts yet again. Kent returns to Edward's side. Isabel and Mortimer in fact become the adulterous lovers that Edward has imagined them to be all along, and their motives shift from selfless patriotism to sexual passion and lust for power.

Without doing a thing Edward emerges as the Noble Sufferer. Thanks to all his practice in role-playing, the master rises to the occasion magnificently. When the rebels come to arrest him, they find him in the pose of a world-weary recluse, his kingly robes exchanged for a monk's garb, his head resting in the lap of an abbot.

> Good father on thy lap
> Lay I this head, laden with mickle care,
> O might I never open these eyes againe,
> Never againe lift up this drooping head,
> O never more lift up this dying hart!

> (4.6.39-43)

Who could resist such a *coup de théâtre*? This scene is typical of how Edward stage-manages his downfall with such stunning effect. When the rebels demand his crown, Edward first hands it to them willingly, then snatches it back, then demands that the most ambitious of the rebels step forward and personally take it off his head, and finally resigns it himself in a speech of sterling Senecan sentiments. "Now sweete God of heaven,/Make me despise this transitorie pompe," says the man who has squandered England's treasury on idle triumphs, masques, lascivious shows, and prodigal gifts. Edward's mastery as an actor makes us forget all that. By the end of the play it is not the rebels' accusations but Edward's own estimate of himself that we find ourselves believing: "how have I transgrest,/Unlesse it be with too much clemencie?" (5.1.122-123).

These shifts in imaginative appeal and moral judgment are reflected in the play's imagery, particularly in sexually charged images of naturalness and unnaturalness. In the first half of the play the imagery portrays Edward as an "unnatural" king. The idea is introduced obliquely in Lancaster's question "My lord, why do you thus incense your peeres,/That naturally would love and honour you,/But for that base and obscure *Gaveston*?" (1.1.99-101). The sexual accusation that lurks in these lines is not forgotten when the word is sounded later. "A desperate and unnaturall resolution," Warwick exclaims when Edward says he would rather fight a civil war than send Gaveston back into exile (3.3.217). When so reliable a judge as Kent calls Edward "unnaturall king, to slaughter noble men/And cherish flatterers" (4.1.8-9), the epithet begins to stick. But then come all the shifts in politics and in poetry that turn Edward into a hero. "Unnatural" becomes a description of the rebel side. It is Kent himself, returned to Edward's cause, who calls the nobles' war "this unnaturall revolt" (4.6.9). For having thrown her own husband into prison Isabel becomes in Edward's eyes, and our own, "that unnaturall Queene" (5.1.17). And young Edward, newly crowned king, cannot believe his mother so "unnaturall" as to have murdered his father (5.6.76). What, then, is "natural"? The conventional order of society? Or a man's emotional needs? Marlowe does not make it easy to decide.

Edward's death is the revenge of men who have readier answers to such questions. Put under arrest, stripped of his royal regalia, shuttled from castle to castle, Edward suffers tortures and indignities that we hear described. Only twice do we actually see them onstage, and both times the tortures are sexual. When Mavis and Gurney shave off the king's beard with cold puddle-water, they are ostensibly trying to keep their prisoner from being recognized. They are also symbolically stripping him of his manhood, as Edward himself realizes. Throughout this inverse rite of passage Edward's mind is on the real motive that enflames his tormentors:

> O *Gaveston*, it is for thee that I am wrongd,
> For me, both thou, and both the *Spencers* died,
> And for your sakes, a thousand wronges ile take.

(5.3.41-43)

When death comes at last, the punishment suits the crime. Lightborne (that is, *Luci-fer*, "light-carrier"), an Italian-trained specialist in techniques of murder, designs a death that is invisible, elegantly efficient—and unmistakably allegorical. He specifically orders his accomplices to "get me a spit, and let it be red hote" (5.5.30). Though the speeches and stage directions mention nothing about this spit while Edward is being crushed under an up-turned table, the cry he lets out leaves little doubt that Lightborne puts the spit to just the use specified in Holinshed's *Chronicles*:

> they came sodenly one night into the chamber where hee lay in bed fast asleepe, and with heavie feather beddes, (or a table as some write) being cast upon him, they kept him downe, and withall put into his fundament an horne, and through the same they thrust up into his bodie a hote spitte, (or as other have through the pype of a Trumpet, a Plumbers instrument of yron made verie hote) the which passing up into his intrayles, and being rolled to and fro, burnt the same, but so as no appearance of any wounde or hurt outwardly might bee once perceyved.

(2:883)

The man who cast himself as Hercules welcoming Hylas dies a catamite's death. At issue here is not the fact that Marlowe's Edward is, in psychological terms, a "homosexual," or that, in legal terms, he has committed acts of sodomy, but that, in political terms if not physical terms, he has chosen to play the "boy."

The troublesome raigne and lamentable death of Edward second, King of England: with the tragicall fall of proud Mortimer ends with the rise of Edward III—and a seeming return to principles of social order and sexual orthodoxy. When the young king orders Mortimer's execution, the rebel lord reads his own career in the terms spelled out in the play's full title in the quarto of 1594: having entrusted himself to Fortune's wheel, proud Mortimer first rose to the top and now has fallen to the bottom. In retrospect his life shapes up as a classic *de casibus* tragedy, and he can stride off the stage to his execution with the confidence and composure of a man sure of his own identity.[31] How we should read the story of Edward's "troublesome raigne" and "lamentable death" is less clear. The passion-crazed author of his own doom? Or the victim of evil manipulators? Edward is both. If Hegel is right that the essence of tragedy is to play out the conflict, not of right against wrong, but of two irreconcilable rights against each other, *Edward II* is a tragedy of the highest mark.[32] On the one hand we see the needs of England as a society and the necessity for right rulership; on the other, the needs of Edward as a man and the necessity for love and companionship. That impasse offers no way out but death. Therein lies the tragedy.

Compared with Shakespeare's plays, *Edward II* may at first seem to be offering a less sympathetic portrayal of homosexual desire. The models that Marlowe has used in drawing his characters have, after all, been appropriated from a highly unsympathetic source: not from classical biography or Hellenistic romance, as they are in Shakespeare, but from satire. And his pattern of tragedy, in this play as in *Doctor Faustus*, comes from the dogmatic scheme of rewards and punishments that governs morality plays. The fascination is in how Marlowe puts these two clichés of Elizabethan culture together. Marlowe's sources may be simplistic; the response that *Edward II* invites is not. It is perhaps a measure of Shakespeare's broader, more inclusive vision that his plays always incorporate ways of distancing oneself from homosexual desire, of reconciling homosexual desire with established structures of ideology and power. Such is decidedly *not* the case with Marlowe. He leaves us no way out of Edward's dilemma emotionally or intellectually, no way of reconciling the judgmental ridicule of satire and the sympathetic tears of tragedy. As always in Marlowe, we have in *Edward II* a *double* perspective. Marlowe is both the satirist and the tragedian, both the oppressor and the victim: his protagonist Edward is both a sodomite and a man who feels homosexual desire. Marlowe takes up where the satirists leave off. He accepts the satirists' dismissal of the sexual maverick as a social outcast; at the same time he lets us know what it is like to *be* that outcast. Stephen Greenblatt has argued that Marlowe always discredits his rebel-heroes by ironizing their goals, by exposing how bankrupt those goals really are. In Greenblatt's view, none of Marlowe's heroes finally succeeds in rebelling against the society that contains him.[33] Faustus's metaphysical longings, Tamburlaine's will to power, Barabas's materialism: isolated and exaggerated on the stage, these traits of Renaissance manhood may indeed turn out to be grotesque and risible. With another trait of Renaissance manhood, Edward's homosexual desire, Marlowe goes beyond satirical caricature. Marlowe's portrayal of homosexual desire in the person of Edward II shows us that power can work in more than one direction, that poetic discourse about sexuality can raise questions beyond the reach of moral discourse and legal discourse. By taking up the role of tragic hero, a sodomite can take revenge on the satirists. In *Edward II* Marlowe dares to let the Myth of Master and Minion lay claims on our imaginative sympathy that equal the claims reason lays on our intellect. The straightforward world of rewards and punishments that Edward III sets up in the play's last scene can seem substantial only to someone who does not know the devious ways of erotic desire. The lines that the youthful king speaks over his father's hearse ring with bright simplicity: "let these teares distilling from mine eyes,/Be witnesse of my greefe and innocencie" (5.6.101-102). That final word of the play reverberates ironically indeed.

Even in the poems and plays that end more conventionally, we sense in Christopher Marlowe's works a way of putting homosexual desire into discourse that differs radically from anything we have encountered before. In the Myth of Combatants and Comrades, in the Myth of the Passionate Shepherd, in the Myth of the Shipwrecked Youth, in the Myth of Knights in Shifts, homosexual desire is always contained within the social rules. Even in Illyria the hero carries with him the memory of his port of embarkation and the confident expectation that he will return there. Marlowe's heroes have none of this surety. They act on their desires with no real sense of where those desires will take them. Friendship that must yield to marriage, the firey desire of adolescence that cools with age, the transvestite disguise that is willingly cast aside at the end of the day, the laughter that drowns out the voice of a "Ganymede," the marginal gloss that turns sexual desire into a philosophical metaphor—all of these strategies for having it both ways, for entertaining homoerotic desire but keeping it firmly placed, are rejected. Each of Marlowe's heroes acts on homosexual desire as if his very life depended on it. In the case of Edward, it does. In *Edward II* we not only *see* the conflict between homosexual desire and the social order; we are invited to *feel* it. Marlowe gives us, side by side, a satirist's exterior view of sodomy and a lyric poet's interior experience of homoerotic desire. Of all the progressions marked by the Myth of Master and Minion this psychological shift is the most crucial: Marlowe introduces us to the possibility of a homosexual subjectivity.

CHAPTER SEVEN

THE SECRET SHARER

M e neither woman now, nor boy doth move,
Nor a too credulous hope of mutuall love;
Nor doth it please me to contend with wine,
Nor with fresh flowers my temples round to twine.
But why, O *Ligurinus, why alas*
Doe my rare seene teares ore my cheekes thus passe?
Wherefore in silence, no way fit at all,
Amids my words dos my smooth tongue thus fall?
Now close-cling'd in my nightly dreames I wooe thee,
Now through the grasse of Mars his field pursue thee
So swift of foote, and cruell-hearted thee
Among the streames that ever-moving bee.[1]

English-made cabinet with drawers,

Early seventeenth century; H: 2', W: 1'7", D: 10 3/4" (*above*)
(Victoria and Albert Museum, London, inventory number W37-1927)

Prominent among the pieces of furniture in private chambers was often a cabinet or chest in which personal treasures could be locked up and hidden away, ready to be taken out, handled, and looked at in private or, as a special favor, shown to a friend.

(Photograph reproduced by permission of the Victoria and Albert Museum)

Shakespeare, sonnet 2

as transcribed by an Oxford University man in the 1630s (*top right*)

In two essential ways the earliest readers of Shakespeare's sonnets were unlike us: they were linked to a circle of friends, and they read the poems in manuscript, in handwriting that was familiar and intimate. The hand that had written out the poems was their own or that of a friend. The voice they heard in their heads as they read belonged to that hand.

(Folger MS V.a.170, p. 163; reproduced by permission of the Folger Shakespeare Library)

Shakespeare, sonnet 20

from *Poems written by Wil. Shakespeare Gent.*, ed. Thomas Benson (*bottom right*)
(London: Thomas Cotes, 1640)

The seventeenth-century owner of the Folger volume was clearly puzzled—until he (or she) decided that the poet must have settled his affections on a most unusual lady.

(Reproduced by permission from a copy in the Folger Shakespeare Library)

The Minde. I. D. g. f. [103]

So polisht, perfect, round, and even,
As it slidde moulded downe from Heaven.
Not swelling, like the Ocean proude,
But stooping gently as a floud:
As smooth as oyle powrd forth: as calme
As flowers: and sweete, as drops of Balme.
Smooth, soft, and sweete, and all a flowd
When it may runne to any good:
And when it stayes, it then becomes
A nest of odours, spice, & gummes.
An action winged as the winde:
In rest, like spirits left behinde
Upon a Banke, or field of flowers
Begotten by the winde and showers.
In the fayre Mansion, lett it rest:
Yet know with what thou art possest,
Thou entertayning in thy breast
By such a Minde makst God thy guest.

To one that would dye a Mayd.

When forty winters shall besiege thy brow,
And trench deepe furrowes in that lovely field:
Thy youthes fayre liberty so accounted new,
Shall be like rotten clothes of no worth held.
Then being askt where all thy beauty lies
Where all the lustre of thy youthfull daies:

To say

Poëms.

O therefore love be of thy selfe so wary,
As I not for my selfe, but for thee will,
Bearing thy heart which I will keepe so chary
As tender nurse her babe from faring ill,
  Presume not on thy heart when mine is slaine,
  Thou gav'st me thine not to give backe againe.

A sweet provocation.

SWeet Cytheria sitting by a Brooke,
With young Adonis lovely, fresh and greene,
Did court the Lad with many a lovely looke,
Such lookes as none could looke but beauties Queene.
She told him stories, to delight his eares:
She show'd him favors, to allure his eye:
To win his heart, she toucht him here and there,
Touches so soft, still conquer chastitie.
But whether unripe yeares did want conceit,
Or he refus'd to take her figured proffer,
The tender nibler would not touch the bait,
But smile, and jest, at every gentle offer:
  Then fell she on her backe, faire Queene, and toward
  He rose and ran away, ah foole too froward.

A constant vow.

IF love make me forsworne, how shall I sweare to love?
O, never faith could hold, if not to beautie vowed:
                                    Though

Poëmes.

Though to my selfe forsworne, to thee Ile constant prove,
Those thoughts to me like Okes, to thee like Osiers bowed,
Studdy his byas leaves, and makes his booke thine eyes,
Where all those pleasures lives, that Art can comprehend:
If knowledge be the marke, to know thee shall suffice:
Well learned is that tongue that well can thee commend,
All ignorant that soule, that sees thee without wonder,
Which is to me some prayse, that I thy parts admire:
Thine eye Ioves lightning seemes, thy voyce his dreadfull
Which (not to anger bent) is musick and sweet fire. (thunder
  Celestiall as thou art, O, doe not loy: that wrong:
  To sing heavens prayse, with such an earthly tongue.

The Exchange.
The Mrs Masculine.

A Womans face with natures owne hand painted,
Hast thou the Master Mistris of my passion,
A womans gentle heart but not acquainted
With shifting change as is false womens fashion,
An eye more bright then theirs, lesse false in rowling:
Gilding the object whereupon it gazeth,
A man in hew all Hews in his controuling,
Which steales mens eyes, and womens soules amazeth,
And for a woman wert thou first created,
Till nature as she wrought thee fell a doting,
And by addition me of thee defeated,
By adding one thing to my purpose nothing.
  But since she prickt thee out for womens pleasure,
  Mine be thy love and thy loves use their treasure.

B 4

In three respects Horace's love lyrics must have startled, bothered, and intrigued Renaissance readers. The Roman poet writes about love, not as an idealistic young suitor eager for ungranted favors and untasted delights, but as a jaded man of the world, someone who has traversed Venus's myrtle groves and come out the other side. Nothing could be less like Petrarch praising Laura or Astrophel gazing upon Stella. Furthermore, Horace writes about sexual desire between males with a matter-of-factness that avoids romanticizing that desire no less than it refuses to be embarrassed by it. He drops all the masks. There, simply, it is. Nothing could be less like Aufidius insinuating his admiration of Coriolanus in ardent metaphors, or Barnfield wooing "Ganymede" in the vestments of pastoral, or Musidorus battling Pyrocles in the disguise of an Amazon, or Sir Voluptuous Beast lusting after goats. Finally, for a Renaissance reader able to buy or to borrow a copy for himself, Horace's love lyrics offered an experience of sexual desire quite unmatched by anything we have encountered so far not only in the intensity of that desire but in its *intimacy*. As texts for private reading, Horace's *Carmina* might seem to invite the same kind of socially licensed fantasizing as romance narratives like Sidney's *Arcadia* and Ovidian *epyllia* like Marlowe's "Hero and Leander." But those texts, after all, are third-person narratives. Storyteller and reader band together in looking at "them." The protagonists of the story exist somewhere else, in a fictional place and time that are home to neither storyteller nor reader. In Beaumont's "Salmacis and Hermaphroditus," the most intimate relationship is not between the lovers or even between the reader and the lovers but between the narrator and the reader. With his sensuous turns of phrase and coy wit Beaumont's persona intrudes between us and the lovers from beginning to end. In lyric poems the intimacy, ostensibly at least, is between poet and lover. The reader, if not an out-and-out eavesdropper, is cast as a secret sharer, a privileged witness to someone else's private life.

All three things that distinguish Horace's *Carmina* distinguish also the love poems that were published in 1609 as *Shake-speares Sonnets. Never before Imprinted*. Verbal echoes of Horace's *Carmina*, heard throughout Shakespeare's plays, suggest that Shakespeare had firsthand acquaintance with the Latin text, probably in one of the editions annotated by Denys Lambin.[2] Echoes of Horace in Shakespeare's sonnets are not so direct as in the plays, but Shakespeare's love poems are unlike any other sonnet sequences written in English during the sixteenth century in the very ways that Horace's love poems also differ: they are focused on what love is like after sexual consummation, not before; many of them (in Shakespeare's case, most of them) are addressed, not to a woman, but to another man; and they are nondramatic, subjective, private. Each of these three features has attracted serious critical notice only in our own day.

Thoroughly unconventional in Shakespeare's sonnets is what amounts to an obsession with sexual experience. Stephen Booth's ingenuity has revealed how charged these poems are— even the most idealistic ones—with sexual puns.[3] It is sexual desire, to be sure, that ignites the freezing fires of Sidney, Spenser, Samuel Daniel, and all the other English disciples of Petrarch, but only in Shakespeare's sonnets does sexual desire remain uncontained by spiritual metaphor. Metaphors connect; puns disjoin. The way in which ideology and power are aligned with feeling in most sonnet cycles of the fourteenth, fifteenth, and sixteenth centuries defines a sexuality that satisfied perfectly the idealistic sensibility of the Renaissance. When we look for the transformations that these poems work on sexual desire, we can see at once why they fascinated Renaissance writers and readers: the scenario of indefatigable male pursuing unattainable female serves to focus, and thus control, sexual desire at the same time that it confirms the structures of power in Renaissance society. By investing the objects of their desire with ideal significance Petrarchan poets manage to deprive sexual energy of some of its frightening power to overwhelm. And by directing that energy into sonnets they confirm, as we shall see, the power of men over women. Amid these well tried ways of harmonizing feeling, ideology, and power Shakespeare, like Horace, sounds a distinctly discordant note.

A second difference in Shakespeare's sonnets concerns the objects of desire. As Horace in his odes, Shakespeare in his sonnets uses erotic images quite indifferently in talking about his affections, whether those affections concern his mistress or the male friend to whom most of the poems are addressed. To Renaissance philologists the homoeroticism of Horace's verses proved even more of a challenge than Ovid's *Metamorphoses* or Virgil's eclogues. Some of the humanists fulminated; some of them philosophized; some of them kept a tactful silence. As the commentators go, Denys Lambin, whose edition of the *Carmina* Shakespeare seems to have read, is remarkably matter-of-fact.

For the lines "Me neither woman now, nor boy doth move" Lambin provides this paraphrase:

> After many words the poet declares that he is unsuited and (if I may say so) no longer equipped for love, and according to his judgment and wish he is giving up such fancies, absurdities, and extravagances. He then confesses that he is still under love's power. Even though he ought, at his enfeebled age, to stay away as far as possible from such softness [*a tali mollitie*] and extravagance [*ac nequitia*], he is nevertheless called back to his former wantonness [*ad pristinas lascivias*], set on fire by his love for the boy Ligurinus.[4]

Mollitia (softness, mildness, effeminacy), *nequitia* (worthlessness, badness, extravagance), and *lascivia* (playfulness, sportiveness, wantonness) are not exactly neutral words, but Lambin refrains from the platonizing ingenuity of Christophoro Landino (Venus should turn her attentions instead to Horace's friend Paulus Maximus—young, noble, handsome, virtuous, and eloquent, a latter-day Aeneas worthy of a latter-day Dido) and the moral outrage of Hermannus Figulus ("These people were accustomed to loving boys dishonorably and foully. This infamous and filthy indecency is mentioned by St. Paul").[5] Hermanus Figulus is incensed by sodomy. What bothers Landino is not that Horace talks so frankly about sexual desire, or even that he talks about sexual desire between men, but that he so conspicuously lacks a Renaissance lover's idealism. What Landino would really like to do is transform Horace's odes into Renaissance sonnets.

But not such sonnets as Shakespeare's. Since the eighteenth century, if not before, the homoerotic images in certain of Shakespeare's sonnets have seemed an embarrassment, something that needs to be explained away. "It is impossible to read this fulsome panegyrick, addressed to a male object, without an equal mixture of disgust and indignation": so George Steevens, writing in 1780, on Shakespeare's playful ways with "prick" in sonnet 20. Edmund Malone's reply, drafted ten years later, has remained the standard academic line ever since: "such addresses to men, however indelicate, were customary in our author's time, and neither imported criminality nor were esteemed indecorous."[6] Only with changes in our own time in what counts as "customary" have homosexual readings of Shakespeare's sonnets come to seem anything other than wild imaginings from the likes of Oscar Wilde in "Portrait of Mr W. H." Despite its legalistic exactitude with Shakespeare's diction, Martin Green's *The Labyrinth of Shakespeare's Sonnets: An Examination of Sexual Ele-*

ments in Shakespeare's Language (1974) failed to change many academic minds at the time it was published. Since Joseph Pequigney's *Such Is My Love* (1985) Malone's argument has finally begun to be questioned, however reluctantly. Pequigney makes no compromises with "Renaissance friendship": Shakespeare's sonnets, Pequigney argues, document a sexually consummated love affair between the persona and the male friend about whom most of the poems are written.

Among academic critics, at least in print, Pequigney's argument is still far from being accepted as dogma.[7] Pequigney takes several critics to task for refusing to acknowledge publicly what they have believed about the poems privately. In a preface that has been read by tens of thousands of undergraduates W. H. Auden, for example, insists on the sonnets' "mystical" and idealistic view of the young man and derides attempts to claim Shakespeare for "the Homintern." Yet Auden himself is reported to have confessed to a gathering at Igor Stravinsky's apartment, in the very year he wrote the preface, that "it won't do just yet to admit that the top Bard was in the homintern."[8] If the report is true, Auden's hypocrisy has had especially unfortunate results, since even open-minded psychoanalytic critics like C. L. Barber and Richard P. Wheeler have used him as a homosexual "authority" to discount any physical relationship between Shakespeare's persona and the fair young man of the first 126 sonnets.[9]

For our purposes here, what is important is not whether particular poems and particular passages "prove" that Shakespeare the man did or did not have sexual relations with a certain other man but how the sonnets as poems insinuate sexual feeling in the bonds men in general made with one another in early modern England. Shakespeare's speaker articulates that connection, not through what he does or what he says to the friend directly, but through what he thinks and what he says to us as readers. Shakespeare may have made his living as a dramatist, but, as Heather Dubrow points out, his sonnets are surprisingly undramatic compared to the sonnets of Sidney, Spenser, and Daniel.[10] Seldom are they addressed to another person as if he or she were actually present. Almost never do they arise out of a specific, immediate incident. Rather, they are personal reflections on events that have taken place at some indefinite time in the past, events that have an existence primarily in the poet's mind. Like Horace with his dreams of Ligurinus, Shakespeare's speaker evokes friend and mistress not as real presences, but as mental images. In several sonnets the friend figures as a "shadow" who disturbs the poet's sleep. As a discourser about homosexual desire, the persona of Shakespeare's sonnets might in some ways seem to resemble Virgil's Corydon and Barnfield's Daphnis. Are they not also men who struggle with their desires in the solitude of lyric verse? There are, however, subtle but important differences in the audience to which these voices speak. Virgil's Corydon and Barnfield's Daphnis speak directly to Alexis and to Ganymede. Shakespeare's persona speaks to himself. In both cases we as readers are privileged to "overhear," but in Shakespeare's case we share with the speaker a privacy and secrecy different in degree and in kind from the much more public performance that goes on in pastoral monologues.

Shakespeare's sonnets are, in a special sense, *confessions*. For putting sex into discourse there are, according to Foucault, two grand strategies: *ars erotica*, in which pleasure for its own sake is the subject, and *scientia sexualis*, in which the subject is not pleasure but truth. It is the second strategy—earnest, cerebral, perplexed—that has dominated western discourse about sex. First in religion, then in science, discourse in pursuit of the truth about sex has most often taken the form of confession:

> The confession was, and still remains, the general standard governing the production of the true discourse on sex. It has undergone a considerable transformation, however. For a long time, it remained firmly entrenched in the practice of penance. But with the rise of Protestantism, the Counter Reformation, eighteenth-century pedagogy, and nineteenth-century medicine, it gradually lost is ritualistic and exclusive localization; it spread; it has been employed in a whole series of relationships: children and parents, students and educators, patients and psychiatrists, delinquents and experts.

In these varied circumstances confession has assumed varied forms: diaries, letters, autobiographical narratives, consultation reports, affadavits. The process of taking an instrument of religious discipline and putting it to secular uses began in the sixteenth century. What has changed about confession in the course of this secularization is where the emphasis falls:

> It is no longer a question simply of saying what was done—the sexual act—and how it was done; but of reconstructing, in and around the act, the thoughts that recapitulated it, the obsessions that accompanied it, the images, desires, modulations, and quality of the pleasure that animated it. For the first time no doubt, a society has taken upon itself to solicit and hear the imparting of individual pleasures.[11]

In Shakespeare's sonnets we have, I believe, just such a record of "thoughts," "obsessions," "images," "desires," "modulations," and "quality of the pleasure" as Foucault describes. At least one of the sonnets (number 62, "Sinne of selfe-love possesseth al mine eie,/And all my soule, and al my every part") reads like a confession in the religious mode. Confession in other sonnets is less direct, perhaps, but all the more compelling in how it situates the speaker and what it asks from a reader.

As a way of putting sex into discourse, confession works in three ways: it individualizes the speaker, it assumes that he or she speaks to some kind of authority figure, and it sets as the goal of his or her speaking a revelation of truth. Confession assumes different forms, depending on who stands as the authority figure. In a religious confession—and in the psychiatric "confession" that is its twentieth-century equivalent—the authority figure is a priest or an analyst. In a legal confession he (only rarely she) is a policeman or a judge. If Shakespeare's sonnets are likewise confessions, who is the authority figure? Who listens as the poet speaks about his thoughts, obsessions, images, and desires? In the specific case of confession, as in more general ways, moral discourse and legal discourse about sexuality differ fundamentally from poetic discourse about sexuality in the relationship they set up between audience and authority. In a nice ambiguity, the "confessor" is the one who listens as well as the one who speaks. Likewise with "taking confession": it is a ritual act that *both* communicants perform. The listener to the confessions recorded in Shakespeare's sonnets is not, in fact, an authority figure at all: he, or she, is a collaborator. We as readers become "confessors"; we ourselves "take confession." Speaker and listener are bound together in a pact of secrecy. The speaker of Shakespeare's sonnets, because he asks for our imaginative complicity, ends up confessing *us*.

In the identity assumed by the speaker and in the response they ask from a reader, Shakespeare's sonnets are homologs to private life. All of the myths we have encountered so far in this book are, as it were, in the public domain. Communal experience is the very subject of the Myth of Combatants and Comrades. The Myth of the Passionate Shepherd articulates the sexual desires and, possibly, the sexual behavior of an entire age-group. "Gentlemen readers" as a social group are the assumed audience in the Myth of the Shipwrecked Youth, just as another social group, the young men of a village, were the actual performers of the morris dances and wooing rites that acted out the same temporarily licensed desires. Society—or at least all the people who presume to speak for society—is a dominating presence in the Myth of Knights in Shifts. And the plays in which Marlowe dramatizes the Myth of Master and Minion were conceived as communal experiences from the ground up, as scripts to be acted, heard, watched, thought about, and remembered by men in groups. Shakespeare's sonnets are different. They situate the speaker and the listener within the enlarging sphere of personal privacy and communal intimacy that was being shaped in the sixteenth and seventeenth centuries by several forces: by the consolidation of state authority and the "privatization" that this new sense of "public" implied for life beyond the state's concern, by the Protestant Reformation with its stress on individual religious experience, by the spread of literacy and printing and the private reading that both technologies made possible.[12]

One way of investigating the "history of private life" in the Renaissance, Orest Ranum proposes, is to take stock of "the sites where intimacy flourished." Increasingly in the course of the sixteenth and seventeenth centuries, the houses of people of means—merchants, professionals, and gentlemen as well as noblemen—acquired a new depth. Beyond the public spaces of such houses, beyond the rooms where one received visitors, carried on business, and entertained, there were private chambers, places where one could be alone, where conversations could be enjoyed with one or two intimates, where public life could be left behind by crossing a threshold.[13] Sir Simonds D'Ewes was sequestered in just such a chamber, within the precincts of the Temple, when he shared with a classmate from Cambridge "things . . . that weere secrett as of the sinne of sodomye, how frequente it was in this wicked cittye, . . . especially it being as wee had probable cause to feare, a sinne in the prince as well as the people."[14] Prominent among the pieces of furniture in such chambers was often a cabinet or chest in which personal treasures could be locked up and hidden away, ready to be taken out, handled, and looked at in private or, as a special favor, shown to a friend. Examples of such cabinets, many of them elaborately carved and marquetted, are preserved in the Victoria and Albert Museum in London.[15] Books, flowers, letters, rings, and miniature portraits in jeweled cases were among the souvenirs of intimacy that might be taken out and shared. To find out the secrets of a friend's love life, symbolized in these carefully guarded objects, one had, literally and figuratively, to penetrate a series of protective enclosures: the outer rooms, the private chamber, the ornamental cabinet, the case made of jewels and precious metal within which the image of the friend's lover was set. One can understand King James's sense of outrage when Sir Edward Coke searched the Earl of Somerset's "caskett" and discovered a letter the king had written to his sometime favorite.[16]

It is to this private space, Patricia Fumerton has argued, that Renaissance sonnets belong.[17] The very diction of the poems tells us that. In her analysis of The "Inward" Language in sonnets by Wyatt, Sidney, Shakespeare, and Donne, Anne Ferry has noted that the two commonest metaphors for examining one's inward state are entering a chamber or closet and reckoning one's accounts. Lacking *our* terms for inward experience—"self" as an independent noun, "inner life," "personality," "consciousness," "feeling"—speakers of early modern English most often referred to the contents of the heart as "secrets." That term implies not only that the heart harbors hidden meanings but that a key exists for unlocking those meanings, for making the heart's contents known in words and for revealing those contents to others.[18] Renaissance sonnets, especially those of Sidney and Shakespeare, present themselves as inventories of the poet's heart, as secrets divulged, as confidences shared. The reader, unless he or she happens to be the beloved person addressed by the poems, becomes perforce the poet's confidant. In the act of reading we share the poet's secrets. We play the role of intimate friend.

The physical and psychological circumstances in which we read these poems today are, to say the least, different. Most twentieth-century readers first encounter Shakespeare's sonnets in a book: neatly printed, most likely annotated, cheaply or luxuriously bound, packaged as a commodity that anyone with the money and the inclination can buy, read or not read, preserve or mark up, keep for oneself or give to someone as a present or sell back to the campus bookstore at the end of term. The poems belong to no one in particular, and the book that contains them can be put to a variety of uses. In two essential ways the earliest readers of Shakespeare's sonnets were unlike us: they were linked to a circle of friends, and they read the poems in manuscript, in handwriting that was familiar and intimate. The hand that had written out the poems was their own or that of a friend. The voice they heard in their heads as they read belonged to that hand. For perhaps fifteen years, from the time Shakespeare wrote them until the London bookseller Thomas Thorpe printed them in 1609, Shakespeare's sonnets were *private* poems in a more than figurative sense. They belonged to what twentieth-century scholars, standing on this side of the Gutenberg revolution, have called the "manuscript culture" of early modern England. Before the fifteenth century, all literary culture was manuscript culture. The technology of print, even while making it possible for individuals to buy books of their own and to read them in solitude, served to heighten the contrast between public and private. A manuscript, what was in it and who got to read it, was a radically more personal affair than a book. In the short run at least, print culture actually helped to strengthen manuscript culture by giving it an identity as something gentlemanly and exclusive.[19] By the end of the sixteenth century, when Shakespeare was writing his sonnets, manuscripts were private concerns in a way they had not been before the invention of movable type. Hence Francis Meres's reference in 1598, eleven years before the poems saw print, to Shakespeare's "sugred Sonnets among his private friends."[20]

Two of the sonnets, in fact, comment directly on the manuscript culture in which the poems were originally written and read. Sonnet 77 ("Thy glass will show thee how thy beauties wear"), the better known of the two, seems to have been penned to accompany the poet's gift of a manuscript book on whose "vacant leaves" the friend can leave his "mindes imprint."[21] The speaker's unflinching gaze at the wrinkles the friend can see by looking in the mirror, implicitly reflected in the lines that the friend will ink on the book's "waste bla[n]ks" (77.10), indicates one use of private manuscripts: the noting down of *sententiae*, of thoughts useful to remember. The catalog of clichés that Polonius dictates to Laertes ("these few precepts in thy memory/See thou character. Give thy thoughts no tongue,/Nor any unproportioned thought his act") explains all too clearly why tablets like the one Shakespeare sends to his friend were sometimes called "commonplace books."[22] Quite another use for such manuscripts is indicated by sonnet 122. Here, five poems short of the disenchanted end of the sonnets addressed to the friend, the poet explains why he has refused the gift of a similar book of blank leaves, why he has made bold "to give them from me" (122.11).[23] "Thy guift, thy tables, are within my braine/Full characterd with lasting memory" (122.1-2). Why, then, write it all down? The poet will remember the friend forever—"Or at the least, so long as braine and heart/Have facultie by nature to subsist" (122.5-6). That qualifier, in such sharp contrast to the grand eternizing claims the poet has earlier made for his verse, and for his love, is one of many galled ironies that give bite to the superficially smooth lines of sonnet 122. Has the friend sent the book with expectations that the poet will fill it up with still more poems in praise of his beauty? If so, sonnet 122 illustrates a second use of poems in manuscript, as tokens of courtship and amorous intrigue.[24] The commonplace book associated with Richard Barnfield contains both kinds of poems, moral *sententiae* like Tichbourne's elegy "My prime of youth is but a frost of cares" and fantasies of sexual adventure like "The Shepherd's Confession."

Both of these conventional uses of manuscript poetry, the didactic use prescribed in sonnet 77 and the amorous use implied in sonnet 122, are exemplified in Shakespeare's sonnets as a whole. Sonnets 1 to 19 are hortatory poems, verses of just the sort the poet urges the friend to copy out in his commonplace book. Is it, perhaps, these very poems about the ravages of time that the poet has in mind in sonnet 77? The wise, knowing speaker of the first nineteen sonnets urges the friend to preserve his beauty, in the first fourteen poems by marrying and begetting children, in sonnets 15 and 16 by begetting children but also by allowing the poet to immortalize him in lines of verse, and finally in the last three sonnets of the group by relying on the poet's verses alone. With sonnet 20, marriage, children, and didactic argument are left behind. The ensuing sonnets read like love poems.

As different as they may be in purpose, sonnets 77 and 122 share a common idea about how inadequate poetry is for telling the truth. Central to both poems is a distinction between the mind of the writer and the text that he writes. "The vacant leaves thy mind's imprint will bear," the poet tells the friend in sonnet 77.

> Look what thy memory cannot contain,
> Commit to these waste blanks, and thou shalt find
> Those children nursed, delivered from thy brain,
> To take a new acquaintance of thy mind.

> (77.9-12)

What is so striking in this image of poems as "brain-children" is the *estrangement* the poet feels from his own offspring. Look again, perhaps at some later time, at what you have written, at what has been "delivered from thy brain," and you may not recognize it; you may be obliged to take up "new acquaintance," as with infants who have been "nursed" into children. Perhaps the poet is intimating his own regret at the fulsome panegyrics he wrote in an earlier frame of mind, but a dissociation between the imagining mind and the writing hand occurs often enough in the sonnets to strike the reader of these poems as a general truth. The whole point of sonnet 122 turns on the difference, the now painful difference, between the poet's mental impressions of the friend and the tablet the friend has given him for putting those impressions on paper. Most often in the sonnets this distinction takes shape as simple truth versus painted illusion. As early in the sequence as sonnet 21, "painted beauty" is contrasted with the friend's natural good looks ("my love is as faire/As any other mothers childe") (21.2, 10-11). The contrast between "true plaine words" and "grosse painting" (82.12-13) comes into its own in sonnets 82 to 99, when the narrative context introduces a rival for the friend's attentions, a more facile poet "by spirits taught to write/Above a mortall pitch" (86.5-6). Through all of the sonnets, even the most ecstatic, we are made to confront again and again the gap between imaginative experience itself and the poems the poet writes about that experience. It is this self-consciousness in the sonnets that prompts Joel Fineman to claim Shakespeare as the inventor of the subjectivity we now take for granted in all lyric poetry.[25]

Shakespeare did not lack models, however. It was from Sidney's sonnets, Anne Ferry argues, that Shakespeare learned how to manipulate "inward language" to create such a powerful sense of subjective presence. A "sense" of presence is precisely what both poets create. After elaborately setting in place all the enclosures that separate viewer from portrait miniature and reader from sonnet, Fumerton finds at the heart of both kinds of objects not the promised secrets themselves but only "the artifice of secrecy." The private self is ultimately "unrepresentable."[26] Ferry is closer to the truth, I believe, in frankly accepting that what Shakespeare creates in his sonnets is not inwardness itself—art, after all, is never the real thing—but an *illusion* of inwardness. Shakespeare manages to do that in four ways: by picking up on Sidney's clue and playing up the inadequacies of poetic rhetoric to tell the heart's secrets; by implying major narrative events that happen *between* sonnets, "offstage" as it were, in an "outward" public world somewhere else; by depicting this outward world as vicious and hostile; and by granting his beloved an "inwardness" as strongly implied as the speaker's own.[27] As a result, Shakespeare's sonnets do not so much *express* an inward life as *imply* it.

Not every reader of Shakespeare's sonnets in manuscript was made privy to all of the poet's secrets; not every reader heard the whole story. To judge from surviving manuscripts, such readers must have been few. Where 69 manuscripts datable to before 1700 contain poems by John Donne, only 20 such manuscripts contain sonnets by Shakespeare. Where 150 different poems by Donne were copied out and passed from friend to friend, only 12 of Shakespeare's sonnets exist in seventeenth-century copies. When the multiple copies of individual poems are added up, we are left with nearly 4,000 separate items for Donne—nearly 4,000 instances of a poem by Donne being read, liked, and copied.[28] With Shakespeare's sonnets, or so the surviving manuscripts attest, that happened only 24 times. Only two of Shakespeare's sonnets appear in more than one manuscript, and one of those two sonnets appears in only one additional copy. For all intents and purposes, it was only the sonnet numbered 2 in the 1609 printing ("When fortie Winters shall besiege thy brow") that seems to have had anything like the currency of Donne's love poems in the manuscript culture of seventeenth-century England. Significantly, perhaps, sonnet 2 contains none of the homoerotic imagery that characterizes so many of the other sonnets. Five of the twelve seventeenth-century manuscripts that include sonnet 2 entitle it "To one that would die a maid," and one other manuscript sets it down as "A lover to his mistress."[29] By a few strokes of a collector's pen, Shakespeare's poem about the tyranny of time, spoken by one man to another, could be made over into a *carpe diem* poem of seduction, spoken by a man to a woman. If it occurred to any of the Oxford students and inns-of-court men who put together most of these collections of verse that sonnet 2 might be a poem addressed *to* a person like himself, rather than a poem that could have been written *by* a person like himself, none of the surviving manuscripts indicates it. The compiler would, in that case, have written the poem down for just the opposite reason. In its sententious solemnity, sonnet 2 might have recommended itself to Polonius, who might in turn have recommended it to his son for its sober advice on marrying and begetting heirs. Which way Margaret Bellasys read the poem (she owned the miscellany that is now British Library Add. MS 10309) remains an open question. "Fortie winters" in her version of the poem have advanced to "threescore."

Two other sonnets by Shakespeare had been put to amorous uses—but in print, not in manuscript—before Thomas Thorpe made all of the poems public in 1609. The sonnets that became numbers 138 and 144 in Thorpe's edition had already been printed, along with verses from *Love's Labors Lost* and poems by other writers, as *The Passionate Pilgrim* in 1599, the whole volume being ascribed by the printer to "W. Shake-speare."[30] As a heterogeneous miscellany of poems about love *The Passionate Pilgrim* is not at all unlike the private manuscript miscellanies that have chanced to survive. The printed volume may, in fact, derive from such a manuscript. Shakespeare's poems are interspersed with poems by other writers that struck the collector's fancy. From *The Passionate Pilgrim*, as from the seventeenth-century manuscripts, one would get no idea that most of Shakespeare's sonnets are addressed to a man. The poem that opens *The Passionate Pilgrim*—"When my love swears she is made of truth,/I do believe her though I know she lies"—is one of the sonnets that comes toward the end of the sequence when it was printed complete seven years later. In the context of the 1609 volume, this particular sonnet figures as the twelfth in a series of sometimes playful but often ascerbic poems about the persona's mistress. In the very different context of the 1599 volume it sets a tone of sportive sensuality that sounds through the whole collection. And it establishes a thoroughly heterosexual image of lovemaking that turns even the four poems about Venus and Adonis into amusements that the poet may have contrived to amuse his mistress. Certainly the first poem in *The Passionate Pilgrim* radically alters our twentieth-century understanding of the second. In this context, "Two loves I have of comfort and dispaire" reads like an allegory in which the poet struggles with a desire that is completely heterosexual. When he declares, "The better angell is a man right faire:/The worser spirit a woman collour'd il," a reader has nothing to make him think that these are persons, not personifications. The choice seems to be between loving and not loving, not between loving a man and loving a woman.

The Passionate Pilgrim seems to have made little if any difference in the manuscript culture to which Shakespeare's sonnets still belonged. Even after all the sonnets were published in 1609, it was the same single sonnet, "When fortie Winters shall besiege thy brow," that continued to appear most often in private manuscripts. Only a few of these manuscripts seem to be based on the 1609 quarto; most of them continue the tradition of friends copying poems from friends. A reprinting of *The Passionate Pilgrim* in 1612 takes no account of the 1609 complete edition and even preserves readings that are thought of today as corrupt, such as the couplet of the first poem: "Therefore Ile lie with Love, and Love with me,/Since that our faults in Love thus smother'd be" (sig. A3). It was in the looser form of the manuscripts and *The Passionate Pilgrim* that John Benson reprinted the sonnets in 1640. In addition to the sonnets from the 1609 quarto Benson includes non-Shakespearean poems from *The Passionate Pilgrim*, and he rearranges them all to suit his own taste.

In looking at Shakespeare's sonnets from the point of view of Renaissance readers we have, then, something much more fluid than the 1609 quarto would suggest. For Renaissance readers these were verses *ad hoc* and *ad hominem* with respect not only to the poet, his friend, and his mistress but to *themselves*. Sixteenth-century manuscripts were "properties" of their owners in both the legal and the psychological senses of the word. In the critical parlance of our own day, Shakespeare's sonnets were constantly being deconstructed and appropriated to the interpretations and the uses of different readers. The history of their dissemination in manuscript and print offers a radical demonstration of how a text, once out of a writer's hands, "belongs" to nobody. *The Passionate Pilgrim* is simply the first of these deconstructions to appear in print. More than any other texts we have considered in this book, Shakespeare's sonnets occupy a highly equivocal position on the border between public and private.

With Shakespeare's sonnets, as with Donne's poems, we should perhaps distinguish *degrees* of privacy. Judging from the number of surviving manuscripts and from the particular poems recurring in them, Arthur Marotti proposes that Donne's satires and elegies enjoyed a much wider circulation in manuscript than did the love lyrics that were collected and printed after his death as *Songs and Sonnets*. Beyond the lady (or ladies) so forcefully addressed in the love poems, only a small coterie of Donne's friends must have seen them and then only in loose sheets, as individual poems, and not as an entire collection.[31] To surmise from the few manuscripts that survive, Shakespeare's "sugred Sonnets among his private friends" must have been very private indeed. *Shake-speares Sonnets. Never before Imprinted*: the subtitle to the 1609 quarto says it all. As a complete group these poems had never been made public, had never been bought and sold, had never passed from one stranger's hand to another in exchange for a coin. From manuscripts limited to Shakespeare's "private friends" to manuscripts containing only one or two of the sonnets to *The Passionate Pilgrim* to *Shake-speares Sonnets* to John Benson's edition of 1640: in that progression we can read a transformation of hand and voice into *things*. Personal utterances are turned into commercial commodities. Topical immediacy fades into literary distance. Particularity becomes universality. J. W. Saunders's metaphor about sixteenth-century publishing seems right:

> All through the period of manuscript circulation there was a steady expansion of the reading audience outwards from the first circle of intimates. The widening circulation was a continuous process, like the circular ripples on a pond when a stone disturbs the surface, from the poet's intimates at the source to the unconnected enthusiasts and ultimately the printers on the fringes.[32]

If sixteenth-century printers were on the fringes and sixteenth-century purchasers were beyond that, where do *we* stand as twentieth-century readers? To situate ourselves in Saunders's metaphor is to realize what a huge imaginative distance we have to bridge to see Shakespeare's sonnets in their original social context.

In printing all of Shakespeare's sonnets in 1609 Thomas Thorpe seems to have gone to extraordinary lengths to preserve the "private" character the poems had in manuscript. The purchaser is invited to feel lucky to have laid hands on poems "never before imprinted." Thorpe cryptically signs himself "T— T—" on the title page and dedicates the volume "TO . THE . ONLIE . BEGETTER . OF . THESE . INSUING . SONNETS . Mr. W. H.," setting up a mystery that was probably no more solvable then than now. In styling himself on the dedication page as a "WELL-WISHING . ADVENTURER" who is "SETTING . FORTH," Thorpe may implicitly be casting the *reader* in that role. There is something clandestine about the whole affair. Thomas Thorpe calculated well. If John Donne's poems were made for New Criticism, William Shakespeare's sonnets were made for the Old Historicism. The vast majority of what has been written about the sonnets in the past three hundred and fifty years has been concerned with sleuthing out who is who and what "really" is going on between the lines. The fact that little is known about Shakespeare the man and absolutely nothing about the people he is talking about makes the game all the more challenging.[33]

One other way in which Thorpe may have played up the sonnets' secrecy, lost entirely in twentieth-century reprintings of the poems, is their orthography. When the subject was love and the purpose at hand was intrigue, Renaissance poets would sometimes write out their sentiments in double-speak. In the diaries he kept while a musician and music tutor in several well-to-do households Thomas Whythorne records doing, more than once, just what Maria, Sir Toby, and Sir Andrew do to Malvolio with a forged letter from Olivia in *Twelfth Night*. Enamoured of a rich widow who employed him, though unsure of how she really felt about him, Whythorne sent her a poem that begins:

> Mizdeem mee not wythout kawz why
> Althouh I talk familiarly
> If thus mery I shuld not bee
> Great pryd thei would then judg in mee
>
> I may keep that eevn all the day
> Altyms and howrz in honest way
> And mean nothing az yee mistrust
> To serv az thrall t'obey their lust[.]

Four more stanzas keep insinuating, and yet denying, desire. "I mad this song sumwhat dark & dowtfull of sens," Whythorne notes in his diary, "bekawz I knew not serteinly how shee wold tak it, nor to whoz handz it miht kumen after that she had read it." If she liked what he intimated, she would keep the poem a secret. If she scorned his sentiments or misunderstood them, she might show the poem to others. Either way, Whythorne was safe: "it is so mad as neither shee nor no other kowld mak any great matter thereof, spesially, if I miht hav kum to th awnswering therof."[34] In the sharing of amorous secrets deniability was all. If the right person read them, poems like Whythorne's were full of secret clues that made the amorous message clear. If the wrong person read them, such poems could be taken "straight," as literary exercises. Whythorne was, after all, a professional writer and performer of songs. On other occasions, in other households, with other women, Whythorne used the same strategem, often with notable success.

Whythorne has entered his verses in his diary in a fair italic hand that differs from the secretary hand in which he has written the rest, setting the verse apart as a different kind of discourse. Writers of verse in manuscript had a number of other ways of indicating such differences in discourse and of signaling the presence of secrets: by giving certain words special emphasis, by writing them larger, by putting them in italics, by using capital letters. Olivia's forged letter, for example, includes these lines:

I may command where I adore,
    But silence like a Lucrece knife
With bloodless stroke my heart doth gore.
    M.O.A.I. doth sway my life.

(2.5.103-106)

It is the "alphabetical position" (2.5.117) of the last line that sends Malvolio's ingenuity running—straight into the trap laid for him by his enemies. Just possibly Thomas Thorpe played similar tricks with capital letters when, in exchange for sixpence a copy, he revealed *Shake-speares Sonnets. Neverbefore Imprinted* to a public readership.[35]

The teasing, if teasing it is, begins on page 1 with the first stanza of the first sonnet:

From fairest creatures we desire increase,
That thereby beauties *Rose* might never die,
But as riper should by time decease,
His tender heire might beare his memory.

(1.1-4)

Modern editions almost invariably turn "beauties *Rose*" into "beauty's rose." That way, the line becomes less distracting for a twentieth-century reader to scan, but distraction may be just what Thorpe intended. As it happens, *Rose* is capitalized, though never again italicized, throughout the entire volume. The names of other flowers—lily, violet, marigold, canker—may or may not be capitalized. Rose always is. Does that signify, or does it not? The first response of anyone who has read early modern manuscripts or books firsthand is to doubt it. Only in the late seventeenth century did the orthography of English begin to assume the rule-bound rationality that is still taught in schools today if not always followed in practice. When they talk about capitalization at all, most sixteenth-century authorities on orthography limit their rules for capitalization to the first word in a sentence and to proper names—and then proceed to ignore what they have just said by capitalizing whatever they want to emphasize! John Hart is virtually alone in including among his rules for capitalization "the appellatives of everi notable thing which is to be referred to the discretion or pleasure, of the writer."[36] Add to that the slapdash speed and sloppy proofreading of much early modern printing, and the case for the significance of "beauties *Rose*" looks weak. Stephen Booth speaks for most twentieth-century scholars in regarding the punctuation, capitalization, and italics of the 1609 quarto as "a printer's whims, errors, or idiosyncracies." George Wyndham was clearly imagining a writer with a Victorian education, working with Victorian printers, when he argued more than a hundred years ago that Shakespeare himself must have edited and proofread the 1609 quarto himself because its orthography bespeaks a mind well acquainted with grammatical niceties and Greek and Latin etymology.[37]

Perhaps it is neither a painstaking Shakespeare nor a whimsical typesetter who is responsible for the volume's orthography but wily Thomas Thorpe. Perhaps the capitalization and italics are part of Thorpe's strategy for marketing *Shake-speare's Sonnets* as a revelation of secrets. A reader's suspicions on page 1 that *Rose* refers to some secret personage, some equivalent to Petrarch's Laura/laurel or Sidney's Stella/star, are confirmed when "Sweet Roses" are set in figurative parallel with "you, beautious and lovely youth" (54.11, 13), when "Roses of shadow" are contrasted with the true "Rose" of the friend's beauty (67.8), when the beauty of the friend's "budding name" is likened to "the fragrant Rose" (95.2, 3), when "the deepe vermillion in the Rose" in the poet's verses is said to be "drawne after you" (98.10, 12), when the poet concludes a sonnet by affirming, "For nothing this wide Universe I call,/Save thou my Rose, in it thou art my all" (109.13-14). To read "beauties *Rose*" aright we need to invoke, not orthography or biography, but *rhetoric*. It is not the rules about how people capitalized words in early modern English that are relevant here, or even proofs about who the person beneath the cipher might be, but the effect of these capitals and italics on readers beyond Shakespeare's immediate circle of intimates. "Great letters" could function as a raised eyebrow, a knowing smile, a sly wink. Other aspects of Thorpe's little book—its title, its dedication, its indecipherable connection with the author—suggest that *certain*, though by no means all, capitalizations and italics in the book may be part of its design as a revelation of secrets. By 1609 "Shake-speare" on the title-page was a personage, a commodity of known value. Whom he was writing about may not have been so well known—or even very important. If J. W. Saunders is right that printing a private manuscript was like dropping a stone into a pond and producing circles ever more remote from the poet and his intimates, we should not assume that every purchaser, or even most purchasers of Thorpe's quarto would know who the poet's "Rose" might be. Less important than knowing for sure was the illusion of getting close to a famous person's secrets.

Such secrets as the sonnets yield are revealed only gradually.

At first reading, the situation in the first nineteen sonnets seems straightforward enough: the poet, old enough to know the ravages that time can wreak on beauty, urges a younger male friend to brave Time's tyranny by marrying and begetting children. The speaker and his friend exist in a social universe of two, in a world divided between "you" and "me." Thus, in sonnet 15 ("When I consider every thing that growes/Holds in perfection but a little moment") the speaker describes his own way of defying Time, by creating poems that "counterfeit" the friend's beauty; in sonnet 16 ("But wherefore do not you a mightier waie/Make warre uppon this bloudie tirant time") the speaker turns to the young man and suggests the "mightier way" in which *he* can defy Time, by procreating living images of himself in "lines of life" that will outdo the persona's "pupil pen." All of the early sonnets turn on this separateness of speaker and friend. Speaking across that great divide, the persona defines for his friend a particular sexuality, one way out of many possible ways of conceptualizing sexual desire. The botanical images Shakespeare uses in sonnet 16 are typical of all nineteen sonnets in the opening sequence:

> Now stand you on the top of happy hours,
> And many maiden gardens yet unset,
> With virtuous wish would bear your living flowers,
> Much liker than your painted counterfeit.

> (16.5-8)

Again and again in these early poems the friend's beauty is imaged as a flower (1, 5, 6, 12, 18); his youthfulness, as morning (7), as spring and summer (1, 3, 5, 6, 13, 18), as the Golden Age in Ovid's account of creation ("this thy golden time," 3.12). The sexual vitality of these images is strongest, perhaps, in sonnets 5 ("Those howers that with gentle worke did frame,/The lovely gaze where every eye doth dwell") and 6 ("Then let not winter's wragged hand deface,/In thee thy summer ere thou be distil'd"), where the friend's semen is likened to perfume with which he should "make sweet some viall" (6.3).

As we have seen more than once in connection with Spenser, this was a vision of sexuality supremely satisfying to the Elizabethan imagination: by relating human sexual activity to the regenerative cycle of nature this particular way of imagining sexual desire fuses the physical and the philosophical. In political terms it subordinates individual desire to a higher authority, to the divinely ordained scheme of the universe. The Epithalamion that Spenser wrote for his own marriage, for example, lovingly describes, stanza by stanza, all the activities of the wedding day, culminating in the elaborate ceremonies of preparing bride, bridegroom, and bedchamber that were one of the most sociable features of sixteenth-century weddings. When the guests have all departed and he turns to the physical initiation of his bride and himself, Spenser casts the climactic rite in the same vegetative images that define sexuality in Shakespeare's first nineteen sonnets. He invokes, first, Diana, goddess of the moon that shines through the bed-chamber window, goddess of chastity, goddess of "wemens labours"; then Juno, goddess of wedlock; then Genius, the patron of generation,

> in whose gentle hand
> The bridale bowre and geniall bed remaine,
> Without blemish or staine,
> And the sweet pleasures of theyr loves delight
> With secret ayde doest succour and supply,
> Till they bring forth the fruitfull progeny.[38]

Spenser in his Epithalamion and Shakespeare in his first nineteen sonnets succeed in the one thing that commentators like Landino were most anxious to do in their readings of Latin love poetry: to combine the physical, philosophical, and political aspects of sexual desire into a viable whole. In Foucault's terms, they have coordinated structures of ideology and power with individual feeling to produce a discourse about sex that was intellectually and emotionally compelling to sixteenth-century readers.

In Shakespeare's first nineteen sonnets, if not in Spenser's Epithalamium, the harmony among ideology, power, and feeling is less settled than it first appears. Discordant questions about power and its relationship to feeling are left unresolved. As gestures of rhetoric, Shakespeare's early sonnets seem to be selfless attempts on the persona's part to convince the young friend of a more experienced vision of sexual desire—a view that sees desire in a wider frame of time than an adolescent can. In that sense each sonnet is a gesture of power directed toward two objects: toward time and toward the friend. The couplet of sonnet 15 nicely catches this complexity: "And all in war with Time for love of you / As he takes from you, I engraft you new" (15.11-12).

Many readers have noted the pun here on "engraft": it suggests the Greek root *graphein*, "to write," at the same time that it sets up the images of horticultural grafting in the next sonnet.

Shakespeare's early sonnets are an attempt to impose his vision simultaneously on time and on the friend. Despite the pun, sonnets 15 and 16 keep the two senses of "engraft" entirely separate: the poet creates, the friend procreates. The persona himself keeps his distance from sexual desire. And that is exactly where most editors and critics since Malone have tried to keep him. Then comes sonnet 20:

> A Woman's face with natures own hand painted,
> Haste thou the Master Mistris of my passion,
> A womans gentle hart but not acquainted
> With shifting change as is false womens fashion,
> An eye more bright than theirs, lesse false in rowling:
> Gilding the object where-upon it gazeth,
> A man in hew all *Hews* in his controwling,
> Which steales mens eyes and womens soules amaseth.
> And for a woman wert thou first created,
> Till nature as she wrought thee fell a dotinge,
> And by addition me of thee defeated,
> By adding one thing to my purpose nothing.
>> But since she prickt thee out for womens pleasure,
>> Mine be thy love and thy loves use their treasure.

With this poem four things change dramatically: the ends to which the poet speaks, the language that he uses, the imaginative setting in which he situates himself, and the self-identity he assumes.

Quite suddenly, hortatory verse starts sounding like amatory verse. A reader who is out for secrets is forced to reconsider what he or she has read already. As Pequigney argues, we can see in the first twenty sonnets a progression in which the poet's sexual feelings for the friend, held carefully in check at first, gradually emerge as the poet's real subject. Homosocial desire changes by degrees into homosexual desire. The word "love" first enters the sonnets very obliquely indeed when the poet appeals to the friend's "selfe love" as a motive for begetting progeny (3.8). In sonnet 5 love is still a property of the friend, though more ambiguously so, when the poet remarks "the lovely gaze where every eye doth dwell" (5.2). The personal significance of that word for the poet becomes increasingly clear—and increasingly physical—as he begs the friend to have a child, to create another self "for love of me" (10.13), as he ventures to call him "love" (13.1) and "deare my love" (13.11), as he goes to war with time "for love of you" (15.13), as he defies time to carve wrinkles in "my loves faire brow" (19.9), as he boasts "My love shall in my verse ever live young" (19.14). Is "my love" in this line a name for the friend, or does it refer to the poet's feelings?

"Love" and "my love" emerge after sonnet 13 as the poet's favorite epithets for the young man. Speaking to him and speaking about him, the poet refers to the young man by that title more than twenty times. Only seven times does the poet refer to him as his "friend." "Love," "lover," and "lovely," as Booth points out, were ambiguous if not ambivalent in sixteenth- and seventeenth-century usage. They might or might not suggest sexual desire, depending on the context.[39] The context in Shakespeare's sonnets is, to say the least, equivocal. "Love," on equal terms with "mistress," is likewise how the poet speaks to and about the woman who is the subject of the 27 sonnets printed toward the end in Thorpe's edition. Only once does he call her his "friend." We have, then, two people—and three terms for talking about them. At one extreme is "mistress," with its explicitly sexual reference. At the other extreme is "friend," with its largely nonsexual reference. In between is "love," which can be sexual, or nonsexual, or both. "Two loves I have," declares the poet in sonnet 144,

> of comfort and dispaire,
> Which like two spirits do sugiest me still,
> The better angell is a man right faire:
> The worser spirit a woman collour'd il.

(144.1-4)

We do no more than respect an ambiguity in early modern English if we follow Shakespeare's example and refer to the young man, not as the poet's "friend," but as his "love."

Questions about love reach a crisis—for the poet, for his readers, and presumably for the young man—in sonnet 20. The issue here is easy enough to state but not so easy to decide: is sonnet 20 a *denial* of sexual desire, or is it an *avowal*? The *literal sense* of what the poet says certainly indicates denial. "Love" versus "love's use": the terms the poet/speaker uses to draw his distinctions derive from Aristotle's *Nicomachean Ethics*. *Philia*, the highest of human bonds, is premised on the *equality* of men as one another's peer; *eros*, a lesser bond, thrives on *inequality*, on needs that each partner fulfills for the other. All of the preceding sonnets, we see in retrospect, have been arguments in an implicit debate. In effect, Shakespeare has been addressing the great question in classical ethics that is posed so often in Shakespeare's comedies about courtship: which has the greater claim on a man, friendship with other men or sexual ties with women? The procreational images of the first nineteen sonnets would seem to place the poet/speaker of the first nineteen sonnets squarely with Daphnaeus, the spokesman in Plutarch's dialogue "Of Love" who urges Bacchon to marry. When Daphnaeus says of marriage that there is "no knot or link in the world more sacred and holy," Protogenes, the critic of women and praiser of pederasty, counters with the "higher" values of male friendship:

> This bond in trueth of wedlocke . . . as it is necessary for generation is by good right praised by Polititians and law-givers, who recommend the same highly unto the people and common multitude: but to speake of true love indeed, there is no jot or part thereof in the societie and felowship of women . . . . For amitie is an honest, civill and laudable thing: but fleshly pleasure, base, vile, and illiberal.[40]

Here is just the distinction between "love" and "love's use" that Shakespeare draws in sonnet 20. In Plutarch's dialogue, Bacchon's marriage transpires during the very time the debaters are having their argument, making their conclusion—or rather their lack of one—a moot point.

In sonnet 20 the issue is likewise left unresolved. *What* Shakespeare's speaker says is above reproach; *how* he says it has left many readers since George Steevens uneasy, whatever Edmund Malone may have said to reassure them. There is something playfully salacious about those puns on "thing" and "prick" that distinctly recalls Richard Barnfield's poems. Indeed, the whole conceit of sonnet 20, casting a male in the role most sonnets would assign to a female, recalls Barnfield's sonnet 11 ("Sighing, and sadly sitting by my Love,/He ask't the cause of my hearts sorrowing"). In Shakespeare's sonnet 20, as so often in Barnfield, sexual innuendo seems to be working at cross purposes to moral innocence. To lament that the friend has "one thing to my purpose no-thing" might seem to imply that friendship and sexual passion, "love" and "love's use," are two separate things. The tone, however, makes one wonder just what the persona's "purpose" is. Does he find other parts of the beloved's anatomy more commodious? If Shakespeare is citing Plutarch, he calls him to witness on both sides of the case.

Shakespeare's speaker may side with Plutarch's Daphneus on the issue of "love" versus "love's use," but he echoes Protogenes, Plutarch's homosexual apologist, when it comes to which kind of beauty is superior, male or female. The diptych

that sonnet 20 forms with sonnet 21 is hinged on a contrast between the young man's fresh face "with natures own hand
painted" (20.1) and the "painted beauty" (21.2) that inspires the
muses of most other poets. The implied contrast *within* both
poems is between male and female, as it may be also *between*
them. Male beauty is superior to female, according to Plutarch's
Protogenes, for just the reasons Shakespeare's speaker cites: "it
is not besmered with sweet ointments, nor tricked up and
trimmed, but plaine and simple alwaies a man shall see it, without any intising allurements" (fol. 1133). Whatever suspicions a
reader may have about the sonnet's tone are encouraged by the
capitalizations and italics in Thorpe's edition. "Woman," "Master Mistris," and *"Hews"* are all tricked out as possible code
words, as possible keys to a closely guarded secret that has been
hinted at since "beauties *Rose*" in sonnet 1. The tone of sonnet
20, so troubling to modern readers, seems perfectly consonant
with the myths we have been exploring in this book. In its social, narrative, and rhetorical contexts, sonnet 20 comes across as
an extremely sophisticated version of "Come live with me and
be my love."

There is a sense, then, in which the early sonnets are gestures
of power not just toward time and toward the friend but toward
the poet's own self: they are attempts to convince not only the
friend but the persona himself that the cosmic heterosexuality
exemplified in Spenser's Epithalamion has highest claims on
erotic desire. They argue Elizabethan orthodoxy. For the friend,
the early sonnets are poems of persuasion; for the persona, they
are poems of renunciation. The whole scenario here seems un-
cannily similar to Barnfield's eclogues. We encounter the same
pair of characters, the same implied setting, the same double
sense of time, the same tension between conventional and unconventional sexualities. Like Barnfield's Daphnis toward the
end of the eclogues, Shakespeare's persona in the first nineteen
sonnets speaks as an older man to a younger, as experience to
innocence, as disciplined desire to overpowering beauty. Both
speakers counsel marriage. Implicit, perhaps, in Shakespeare's
luxuriant images of flowers and trees is the pastoral landscape
in which Barnfield plays out his erotic fantasies to their ultimately chaste end. There is the same sharply divided attitude
toward time: both poets celebrate the pleasures of morning, of
spring, of "this thy golden time," but both are just as keenly
conscious of time's destructive power. Finally, both sets of
poems turn on the same conflict between male-male attachments

and heterosexual passion. That is to say, Shakespeare's early sonnets, like Barnfield's eclogues and sonnets, enact the rites of wooing that make up the Myth of the Passionate Shepherd.

Sonnet 20 may be a poem of courtship, but Shakespeare does not stop there. Like Horace, but unlike most Renaissance poets who write about love, Shakespeare goes on to write about what happens when emotional desire becomes physical act. John Donne's love poems, infamous as they may be in this regard, are all about the before ("Come, Madame, come, . . . / Off with that girdle") and the after ("Busie old foole,/unruly Sunne,/Why dost thou thus,/Through windowes, and through curtaines call on us?").[41] They *imply* the physical and emotional realities of lovemaking, but they do not talk about them directly. Those emotional and physical realities are Shakespeare's very subject in the poems that succeed sonnet 20. Quite in keeping with all the other ways in which the sonnets play off experience itself against the words that would inscribe it, sexual experience in the sonnets resides largely in puns. Many of the puns that Stephen Booth has caught and cataloged occur not just once, in individual sonnets, but are sustained through the whole sequence: "have" (52.14, 87.13, 110.9-12, 129.6), "use" (2.9, 4.7, 6.5, 20.14, 40.6, 48.3, 78.3, 134.10), "will" (for male and female sexual organs as well as for sexual desire: 57.13, 112.3, 134.2, 135.passim, 136.passim, 143.13, 154.9), "pride" (for penis: 64.2, 52.12, 151.9-11), and "all" (for penis, likely by analogy with "awl": 26.8, 75.9-14, 109.13-14). As heard by Booth, the couplet to sonnet 109 embodies something more substantial than sentiment:

> For nothing this wide Universe I call,
> Save thou my Rose, in it thou art my all.

(109.13-14)

"All" or "no-thing": when it comes to homosexual puns, most academic readers of Shakespeare's sonnets have insisted on the nothing. Booth gallantly tries to have it both ways, noting the possibility of homosexual doubles entendres but finding a metaphorical excuse for their presence. Of sonnet 98 ("From you have I beene absent in the spring") he says, for example:

> The language of this sonnet and of sonnet 99 ["The forward violet thus did I chide"] is full of unexploited relevance to sexual love . . . . All these senses remain dormant throughout the poem; they function only to the extent that such a concentration of potentially suggestive terms gives a vague aura of sexuality

to the poem and thus . . . reinforces the persistent and essential analogy Shakespeare draws between the speaker's relationship with a beloved and the traditional courtly love poet's relationship with a mistress.[42]

Joseph Pequigney will have none of this. The sonnets to the young man trace the course of a sexually consummated love affair, Pequigney argues, and in the sexual puns of the sonnets about the young man, no less than in the sexual puns of the sonnets about the mistress, Shakespeare is talking about the psychological and anatomical realities of sexual love. As a record of a love affair, the sonnets about the young man tell a three-part story, with a beginning (sonnets 1-19, in which the poet falls in love), a middle (sonnets 20-99, in which the poet's passion "finds fruition in sexual acts"), and an end (sonnets 100-126, in which the poet's love wanes).[43]

In this story of wooing, winning, and ruing, the diptych of sonnets 20/21 is the turning point. Sexual puns introduced in the next several sonnets continue through the one hundred twenty-five that follow. The rite of passage from sexual innocence to sexual experience is marked ceremonially in sonnet 22 ("My glass shall not persuade me I am old/So long as youth and thou are of one date"), with its exchange of hearts from one lover's breast to the other's and its echoes of St. Paul's text on man and wife as "one flesh," appointed in the *Book of Common Prayer* to be read during the marriage rite:

> For all that beauty that doth cover thee,
> Is but the seemely rayment of my heart,
> Which in thy brest doth live, as thine in me.
> How can I then be elder then thou art?
>
> (22.5-8)

If the application of the biblical text seems metaphorical here, it persists as the subtext in all the later sonnets that imagine the friend's relations with the poet's mistress in blatantly fleshly terms, as body closing with body and shutting the poet out. The next sonnet in the sequence worries the distinction between figures of speech and things themselves until it becomes hard to say just where words give place to bodies. With its wordplay on "actor," "part," "fierce thing," "love's strength," and "decay," sonnet 23 makes us see how being (1) an actor in the theater, (2) a player of lovers' word games, (3) a writer of poems, and (4) a performer in bed are all aspects of the same thing:

As an unperfect actor on the stage,
Who with his feare is put besides his part,
Or some fierce thing repleat with too much rage,
Whose strengths abondance weakens his owne heart;
So I for fear of trust, forget to say,
The perfect ceremony of loves right,
And in mine owne loves strength seeme to decay,
Ore-charged with burthen of mine owne loves might.

(23.1-8)

The rival poet who later emerges in sonnets 78 to 86 thus poses a threat to the persona on two fronts: sexual as well as rhetorical. The nine poems in this group are packed with sexual puns on "pen," "will," "spirit," and "pride." The rival poet finds it much easier than Shakespeare's speaker/poet/lover both to make love and to make poems out of love. Alerted by sonnet 23, a reader who is looking out for secrets should be ready by the time he gets to sonnet 26 ("Lord of my love, to whome in vassalage/Thy merrit hath my dutie strongly knit") to see the puns for penis that Booth finds in "show my wit" (26.4), "all naked" (26.8), "tottered loving" (26.11), and "show my head" (26.14).[44] In this context, the linked paired formed by sonnets 27 ("Weary with toyle, I hast me to my bed") and 28 ("How can I then returne in happy plight/That am debard the benifit of rest?"), in which the friend's "shadow" (27.10) haunts the poet in his bed and keeps him from sleeping, figures as Shakespeare's version of Horace toiling in his dreams after Ligurinus. What emerges in the sonnets that follow immediately after 20/21 is not so much a narrative context as a rhetorical one: these poems invite us not only to read *between* the lines, to deduce the story that has inspired them, but in a quite particular way to read *within* the lines, to decode puns and so make ourselves privy to secrets—secrets that are specifically sexual.

Along with the shifts in sonnet 20 in purpose and in language comes a shift in the the implied world of the poems, in the imagined setting within which the persona and his two loves, male and female, play out their drama of sexual desire. The pastoral images of the first twenty sonnets are replaced by chambers and closets (46), beds (27, 142), chests (48, 52, 65), mirrors (63, 77), and clocks (57). The delights of the *locus amoenus* give way to the confidences of the bedchamber. It is in just such a setting that we often overhear Shakespeare's persona in the confessions that succeed sonnet 20. In sonnet 27 ("Weary with toyle, I hast me to my bed") the love appears to the poet in his bed "like a jewell (hunge in ghastly night)" (27.11). The cabinet of secrets that is implicit in this conjunction of bedchamber, jewel, and the sonnet itself as secrets committed to paper is noted explicitly when the poet returns to the same scene later in the sequence. Once the persona begins to imagine his love betraying him, the love-as-jewel turns into something to be locked up, something that must be protected from theft. Setting out on a journey, the persona tells his love in sonnet 48, he carefully stowed away his valuables. But his love—"thou, to whom my jewels trifles are"—cannot be secured so easily:

> Thee have I not lockt up in any chest,
> Save where thou art not though I feel thou art,
> Within the gentle closure of my brest,
> From whence at pleasure thou maist come and part.

(48.5, 9-12)

The image here is like a figure-ground puzzle: it wavers between the figurative idea of the friend's image locked away in the persona's heart and the physical reality of his love enclosed in the persona's embrace. By sonnet 52 images of jewels and chests, of locking things up, have taken on specifically sexual meanings:

> So am I as the rich whose blessed key,
> Can bring him to his sweet up-locked treasure,
> The which he will not ev'ry hour survay,
> For blunting the fine point of seldome pleasure.

(52.1-4)

The jewels here may recall the persona's mental image of his love in sonnets 27 and 48, but the suggestion of appetite in the fourth line, the fear of "blunting the fine point of seldome pleasure," invites us to read the poem in graphically physical terms. The "sweet up-locked treasure" may be not so much an idealized image of his love as a very real part of his love's anatomy.

In this new imaginative space after sonnet 20, questions of public versus private take on an urgency that is absent entirely from the first nineteen poems. As early as sonnet 25 ("Let those who are in favor with their stars,/Of publike honour and proud titles boast") the poet sets up a contrast, often to be repeated, between worldly ostentation and the homely fact of the friends' love for one another. Not always is that separation between public and private felt so happily. Troubled imaginings in sonnet 36 ("Let me confesse that we two must be twaine,/Although our undivided loves are one") of a time when the poet may not

"acknowledge" the friend nor the friend show "publike kind-
nesse" to the poet seem to have less to do with the young man's
possibly higher social station than with "bewailed guilt" on the
part of the poet—dark hints of wrongdoing that are sounded
again in sonnets 88 ("With mine owne weakenesse being best
acquainted,/Upon thy part I can set downe a story/Of faults
conceald" [5-7]), 89 ("Say that thou didst forsake mee for some
falt,/And I will comment upon that offence"), 90 ("Then hate me
when thou wilt, if ever, now,/Now while the world is bent my
deeds to crosse"), 112 ("Your love and pittie doth th'impression
fill,/Which vulgar scandall stampt upon my brow"), 120 ("That
you were once unkind be-friends mee now"), and 121 ("Tis better to be vile then vile esteemed,/When not to be, receives reproach of being").

After the persona's first avowal of sexual desire in sonnet 20,
we would expect, according to the progression of myths we have
been following in this book, a moral or legal intervention, on the
part of the poet's conscience if not from some other person. Even
Barnfield, for all his salacious imaginings, lays aside his illicit
desires for the "higher" concerns of epic poetry—and for marriage. In Shakespeare's sonnets no such thing happens. We hear
nothing about moral reservations. No thought of the law provokes fear. In the course of his self-confessions after sonnet 20
Shakespeare's speaker struggles with problems of authority, to
be sure, but those problems have nothing to do with moral philosophy or the law. They concern instead authority in being the
lover of another man and authority in writing about homosexual
love.

The familiar, even complacent role the poet enjoys in the first
nineteen sonnets ends abruptly after sonnets 20/21: to declare
homosexual desire—and to *act* on it—changes everything. Conventional structures of ideology and power explode; the fragile
proprieties of the first nineteen poems are shattered. In the early
sonnets power is all on the persona's side. His age, his experience, above all his powers as a poet put him in command of the
situation at hand. Both the sonnet as a medium and orthodox
heterosexuality as the message are firmly under his control. As
long as he plays the sage older friend, it is he who is doing the
acting; the young friend's role is to react. Admitting his passion
changes all that. "I" and "you" no longer have their comfortable
separate identity. The poet who doubts his own abilities in sonnet 23 ("As an unperfect actor on the stage") is quite another
person from the poet who confidently went to war with time in

sonnet 15 ("When I consider every thing that growes,/Holds in perfection but a little moment"). Critics customarily speak of the young man as the poet's "friend," but the perplexed relationship described in the sonnets after 20/21 is anything but Aristotle's *philia*, with its easy mutuality between men who are equals.

Different from the first nineteen poems in the relationship they imply between speaker and listener, the love sonnets to the young man differ just as much from the sonnets about the mistress. The frustrated idealism of sonnets 20 through 126 stands in the sharpest possible contrast to the resigned cynicism of the sonnets addressed to the so-called "dark lady." Many of the latter have, indeed, something of Horace's genial urbanity about them. "Therefore I lye with her, and she with me,/And in our faults by lyes we flattered be" (138.12-14): for all their cynicism, sonnets 127 to 154 communicate a mutuality, a sensual understanding between speaker and listener, that so often is painfully not the case in sonnets 20 through 126. Shakespeare devotes 126 highly varied sonnets to the young man and only 28 alternately affable and sarcastic sonnets to the mistress for the same reason that the fourth- and fifth-century Greeks devoted so much more attention in their philosophical writings to the love between men and boys than to the love between men and women: in each case it was the bond between male and male that seemed the more complicated and problematic.[45] Once Shakespeare's poet has declared his passion, the rhetoric of friendship no longer seems adequate. Rapture, jealousy, self-advertisement, self-denigration: the shifting moods and shifting roles of sonnets 20 through 126 run absolutely counter to Renaissance ideas of friendship. Apologists for the sonnets as testimonials to friendship have not read their Aristotle, Cicero, and Montaigne.

Lacking a ready-made rhetoric, Shakespeare's poet has to find his own. With respect to social class, gender, and the rest of society the poet keeps positioning and repositioning himself and the young man he calls "love." The fact that the youth is addressed several times as if he were a nobleman, while Shakespeare himself was at best an upstart gentleman, has been seized upon by all the detectives in pursuit of "Mr. W. H." More important than the friend's actual social status, however, is how the persona uses the language of social difference: he subjectifies it and ironizes it. When the object of his passion was female, a male poet in early modern England faced no such existential problems. He did not have to choose what to say, only how to say it. In sonnet 106 Shakespeare's poet casts himself in the conventional poet's role, as a pillager of the past, as a browser through old manuscripts who puts dusty clichés to fresh uses:

> When in the Chronicle of wasted time,
> I see discriptions of the fairest wights,
> And beautie making beautifull old rime,
> In praise of Ladies dead, and lovely Knights,
> Then in the blazon of sweet beauties best,
> Of hand, of foote, of lip, of eye, of brow,
> I see their antique Pen would have exprest,
> Even such a beauty as you maister now.

(106.1-8)

In "old rimes" it is "Ladies," not "lovely Knights," who are customarily the object of the poet's attentions. If we have let ourselves be seduced by the rhetoric of courtly love, we may be a little startled by the last line of these two glib quatrains, by the incongruity between that distinctly odd verb "master" and the conventional "beauty" that is its syntactical object. Here, in fact, is the same arch tone, the same playful teasing about gender that we encountered in sonnet 20. Is there a pun on that capitalized "Pen" that parallels sonnet 20's pun on "prick"?

"Master Mistris": ambiguities of syntax in that epithet in sonnet 20 are bound up with ambiguities of power in the sonnets as a whole. Are the two words in apposition? Is it "master-mistress" with a hyphen? The line is then a kind of in-joke between persona and friend, as the persona quips about the young man's gender. Is one word subordinated, grammatically and sexually, to the other? Is the young man "the *master* mistress of my passion," as opposed to the persona's "lesser" mistress, the woman of sonnets 127 to 154? The line in that case becomes a witty compliment of the sort the persona has been serving up in the previous nineteen poems, but it also foreshadows the dark jealousies of persona-love-mistress as a *ménage à trois*. If we bite Thomas Thorpe's bait and accept "W. H." as a cipher for the young man addressed in these poems, it is worth remembering that the abbreviation "Mr." in late sixteenth-century orthography more likely stands for "Master" than "Mister."

Whichever way we read the phrase, the word "master" points up the reversal of meaning that has overtaken the word "mistress" since the Middle Ages. In the context of courtly love "mistress" originally designated the lady as a setter of tasks for her servant-knight. By Shakespeare's time, however, the word had taken on the specifically sexual meaning of "a woman who illicitly occupies the place of wife" (OED 11)—and with that meaning all the Judeo-Christian assumptions about the husband as "head" of the wife (Ephesians 5:22-23). The earliest citations in the *Oxford English Dictionary* all occur in contemptuous contexts that see compliant woman as a source of pleasure for predatory man. Mistress Quickly fails to make the OED, but the title fits her perfectly. The difference between the literal and the secondary meanings of the word "mistress" turns, indeed, on whether the lady has granted sexual favors or not. If she holds off, she remains in control, a "mistress" in the original courtly sense; if she gives in to the suitor's desires, she gives up her power and becomes a "mistress" in the secondary sexual sense. Questions of power are neatly decided by the question of sex or no sex.

If *Paradise Lost* celebrates the fortunate fall, Petrarchan sonnets celebrate the fortunate refusal. At first glance, the scenario of suitor prostrate before his mistress would seem to give all the power to the lady. She, after all, has the prerogative of saying no. That much is only natural. Among animals at least, it is females that do the choosing of sexual partners. There is a very good biological reason why that should be the case: in the great scheme of things sperm are plentiful, eggs are scarce. The physical consequences of sexual activity are much more serious for a female animal than for a male. Females have a right to be choosy.[46] From the social games they played if not from the observations they made of animals, Renaissance sonneteers seem to have recognized this basic fact about rituals of courtship. At the very beginning of the sonnet tradition, in Dante's *La Vita Nuova*, we discover a fundamental anomaly: the poet may be firmly in control of his medium, but he is not in control of the lady. The medium becomes, then, a way of extending control from poem to person. A sonnet shows us poetry in just the terms that Renaissance critics like Sidney and Puttenham best understood it: as a species of oratory, an art of persuasion.[47] It is a strategem on the suitor's part to bend the lady's will to his own. It is a male's attempt to defy the dictates of biology. It is Art's revenge on Nature.

The lady may have the prerogative of saying no, but, for the persona at least, her power stops there. In holding off she in fact gives the male speaker just the opportunity he needs to celebrate his own prowess: to make a public display of his feelings, to show off his ingenuity as a poet, to turn the woman with her disconcerting *otherness* into a manageable image in a poem. The dramatic conventions of the Renaissance sonnet grant the lady a reality only as an object of the male persona's desires. "Look into thy heart and write": Sidney's advice to himself indicates just where the writer's interest—and the reader's—lies, not on the lady but on the suitor. The poet, not the mistress, is the *subject*, in every sense of the word. Seen in its rhetorical context, a Petrarchan sonnet is a power ploy of speaker over listener; seen in its social context, it is a power-ploy of a man over a woman; seen in its sexual context, it is power-ploy of male over female. Change the gender of the listener from female to male, and all of the delicate alliances of feeling, ideology, and power are called into question. "Master Mistris": Shakespeare's yoking together of those two words reminds us that there is no real equivalent in English for a man as a lover of a man. "Master" comes with all the suggestion of superior power that "mistress" implies, but with none of the suggestion of sexual subjection. In a relationship between two men, of what use are the conventional terms "master" and "mistress"? Who exercises power over whom?

If the rhetoric of courtly love fails him, Shakespeare's poet is equally dissatisfied with the roles assigned to lovers by the Myth of Master and Minion. "Lord of my love," the persona addresses the friend in sonnet 26, "to whome in vassalage/Thy merrit hath my dutie strongly knit." Only when the friend returns some mark of favor will the persona "boast how I doe love thee" (26.1-2, 13). So humble is the persona's posture that one might take sonnet 26 as an exercise in polite convention, as an appeal for money perhaps or as a cover letter for other poems, if the persona did not elsewhere present himself even more abjectly—and even more sarcastically. Sonnet 57 asks in mock-sincerity,

> Being your slave what should I doe but tend,
> Upon the houres, and times of your desire?
> I have no precious time at al to spend;
> No services to doe til you require.

(57.1-4)

If we trust our ears, we may suspect that the nature of those "services" is sexual. Sixteenth-century pronunciation facilitates a pun on "hours"/"whores" (the friend may require such services from other retainers besides the speaker), spending time "at all" can be read as a noun as well as an adverb, and "to do" is one of the sonnets' commonest circumlocutions for "the act of generation." Sonnet 58 continues the conceit of vassal/slave—and the pun on "hour" that renders it sexual:

> That God forbid, that made me first your slave,
> I should in thought controule your times of pleasure
> Or at your hand th'account of houres to crave,
> Being your vassail bound to staie your leisure.

(58.1-4)

With the same edge of irony sonnet 110 ("Alas 'tis true, I have gone here and there,/And made my selfe a motley to the view") casts the friend as "a God in love" to whom the persona is "confin'd" as a votary (110.12). The persona is at his most vulnerable, perhaps, in sonnet 94 ("They that have powre to hurt, and will doe none"). His willingness to put down his guard, to give himself up to his love's frightening power, seems all the more remarkable when compared with the persona's self-containment in the first nineteen sonnets. One hears in sonnets 26, 57-58, and 94 proof of Sir William Cornwallis's warning in his essay "Of Friendship and Factions": "That part of Friendship which commaunds secrets I would not have delivered too soone, this is the precioussest thing you can give him, for thereby you make your selfe his prisoner."[48] In other sonnets the poet tries on the roles of lord and vassal the other way around. During love-making (if we grant "have" its sexual force) it is the persona who plays the monarch: "Thus have I had thee as a dreame doth flatter,/In sleepe a King, but waking no such matter" (87.13-14). And in 114 the persona wonders whether he always puts the best appearance on whatever his love has done because, "being crown'd with you," his mind "doth . . . drinke up the monarks plague this flattery" (114.1-2).

On other occasions, in other moods, Shakespeare's poet turns from the political roles of lord/vassal and vassal/lord to roles inscribed by the family. Is there something of the father, as well as the friend, in the persona who speaks in sonnets 1 through 19? That role is implicit later on, in paired sonnets 33 ("Full many a glorious morning have I seene,/Flatter the mountaine tops with soveraine eie" and 34 ("Why didst thou promise such a beautious day"), both of which turn on a pun between "Sun" and "son." In general, however, the heavy mantle of father does not rest well on the speaker's shoulders after sonnet 20. Being older and wiser serves his purpose as long as he is emotionally disengaged, but once he has given in to desire years and experience become a cause for regret. Among the most bitter of the sonnets is 37, in which the persona looks at his love's sexual exploits "as a decrepit father takes delight/To see his active childe do deeds of youth" (37.1-2).

If not friend and friend, if not knight and lady, if not master and minion, if not father and son, who *are* the lovers to one another? A more complicated tie than all the rest is implied in sonnet 82. Complaining about the rival poet who has threatened his sovereignty since sonnets 20/21, Shakespeare's poet concedes,

> I Grant thou wert not married to my Muse,
> And therefore maiest without attaint ore-looke
> The dedicated words which writers use,
> Of their faire subject, blessing every booke.

> (82.1-4)

It may, in this instance, be the gender of the poet's muse that inspires an allusion to marriage, but in other sonnets the poet needs no such excuse. "So shall I live, supposing thou art true,/Like a deceived husband" (93.1-2), he confesses in sonnet 93. The poet as husband and his love as wife keep their metaphorical identities through the whole sonnet, until they acquire truly mythic dimensions at the end: "How like *Eaves* apple doth thy beauty grow,/If thy sweet vertue answere not thy show" (93.13-14). In the very next poem the roles are reversed. As a gesture of submission, as an act of obeisance spoken in third person, as a return to the argument of the earliest sonnets in urging the poet's love to "husband natures ritches from expence," sonnet 94 implicitly casts the *love* as husband and the *poet* as wife. Sonnet 97 ("How like a Winter hath my absence beene") seems to do the same, as the poet contrasts "the teeming Autumne big with ritch increase" with his own feelings of sterility and emptiness:

> Yet this aboundant issue seem'd to me,
> But hope of Orphans, and un-fathered fruite,
> For Sommer and his pleasures waite on thee,
> And thou away, the very birds are mute.

> (97.5-8)

In the metaphors of sonnets 82, 93, 94, and 97 we find overt expression of a subtext that Stephen Booth sees running through the whole sequence. The paradox avowed in sonnet 36 ("Let me confesse that we two must be twaine,/Although our undevided loves are one") and affirmed in the exchange of hearts and the sharing of one identity in sonnets 22, 34, 39, 42, 62, 109, 134, and 135 is the very mystery that makes a sacrament of human marriage. "Ye husbands love your wives, even as Christ loved the Church and hath given himself for it": St. Paul's words in Ephesians 5:25-33 were appointed in the Elizabethan *Book of Common Prayer* to be read at the end of the marriage rite when there was to be no sermon.

> For this cause shall a man leave father and mother, and shall be joined unto his wife, and they two shall be one flesh. This mystery is great, but I speak of Christ and the congregation. Nevertheless, let every one of you so love his own wife, even as himself.[49]

St. Paul may have been talking primarily about a religious mystery; the 1559 *Book of Common Prayer* is quite explicit—much more explicit than its twentieth-century counterpart—in talking about the mysteries of sex. Matrimony, the priest says in his greeting,

> is not to be enterprised nor taken in hand unadvisedly, lightly, or wantonly, to satisfy men's carnal lusts and appetites, like brute beasts that have no understanding, but reverently, discreetly, advisedly, soberly, and in the fear of God, duly considering the causes for which matrimony was ordained.
>
> (p. 290)

Of those three causes—procreation, avoiding fornication, and giving "mutual society, help, and comfort" (pp. 290-291)—the first two are concerned with sex. After such a preamble, one can understand why the spiritual metaphor of "one flesh" in Ephesians 5 would have such physical force, why listeners like Shakespeare would find it easier to remember the fleshly vehicle than the spiritual tenor. It is Ephesians 5, and "The Form of Solemnization of Matrimony" in which it is embedded, that provides the context for one of Shakespeare's most famous sonnets. "Let me not to the marriage of true mindes/Admit impediments": sonnet 116 is an implicit answer to what the priest is instructed to say before anything else to the man and the woman who have presented themselves for marriage:

> I require and charge you (as you will answer at the dreadful day of judgment, when the secrets of all hearts shall be dis-

closed) that if either of you do know any impediment why ye may not be lawfully joined together in matrimony, that ye confess it.

(p. 291)

One word of the priest's charge, "impediment," sounds out in sonnet 116. Two other words, "secrets" and "confess," inspire the sonnets as a whole. Like the marriage of man and wife in the *Book of Common Prayer*, "The marriage of true minds" in sonnet 116 may have a physical as well as a spiritual aspect. "True minds" can mean not only the true "affections" (OED II.15.b) that readers conventionally find in the phrase, but the true "intentions" (OED II.14) of two people who present themselves for marriage before a priest. Only twice in the sonnets addressed to the mistress does Shakespeare's poet make even the remotest allusion to these marriage texts from the *Book of Common Prayer*.[50]

What we can observe in the course of the first 126 sonnets is, then, a constantly shifting attempt on Shakespeare's part to bring structures of ideology and structures of power into the kind of viable alignment with feeling that we find in more conventional love poetry. In the sonnets Shakespeare seeks to speak about homosexual desire with the same authority that Petrarch assumes in speaking about heterosexual desire. In pursuit of that end Shakespeare invokes three different modes of discourse: Horace's language of erotic experience, the traditional language of courtly love, and the language of Christian marriage. On very few points are those three languages in accord. Shakespeare's sonnets to the young man not only record what happens between the speaker and his love; the sonnets also play out the conflicts and inconsistences in the conventional ways the poet has for explaining what happens—to himself, to his love, to us as sharers of his sexual secrets. Shakespeare's sonnets test the limits of the love sonnet as a genre. In the hands of other sixteenth-century poets, sonnets serve to confirm those interlocking structures of power and ideology—and feeling—that define Renaissance heterosexuality. In testing the soundness of those structures Shakespeare tests also the verse form in which the structures that define sexuality are turned into words and are made accessible to the imagination. To take the terms of courtly love and Christian marriage and apply them to a subject to which they do not conventionally belong is to force a reexamination of both the terms and the subject. Society may dictate the terms, but the use to which Shakespeare has put those terms is a radical choice. The result is, or can be, something *new*. In *Shakespeares Sonnets. Never before Imprinted*. we have an exercise in the "conditioned and conditional freedom" held out by Pierre Bourdieu's idea of social *habitus*. Out of the already tried "strategies" open to him as a writer, out of the "matrix of perceptions, appreciations, and actions" that he shared with his contemporaries, Shakespeare improvised a new form of discourse.[51] It will not do to say that Shakespeare's sonnets cannot be about homosexual desire since no one else in early modern England addressed homosexual desire in just these terms.

Using a new imaginative vocabulary to talk about an old subject brings Shakespeare to a conclusion altogether different from that of poets in other sequences of sonnets. Traditional sonnet sequences control sexual desire by transcending it: caught up in an impossible conflict between his own hot desire and the lady's cold disdain, the Petrarchan poet turns desire into art and lover's lust into philosopher's zeal. Only Spenser manages to have it both ways by actually marrying the lady in question. In the matter of closure, as in everything else, Shakespeare's sonnets present an anomaly. How critics read the ending seems to depend very much on how they have been filling in the narrative gaps along the way. C. S. Lewis speaks for older, idealistic critics when he singles out sonnet 144 ("Two loves I have of comfort and dispaire") and sees a psychomachia between Comfort and Despair going on through all the poems. The sequence ends "by expressing simply love, the quintessence of all loves whether erotic, parental, filial, amicable, or feudal."[52] From a psychoanalytical point of view C. L. Barber and Richard P. Wheeler find special significance in sonnet 114 ("Or whether doth my minde being crown'd with you/Drinke up the monarks plague this flattery?") and its articulation of the persona's hard-won "self-*regard*, with all that implies as against entire dependence on the regard of the friend."[53] For Pequigney the sonnets' end is the affair's end. The two pairs of parentheses that take the place of a final couplet in the quarto printing of sonnet 126 ("O Thou my lovely Boy who in thy power,/Doest hould time's fickle glasse[,] his sickle, hower") are, Pequigney proposes, pregnant with meaning. They imply that "the poet is entering upon a course of gradual detachment or falling out of love. The parenthetical message might then be translated, 'the rest is silence.'"[54] Showing how rhetorical devices in the poems serve to communicate psychological states, Heather Dubrow compares the last two poems printed in the quarto, verses whose ultimate inspiration is not Petrarch but Anacreon, with the Epithalamium that Spenser puts at the end of the *Amoretti*. In both cases the reader encounters a shift in genre and a stepping back from the intense emotionality of the earlier poems. But the subject of sonnets 153 ("*Cupid* laid by his brand and fell a sleepe") and 154 ("The little Love-God lying once a sleepe,/Laid by his side his heart inflaming brand") is "the very impossibility of achieving distance from love and the inaccessibility of any finality, any cure." Perhaps, then, there *is* no closure.[55]

If, on the other hand, we look at the poems as an attempt to read homosexual experience in the idiom of courtly love and according to the ideals of Christian marriage, the volume of *Shake-speares Sonnets* ends by making us realize, and feel, the void between sexual experience and the metaphors we have to talk about it. "O Thou my lovely Boy": the poet's parting gesture toward the lover whose fickleness has caused him such anguish is to give up the whole enterprise, to fall back on a cant term, to look at sodomy from the outside and to see it as an act of aggression. The fact that Shakespeare's poet takes the power on himself makes the ending all the bleaker. Once he took up arms against Time in defense of the young man's beauty. Now he joins forces with Nature, "soveraine mistress over wrack" (126.5), in envisioning the young man's destruction. "O thou minnion of her pleasure," he sneers as he gives up the struggle and lays down his pen (126.9). Here is anything but the "mutuall render only me for thee" (125.12) that the poet has desired and the lover has refused. The other person, Shakespeare's poet discovers, remains an*other* person, forever fugitive from all attempts to fix him in imagination. We come away from the sonnets with a sense that the conflicts of ideology and power are never really resolved. Horatian odes, Petrarchan sonnets, the Christian marriage rite: none of these can tell the whole truth about sex. Out of all the homosexualities studied in this book, the homosexuality inscribed in Shakespeare's sonnets is the most compelling because it is not end-stopped. The enjambment of Shakespeare's lines with life continues even when we have come to the sonnets' end.

What is *not* cast aside at the end of the sonnets is the fact of sexual desire. In this respect the Myth of the Secret Sharer is different from all the other modes of poetic discourse in this book. If these myths do not close with an absolute denial of homosexual desire, as with The Shipwrecked Youth and Knights in Shifts, they end with the isolation of the hero who persists in acknowledging that desire. One thinks of Antonio in the Myth of Combatants and Comrades, of Virgil's Corydon and his English-speaking imitators in The Passionate Shepherd, of Edward II in Master and Minion. "Me neither woman now, nor boy doth move,/Nor a too credulous hope of mutuall love": if by the end Shakespeare's persona finds himself in the position of Horace's urbane lover, he does so not for any of the reasons that isolate the other heroes. It is not structures of power or structures of ideology, social disapproval or moral dogma, that set him apart, but problems of authority. He is alone in his subjectivity. Like Montaigne, Shakespeare remains acutely aware, as none of his English contemporaries seem to be, that sexuality is something we can know only "in circumlocution and picture." It is this self-conscious subjectivity that puts the Myth of the Secret Sharer closest of all six myths to our own experience of sexual desire in the twentieth century.

With Shakespeare's sonnets the several progressions outlined in chapter 1 come to an end. From the universal ways of express-ing male bonding in human society that we surveyed in chapter 2 we have arrived at an eroticized form of male bonding specific to the culture of early modern England. The sexual potentiality in male bonding, steadily mounting through the sequence of six myths, reaches a literal and figurative climax in Shakespeare's sonnets. Devious metamorphoses of desire in the first five myths end in the confidences of the Secret Sharer. When homosexual desire has become its own explicit subject, we have completed the move, in social terms, from license to licentiousness. We have moved also from public ways of playing out homosexual desire to private ways, and from forms of symbolic discourse that were "legible" to all early modern Englishmen, illiterate and literate alike, to forms of discourse that were accessible only to a small, highly sophisticated readership. In psychological terms, that narrowing of social focus entails a move from con-scious control of sexual desire toward greater daring and risk, not only politically but artistically. In the Myth of the Secret Sharer we witness the invention of a new mode of discourse about homosexual desire where none existed before. In chrono-logical terms, finally, we have moved from seasonal rituals that antedate written records to an experience of sexual desire that seems distinctively modern. Our survey has extended from ex-pressions of desire that were current throughout the sixteenth and seventeenth centuries to one that is highly idiosyncratic to its author and to its historical moment. Shakespeare's sonnets could not have been written thirty years earlier. Thirty years later they were not being understood.

It would be nice to end this book on a triumphant note, to celebrate the fact that Shakespeare, once and for all, broke through the cultural constraints of his time in portraying homosexual desire with such candor and subtlety. Sadly, that is not case. Shakespeare may have subverted the sexual rules of early modern English society, but most writers and readers have not been able to follow him in that act of rebellion. The anomalous quality of Shakespeare's sonnets seems to have been apparent from the very beginning. References to them among contemporary readers are in fact few; transcriptions into commonplace books are rare; imitations by other poets are almost nonexistent. The 1609 first printing was apparently enough to satisfy demand until 1640, when John Benson published *Poems written by Wil. Shakespeare Gent.*[56] To produce a marketable commodity Benson tried several ways of bringing Shakespeare's sonnets in line with Caroline taste. First, he rearranged them, so that any sense of an underlying plot is destroyed. Next, he supplied many of the sonnets with a title (e.g., Sonnet 122, "Upon the receit of a Table Booke from *his Mistris*"), turning each poem into a little move in the game of courtly love, into a conventional task that the poet has set for himself. Other sonnets he regrouped under thematic headings: "The glory of beautie," "Injurious Time," "True Admiration," to take the first three. Sonnets treating the same theme he sometimes printed continuously, sometimes singly, so as to give an impression of formal variety. From *The Passionate Pilgrim* he incorporated Shakespeare's verses from *Love's Labours Lost* as well as poems attributed to Shakespeare but assigned today to other writers. Finally, Benson changed certain of the masculine pronouns to feminine. Given Benson's other manipulations of Shakespeare's text, it is surprising how seldom this radical editing is necessary. In addition to sonnet 122, he supplies misleading titles for sonnet 125 ("An entreatie for her acceptance") and sonnets 113-114-115 (printed continuously as "Selfe flattery of her beautie"). In effect, Benson depersonalizes and "de-privatizes" the poems, turning the "I" who speaks them into a generic type, into a universal Lover. The object of this Lover's desires becomes an equally unspecific Mistress. The success of Benson's editing can be witnessed in a copy of *Poems written by Wil. Shakespeare Gent.* now in the Folger Shakespeare Library. Manuscript notes in an almost contemporary hand amplify the spirit of the editor's own emendations. Benson's title for sonnet 20 ("The exchange") was not quite enough, however, to explain away all the paradoxes of the "master mistress." The seventeenth-century owner of the Folger volume was clearly puzzled—until he (or she) decided that the poet must have settled his affections on a most unusual lady. "The M^{ris} Masculine" reads the owner's clarification.

All in all, Benson's Shakespeare would have been quite at home on the shelf next to Edmund Waller. That was just the form in which readers of the sonnets, such readers as there were, encountered the text until George Steevens reprinted the 1609 quarto more than a century later, in 1766. Steevens's disgust at sonnet 20 has been noted already. Edmond Malone's edition of 1790, with its reassuring remarks on what was "customary" in Elizabethan England, helped to ease such doubts. With his full critical apparatus of preface and notes, Malone reinstated the "I" who had been obliterated by Benson—but in a guise that was acceptable to the middle-class readers of late eighteenth-century England.[57] By and large, that is still the guise in which most readers imagine the persona today. To us, the poet of Shakespeare's sonnets may seem much more sophisticated psychologically and rhetorically than he did to Malone, but the "I" who speaks in these poems has never quite shed the middle-class values that Malone attributed to him in 1790. It was with thanks to Malone that Wordsworth could say of the sonnets, "With this key Shakespeare unlocked his heart," and open up these formerly closed texts to Romantic and post-Romantic readers, who imagine the persona of the sonnets to be just such a person as themselves. Until they were taken in hand by Malone, Shakespeare's sonnets were "marginal" texts like those that feminist critics of the past twenty years have been excavating and rehabilitating, or in many cases habilitating for the first time. We don't have to rediscover Shakespeare's sonnets as texts, but we do have to rediscover them in their sixteenth-century cultural context, as discourses of homosexual desire. Malone, and most readers after him, have not been quite so outspoken as Steevens in their responses to the sexual subject of the sonnets. Instead, they have quietly contrived to *contain* these poems, not within the culture of sixteenth-century England, but within their own culture's ways of understanding the relationship between male bonding and homosexual desire. The most recent is Joel Fineman, who argues that Shakespeare uses the *rhetoric* of Platonizing homosexual desire to create a thoroughly heterosexual subjectivity.

Benson's edition of 1640 is a sign that the cultural moment of Shakespeare's sonnets had passed, that the ambivalent alliances between male bonding and sexual desire that demanded such sensitive and varied treatment in poetic discourse was beginning to assume the schematic opposition that finally emerged as social dogma in the late eighteenth century and has remained in effect until today: a supposition that male bonding and male homosexuality are opposites, not different aspects of the same psychological and social phenomenon. Shakespeare's sonnets address the connection between male bonding and male homosexuality with a candor that most readers, most male readers at least, have not been willing to countenance. If that connection now seems clearer, this book will have done in a small way what Shakespeare's sonnets did so much more expansively in the sixteenth century: out of already familiar characters and plots, ideas and feelings it will have created a more liberally imagined world for one of the many modes of human sexual desire.

NOTES

CHAPTER ONE

1. Henry Hawkes, *A relation of the commodities of Nova Hispania, and the maners of the inhabitants* (1572), printed in Richard Hakluyt, *The Principall Navigations, Voiages and Discoveries of the English Nation* (London, 1589), facsimile reprint, intro. David Beers Quinn and Raleigh Ashlin Skelton (Cambridge: Cambridge Univ. Press, 1965), 2:548.

2. Roger Scruton, *Sexual Desire* (London: Weidenfeld and Nicolson, 1986), p. 187. R. A. Padgug advances a similar argument, but substitutes "human culture" for "rationality" in "Sexual Matters: On Conceptualizing Sexuality in History," *Radical History Review* 20 (1979): 3-23.

3. *Essais*, 3.5 (1580-1588), trans. John Florio (1603), ed. Thomas Seccombe (London: Grant Richards, 1908), 3:81. Compare Donald Frame: "this is an action that we have placed in the sanctuary of silence, from which it is a crime to drag it out even to accuse and judge it. Nor do we dare to chastise it except roundaboutly and figuratively." *The Complete Works of Montaigne* (Stanford: Stanford University Press, 1967), p. 644.

4. Montaigne, *Essais*, trans. Florio, ed. Seccombe, 3:82, 83. The last sentence reads in the original: "Mais de ce que je m'y entends, les forces et valeur de ce Dieu se trouvent plus vives et plus animées en la peinture de la poësie qu'en leur propre essence." *Oeuvres complètes*, ed. Albert Thibaudet and Maurice Rat (Paris: Éditions Gallimard, 1962), 826.

5. Michel Foucault, *The History of Sexuality*, vol. 1: *An Introduction* (1976), trans. Robert Hurley, (New York: Pantheon, 1978): 105-106. Vol. 2: *The Use of Pleasure*, trans. Robert Hurley (New York: Pantheon, 1986), shifts the beginning of an analytical interest in sex from the nineteenth century to fifth-century Greece. Vol. 3: *The Care of the Body*, trans. Robert Hurley (New York: Pantheon, 1986), takes up Greek and Roman discourse written under Roman rule, including Galen, Plutarch, and Seneca. In Vol. 4: *L'Aveu de la chair* (English translation still forthcoming in 1990), Foucault traces the transformation of Greek and Roman ideas in early Christianity, with St. Paul, Tertullian, and St. Augustine.

6. Quoted in A. L. Rowse, *Simon Forman: Sex and Society in Shakespeare's Age* (London: Weidenfeld and Nicolson, 1974), p. 20. For a detailed analysis of Forman's dream see Louis Adrian Montrose, "'Shaping Fantasies': Figurations of Gender and Power in Elizabethan Culture," rpt. in *Representing the English Renaissance*, ed. Stephen Greenblatt (Berkeley: Univ. of California Press, 1988), pp. 31-64.

7. The classic account of Renaissance ideas about the four humors is

E. M. W. Tillyard's in *The Elizabethan World Picture*, Vintage Books ed. (New York: Random House, n.d.), pp. 66-79. See also Julia Briggs, *This Stage-Play World: English Literature and Its Background 1580-1625* (Oxford: Oxford Univ. Press, 1983), pp. 20-24.

8. Transcribed in Rowse, *Simon Forman*, p. 79. Translations from Forman's Latin are mine.

9. *The History of King Lear*, Sc. 2, 123-128, in William Shakespeare, *The Complete Works*, gen. ed. Stanley Wells and Gary Taylor (Oxford: Clarendon Press, 1986), p. 1031.

10. Foucault, *History of Sexuality*, 1:100.

11. John Boswell, "Revolutions, Universals, and Sexual Categories," *Salmagundi* 58-59 (1982-83): 89-113; rpt. in *Hidden from History: Reclaiming the Gay and Lesbian Past*, ed. Martin Bauml Duberman, Martha Vicinus, and George Chauncey, Jr. (New York: New American Library, 1989), pp. 17-36.

12. Vern L. Bullough, *Homosexuality: A History* (New York: New American Library, 1979), p. 2: "Even if homosexuals returned to their anonymity, homosexuality would not disappear; it would simply give those segments of society that do not want to face the reality the illusion that it had. It does exist, however, and as far as history can tell us, it has always existed." Bullough's assumptions are even more clearly stated in *Sexual Variance in Society and History (Chicago: Univ. of Chicago Press, 1976), where Bullough defines his subject as "a history of attitudes* toward sex and their relationship to certain forms of stigmatized sexual *behavior*" (p. viii, emphasis added).

13. In addition to Foucault's *History of Sexuality*, see Jonathan Katz, *Gay American History* (New York: Thomas & Crowell, 1976); Jeffrey Weeks, *Coming Out: Homosexual Politics in Britain from the 19th Century to the Present* (London: Quartet, 1977), and "Discourse, Desire, and Sexual Deviance: Some Problems in the History of Homosexuality," in *The Making of the Modern Homosexual*, ed. Kenneth Plummer (Totowa, N.J.: Barnes & Noble, 1981), pp. 76-111; David M. Halperin, "Sex Before Sexuality: Pederasty, Politics, and Power in Classical Athens," in *Hidden from History*, pp. 37-53; Robert Padgug, "Sexual Matters: Rethinking Sexuality in History," rpt. in *Hidden from History*, pp. 54-66; and David F. Greenberg, *The Construction of Homosexuality* (Chicago: Univ. of Chicago Press, 1988), especially pp. 482-499. A good account of the essentialist versus constructionist debate, with full bibliographical references, is provided in the editors' Introduction to *Hidden from History*, pp. 1-13. See also Stephen O. Murray, "Homosexual Acts and Selves in Early Modern Europe," in *The Pursuit of Sodomy: Male Homosexuality in Renaissance and Enlightenment Europe*, ed. Kent Gerard and Gert Hekma (New York: Harrington Park Press, 1989), pp. 457-477, and Gregory A. Sprague, "Male Homosexuality in Western Culture: The Dilemma of Identity and Subculture in Historical Research," *Journal of Homosexuality* 10.3/4 (1984): 29-43. The issues are not without contemporary political implications, as Steven Epstein points out in "Gay Politics, Ethnic

Identity: The Limits of Social Constructionism," *Socialist Review* 17 (1987): 9-54. On the one hand, academic writers seem to be moving toward a consensus that "homosexuality" is a cultural construct; on the other hand, political activitists are implicitly assuming that homosexuality defines an essential category when they campaign for the civil rights of "gay people" as an ethnic minority.

14. All three taxonomies, Boswell argues, were known in Western Europe during the Middle Ages. Boswell's book on *Christianity, Social Tolerance, and Homosexuality* (Chicago: Univ. of Chicago Press, 1980) demonstrates how the Type A polymorphous assumptions of classical antiquity gave way to rigid Type C condemnations of homosexuality during the thirteenth century and after.

15. Foucault, *History of Sexuality*, 1:23-24, 33-34, 54-55. See also George Chauncey, Jr., "From Sexual Inversion to Homosexuality: Medicine and the Changing Conceptualization of Female Deviance," *Salmagundi* 58-59 (1982-83): 114-146.

16. Alan Bray, *Homosexuality in Renaissance England* (London: Gay Men's Press, 1982), pp. 16-17. On ways of conceptualizing homosexuality see pp. 12-32. The same warning against being blinded by our own typology is voiced by Arthur N. Gilbert, "Concepts of Homosexuality and Sodomy in Western History," in *Historical Perspectives on Homosexuality*, ed. Salvatore J. Licata and Robert P. Petersen (New York: Stein & Day, 1981), pp. 57-68.

17. Eve Kosofsky Sedgwick, "Across Gender, Across Sexuality: Willa Cather and Others," *South Atlantic Quarterly* 88 (1989): 53-72.

18. Martin Bauml Duberman, Martha Vicinus, and George Chauncey, Jr., eds., *Hidden from History: Reclaiming the Gay and Lesbian Past* (New York: New American Library, 1989).

19. "Celle-ci, il ne faut pas la concevoir comme une sorte donnée de nature que le pouvoir essaierait de mater, ou comme un domaine obscur que *le savoir* tenterait, peu à peu, dévoiler. C'est le nom qu'on peut donner à un dispositif historique: non pas réalité d'en dessous sur laquelle on exercerait des prises difficiles, mais grand réseau de surface où la stimulation des corps, l'intensification des plaisirs, l'incitation au discours, la formation *des connaissances*, le renforcement des contrôles et des résistances, s'enchaînent les uns avec les autres, selon quelques grandes stratégies de *savoir* et de pouvoir." Michel Foucault, *Histoire de la sexualité*: vol. 1: *Le volonté de savoir* (Paris: Gallimard, 1976), p. 139, emphasis added.

20. *Basilicon Doron. Or His Majesties Instructions to His Dearest Sonne, Henry The Prince*, 2d ed. (1603), ed. James Craigie, Scottish Text Society 3d ser., no. 16, 1 (Edinburgh: Blackwood, 1944): 65.

21. Reprinted from the original letter in James's own hand (Bodleian MS Tanner 72.f.14 and dated conjecturally to December 1623) in *Letters of King James VI & I*, ed. G. P. V. Akrigg (Berkeley: Univ. of California Press, 1984), p. 431. See also James's letter to Robert Carr, Earl of Somerset, written after Carr had turned on the king: "For I am far from

thinking of any possibility of any man ever to come within many degrees of your trust with me, as I must ingenuously confess ye have deserved more trust and confidence of me than ever man did: in secrecy above all flesh, in feeling and unpartial respect, as well to my honour in every degree as to my profit. And all this without respect either to kin or ally or your nearest or dearest friend whatsomever, nay immovable in one hair that might concern me against the whole world. And in those points I confess I never saw any come towards your merit: I mean in the points of an inwardly trusty friend and servant." P. 336, from a copy (Lambeth Palace Library MS 930), apparently of a lost holograph, dated by Akrigg to early 1615.

22. Here is Phillip Stubbes's account in *The Anatomy of Abuses*: "In the fields and suburbs of the cities they have gardens, either paled or walled around about very high, with their arbours and bowers fit for the purpose . . . . And for that their gardens are locked, some of them have three or four keys a-piece, whereof one they keep for themselves, the other their paramours have to go in before them, lest haply they should be perceived, for then were all their sports dashed . . . . These gardens are excellent places, and for the purpose; for if they can speak with their darlings nowhere else, yet there they may be sure to meet them and to receive the guerdon of their pains: they know best what I mean." Quoted in Rowse, *Simon Forman*, p. 55.

23. John H. Gagnon and William Simon's general ideas about sexual scripts are set forth in chapter 1, "The Social Origins of Sexual Development," in *Sexual Conduct: The Social Sources of Human Sexuality* (Chicago: Aldine Press, 1973), pp. 1-26; the three "levels" of scripts are introduced in their article "Sexual Scripts," *Society* 22 (1984): 53-60.

24. Wolfgang Iser, "Representation: A Performative Act," rpt. in *Prospecting* (Baltimore: Johns Hopkins Univ. Press, 1989), pp. 236-248; "The Play of the Text," rpt. in *Prospecting*, pp. 249-261; and *The Act of Reading: A Theory of Aesthetic Response* (Baltimore: Johns Hopkins Univ. Press, 1978), pp. 53-106.

25. In Sidney's view a "poet" is both a "prophet" and a "maker": "The Greeks called him a 'poet,' which name hath, as the most excellent, gone through other languages. It cometh out of this *poiein*, which is, to make . . . ." Sir Philip Sidney, *A Defence of Poetry* (c. 1581, ptd. 1595), ed. J. A. Van Dorsten (Oxford: Oxford Univ. Press, 1966), p. 22. Implicitly at least, Sidney extends his ideas to oral tradition when he confesses his delight in the ballad of Chevy Chase. The verbs he uses in his discussion of stage-plays suggest that he thinks of them as being seen and heard rather than read.

26. This distinction between deeds and desires is central to James A. Brundage's consideration of *Law, Sex, and Christian Society in Medieval Europe* (Chicago: Univ. of Chicago Press, 1987). In *Homosexuality: A Philosophical Inquiry* (Oxford: Basil Blackwell, 1988) Michael Ruse, like Brundage, makes a distinction between feelings and behavior, between inclination and acts, in his survey of the moral positions that philoso-

phers have taken on homosexuality, pp. 176-202. It was not until the late eighteenth century, when Jeremy Bentham sat down to consider the matter privately on paper, that any post-classical philosopher seems to have thought about the desires that inform the deeds that generate such moral controversy. For a full account of Bentham's writings on the need for reform in the laws against homosexuality—writings that remain unpublished to this day—see Louis Crompton, *Byron and Greek Love: Homophobia in 19th-century England* (Berkeley and Los Angeles: Univ. of California Press, 1985), pp. 12-62.

27. Ruse, *Homosexuality*, p. 17.

28. David F. Grenberg,*The Construction of Homosexuality* (Chicago: Univ. of Chicago Press, 1988).

29. *Middle English Dictionary*, ed. Sherman M Kuhn and John Reidy, Pt. G (Ann Arbor: Univ. of Michigan Press, 1963), p. 9, offers this as the primary definition of the noun "gai": "Joyous, merry, gay; light-hearted, carefree; also, wanton, lewd, lascivious." In the *Oxford English Dicitonary* citations of uses in modern English ("Addicted to social pleasures and dissipations. Often *euphemistically*: Of loose or immoral life") are dated no earlier than 1637 (OED, s.v. "gay.")—leaving a curious gap for the sixteenth century. Roger Scruton's lament over "the kidnapping and debauching of the innocent word 'gay'" in a *Times Literary Supplement* review of *The State of the Language,* ed. Leonard Michaels and Christopher Ricks (Berkeley: Univ. of California Press, 1980), prompted a series of letters pointing out sexually defined uses of the word "gay" long before it was appropriated in the twentieth century by homosexual men and women to define themselves. Scruton's review, "English and where it's at," appeared in *TLS* no. 4013 (22 February 1980), pp. 211-212. Letters followed from Wayne Dynes, *TLS* no. 4016 (14 March 1980), p. 294; Michael Cameron Andrews, *TLS* no. 4021 (18 April 1980), p. 441; Colin Watson, *TLS* no. 4025 (16 May 1980), p. 556; J. C. Bryce and Derek Parker, *TLS* no. 4027 (30 May 1980), p. 614. Dynes's letter makes a particularly important point: "The tendency toward semantic shift is a universal property of natural languages. Statistically, it follows that changes in meaning are not accomplished primarily by minorities, but only with the consensus of the (presumably) heterosexual majority. The word 'bad' is a case in point. As Zupicka noted, in an opinion followed by the majority of etymologists, this commonest of all modern English pejorative adjectives derives from the Old English for 'hermaphrodite: male homosexual.' The evil originally imputed to a sexual minority has been universalized. Could one ask for a clearer case of the linguistic oppression imposed by the majority on a sexual minority?" Far from violating an innocent word, then, men and women who describe themselves as "gay" have made a violent word innocent: they have taken what was, in effect, an insult and turned it into a badge of pride. (In connection with Dynes's example, one thinks of the way "bad" has been transformed in Black American slang into a superlative for "good.")

30. Denis De Rougemont, *Love in the Western World*, trans. Montgomery Belgion, rev. ed. (New York: Harper, 1974), p. 18.

31. Pierre Bourdieu, *Outline of a Theory of Practice*, trans. Richard Nice (Cambridge: Cambridge Univ. Press, 1977), pp. 72-95. Bourdieu himself puts his general concept to specifically literary use in "Flaubert's Point of View," in *Literature and Social Practice*, ed. Philippe Desan, Priscilla Parkhurst Ferguson, and Wendy Griswold (Chicago: Univ. of Chicago Press, 1988), pp. 211-234.

32. Robert Padgug, "Sexual Matters: Rethinking Sexuality in History," rpt. in *Hidden from History*, pp. 54-66.

33. "Homology" is Lucien Goldmann's way of answering the huge question left open by Marx: just *how* material reality interacts with intellectual and artistic culture. See *Towards a Sociology of the Novel*, trans. Alan Sheridan (London: Tavistock, 1977), pp. 156-160.

34. D. W. Robertson's argument in *A Preface to Chaucer: Studies in Medieval Perspectives* (Princeton: Princeton Univ. Press, 1962) that medieval literature is to be understood as an illustration of medieval moral doctrine has inspired a whole school of criticism of Renaissance literature as well. After studying nearly one thousand years of evidence in *Law, Sex, and Christian Society in Medieval Europe*, James A. Brundage concludes that the history of the religious and secular laws governing sexuality in Western Europe is by and large the story of the church and the state adapting to changes in society (p. 5).

35. "The philosopher, therefore, and the historian are they which would win the goal, the one by precept, the other by example. But both, not having both, do both halt. For the philosopher, setting down with thorny arguments the bare rule, is so hard of utterance and so misty to be conceived, that one that hath no other guide but him shall wade in him till he be old before he shall find sufficient cause to be honest. For his knowledge standeth so upon the abstract and general, that happy is that man who may understand him, and more happy that can apply what he doth understand. On the other side, the historian, wanting the precept, is so tied, not to what should be but to what is, to the particular truth of things, that his example draweth no necessary consequence, and therefore a less fruitful doctrine. Now doth the peerless poet perform both: for whatsoever the philosopher saith should be done, he giveth a perfect picture of it in someone by whom he presupposeth it was done, so as *he coupleth the general notion with the particular example*." *A Defence of Poetry*, ed. Van Dorsten, pp. 31-32, emphasis added.

36. "The ideas of the ruling class are in every epoch the ruling ideas: i.e., the class which is the ruling *material* force of society, is at the same time its ruling *intellectual* force. The class which has the means of material production at its disposal, has control at the same time over the means of mental production, so that thereby, generally speaking, the ideas of those who lack the means of mental production are subject to it." *The German Ideology* (1846), in *The Marx-Engels Reader*, ed. Robert C. Tucker (New York: Norton, 1972), p. 136.

37. William H. Masters and Virginia E. Johnson, *Human Sexual Response* (Boston: Little, Brown, 1966), pp. 3-8.

38. In addition to the works by Bray, Boswell, and Bullough, already cited, see James M. Saslow, "Homosexuality in the Renaissance: Behavior, Identity, and Artistic Expression," in *Hidden from History*, pp. 90-105.

39. "There is no art delivered to mankind that hath not the works of nature for his principal object, without which they could not consist, and on which they so depend, as they become actors and players, as it were, of what nature will have set forth. . . . Only the poet, disdaining to be tied to any such subjection, lifted up with the vigour of his own invention, doth grow in effect another nature, in making things either better than nature bringeth forth, or, quite anew, forms such as never were in nature, as the Heroes, Demigods, Cyclops, Chimeras, Furies, and such like: so as he goeth hand in hand with nature, not enclosed within the narrow warrant of her gifts, but freely ranging only within the zodiac of his own wit." *A Defence of Poetry*, ed. Van Dorsten, pp. 23-24.

40. Rictor Norton, *The Homosexual Literary Tradition: An Interpretation* (New York: Revisionist Press, 1974), p. 17.

41. Joseph Pequigney, *Such Is My Love: A Study of Shakespeare's Sonnets* (Chicago: Univ. of Chicago Press, 1985), p. 1.

42. A. L. Rowse, *Homosexuals in History: A Study of Ambivalence in Society, Literature, and the Arts* (New York: Carroll & Graf, 1977). On the Renaissance see pp. 6-69.

43. Robert K. Martin, *The Homosexual Tradition in American Poetry* (Austin: Univ. of Texas Press, 1979), pp. 51-52.

44. The issues of subjectivity and hidden agendas are addressed by several anthropologists in James Clifford and George E. Marcus, eds., *Writing Culture: The Poetics and Politics of Ethnography* (Berkeley: Univ. of California Press, 1986). See particularly the essays by Mary Louise Pratt, pp. 27-50; Renato Rosaldo, pp. 77-97; and James Clifford, pp. 98-121. Linda Hutcheon regards the writer's frankness about his or her situatedness as one of the strengths of postmodern ways of writing history and literary criticism. See *A Poetics of Postmodernism: History, Theory, Fiction* (New York: Routledge, 1988), pp. 74-86. On the question of whether one has to be gay to write gay criticism see the exchange between David Van Leer, "The Beast of the Closet: Homosexuality and the Pathology of Manhood," *Critical Inquiry* 15 (1989): 587-605, and Eve Kosovsky Sedgwick, "Tide and Trust," *Critical Inquiry* 15 (1989): 745-757.

45. The study I have undertaken here is "historicist" because, unlike formalist New Criticism in the 1930s or Deconstructionism in the 1970s, it insists on putting literary texts in historical context, "new" because it asks questions that seem vital to us in our own moment in history. Stephen Greenblatt introduces the term "New Historicism" and discusses the critical method it entails in *Genre* 15 (1982): 1-4. Greenblatt's

own book on *Renaissance Self-Fashioning* (Chicago: Univ. of Chicago Press, 1980) draws on social history and psychoanalytic theory to explore how six English writers arrive at a sense of self in their works. Cf. also Louis Adrian Montrose's review of Greenblatt's book, "A Poetics of Renaissance Culture," *Criticism* 23 (1981): 349-359. In effect, the New Historicism is a kind of "historical anthropology" that takes imaginative literature, rather than living informants, as its subject. New Historicist critics seem to be divided on the question of whether the cultures they study are closed systems or whether they are open to improvisation, innovation, and change. On this issue see Jean Howard, "The New Historicism in Renaissance Studies," *English Literary Renaissance* 16.1 (1986): 13-43. On the grounding of these theoretical differences in Saussure's linguistic distinction between *langue* and *parole* see Stuart Hall, "Cultural Studies: Two Paradigms (1980), rpt. in *Culture, Ideology, and Social Process: A Reader*, ed. Tony Bennett, Graham Martin, Colin Mercer, and Janet Woollacott (London: Batsford, 1981), pp. 19-37, and Jonathan Culler, "Semiology: The Sausserian Legacy," pp. 129-143, in the same volume.

46. In addition to Foucault and Bray, see Guido Ruggiero, *The Boundaries of Eros: Sex Crime and Sexuality in Renaissance Venice* (New York: Oxford Univ. Press, 1985), and Judith Brown, *Immodest Acts: The Life of a Lesbian Nun in Renaissance Italy* (New York and Oxford: Oxford Univ. Press, 1986).

47. On women's sexual mores as a reflection of male, not female, values see Juliet Dusinberre, *Shakespeare and the Nature of Women* (London: Macmillan, 1975), pp. 51-62, 110-136; Lisa Jardine, *"Still Harping on Daughters": Women and Drama in the Age of Shakespeare* (Brighton: Harvester Press, 1983), pp. 37-67; and Coppélia Kahn, "The Cuckoo's Note: Male Friendship and Cuckoldry in *The Merchant of Venice*," in *Shakespeare's "Rough Magic,"* ed. Peter Erickson and Coppélia Kahn (Newark: Univ. of Delaware Press, 1985), pp. 104-112.

48. Bray reaches similar conclusions: "Female homosexuality was rarely linked in popular thought with male homosexuality, if indeed it was recognized at all. Its history is, I believe, best to be understood as part of the developing recognition of a specifically female sexuality." *Homosexuality in Renaissance England*, p. 17. Judith Brown is nonplused about the scant attention the subject received from men: "In light of the knowledge that Europeans had about the possibility of lesbian sexuality, their neglect of the subject in law, theology, and literature suggests an almost active willingness to *disbelieve*." *Immodest Acts*, p. 9. She attributes this lack of attention to the phallocentrism of Renaissance sexuality, to the male assumption that lesbianism was merely an attempt to emulate their own sexual behavior.

49. Included in *The Passionate Pilgrim* (1599), facsimile edition ed. Joseph Quincy Adams (New York: Scribners, 1939), sig. C6^v.

CHAPTER TWO

1. Plutarch, *Lives of the Noble Grecians and Romans*, trans. Sir Thomas North (1579), intro. George Wyndham, The Tudor Translations (1895; rpt. New York: AMS Press, 1967), 1:60. Further references are cited in the text by volume number and page number.

2. Lionel Tiger, *Men in Groups* (New York: Random House, 1969). Tiger's aggressive attempt to bring together biology, anthropology, and sociology to form an "ethology" of male bonding has provoked criticism from biologists, anthropologists, and sociologists roused to defend their territories. On "The Male Bond and Human Evolution" see pp. 41-54; on politics and war, pp. 55-92. A coinage from the social sciences, "homosociality" owes its current critical currency to Eve Kosofsky Sedgwick in *Between Men: English Literature and Male Homosocial Desire* (New York: Columbia Univ. Press, 1985). Only in the last few pages of *Men in Groups*, as a kind of afterthought, does Lionel Tiger entertain the possibility that male homosexuality may be "a specific feature of the more general phenomenon of male bonding" (p. 216).

3. Coppélia Kahn, *Man's Estate: Masculine Identity in Shakespeare* (Berkeley: Univ. of California Press, 1981), pp. 151-192, links *Coriolanus* with *Macbeth* in this regard and sees each of these "bloody" heroes as tragically dependent on a strong woman for his identity.

4. William Shakespeare, *Coriolanus*, 1.7.29-33, in *The Complete Works*, ed. Stanley Wells and Gary Taylor (Oxford: Clarendon Press, 1986), p. 1207. Further quotations from Shakespeare's plays are taken from this edition and are cited in the text by act, scene, and line numbers.

5. "He was wonderfull fayer, being a child, a boye, and a man, and that at all times, which made him marvelous amiable, and beloved of every man. . . . Alcibiades stoode in awe of no man but of Socrates only, and in deede he dyd reverence him, and dyd despise all other. And therefore Cleanthes was wont to saye, that Alcibiades was held of Socrates by the eares: but that he gave his other lovers holde, which Socrates never sought for: for to saye truely, Alcibiades was muche geven over to lust and pleasure. And peradventure it was that Thucydides ment of him, when he wrote that he was incontinent of bodie, and dissolute of life." Plutarch, *Lives*, trans. North, 2.90, 95.

6. Aristotle, *Ethica Nicomachea*, 8.3-5, ed. and trans. W. D. Ross, in *The Works of Aristotle*, 9 (Oxford: Clarendon Press, 1915): 1155^b-1157^b. There is a full discussion of *philia* in Irving Singer, *The Nature of Love*, 1, rev. ed. (Chicago: Univ. of Chicago Press): 91-114. See also A. W. Price, *Love and Friendship in Plato and Aristotle* (Oxford: Clarendon Press, 1989), pp. 103-130.

7. Cicero, *De Amicitia*, trans. John Harington (1550), rpt. in Ruth Hughey, *John Harington of Stepney: Tudor Gentleman: His Life and Works* (Columbus: Univ. of Ohio Press, 1971), p. 179.

8. Michel de Montaigne, *Essais*, 1.27, trans. John Florio (1603), ed. Thomas Seccombe (London: Grant Richards, 1908), 1:232. Compare

Montaigne's English imitator Sir William Cornwallis in his own essay "Of Love": "I hope I shall not offend Divinitie, if I say the conjunction of man and wife, is not Love; It is an allowance of Gods, and so good: and the name of it, I thinke, two honest Affections united into one . . . . *Love thy neighbour as thy selfe*, that which comes nearest to Love is this, man with man agreeing in sexe: I cannot thinke it is so betweene man and women, for it gives opportunitie to lust, which the purenesse of Love will not endure." *Essayes* (London: Edmund Mattes, 1600), sigs. D7^v-D8.

9. Michel Foucault, *A History of Sexuality*, vol. 3: *The Care of the Self*, trans. Robert Hurley (New York: Pantheon, 1986): 189-232.

10. Plutarch, *Moralia*, trans. Philemon Holland as *The Philosophie* (London, 1603), fols. 1132-1133. Future references are cited in the text by folio number.

11. "Chariclem illum Corinthium, adolescentem haudquaquam deformem, deditum nonnihil comendi & fucandi corporis studio, ut qui mulieribus, opinor, forma atque elegantia ista commendari affectaret. Una autem cum ipso & Callicratidem istum Atheniensem, moribus ac habitu simpliciorem." Lucian, *Opera* (Greek text and Latin translations by various hands), ed. Gilbert Cousin and Johannes Sambucus (Basel: Henricus Petrus, 1563), 4:179-180, my translation. A full—and, for once, faithful—English translation of "*Erotes*" as "Affairs of the Heart" is available in Lucian, *Works*, ed. and trans. M. D. Macleod, Loeb Library, 8 (London: Heinemann, 1967): 150-235.

12. "Quando enim a puero dignus ac serius ille amor simul enutritus, in eam aetatem quae iam ratione uti, aliaque ex aliis colligere potest, confirmatus fuerit: id quod olim amatum est, mutuos atque alternos amores vicissim reddit: adeoque difficile est sentire uter alterius amator existat, perinde ut e speculo, simili amantis benevolentiae, in amatum recidente imagine." Lucian, *Opera*, 4:231-232.

13. "Solus enim masulus amor, commune virtutis ac voluptatis opus est." Lucian, *Opera*, 4:210.

14. Lawrence Stone, *The Past and the Present Revisited* (London: Routledge and Kegan Paul, 1987), pp. 378-380. The causes for these four waves of homophobia were different. The third century A.D. witnessed the political triumph of Christianity. Thomistic philosophy, with its elevation of "nature" as an ethical criterion, is cited as the cause for increasing homophobia during the thirteenth century and after by John Boswell in *Christianity, Social Tolerance, and Homosexuality* (Chicago: Univ. of Chicago Press, 1980), pp. 303-332. Stone proposes four causes for the official homophobia of the sixteenth century: the religious crisis of the Reformation and Counter-Reformation, the epidemic spread of syphilis, the rise of the unified political state, and social and economic upheavals. For the period after 1790, Louis Crompton, *Byron and Greek Love: Homophobia in 19th-Century England* (Berkeley: Univ. of California Press, 1985), pp. 12-62, demonstrates how prosecution of homosexuals in England reached unprecedented levels at the very time when same-

sex relations were being decriminalized on the Continent. Only a few executions are known to have taken place in England before the eighteenth century; after 1805 executions were averaging two *per year*, with as many as six or seven in some years. Crompton attributes this homophobia to British xenophobia—to a fear of French invasion in particular and to an insular sense of moral superiority in general.

15. Boswell's general thesis is borne out by James A. Brundage's detailed examination of *Law, Sex, and Christian Society in Medieval Europe* (Chicago: Univ. of Chicago Press, 1987). Sexual behavior had always had its theological aspect and its social aspect, Brundage observes. The effect of the Reformation was to shift the relative importance from the theological to the social, to turn a religious issue into a civil issue (pp. 551-575).

16. Alan Bray, *Homosexuality in Renaissance England* (London: Gay Men's Press, 1982), pp. 13-32; Guido Ruggiero, *The Boundaries of Eros: Sex Crime and Sexuality in Renaissance Venice* (New York: Oxford Univ. Press, 1985), pp. 109-145.

17. *Fleta*, ed. and trans. H. G. Richardson and G. O. Sayles, Selden Society 72 (London: Quaritch, 1955), 2:89-90.

18. *The Mirror of Justices*, ed. and trans. William Joseph Whittaker, Selden Society 7 (London: Quaritch, 1895), pp. 15-16.

19. *Britton*, ed. and trans. Francis Morgan Nichols (Oxford: Clarendon Press, 1865), 1:41-42. A marginal note in an early fourteenth-century manuscript of "Britton" (Cambridge Univ. Library, MS Dd.vii.6) makes this connection explicit: "Burners of corn and houses, wives guilty of treason against their husbands, sorcerers, sodomites, renegates, and misbelievers, run in a leash (*currunt en une leesse*) as to their sentence of being burned."

20. Genesis 19:24-25 in *The Geneva Bible* (1560), intro. Lloyd E. Berry (Madison: Univ. of Wisconsin Press, 1969), fol. 8ᵛ.

21. Quotations from 15 Henry VIII, c. 6, are taken from *The Whole volume of statutes at large, which at anie time heeretofore have beene extant in print, since Magna Charta, untill the XXIX. yeere of the reigne of our most gratious sovereigne Ladie Elizabeth* . . . (London: Christopher Barker, 1587), 1:637. The parliamentary history of the bill is narrated in Stanford E. Lehmberg, *The Reformation Parliament 1529-1536* (Cambridge: Cambridge Univ. Press, 1970), pp. 184-187. David Knowles, *The Religious Orders in England*, 3 (Cambridge: Cambridge Univ. Press, 1961): 198-205, narrates the legal planning of the dissolution of the monasteries and, 3:268-290, the visitation of 1535-36 that produced the evidence necessary to carry out the dissolution. The journal of the House of Lords for 17 January 1534 records: "*Memorandum*, quod cum diversa scelera detestabilia nuper per eos, qui, ut videntur, morte digni perpetrata fuerunt, quibus ex ordine Juris regni (ut Juris periti aiunt) nulla condigna imponi potest pena; ideo conducibile esse excogitatum est, quod quicunque in Sanctuaria trahens moram, egrediens, et extra, scelus morte dignum perpetrans, ac in Sanctuarium regressus pro

sufragio et corporis tuitione, Ecclesiasticum beneficium amittet; ac etiam qui Sodomiam committit, penam Capitis permittet; de quibus rebus Justiciariis committitur duas conficere Billas." *Journals of the House of Lords, Beginning Anno Primo Henrici Octavi*, 1 (place un-specificed: publisher unspecified, 1800): 59. The bill passed the House of Lords in just five days.

22. Michael Goodich, "Sodomy in Ecclesiastical Law and Theory," *Journal of Homosexuality* 1 (1976): 427-434.

23. Quoted in Knowles, *The Religious Orders in England*, p. 204.

24. Quoted in Knowles, *The Religious Orders in England*, p. 289.

25. Reprinted in *The Whole volume of statues at large*, 1:797.

26. Reprinted in *The Whole volume of statutes at large*, 2:199. Mary's relations with Parliament are considered in D. M. Loades, *The Reign of Mary Tudor: Politics, Government, and Religion in England, 1553-1558* (New York: St. Martin's Press, 1979), pp. 270-277.

27. Reprinted in *The Whole volume of statutes at large*, 2:72-73. At least one of the provisos had its origin in the House of Commons (*Journals of the House of Lords*, 1:353). Entries in the Lords journal indicate that it took twelve days for the buggery bill to pass from the House of Lords to the House of Commons and back again to the House of Lords—a far more complicated procedure than the five days it took to pass 25 Henry VIII, c. 6. The second session of Edward's first Parliament is studied by W. K. Jordan, *Edward VI*, vol. 1: *The Young King* (Cambridge, Mass.: Harvard Univ. Press, 1968): 305-323.

28. Michel Foucault, *The History of Sexuality*, vol. 1: *An Introduction*, trans. Robert Hurley (New York: Pantheon, 1978): 124.

29. Reprinted in *The Whole volume of statutes at large*, 2:449.

30. G. R. Elton, *The Parliament of England 1559-1581* (Cambridge: Cambridge Univ. Press, 1986), pp. 110-111.

31. Stone, *The Past and the Present Revisited*, pp. 368-369. From the sixteenth century through the seventeenth and the eighteenth, Stone sees a change from concern with public *order* to concern with public *decency*. Important also in this attempt to bring sexual behavior under control of the civil law is the legal shift that Brundage (*Law, Sex, and Christian Society*, pp. 551-575) notes with respect to marriage itself. In the Protestant view, marriage was a civil matter, not a sacrament, and hence should be subject to civil, not ecclesiastical jurisdiction. Among Protestant countries England remained an exception, however, in the power that ecclesiastic courts continued to enjoy down through the eighteenth century.

32. Sir Simonds D'Ewes, *The Journals of all the Parliaments During the Reign of Queen Elizabeth*, rev. Paul Bowes (London: John Starkey, 1682), p. 84.

33. Transcribed in J. S. Cockburn, ed., *Calendar of Assize Records . . . Elizabeth I*, 4 [Kent] (London: Her Majesty's Stationery Office, 1979): 88. Other volumes covering Elizabeth's reign are 1 [Sussex] (London: HMSO, 1975), 2 [Hertfordshire] (London: HMSO, 1975), 3 [Essex] (Lon-

don: HMSO, 1978), and 5 [Surrey] (London: HMSO, 1980). For James's reign, 1 [Hertfordshire] (London: HMSO, 1975), 2 [Sussex] (London: HMSO, 1975), 3 [Kent] (London: HMSO, 1980), 4 [Essex] (London: HMSO, 1982), and 5 [Surrey] (London: HMSO, 1982). In his indexes to these volumes Cockburn distinguishes between "sodomy" (homosexual relations between males) and "buggery" (bestiality). For Bray's assessment of these and other court records see *Homosexuality in Renaissance England*, pp. 38-42 and 70-80.

34. On abstract "rule-dominated" legal ideology versus pragmatic "realist" ideology see Elizabeth Mertz and Bernard Weissbourd, "Legal Ideology and Linguistic Theory: Variability and Its Limits," in *Semiotic Mediation: Sociocultural and Psychological Perspectives*, ed. Elizabeth Mertz and Richard J. Parmentier (Orlando, Fla.: Academic Press, 1985), pp. 261-285; on the workings of the Jacobean justice system see Cynthia B. Herrup, "Law and Morality in Seventeenth-Century England," *Past and Present* no. 106 (1985): 102-123.

35. B. R. Burg, "Ho Hum, Another Work of the Devil: Buggery and Sodomy in Early Stuart England," *Journal of Homosexuality* 6.1/2 (1980/81): 69-78.

36. Sir Edward Coke, *The Third Part of the Institutes Of the Laws of England*, 3d ed. (London: J. Fleshner, 1660), p. 58.

37. Renaissance English legal scholarship in general and Coke's scholarship in particular are contrasted with humanistic scholarship on the Continent in Donald R. Kelley, "History, English Law and the Renaissance," *Past and Present* no. 65 (1974): 24-51.

38. Sir Edward Coke, *A Booke of Entries: Containing Perfect and approved Presidents . . . concerning the practique part of the Laws of England . . . necessarie to be knowne, and of excellent use for the moderne practise of the Law . . .* (London: Society of Stationers, 1614), fol. 351ᵛ-352, my translation. The original reads: "instigatione diabolica seduct[us] duodecimo die Maii ultimo preterito apud parochiam Sancti Andree in high Holborne in Comitat[u] Middl[esex] predict[us], videlicet in domo mansional[i] cuiusdam M. ibidem vi et armis in quenda[m] K. B. puerum masculu[m] circa etatem sexdecim annoru[m] insultum fecit, Et cum eodem K. B. adtunc et ib[ide]m nequit[er] diabolice, felonice, ac contra naturam rem veneream h[ab]uit ipsumque K. adtunc & ib[ide]m carnaliter cognovit, peccatu[m]que illud Sodomiticum detestabile et abhominand[um], Anglice dicit[um] Buggarie (inter Christianos non nominand[um]) adtunc & ib[ide]m cum eodem K. B. nequiter, diabolice, felonice, ac contra naturam commisit ac perpetravit, in magni Dei omnipotent[i] displicent[um], ac totius generis humani dedecus, contra pacem dicti d[omi]ni Regis coronam & dignitatem suas, et contra formam statuti in h[uius]modi casu edit[i] & p[ro]vis[i], etc." Under the heading "Indictments" in the Table of Contents, "Buggary" is misprinted as "Burglary." The fact that *vi et armis* was a standard formula is indicated by a special statute, 37 Henry VIII, c. 8, that allowed indictments for felony to stand even if this phrase happened to have been

omitted. Cf. *The Whole volume of statutes at large*, 1:1020-1021.

39. A full account of the Castlehaven trial is offered by Caroline Bingham, "Seventeenth-Century Attitudes Toward Deviant Sex," *Journal of Interdisciplinary History* 1 (1971): 447-472. See also Burg, "Another Work of the Devil," pp. 72-74.

40. Atherton's trial is described in Burg, "Another Work of the Devil," pp. 74-75. Bray (*Homosexuality in Renaissance England*, p. 15) reproduces the woodcut illustrations that accompanied *The Life and Death of John Atherton*, a pamphlet published shortly after the execution of Atherton and Childe in 1640.

41. Stephen O. Murray's argument seems true: "Contemporary sociologists and criminologists do not generalize about 'gay people' or 'criminals' from examining clinical or incarcerated people: being caught or being treated indicates someone is not a typical member of these conceptual classes. I can think of no reason to suppose that the set of those who came to the attention of the criminal justice system in earlier, less rationalized epochs is any less biased a sample from which to extrapolate." See "Homosexual Acts and Selves in Early Modern Europe," in *The Pursuit of Sodomy: Male Homosexuality in Renaissance and Enlightenment Europe*, ed. Kent Gerard and Gert Hekma (New York: Harrington Press, 1989), pp. 457-477.

42. Robert L. Caserio makes a very similar argument about our own times in "Supreme Court Discourse v. Homosexual Fiction," *South Atlantic Quarterly* 88 (1989): 267-299.

43. Martin Green, *The Labyrinth of Shakespeare's Sonnets: An Examination of the Sexual Elements of Shakespeare's Language* (London: Charles Skilton, 1974).

44. The issue of sexual or nonsexual meaning in rhetoric about friendship seems not to have been stated explicitly until the eighteenth century. George Steevens, for example, registered "disgust and indignation" at the sexual imagery in Shakespeare's sonnet 20. Apropos Steevens's remark Edmund Malone declares, "Some part of this indignation might perhaps have been abated, if it had been considered that such addresses to men, however indelicate, were customary in our author's time, and neither imported criminality nor were esteemed indecorous." Quoted by Joseph Pequigney in *Such Is My Love: A Study of Shakespeare's Sonnets* (Chicago: Univ. of Chicago Press, 1985), p. 30, who offers a full account, pp. 30-32, 74-80, of how later editors and critics have accepted Malone's apologia as dogma.

45. Aristotle, *Poetics*, 57.b.1, trans. Gerald F. Else (Ann Arbor: Univ. of Michigan Press, 1967), pp. 57-58. On Aristotle's categories and on distinctions between metaphor and logic see Colin Murray Turbayne, *The Myth of Metaphor*, rev. ed. (Columbia: Univ. of South Carolina Press, 1970), pp. 11-27.

46. Wolfgang Iser, "Representation: A Performative Act," rpt. in *Prospecting* (Baltimore: Johns Hopkins Univ. Press, 1989), p. 239. In an essay that appeared just as *Homosexual Desire in Shakespeare's England* was

going to press, Alan Bray uses evidence from letters, diaries, and other private papers to argue for the same ambiguity that I am proposing here. "The Sodomite" and "The Masculine Friend" may have constituted two contrasted images, two distinct codes, but the similarities between the two could be turned into a powerful political weapon—especially toward the end of the sixteenth century, when the altruistic ideals of friendship had less and less to do with the political and economic ties that men made with one another in fact. See Alan Bray, "Homosexuality and the Signs of Male Friendship in Elizabethan England," *History Workshop*, no. 29 (1990): 1-19.

47. See Retha M. Warnicke, *Women of the English Renaissance and Reformation* (Westport, Conn.: Greenwood Press, 1983), and Margaret W. Ferguson, Maureen Quilligan, and Nancy J. Vickers, eds., *Rewriting the Renaissance: The Discourses of Sexual Difference in Early Modern Europe* (Chicago: Univ. of Chicago Press, 1986), especially the esssays in part 1, "The Politics of Patriarchy: Theory and Practice," pp. 3-144.

48. David Cressey, *Literacy and the Social Order: Reading and Writing in Tudor and Stuart England* (Cambridge: Cambridge Univ. Press, 1980), pp. 1-18, 42-61. For early modern England we still lack the kind of detailed analysis of who read what that Keith Basso proposes in "The Ethnography of Writing," in *Explorations in the Ethnography of Speaking*, ed. Richard Bauman and Joel Sherzer (Cambridge: Cambridge Univ. Press, 1974), pp. 425-432, and that Roger Chartier provides for early modern France in "Publishing Strategies and What People Read, 1530-1660," in *The Cultural Uses of Print in Early Modern France*, trans. Lydia G. Cochrane (Princeton: Princeton Univ. Press, 1987), pp. 145-182.

49. This feature of Shakespeare's history plays has been remarked by a variety of critics: Coppélia Kahn, *Man's Estate*, pp. 47-81; David Sundelson, *Shakespeare's Restorations of the Father* (New Brunswick: Rutgers Univ. Press, 1983), pp. 53-70; Peter Erickson, *Patriarchal Structures in Shakespeare's Drama* (Berkeley: Univ. of California Press, 1985), pp. 39-65.

50. Walter J. Ong, *Fighting for Life: Contest, Sexuality, and Consciousness* (Ithaca: Cornell Univ. Press, 1981), p. 81.

51. Compare Lydgate, *The Historye[,] Sege[,] and Dystruccyon of Troye* (printed 1513): "But Achylles firste began abreyde,/And unto hym even thus he seyde: Ector (quod he) full pleasynge is to me/That I at leyser naked may the[e] se[e],/Syth I of the[e] never myght have syght/But whan thou were armed as a knyght . . . ." Rpt. in Geoffrey Bullough, ed. *Narative and Dramatic Sources of Shakespeare*, 6 (London: Routledge and Kegan Paul, 1966): 165.

52. The classic account is that of Stanley Edgar Hyman, *Iago: Some Approaches to the Illusion of His Motivation* (New York: Atheneum, 1970), pp. 101-121.

53. Though she defines herself as a "Desdemona-critic" rather than an "Othello-critic" or an "Iago-critic," Carol Thomas Neely, *Broken Nuptials in Shakespeare's Plays* (New Haven: Yale Univ. Press, 1985), pp. 105-135, provides a brilliant account of Iago as a sexual politician.

54. On the violence of male bonding in *Romeo and Juliet* see Coppélia Kahn, "Coming of Age: Marriage and Manhood in *Romeo and Juliet* and *The Taming of the Shrew*," in *Man's Estate*, pp. 82-118, and Marianne V. Novy, "Violence, Love, and Gender in *Romeo and Juliet* and *Troilus and Cressida*," in *Love's Argument: Gender Relations in Shakespeare* (Chapel Hill: Univ. of North Carolina Press, 1984), pp. 99-124. Mercutio's obsession with phallic puns—specifically with puns related to Romeo's phallus—has been remarked by Joseph A. Porter, *Shakespeare's Mercutio: His History and Drama* (Chapel Hill: Univ. of North Carolina Press, 1988), pp. 143-163, and by Donald W. Foster, "'Believe not that the dribbling dart of love/Can pierce a complete bosom': Shakespeare's Chaste Male Lovers," unpublished essay presented at the Shakespeare Association of America meeting, April 1988.

55. "Companionate" is Lawrence Stone's term for the ideal of marriage that, in his view, supplanted a patriarchal model of marriage in the sixteenth and seventeenth centuries. See *The Family, Sex and Marriage in England 1500-1800* (New York: Harper & Row, 1977), pp. 135-142. The conflict between marriage and male friendship is the subject of Eugene M. Waith's essay "Shakespeare and Fletcher on Love and Friendship," *Shakespeare Studies* 18 (1986): 235-250.

56. William Segar, *Honor Military, and Civil* (London: Robert Barker, 1602), p. 248. Stone's argument in *The Family, Sex and Marriage*, pp. 180-195, that pragmatic calculation of family interest was the accepted viewpoint on marriage in the sixteenth century has been challenged by Keith Wrightson, who argues that the patriarchal and companionate models should be seen as "the poles of a continuum in marital relations in a society which accepted both the primacy of male authority and the ideal of marriage as a practical and emotional partnership." See Wrightson, *English Society 1580-1680* (New Brunswick, N.J.: Rutgers Univ. Press, 1982), p. 104. In *The World We Have Lost*, 3d ed. rev. (London: Methuen, 1983), pp. 1-21, Peter Laslett stresses the practical advantages—indeed the practical necessity—of marriage. For nobility and commoners alike, the economic realities were such that it was impossible to become a full member of society until one married and became the head of one's own household. And the age when one could do that was, by our standards, high. Between 1580 and 1680 the average age at which men married, according to Wrightson (*English Society*, pp. 67-70), was 27 to 30. In general, the aristocracy and upper gentry married somewhat younger than their social inferiors.

57. Antoine de La Sale, *The fyftene Joyes of maryage*, trans. attributed to Robert Copland (London: Wynkyn de Worde, 1509), sigs. L3ᵛ-L4. Only fragments survive of the 1507 edition. "*The xv joyes of marriage*" is listed along with "The booke againste woemen viz., *of marriage and wyvynge*" among the nine titles that the Archbishop of Canterbury and the Bishop of London ordered the Stationers Company to round up and to bring to the bishop for a public burning in 1599. Adam Islip had only recently been fined two shillings and six pence for the disorderly print-

ing of *The xv joyes*. The churchmen's ban must have been successful, since no known copies survive of the new edition of *The xv joyes*. See Edward Arber, *A Transcript of the Registers of the Company of Stationers of London, 1554-1640 A.D.*, 3 (London: privately printed, 1876): 677-678. Four years after the Archbishop's ban a new translation in prose, possibly by Robert Tofte, appeared under the title *The batchelars banquet: or a banquet for batchelars: wherein is prepared sundry dainties [sic] dishes. Pleasantly discoursing the variable humours of women* (London: Thomas Creede, 1603). The book must have been extremely popular, since it was reprinted later the same year, as well as in 1604, 1630, and 1631. As F. P. Wilson argues in the introduction to his modern edition of the text (Oxford: Clarendon, 1929), *The batchelars banquet* may well be the new translation that was suppressed in 1599.

58. I Corinthians 7:1 in *The Geneva Bible* (1560), p. 78ᵛ. Further quotations from this chapter on marriage are taken from this translation and are cited in the text.

59. Leslie A. Fiedler, *The Stranger in Shakespeare* (New York: Stein and Day, 1972), pp. 15-81; Janet Adelman, "Male Bonding in Shakespeare's Comedies," in *Shakespeare's "Rough Magic": Renaissance Essays in Honor of C. L. Barber*, ed. Peter Erickson and Coppélia Kahn (Newark: Univ. of Delaware Press, 1985), pp. 73-103; Peter Erickson, *Patriarchal Structures in Shakespeare's Drama* (Berkeley: Univ. of California Press, 1985); Catherine Belsey, "Disrupting Sexual Difference: Meaning and Gender in the Comedies," in *Alternative Shakespeares*, ed. John Drakakis (London: Methuen, 1985), pp. 166-190; Kahn, *Man's Estate*; W. Thomas MacCary, *Friends and Lovers: The Phenomenology of Desire in Shakespearean Comedy* (New York: Columbia Univ. Press, 1985). In an attempt to link these matters with changing political conditions, Marilyn L. Williamson, *The Patriarchy of Shakespeare's Comedies* (Detroit: Wayne State Univ. Press, 1987), distinguishes three sequential groups of plays: "comedies of courtship" during the reign of Elizabeth when men entertained the fantasy of courting and marrying a powerful woman, the "problem plays" when James came to the throne and began to reassert male control, and the "romances" of James's later reign with their celebration of patriarchy as something natural and unchanging.

60. Adelman, "Male Bonding," p. 88.

61. Adelman, "Male Bonding," p. 91.

62. Belsey, "Disrupting Sexual Difference," p. 190.

63. In his edition of the play G. R. Proudfoot (Lincoln: Univ. of Nebraska Press, 1970) considers the question of divided authorship and remarks that, though the precise shares of Shakespeare and John Fletcher remain disputed, the play "achieves a degree of coherence sufficient to have made it a success in its own day" (p. xix).

64. Charles Edward Mallet, *A History of the University of Oxford* (1924; rpt. London: Methuen, 1968), 2:141; Wilfrid R. Prest, *The Inns of Court under Elizabeth I and the Early Stuarts 1590-1640* (London: Longman, 1972), p. 9.

65. Bray, *Homosexuality in Renaissance England*, pp. 13-32.

66. B. R. Burg, "Ho Hum, Another Work of the Devil: Buggery and Sodomy in Early Stuart England," *Journal of Homosexuality* 6.1/2 (1980/81): 69-78, and chapter 1, "Sodomy and Public Perception: Seventeenth-Century England," in *Sodomy and the Pirate Tradition: English Sea Rovers in the Seventeenth-Century Caribbean* (New York: New York Univ. Press, 1984), pp. 1-42.

67. Sedgwick, *Between Men*, p. 25.

68. Bray, *Homosexuality in Renaissance England*, p. 76.

69. Philippe Ariès, "Thoughts on the history of homosexuality," in *Western Sexuality: Practice and Precept in Past and Present Times*, ed. Philippe Ariès and André Béjin, trans. Anthony Forster (Oxford: Basil Blackwell, 1985), p. 71.

70. Jonathan Goldberg, "Colin to Hobbinol: Spenser's Familiar Letters," *South Atlantic Quarterly* 88 (1989): 107-126, taking up the term from D. A. Miller, "Secret Subjects, Open Secrets," in *The Novel and the Police* (Berkeley: Univ. of California Press, 1988), pp. 192-220.

71. On this issue see Stephen Murray and Kent Gerard, "Renaissance Sodomitical Subcultures?" in *Among Men, Among Women: Sociological and Historical Recognition of Homosexual Arrangements*, ed. Dirk Jaap Noordam (Amsterdam: Univ. of Amsterdam Press, 1983); Gregory Sprague, "Male Homosexuality in Western Culture: The Dilemma of Identity and Subculture in Historical Research," *Journal of Homosexuality* 10 (1984): 29-43; Ruggiero, *The Boundaries of Eros*, pp. 113-115, 135-141; and James M. Saslow, "Homosexuality in the Renaissance: Behavior, Identity, and Artistic Expression," in *Hidden from History: Reclaiming the Gay and Lesbian Past*, ed. Martin Bauml Duberman, Martha Vicinus, and George Chauncey, Jr. (New York: New American Library, 1989), pp. 90-105.

72. The terms that Geoffrey Gorer first proposed in *The Danger of Equality and Other Essays* (London: Cressett, 1966), have been put to influential use not only by Stephen O. Murray, *Social Theory, Homosexual Realities* (New York: Gay Academic Union, 1984), but by Randolph Trumbach, "London's Sodomites: Homosexual Behavior and Western Culture in the Eighteenth Century," *Journal of Social History* 11 (1977): 1-33; Barry D. Adam, "A Social History of Gay Politics," in *Gay Men: The Social History of Male Homosexuality*, ed. Martin P. Levine (New York: Harper and Row, 1979), pp. 285-300; and, on a global scale, by David F. Greenberg, *The Construction of Homosexuality* (Chicago: Univ. of Chicago Press, 1988).

73. Stephen O. Murray, *Social Theory, Homosexual Realities*, and "Homosexual Acts and Selves in Early Modern Europe"; Randolph Trumbach, "Sodomitical Subcultures, Sodomitical Roles, and the Gender Revolution of the Eighteenth Century," *Eighteenth-Century Life* 9 (1984): 109-121, and "Sodomitical Assaults, Gender Role, and Sexual Development in Eighteenth-Century London," in *The Pursuit of Sodomy*, pp. 407-429; Bray, *Homosexuality in Renaissance England*, pp. 81-114; Gert

Hekma, "Sodomites, Platonic Lovers, Contrary Lovers: The Backgrounds of the Modern Homosexual," in *The Pursuit of Sodomy*, pp. 433-455; Greenberg, *The Construction of Homosexuality*, pp. 301-481.

CHAPTER THREE

1. *The Bucoliks of Publius Virgilius Maro, Prince of All Latine Poets; otherwise called his Pastoralls, or shepeherds meetings*, trans. Abraham Fleming, 2d ed. (London: Thomas Woodcocke, 1589), pp. 4-6. Fleming's translation was first printed in 1575. The square brackets that Fleming uses to indicate English words added to round out the sense of the Latin original have been removed. All further quotations from Virgil's second eclogue are from this second printing of Fleming's translation. The second eclogue was also translated by Abraham Fraunce for inclusion in *The Lawyer's Logick* (1588), pp. 121^v-122^v, as an example of logical organization. John Dryden's translation of the poem (1697) is reprinted in Stephen Coote, ed., *The Penguin Book of Homosexual Verse* (Harmondsworth: Penguin, 1983), pp. 83-85.

2. Ovid, *Metamorphoses*, 1.107-112, trans. Arthur Golding (1567), ed. J. F. Nims (New York: Macmillan, 1965), pp. 6-7.

3. Ernst Robert Curtius, *European Literature and the Latin Middle Ages*, trans. W. R. Trask (New York: Harper, 1963), pp. 195-200.

4. *As You Like It*, 1.1.109-113, in William Shakespeare, *The Complete Works*, ed. Stanley Wells and Gary Taylor (Oxford: Clarendon Press, 1986), p. 708. Further quotations from Shakespeare's plays are taken from this edition and are cited in the text by act, scene, and line numbers.

5. In *Oxford and Cambridge in Transition 1558-1642* (Oxford: Clarendon Press, 1959) Mark H. Curtis pursues two theses: that the universities brought together a much wider social range than formerly and that an expanded curriculum gave the universities greater interconnectedness with Tudor and Stuart society at large.

6. Keith Wrightson, *English Society 1580-1680* (New Brunswick, N.J.: Rutgers Univ. Press, 1982), pp. 191-199. Curtis also remarks on the fact that the universities imparted a common culture, "a mutuality of outlook and feeling among all important segments of English society" (*Oxford and Cambridge in Transition*, p. 269).

7. Walter J. Ong, *Fighting for Life: Contest, Sexuality, and Consciousness* (Ithaca: Cornell Univ. Press, 1981), pp. 119-148.

8. Ong, *Fighting for Life*, p. 130. See also Ong's *Rhetoric, Romance, and Technology: Studies in the Interaction of Expression and Culture* (Ithaca: Cornell Univ. Press, 1971), pp. 113-141, where these ideas about Latin are developed more fully.

9. Louis Crompton, *Byron and Greek Love: Homophobia in 19th-Century England* (Berkeley: Univ. of California Press, 1985), pp. 91-93, notes that this was still true in Byron's day. Byron's knowledge about homosexu-

ality in the ancient world came through the Latin and Greek texts in his library—certainly not through the crudely bowdlerized English versions of these texts.

10. Lawrence Stone, *The Family, Sex and Marriage in England 1500-1800* (New York: Harper & Row, 1977), pp. 492-493.

11. William L. Edgerton, *Nicholas Udall* (New York: Twayne, 1966), pp. 37 ff, records the debate of modern scholars about Udall's supposed offense—including the laughable rationalization that the clerk who was recording the Privy Council's investigation intended to write "burglary" but because of fatigue wrote "buggery." Theft was the original charge for which Udall was summoned. The misprint of "burglary" for "buggary" in the Table of Contents of Coke's *Booke of Entries* (London: Society of Stationers, 1614) suggests that a typesetter's fatigue could cause the opposite error just as easily.

12. Roger Ascham, *The Schoolmaster*, ed. Lawrence V. Ryan (Ithaca: Cornell Univ. Press, 1967), p. 80, quoted in Jonathan Goldberg, "Colin to Hobbinol: Spenser's Familiar Letters," *South Atlantic Quarterly* 88 (1989): 122.

13. John Earle, *Micro-cosmographie. Or, a Peece of the World Discovered: In Essayes and Characters* (London: Edward Blount, 1628), sig. E5-E6ᵛ. An "ingle," in the OED's fastidious definition, was "a boy-favourite (in bad sense); a catamite." Wearers of fancy hatbands were gentry or would-be gentry, according to John Stowe's *Annales* (1592): "As well women as men did wear borders of great cristall buttons about their cappes as hat bands, as a worthy garment to distinguish betweene the Gentry and others." Cited in C. Willett and Phillis Cunnington, *Handbook of English Costume in the Sixteenth Century* (London: Faber, 1954), p. 138. In Ben Jonson's *Everyman Out of his Humour* (1600) a gold hatband distinguishes the appearance of Fastidius Briske (cf. 3.6.83-89 in *Ben Jonson*, 3, ed. C. H. Herford and P. Simpson [Oxford: Clarendon Press, 1927]: 549), who is described in Jonson's prefatory remarks as "A Neat, spruce, affecting Courtier, one that weares clothes well, and in fashion . . . " (3:424). Cited in Willett and Cunnington, *Handbook of English Costume in the Seventeenth Century* (London: Faber, 1955), p. 69.

14. Richard C. Trexlar, "Ritual in Florence: Adolescence and Salvation in the Renaissance," in *The Pursuit of Holiness in Late Medieval and Renaissance Religion*, ed. Charles Trinkaus and Heiko A. Oberman (London: Brill, 1974), pp. 200-264; Natalie Zemon Davis, "The Reasons of Misrule: Youth Groups and Charivaris in Sixteenth-Century France," *Past and Present*, no. 50 (1971): 41-75, and "Some Tasks and Themes in the Study of Popular Religion," in *The Pursuit of Holiness*, pp. 307-336; and Maurice Aymard, "Friends and Neighbors," in *A History of Private Life*, vol. 3: *The Passions of the Renaissance*, ed. Roger Chartier, trans. Arthur Goldhammer (Cambridge: Harvard Univ. Press, 1989), pp. 447-491, who comments particularly on the gender-exclusiveness of these adolescent youth groups (pp. 477-484).

15. Steven R. Smith, "The London Apprentices as Seventeenth-Cen-

tury Adolescents," *Past and Present*, no. 61 (1973): 149-161. Smith has designed his article as a follow-up to Natalie Zemon Davis's "The Reasons of Misrule," which had appeared in *Past and Present* two years earlier. Adolescence, Smith asserts, is "a constant feature of history."

16. Philippe Ariès, "Thoughts on the History of Homosexuality," in Philippe Ariès and André Béjin, eds., *Western Sexuality: Practice and Precept in Past and Present Times*, trans. Anthony Forster (Oxford: Basil Blackwell, 1985), p. 67.

17. Lemnus Lemnius, *The Touchstone of Complexions: Expedient and profitable for all such as bee desirous and carefull of their bodily health*, trans. Thomas Newton, 3d ed. (London: Michael Sparke, 1633), pp. 168-172 (on the seven stages), pp. 46-47 (on the sanguinary humor). There had been earlier editions of Lemnius in English translation in 1576 and 1581. For an overview of English Renaissance books on medicine and health, see Paul Slack, "Mirrors of health and treasures of poor men: the uses of the vernacular medical literature of Tudor England," in *Health, Medicine, and Mortality in the Sixteenth Century*, ed. Charles Webster (Cambridge: Cambridge Univ. Press, 1979), pp. 237-273.

18. Thomas Coghan, *The Haven of Health. Chiefly gathered for the comfort of Students, and consequently of all those that have a care of their health*, 4th ed. (London: Anne Griffin, 1636), pp. 283-285 (on the three remedies), pp. 281-282 (on marriage and masturbation). There had been earlier printings of Coghan's manual in 1584, 1588, 1589, 1596, 1605, and 1612. Less sophisticated manuals offer, in addition to the habits of life that Coghan recommends, more concrete remedies for sexual problems. Here is Andrew Boorde's advice on what to do for "involuntary standing of a mans yerde": "Fyrst anoynt the yerde and coddes with the oyle of Juneper, and the oyle of Camphory is good. And so is Agnus castus brayed and made in a playster and layde upon the stones, and let priestes use fasting, watching, evill fare, hard lodging, and great study, and flee from all maner occasion of lechery, and let them smell to Rue, Vinegar, and Camphire." *The Breviarie of Health* (London: Thomas East, 1575), p. 93ᵛ. In an earlier chapter on impotence he offers some additional counsel on what to do about its opposite: "A remedy for that is to leape into a great vessell of cold water or put nettles in the codpece about the yerde and stones" (p. 102).

19. *The Problems of Aristotle, with other Philosophers and Phisitians* (London: Arnold Hatfield, 1597), sigs. E-E2ᵛ.

20. Cited in Lloyd De Mause, "The Evolution of Childhood," in *The History of Childhood*, ed. Lloyd De Mause (New York: Psychohistory Press, 1974), p. 48. It should be noted, however, that Follopius is talking about infants, not adolescents. His advice is extended to parents who want to correct the unnaturally small penises of their male children.

21. Alston's collection is now MS Osborn b197 in the Beinecke Library at Yale University. My quotation is taken from an edited transcription of fols. 152-153 by Donald Foster, to whom I am grateful not only for this transcription but for information about other manuscripts

containing sexually explicit verse, much of it unpublished: Bodleian MS Rawlinson poetry 216, which includes a translation of Ovid's *De Arte Amandi* as well as "The Merrie Ballad of Nashe His Dildo," the most famous pornographic poem of the English Renaissance; MS Rawl. poet. 26, which includes "My Mistress is a Shuttle-Cock," as well as poems relating to both Oxford and Cambridge; MS Rawl. poet. 214, which juxtaposes "A-Dallying with a Lady" and "The Bride's First Night" with Phineas Fletcher's piscatorial *Sicelides*, acted at Kings College, Cambridge, in 1615. Some individual poems from these MSS are printed in E. J. Burford, ed., *Bawdy Verse* (Harmondsworth: Penguin, 1982).

22. Without using the terms "hard" and "soft," Annabel Patterson draws out these distinctions in *Pastoral and Ideology: Virgil to Valery* (Berkeley: Univ. of California Press, 1987), pp. 127-132. The fullest critical treatment of the "soft" version is to be found in Thomas G. Rosenmeyer, *The Green Cabinet: Theocritus and the European Pastoral Lyric* (Berkeley: Univ. of California Press, 1969).

23. George Puttenham, *The Arte of English Poesie*, ed. Gladys Doidge Willcock and Alice Walker (Cambridge: Cambridge Univ. Press, 1936), pp. 38-39.

24. Though critical essays in "hard" pastoral are numerous, Louis A. Montrose offers particularly provocative instances in "'Eliza Queene of shepheardes' and the Pastoral of Power," *English Literary Renaissance* 10 (1980): 153-182, and "Of Gentlemen and Shepherds: The Politics of Elizabethan Pastoral Form," *ELH* 50 (1983): 415-459.

25. Philip Melanchthon, *Opera*, ed. C. G. Bretschneider, 19 (Braunschweig: Schwetschke, 1853): cols. 299-300. Melanchthon identifies Alexis with Augustus Caesar.

26. Erasmus, *De ratione studii*, in *The Collected Works of Erasmus*, ed. Craig R. Thompson, 24 (Toronto: Univ. of Toronto Press, 1978): 683-685.

27. Rpt. in Virgil, *Opera* (Venice: Giunta, 1533), fol. 6.

28. *The Complete Works of Christopher Marlowe*, ed. Fredson Bowers (Cambridge: Cambridge Univ. Press, 1973), 2:537. The poem was first printed in an anthology of love lyrics by various hands, *Englands Helicon*, in 1600.

29. See "The Nimphs Reply to the Sheepheard" in *The Poems of Sir Walter Ralegh*, ed. Agnes M. C. Latham (London: Constable, 1929), p. 40. Raleigh's parody was first printed as a companion piece to Marlowe's poem in *Englands Helicon*.

30. *The Shepheardes Calender*, "Januarye," ll. 55-60, in *The Works of Edmund Spenser: A Variorum Edition*, ed. Edwin Greenlaw, et al., 7 (Baltimore: Johns Hopkins Univ. Press, 1943): 17. Further quotations are taken from this edition and are cited in the text by line number. On Spenser's eclogues as a portrait of the artist as a young man see Bruce R. Smith, "On Reading *The Shepheardes Calender*," *Spenser Studies* 1, ed. Patrick Cullen and Thomas P. Roche Jr. (Pittsburgh: Univ. of Pittsburgh Press, 1980): 69-93.

31. Jonathan Goldberg, "Colin to Hobbinol: Spenser's Familiar Letters," *South Atlantic Quarterly* 88 (1989): 107-126.

32. *The Faerie Queene*, 4.10.26, 41, ed. Ray Heffner in *The Works of Edmund Spenser: A Variorum Edition*, ed. Edwin Greenlaw, et al., 4 (Baltimore: Johns Hopkins Univ. Press, 1935): 128, 132.

33. E.K. makes an extravagant point of this odd spelling in "The generall argument of the whole booke": "They were first of the Greekes the inventours of them called Aeglogai as it were *aigon* or *aigonomon. logoi*. that is Goteheards tales. . . . This being, who seeth not the grossenesse of such as by colour of learning would make us beleeve that they are more rightly termed Eclogai, as they would say, extraordinary discourses of unnecessarie matter, which difinition albe in substaunce and meaning it agree with the nature of the thing, yet nowhit answereth with the *analysis* and interpretation of the word. For they be not termed Eclogues, but Aeglogues. which sentence this authour very well observing, upon good judgement, though indeede few Goteheards have to doe herein, netheless doubteth not to cal them by the used and best knowen name" (*The Works of Edmund Spenser*, 7:12).

34. Richard Barnfield, *The Complete Poems*, ed. Alexander B. Grosart, Roxburghe Club ed. (London: J. B. Nichols and Sons, 1876), p. 47. Since Grosart's edition lacks line numbers, references are cited in the text by stanza number and page number.

35. I John 1:8 in *The Geneva Bible* (1560), intro. Lloyd Berry (Madison: Univ. of Wisconsin Press, 1969), p. 111^v. Future quotations from the Bible are taken from this translation and are cited in the text.

36. John H. Gagnon and William Simon, *Sexual Conduct: The Social Sources of Human Sexuality* (Chicago: Aldine Press, 1973), pp. 1-26.

37. Eric Partridge, *Shakespeare's Bawdy*, rev. ed. (New York: Dutton, 1969), pp. 80 ("cock"), 134 ("let in" and "let out"), 147 ("meat"), 182 ("shoot"), 186 ("sparrow"), 200-201 ("thrust").

38. Harry Morris, *Richard Barnfield, Colin's Child* ([Tallahassee]: Florida State Univ. Press, 1963), pp. 9-11, notes that both of Barnfield's nineteenth-century editors, Grosart (1876) and Edward Arber (1896), connect Barnfield with Gray's Inn. Morris discusses the strong possibility that Barnfield was a friend and protégé of his Shropshire neighbor Abraham Fraunce, who was a member of Gray's Inn. The only certain evidence is that Barnfield dedicated *Lady Pecunia* (1598) to two members of Gray's Inn as well as to another Shropshire acquaintance.

39. There are two general accounts of the inns of court in the sixteenth century, each written from a different perspective. Wilfrid R. Prest, *The Inns of Court under Elizabeth I and the Early Stuarts 1590-1640* (London: Longman, 1972) presents a full factual history. Philip J. Finkelpearl, *John Marston of the Middle Temple: An Elizabethan Dramatist in his Social Setting* (Cambridge: Harvard Univ. Press, 1969), pp. 3-80, offers a discussion of the social and intellectual life of the inns. By the late sixteenth century about half of the newly admitted members had spent some time at the universities (Finkelpearl, pp. 6-7); most of those

admitted were between 16 and 20 years old (Prest, p. 9); although membership was for life, 70 percent of those actually in residence were between 17 and 30 years old (Finkelpearl, p. 6.).

40. Finkelpearle, *John Marston*, pp. 19-31, 44, 61, 80.

41. Webster is the attributed author of this and other pieces collected as *An Addition of Other Characters, or Lively Descriptions of Persons* appended to Sir Thomas Overbury, *New and Choise Characters, of severall Authors*, 6th ed. (London: Thomas Creede, 1615), pp. 337-338.

42. Arthur F. Marotti, *John Donne, Coterie Poet* (Madison: Univ. of Wisconsin Press, 1986), pp. 25-95.

43. Finkelpearle, *John Marston*, p. 42.

44. Alan Bray, *Homosexuality in Renaissance England* (London: Gay Men's Press, 1982), pp. 60-61.

45. The objective facts about MS Folger V.a.161 are set forth in Peter Beal, *Index of English Literary Manuscripts*, 1.1 (London: Mansell, 1980): 65, who rejects Grosart's claim in *The Complete Poems of Richard Barnfield* that the manuscript is in Barnfield's hand. Grosart prints an accurate transcript of the manuscript as an appendix to his edition of Barnfield's poems, pp. 202-220. Without having actually seen the manuscript, Harry Morris also rejects Grosart's claim in *Richard Barnfield, Colin's Child*, pp. 132-147. I am grateful to Laetitia Yeandle, Curator of Manuscripts at the Folger Library, for discussing with me and confirming my impressions about the presence of two hands in the manuscript.

46. The elaborate "Pardon" issued by the "Prince" to all his subjects is mainly a catalog of exceptions so detailed as to exclude *everybody*. Many of the regulations have to do with sexual misdemeanors. For example: All the Prince's subjects shall be pardoned "*Except*, All such Persons as by any Force, or Fraud and Dissimulation, shall procure, be it by Letters, Promises, Messages, Contracts, and other Inveaglings, any Lady or Gentlewoman, Woman or Maid, Sole or Covert, into his Possession or Convoy, and shall convey her into any place where she is, or shall be of full power and opportunity to bargain, give, take, buy, sell, or change; and shall suffer her to escape and return at large, without any such Bargain, Sale, Gift, or Exchange performed and made, contrary to former expected, expressed, employed Contract or Consent." *Gesta Grayorum: Or the History of the High and Mighty Prince Henry Prince of Purpoole Anno Domini 1594*, ed. Desmond Bland (Liverpool: Liverpool Univ. Press, 1968), p. 24.

47. Folger MS V.a.161, fol. 11. I have expanded abbreviations within square brackets.

48. Byrne R. S. Fone, "This Other Eden: Arcadia and the Homosexual Imagination," *Journal of Homosexuality*, 8.3/4 (1983): 13-34.

49. Michel Foucault, *The History of Sexuality*, vol. 1: *An Introduction*, trans. Robert Hurley (New York: Random House, 1978): 100-101.

50. David F. Greenberg, *The Construction of Homosexuality* (Chicago: Univ. of Chicago Press, 1989), pp. 26-40, and Arnold Van Gennep. *The*

Rites of Passage (1909), trans. Monika B. Vizedom and Gabrielle L. Caffee (Chicago: Univ. of Chicago Press, 1960).

CHAPTER FOUR

1. Achilles Tatius, *The Most Delectable and Plesant Historye of Clitiphon and Leucippe*, trans. William Burton (1597), ed. Stephen Gaselee and H. F. B. Brett-Smith (Oxford: Basil Blackwell for Shakespeare Head Press, 1923), chap. 2, p. 41. Future quotations from *Clitiphon and Leucippe* are taken from this translation and are cited in the text by page number.

2. Michel Fokine's scenario for Ravel's ballet is summarized in Rollo H. Myers, *Ravel: Life and Works* (1960; rpt. Westport, Conn.: Greenwood Press, 1973); in my possession is an edition of *The Pastoral Loves of Daphnis and Chloe*, trans. George Moore (n.p.: Boar's Head Books, 1954), part of a series described on the dustjacket as including Guy de Maupassant's *Parisian Nights*, Lucian's *The Pleasures of Being Beaten* ("Fabulously illustrated"), Norman Lockridge's *Lese Majesty: The Private Lives of the Duke and Duchess of Windsor*, and Friedrich Nietzsche's *My Sister and I* ("Dramatic self-revelation by the great philosopher of how he was driven to madness by his sister's abnormal passion for him").

3. Carol Gesner, *Shakespeare and the Greek Romance* (Lexington: Univ. of Kentucky Press, 1970), pp. 1-79, considers in detail the distinctive features of the romances and their currency during the Middle Ages and Renaissance. As an appendix she supplies a bibliographic survey of editions and translations, pp. 145-162. Cf. also Gerald N. Sandy, *Heliodorus* (Boston: Twayne, 1982), pp. 33-74.

4. In *The Greek Romances of Heliodorus, Longus, and Achilles Tatius* (London: Bohn, 1855), pp. 398-399, the Rev. Rowland Smith provides a one-sentence paraphrase in English, relegates the full passage to the bottom of the page in a Latin translation, and gives literary legitimacy to the whole thing with a footnote to Byron's poem "A long, long kiss, a kiss of youth and love." At just the same point, virtually in mid-sentence, Stephen Gaselee switches to Latin in *Achilles Tatius of Alexandria: The Adventures of Leucippe and Clitiphon*, Loeb Library (London: Heinemann, 1917), pp. 129-133.

5. Robert Laneham's eyewitness account of the Kenilworth revels is quoted in David Wiles, *The Early Plays of Robin Hood* (Cambridge: D. S. Brewer, 1981), p. 22.

6. William Shakespeare and John Fletcher, *The Two Noble Kinsmen*, 3.5.119-122, in William Shakespeare, *The Complete Works*, ed. Stanley Wells and Gary Taylor (Oxford: Clarendon Press, 1986), p. 1398. Future quotations from Shakespeare's plays are taken from this edition and are cited in the text by act, scene, and line numbers.

7. Judith Lynne Hanna, *Dance, Sex and Gender: Signs of Identity, Domi-*

nance, Defiance, and Desire (Chicago: Univ. of Chicago Press, 1988), pp. 46-47.

8. Thomas Nashe, *The Returne of Pasquill* (1589), quoted in Wiles, *The Early Plays of Robin Hood*, p. 5, who provides a full account of Maid Marian, pp. 21-24.

9. Quoted from *Plain Percival the Peacemaker* (1589) in Wiles, *The Early Plays of Robin Hood*, p. 18. On Robin Hood and Maid Marion as king and queen of May, see also Peter Burke, *Popular Culture in Early Modern Europe* (London: Temple Smith, 1978), p. 180.

10. Alan Brody, *The English Mummers and Their Plays: Traces of Ancient Mystery* (Philadelphia: Univ. of Pennsylvania Press, 1970), pp. 99-116.

11. E. K. Chambers, *The English Folk-Play* (1933; rpt. New York: Russell and Russell, 1964), p. 113. Further quotations from the Revesby play are taken from Chambers's version and are cited in the text. Though it is the earliest written text to survive, the Revesby play presents three anomalies that have caused some folklorists to doubt its usefulness as a record of oral tradition: it is an amalgam of three distinctly different types of folk play; it was performed, not at the traditional time in January, but in October; and it was acted, not in the village, but at a nobleman's house. Michael J. Preston, "The Revesby Sword Play," *Journal of American Folklore* 75 (1972): 51-57, reports, furthermore, that a computer analysis of the text, along with 156 other folk-play texts and 38 fragments, showed only a small percentage of lines in the Revesby play to bear any resemblance to texts with a more certain relationship to oral tradition. A vigorous defense of the text, however, is offered by Thomas Pettit, "English Folk Drama in the Eighteenth Century: A Defense of the *Revesby Sword Play*," *Comparative Drama* 15 (1981): 3-29. The occasion for the play's performance, tenants putting on their traditional entertainment for a landlord, *was* typical of how folk-plays in the oral tradition were performed. (One thinks of the Warwickshire villagers at Kenilworth in 1575.) Pettit cites arguments from other scholars that the text we have is not the invention of an eighteenth-century antiquarian but a fair copy of a transcript of the play as performed, made either at the time of performance or reconstructed by one or more of the players afterwards. Finally, the eighteenth-century text does not represent a corruption of some lost "original." There never *was* such a thing. Drama in the oral tradition is a series of recreations, using stock characters, stock events, stock speeches. Sexual horseplay, I submit, was among those stock strategies. C. R. Baskervill's essay "Mummers' Wooing Plays in England," *Modern Philology* 21 (1924): 225-272, traces connections between the traditional oral type and the sixteenth-century printed drama.

12. Robert Weimann, *Shakespeare and the Popular Tradition in the Theater: Studies in the Social Dimension of Dramatic Form and Function*, ed. Robert Schwartz (Baltimore: Johns Hopkins Univ. Press, 1978), pp. 15-48; Mikhail Bakhtin, *Rabelais and His World*, trans. Helene Iswolsky

(Cambridge, Mass: MIT Press, 1968), esp. pp. 1-58. On Robin Hood and the tradition of stealing the maypole, see Wiles, *The Early Plays of Robin Hood*, pp. 19, 55-58.

13. Arnold Van Gennep, *Rites of Passage* (1909), trans. Monika B. Vizedom and Gabrielle L. Caffe (Chicago: Univ. of Chicago Press, 1960).

14. Walter Kaufmann, *Tragedy and Philosophy* (New York: Doubleday, 1968), pp. 49-52.

15. On romance as the preeminent mode of Elizabethan culture see F. P. Wilson, *Elizabethan and Jacobean* (Oxford: Clarendon, 1945). Mark Girouard, *Robert Smythson and the Elizabethan Country House* (New Haven: Yale Univ. Press, 1983), demonstrates how the incipient classicism in architecture fostered by a passion for things Italian at the court of Henry VIII gave way to neo-medievalism in architecture under Elizabeth I. A similar shift in styles of portraiture is noted by Roy Strong, *The English Icon* (New Haven: Yale Univ. Press, 1969), pp. 5-21. C. R. Baskervill's two long essays "Some Evidence for Early Romantic Plays in England," *Modern Philology* 14 (1916-17): 229-251, 467-521, remains the fullest account of the vogue for romantic drama at the court of Elizabeth I. In "Elizabethan Chivalry: The Romance of the Accession Day Tilts" (1957), rpt. in *Astraea: The Imperial Theme in the Sixteenth Century* (London: Routledge and Kegan Paul, 1975), pp. 88-111, Frances Yates examines the evidence and explores the mythology for these grand occasions of fiction making. Finally, David M. Bergeron, *English Civic Pageantry 1557-1642* (London: Edward Arnold, 1971) narrates the entries into cities and the countryhouse entertainments that marked Queen Elizabeth's annual summer progresses. In my own essay, "Landscape with Figures: The Three Realms of Queen Elizabeth's Countryhouse Revels," *Renaissance Drama* n.s. 8 (1977): 57-115, I point out how often the romance elements in these entertainments are localized in the woods that surrounded countryhouse estates.

16. See Walter J. Ong, *Fighting for Life: Contest, Sexuality, and Consciousness* (Ithaca: Cornell Univ. Press, 1981), and chapter 2, above.

17. William Segar, *Honor Military, and Civill* (London: Robert Barker, 1602), p. iii. Page references for future quotations from Segar are cited in the text.

18. "For many respects also the vice of adultery ought to be severely punished, as well in warre as peace: which caused *Lucius Cautilius Scriba*, the same yeere the Romanes were defeated at *Canna* (by commaundement of the chiefe Bishop) to be beaten extreamely, for having committed that crime with *Florina. Julius Caesar* likewise caused a speciall favorite of his to be capitally punished, for dishonoring the wife of a Romane gentleman, though no complaint was made thereof. *Papinianus* the doctor sayth, That if any souldier doe keepe in his house his owne sisters daughter, hee may be reputed an adulterer. And as a Maxime or Rule it was decreed by all doctors of Law, That no souldier condemned of adultery may after beare Armes. By the law *Julia* the crime of adultery was thought worthy of infamie, and the offenders

disabled to beare Armes. *Aurelianus* commanded, that if any souldier did ravish the wife of his host, he should be tyed unto two trees, and torne in pieces. *Frotho* king of Scots made a law, That if any man by force defloured a virgine, he should be gelded. The Egyptians proclaimed, That whosoever was found in adultery (although it were with consent) yet the man should be beaten with a thousand stripes, and the woman have her nose cut off" (Segar, *Honor*, p. 21).

19. Roger Chartier, "Culture as Appropriation: Popular Cultural Uses in Early Modern France," in *Understanding Popular Culture: Europe from the Middle Ages to the Nineteenth Century*, ed. Steven L. Kaplan (Berlin: Mouton, 1984), pp. 229-253. Burke, *Popular Culture*, pp. 58-64, makes a similar argument.

20. The literal truth of these accusations has been argued in a full but controversial book by Gershon Legman, *The Guilt of the Templars* (New York: Basic Books, 1966).

21. "Hero and Leander," 1.5-6 and 1.61-62, in *The Complete Works of Christopher Marlowe*, ed. Fredson Bowers, 2d ed. (Cambridge: Cambridge Univ. Press, 1979), 2:431-432. Future references are cited in the text by line number.

22. Suetonius, *The Historie of Twelve Caesars, Emperours of Rome*, trans. Philemon Holland (London: Matthew Lownes, 1606), p. 99.

23. The phrase is Venus's, l. 9.

24. "The Author to the Reader," ll. 9-10, as reprinted in *Elizabethan Narrative Verse*, ed. Nigel Alexander (Cambridge, Mass.: Harvard Univ. Press, 1967), pp. 168-191. Further quotations from Beaumont's "Salmacis and Hermaphroditus" are taken from Alexander's edition and are cited in the text by line number.

25. Robert P. Merrix, "The Vale of Lillies and the Bower of Bliss: Soft-Core Pornography in Elizabethan Poetry," *Journal of Popular Culture* 19.4 (1986): 3-16.

26. *Menaphon* (1589), in *The Life and Complete Works in Verse and Prose of Robert Greene, M.A.*, ed. Alexander B. Grosart (1881-83; rpt. New York: Russell & Russell, 1964), 6:31. Further quotations from *Menaphon* come from Grosart's edition and are cited in the text.

27. *The Countess of Pembroke's Arcadia (The New Arcadia)*, book 1, chapter 1, ed. Victor Skretkowicz (Oxford: Clarendon Press, 1987), pp. 7-9. Future references will be cited in the text by book number, chapter number, and page number.

28. *The Countess of Pembroke's Arcadia (The Old Arcadia)*, ed. Jean Robertson (Oxford: Clarendon Press, 1973), p. 27. Future references will be cited in the text by page number. On differences between the complete five-book "old" *Arcadia* that Sidney wrote for the amusement of his sister and her friends and the "new" *Arcadia* that he left unfinished at his death, see the introductions to the editions of Skretkowicz and Robertson. Both editors explain the complicated publication history of the text, which most readers have encountered in the amalgamation of the

"old" and "new" versions that Fulke Greville first saw through the press in 1593.

29. Thomas Lodge, *Rosalynde* (1590), rpt. in Geoffrey Bullough, ed. *Narrative and Dramatic Sources of Shakespeare*, 2 (London: Routledge and Kegan Paul, 1958): 159-160. Further quotations are taken from Bullough's reprinting and are cited in the text.

30. Deuteronomy 22:5, in *The Geneva Bible* (1560), facsimile rpt., intro. Lloyd E. Berry (Madison: Univ. of Wisconsin Press, 1969), p. 90.

31. John Rainolds, *Th'Overthrow of Stage-Playes* (1599), quoted in Lisa Jardine, *Still Harping on Daughters: Women and Drama in the Age of Shakespeare* (Brighton: Harvester Press, 1983), p. 13. See also Jonas Barish, *The Antitheatrical Prejudice* (Berkeley: Univ. of California Press, 1981), pp. 80-131.

32. Stephen Orgel, "Nobody's Perfect: On Why Did the English Stage Take Boys for Women," *South Atlantic Quarterly* 88 (1989): 7-29.

33. See, for example, Jardine, *Still Harping on Daughters*, pp. 9-36; Laura Levine, "Men in Women's Clothing: Anti-theatricality and Effeminization from 1579 to 1642," *Criticism* 28 (1986): 121-143; Jean E. Howard, "Crossdressing, The Theatre, and Gender Struggle in Early Modern England," *Shakespeare Quarterly* 39 (1988): 418-429; and Marjorie Garber, *Vested Interests: Cross-Dressing and Cultural Anxiety* (forthcoming).

34. *Thomas Platter's Travels in England 1599*, trans. Clare Williams (London: Jonathan Cape, 1937), p. 166.

35. Thomas Coryate, *Coryate's crudities. Hastily gobled up in five monenths travells in France, Savoy, Italy, Rhetia . . . Switzerland, some parts of high Germany, and the Netherlands . . .* (London: William Stansby, 1611), pp. 247-248.

36. George Sandys, *A Relation of a Journey begun Anno Domini 1610*, 2d ed. (London: W. Barrett, 1615), pp. 245-246.

37. Quoted and discussed, along with the other reference, in Michael Shapiro, "Lady Mary Wroth Describes a 'Boy Actress,'" *Medieval and Renaissance Drama in England*, 4, ed. J. Leeds Barroll (New York: AMS, 1987): 187-194.

38. Among the most sophisticated proponents of this view is G. K. Hunter, "Flatcaps and Bluecoats: Visual Signals on the Elizabethan Stage," in *Essays and Studies*, ed. Inga-Stina Ewbank (London: John Murray, 1980), pp. 16-47. Of "Shakespeare's *travesti* roles" Hunter says, "The praise of the boys playing these parts must always have been praise for a role *used* rather than a role *achieved*. Portia does not disappear into Balthazar, nor Rosalind into Ganymede, but makes us conscious of the actor's capacity to invent new characteristics to answer new responsibilities, weakening our sense of a central core of character in order to strengthen our wonder at the co-existence of separate effects" (pp. 38-39).

39. Michael Shapiro reaches this utterly plausible and unpolemical

conclusion in chapter 1 of *Shakespeare and the Tradition of Boy Heroines in Male Disguise* (forthcoming).

40. Differences among playwrights is emphasized by Phyllis Rackin, "Androgyny, Mimesis, and the Marriage of the Boy Heroine on the English Renaissance Stage," *PMLA* 102 (1987): 29-41, who sees Shakespeare as being somewhere in between Lyly's romantic fantasy of androgyny and Jonson's satiric vindication of the reality principle. Nancy Hales insists on the differences among Shakespeare's comedies in "Disguise in *As You Like It* and *Twelfth Night*," *Shakespeare Survey* 32 (1979): 63-72. See also Robert Kimbrough, "Androgyny Seen through Shakespeare's Disguise," *Shakespeare Quarterly* 33 (1982): 17-33.

41. Shapiro, *Shakespeare and the Tradition of Boy Heroines in Male Disguise*, drawing on a catalog of plays compiled by Victor O. Freeburg, *Disguise Plots in Elizabethan Drama* (New York: Columbia Univ. Press, 1915), pp. 101-20.

42. On parallels between *Cymbeline* and *Clitiphon and Leucippe* see Gesner, *Shakespeare and the Greek Romance*, pp. 95-98. None of these is so specific, however, as to make Achilles Tatius a direct source.

43. The most circumspect treatment of this view is to be found in Linda Bamber, *Comic Women, Tragic Men: A Study of Gender and Genre in Shakespeare* (Stanford: Stanford Univ. Press, 1982), pp. 1-43, 109-133. See also Juliet Dusinberre, *Shakespeare and the Nature of Women* (London: Macmillan, 1975), pp. 231-271; Marianne Novy, *Love's Argument: Gender Relations in Shakespeare* (Chapel Hill: Univ. of North Carolina Press, 1984), pp. 21-44; and Catherine Belsey, "Disrupting Sexual Difference: Meaning and Gender in the Comedies," in *Alternative Shakespeares*, ed. John Drakakis (London: Methuen, 1985), pp. 166-190.

44. Ian MacLean, *The Renaissance Notion of Woman* (Cambridge: Cambridge Univ. Press, 1980) offers a summary of the antitheses between male and female that Aristotle attributes to the Pythagoreans (pp. 2-3) and a discussion of the Renaissance debate as to whether women are inferior to men (pp. 28-46).

45. Cf. Jeanne Addison Roberts, *Shakespeare's English Comedy: The Merry Wives of Windsor in Context* (Lincoln: Univ. of Nebraska Press, 1979): "In the broad spectrum of comedy, a sex change in one direction moves the action toward high comedy. In the other direction it propels the characters toward farce" (p. 119).

46. W. Thomas MacCary, *Friends and Lovers: The Phenomenology of Desire in Shakespearean Comedy* (New York: Columbia Univ. Press, 1985), pp. 13-70. MacCary's theory fits *Love's Labors Lost*, pp. 110-120, and *As You Like It*, pp. 171-176, especially well; other plays, less so.

47. C. L. Barber, *Shakespeare's Festive Comedy: A Study of Dramatic Form and its Relation to Social Custom* (Princeton: Princeton Univ. Press, 1959), pp. 3-15, provides a classic account of the seasonal festivals of Elizabethan England and their connections with plays for the public stage. The political implications of these "plebeian" connections are explored in Robert Weimann, *Shakespeare and the Popular Tradition in the*

Theater, pp. 15-48; Michael D. Bristol, *Carnival and Theater: Plebeian Culture and the Structure of Authority in Renaissance England* (London: Methuen, 1985); and Walter Cohen, *Drama of a Nation: Public Theater in Renaissance England and Spain* (Ithaca: Cornell Univ. Press, 1985), pp. 186-253. See also Burke, *Popular Culture*, pp. 178-204, who draws together evidence from all over Renaissance Europe.

48. Phillip Stubbes, *The Anatomie of Abuses*, ed. F. J. Furnivall (London: New Shakespeare Society, 1877-79), pp. 144-145.

49. Most scholars of Renaissance drama have paid more attention to attempts to repress the public theaters than attempts to repress folk drama. David McPherson isolates the issues in "Three Charges against Sixteenth- and Seventeenth-Century Playwrights: Libel, Bawdy, and Blasphemy," in *Medieval and Renaissance Drama in England*, ed. J. Leeds Barroll, 2 (New York: AMS Press, 1985): 269-282. At least two of these issues, bawdy and blasphemy, lie behind attempts to repress the traditional nonprofessional drama in town and country. The fullest and subtlest account of these matters is to be found in Jonas Barish, *The Antitheatrical Prejudice* (Berkeley: Univ. of California Press, 1981), pp. 80-131. James's list of "lawful recreations" is to be found in *King Charles the First's Declaration to His Subjects Concerning Lawfull Sports to be Used on Sundays* (1633) (rpt. London: Quaritch, 1862), p. 11. The "unlawfull games" that James disallows are "Beare and Bullbaitings, Interludes [i.e., plays], and at all times in the meaner sort of people by Law prohibited, Bowling" (p. 12). On the historical circumstances of these two royal proclamations see Robert W. Henderson, "The King's Book of Sports in England and America," *Bulletin of the New York Public Library* 52 (1948): 539-553. David Underdown considers the controversy at large in *Revel, Riot, and Rebellion: Popular Politics and Culture in England 1603-1660* (Oxford: Clarendon Press, 1985). See esp. pp. 46-72.

50. Quoted in G. R. Quaife, *Wanton Wenches and Wayward Wives: Peasants and Illicit Sex in Early Seventeenth-Century England* (New Brunswick: Rutgers Univ. Press, 1979), p. 175. Despite its all-embracing title, Quaife's book is concerned only with records for Somerset.

51. On the importance of solitary reading in the creation of "private life" in early modern Europe see Roger Chartier, "The Practical Impact of Writing," in *A History of Private Life*, vol. 3: *The Passions of the Renaissance*, ed. Chartier, trans. Arthur Goldhammer (Cambridge: Harvard Univ. Press, 1989), pp. 111-159. In particular, "silent, secret, private reading paved the way for previously unthinkable audacities. In the late Middle Ages, even before the invention of the printing press, heretical texts circulated in manuscript form, critical ideas were expressed, and erotic books, suitably illuminated, enjoyed considerable success" (pp. 125-126).

1. Juvenal, 2.8-13, in *Juvenal's Sixteen Satyrs or, A Survey of the Manners and Actions of Mankind*, trans. Sir Robert Stapylton (London: Humphrey Mosley, 1647), p. 18. Further quotations from Juvenal's second satire come from Stapylton's translation and are cited by page number in the text. Stapylton published a translation of the first six satires in 1644, with a second edition in 1646. The complete translation of 1647 was followed by editions in 1660 and 1673, with illustrations by Wenceslas Hollar.

2. Alvin B. Kernan, *The Cankered Muse: Satire of the English Renaissance* (New Haven: Yale Univ. Press, 1959), pp. 37-140.

3. Michel Foucault, *The History of Sexuality*, vol. 1: *An Introduction*, trans. Robert Hurley (New York: Pantheon, 1978): 45.

4. Lawrence Stone in *The Past and the Present Revisited* (London: Routledge and Kegan Paul, 1987), pp. 366-370, takes Guido Ruggiero's findings in the judicial archives of Venice, *The Boundaries of Eros: Sex Crime and Sexuality in Renaissance Venice* (New York: Oxford Univ. Press, 1985), pp. 109-145, to be typical of early modern Europe generally: in the course of the sixteenth century there was not only a rise in prosecutions for homosexuality but a shift in focus from the passive enjoyer of homosexual relations to the sexual aggressor.

5. Sir Edward Coke, *The Third Part of the Institutes of the Laws of England*, 3d ed. (London: J. Fleshner, 1660), p. 59.

6. Michael Goodich, *The Unmentionable Vice: Homosexuality in the Later Medieval Period* (Santa Barbara, Calif.: Clio Press, 1979).

7. Winfried Schleiner, "'That Matter Which Ought Not Be Heard Of': Remarks on the Archaeology of Homophobia in the Renaissance" (paper delivered at the Folger Shakespeare Library, November 1989).

8. David F. Greenberg, *The Construction of Homosexuality* (Chicago: Univ. of Chicago Press, 1989), pp. 294-295. On the connections among urbanization, capitalism, and homosexuality in early modern Europe, see pp. 301-396.

9. "*Bugeria* is an Italian word . . . . It was complained of in Parliament, that the Lumbards had brought unto the Realm the shamefull sin of Sodomy that is not to be named, as there it is said" (Sir Edward Coke, *The Third Part of the Institutes*, 3d ed., p. 58, paraphrasing a parliamentary record from the reign of Edward I, when the common law was being codified).

10. Horace, *Satires*, 1.2.25-28, trans. Thomas Drant as *A Medicinable Morall, that is, the two Bookes of Horace his Satyres, Englyshed* . . . (London: Thomas Marshe, 1566), sigs. B1^v-B2.

11. K. J. Dover, *Greek Homosexuality* (Cambridge: Harvard Univ. Press, 1978), pp. 60-109. To Dover's careful compilation of legal facts and visual evidence David M. Halperin brings theoretical adroitness in *One Hundred Years of Homosexuality and Other Essays on Greek Love* (New York: Routledge, 1990).

12. Paul Veyne, "Homosexuality in Ancient Rome," in Philippe Ariès and André Béjin, eds., *Western Sexuality: Practice and Precept in Past and Present Times*, trans. Anthony Forster (Oxford: Basil Blackwell, 1985), pp. 26-35. Veyne emphasizes masculinity and power as the key concepts in Roman attitudes toward homosexuality: "The passive homosexual was not rejected for his homosexuality but for his passivity, a very serious moral, or rather political infirmity. The passive individual's effeminacy was not the result of his perversion, far from it: it was simply one of the results of his lack of virility, and this was still a vice, even where no homosexuality was present" (p. 30). Veyne's general conclusions are confirmed in Beert C. Verstreete, "Slavery and the Social Dynamics of Male Homosexual Relations in Ancient Rome," *Journal of Homosexuality* 5 (1980): 227-236; Greenberg, *Construction of Homosexuality*, pp. 152-160; and Aline Rouselle, "Personal Status and Sexual Practices in the Roman Empire," in *Fragments for a History of the Human Body*, Part 3, ed. Michel Feher (New York: Zone, 1989), pp. 300-333.

13. Ovid, *De Arte Amandi*, 1.505-513, 3.433-436, trans. attributed to Thomas Heywood (n.p. [London?], n.d. [1600?]), pp. 22, 82.

14. Suetonius, *The Historie of Twelve Caesars, Emperours of Rome*, trans. Philemon Holland (London: Matthew Lownes, 1606), p. 192. Future quotations from this translation are cited in the text. Holland's preface "To the Readers" cautions that Suetonius "penned their lives, who were lately deceased, as one said very well, *eadem libertate qua ipsi vixerunt*: if happlie in prosecuting of this point, he hath recorded ought that may be offensive to chast and modest mindes, yee shal do well to glaunce over with your eye such places lightly, as I with my pen touched unwillingly" (sig. *2).

15. Veyne, "Homosexuality in Ancient Rome," pp. 30-31.

16. Eve Kosofsky Segwick, *Between Men: English Literature and Male Homosocial Desire* (New York: Columbia Univ. Press, 1985), p. 25.

17. Nicholas Breton, *The Good and the Badde, or Descriptions of the Worthies and Unworthies of this Age* (London: George Purslowe, 1616), pp. 30-31. Cf. OED under "gay": "2. Anything that looks gay or showy; an ornament; *esp.* one that is used to amuse a child. b. *fig.* A 'toy,' childish amusement" (with citation of another text by Breton).

18. Randolph Trumbach, "London's Sodomites: Homosexual Behavior and Western Culture in the Eighteenth Century," *Journal of Social History* 11 (1977): 1-33.

19. Louis Crompton, *Byron and Greek Love: Homophobia in 19th-Century England* (Berkeley: Univ. of California Press, 1985), pp. 21-22.

20. John Boswell, *Christianity, Social Tolerance, and Homosexuality* (Chicago: Univ. of Chicago Press, 1980), pp. 303-332.

21. Romans 1:24-28 in *The Geneva Bible* (1560), facsimile rpt., intro. Lloyd E. Berry (Madison: Univ. of Wisconsin Press, 1969), p. 70ᵛ. Further quotations from the Bible are taken from this, the most widely used translation before the King James Version, and are cited in the text.

22. Alan Bray, *Homosexuality in Renaissance England* (London: Gay Men's Press, 1982), p. 25.

23. Richard Baines's "note Containing the opinion of on[e] Christopher Marly his damnable [opini] Judgment of Religion, and scorn of Gods word" is printed in full in Paul H. Kocher, "Marlowe's Atheist Lecture," in *Marlowe: A Collection of Critical Essays*, ed. Clifford Leech (Englewood Cliffs, N.J.: Prentice-Hall, 1964), pp. 159-161. On the suspicious circumstances of Marlowe's death see Frederick S. Boas, *Christopher Marlowe: A Biographical and Critical Study* (Oxford: Clarendon Press, 1940), pp. 265-283, and John Bakeless, *The Tragicall History of Christopher Marlowe* (Cambridge: Harvard Univ. Press, 1942), 2:141-189.

24. John Donne, *The Satires, Epigrams, and Verse Letters*, ed. W. Milgate (Oxford: Clarendon Press, 1967), p. 44. Future quotations from Donne's satiric verse are taken from this edition and are cited by satire number and line number in the text.

25. *The Diary of Sir Simonds D'Ewes 1622-1624*, ed. Elisabeth Bourcier (Paris: Didier, 1974), pp. 92-93. See also Simonds's entry for 20 July 1622: "Saturday morning my brother Elliott and my sister whoe had been heere some fowre dayes, departed and I gott a little studye. I was enformed of manye things, as that the King hearing the Marquess [Buckingham] was not well, went to visite him and asking him what hee ailed, he tolde him a tooth aked, 'and what then man?' quoth hee, and being enformed that hee would pull it out, hee presentlye swore that hee should not and searching for the tooles and finding them, hee threw them all away and swore that hee wound hang the barbarr whoe hidd himselfe under Sr George Gorings cloake. And then halfe breathles 'Whye, man' quoth the King, 'What doost thou meane to doe to spoile and kill thy selfe and then becott (swearing Scottishlye) I shall not joy one good day after.' And a little before, hugging him one time verye seriouslye, hee burst foorth, 'Begott man, never loved another moore then I doe thee and lett God leave mee when I leave thee'" (p. 87). For these references I am grateful to Roger Lockyer, who cited them in the course of a talk on "The Reputation of King James I" at the Folger Shakespeare Library, October 1989.

26. Printed from a copy (Lambeth Palace Library MS 930), apparently of a lost holograph, in *Letters of King James VI & I*, ed. G. P. V. Akrigg (Berkeley: Univ. of California Press, 1984), pp. 335-341. This and the two other surviving letters to Carr are all datable to 1615, just before Carr came under investigation for the murder of Sir Thomas Overbury. Simonds's diary entry is dated seven years later, but Coke's search of Somerset's possessions must have occurred in connection with the Overbury case.

27. Osborn MS b197, pp. 187-189, in the Beinecke Library, Yale University. I am grateful to Donald Foster for sharing his transcription with me. According to Foster, the poem also appears in Bodleian MS Douce 357, fol. 16, where it is entitled "The Duke of Bucks. kin-

dred . . . 1622"; MS Rawlinson poetry 160, fol. 178ᵛ; and MS Tanner 306, fol. 257.

28. *Certaine Satyres* (hereafter cited as *CS*), 3.31-38, in *The Poems of John Marston*, ed. Arnold Davenport (Liverpool: Liverpool Univ. Press, 1961), p. 112. Further quotations from Marston are taken from this edition and are cited by satire number and line number in the text.

29. For the anecdote about Diogenes, see Diogenes Laertius, *Lives of Eminent Philosophers*, 6.2.46, where the following story comes next: "When a youth effeminately attired put a question to him, he declined to answer unless he pulled up his robe and showed whether he was a man or a woman." Trans., R. D. Hicks, Loeb Library (London: Heinemann, 1925), 2:46-49.

30. *Micro-cynicon. Sixe Snarling Satyres* (London: Thomas Creede, 1599), sig. C4ᵛ. Further quotations are cited by signature number in the text.

31. *Epicoene, or The Silent Woman*, 1.1.9-18, in *Ben Jonson*, 5, ed. C. H. Herford and Percy Simpson (Oxford: Clarendon Press, 1937): 165. Further quotations from *Epicoene* are taken from this edition and are cited in the text by act, scene, and line numbers.

32. Michael Shapiro, *Children of the Revels: The Boy Companies of Shakespeare's Time and Their Plays* (New York: Columbia Univ. Press, 1977), pp. 103-138.

33. Phyllis Rackin draws the same distinction between Shakespeare and Jonson in "Androgyny, Mimesis, and the Marriage of the Boy Heroine on the English Renaissance Stage," *PMLA* 102 (1987): 29-41.

34. *Epigrammes*, XXIV, in *Ben Jonson*, 8, ed. C. H. Herford, Percy Simpson, and Evelyn Simpson (Oxford: Clarendon Press, 1947): 34. Further quotations are taken from this edition and are cited in the text.

35. *Volpone, or The Fox* (1605), 3.7.234-239, in *Ben Jonson*, 5:84.

36. Cited in *Ben Jonson*, 11, ed. C. H. Herford, Percy Simpson, and Evelyn Simpson (Oxford: Clarendon Press, 1952): 5.

37. Quoted in G. R. Quaife, *Wanton Wenches and Wayward Wives: Peasants and Illicit Sex in Early Seventeenth-Century England* (New Brunswick: Rutgers Univ. Press, 1979), p. 176. I have altered the punctuation slightly and have added the emphasis.

CHAPTER SIX

1. Ovid, *Metamorphoses*, 10.148-161, trans. Arthur Golding (1567), ed. John Frederick Nims (New York: Macmillan, 1965), p. 253. Future quotations are cited in the text according to the book and line numbers of Ovid's Latin and the page numbers of Golding's translation.

2. James M. Saslow, *Ganymede in the Renaissance: Homosexuality in Art and Society* (New Haven: Yale Univ. Press, 1985), pp. 1-5, and 155-160, discusses the myth's appeal on social as well as intellectual grounds.

3. On Ovid's fortunes in the Renaissance see Douglas Bush, *Mythology and the Renaissance Tradition in English Poetry* (1937), new rev. ed. (New York: Norton, 1963), pp. 69-88, and Lee T. Pearcy, *The Mediated Muse: English Translations of Ovid 1560-1700* (Hamden, Conn.: Archon, 1984).

4. *Ovid's Metamorphosis* [sic], trans. George Sandys (1632), ed. Karl K. Hulley and Stanley T. Vandersall (Lincoln: Univ. of Nebraska Press, 1970), p. 481.

5. Cited in Keith Wrightson, *English Society 1580-1680* (New Brunswick, N.J.: Rutgers Univ. Press, 1982), p. 21. See also William Segar's categorization in *Honor Military, and Civill* (London: Robert Barker, 1602), p. 51: "we in England doe divide our men into five sorts: Gentlemen, Citizens, Yeomen, Artificers, and Labourers." And William Camden's in *Britannia*, trans. Philemon Holland (London: George Bishop and John Norton, 1610), p. 163: "As touching the division of our Common-wealth, it consisteth, of a King or Monarch, Noblemen or Gentry, Citizens, Free-borne, whom we call, Yeomen, and Artisans or Handicraftsmen."

6. David F. Greenberg, *The Construction of Homosexuality* (Chicago: Univ. of Chicago Press, 1988), pp. 25-88; Barry D. Adam, "Age, Structure, and Sexuality: Reflections on the Anthropological Evidence on Homosexual Relations," *Journal of Homosexuality* 11.3/4 (1986): 19-33; C. A. Tripp, *The Homosexual Matrix* (New York: Signet, 1975), pp. 68-69.

7. Alan Bray, *Homosexuality in Renaissance England* (London: Gay Men's Press, 1982), p. 56. On homosexuality and the social order see pp. 33-57.

8. On James see Caroline Bingham, *James I of England* (London: Weidenfeld and Nicolson, 1981), pp. 83-84, 134-136, 207-212; on Bacon (in the absence of a critical modern biography), A. L. Rowse, *Homosexuals in History* (New York: Carroll & Garf, 1977), pp. 48-69; on Castlehaven, Caroline Bingham, "Seventeenth-Century Attitudes Toward Deviant Sex," *Journal of Interdisciplinary History* 1 (1971): 447-472.

9. Records of Richard Williams's trial and its aftermath are transcribed in Jonathan Katz, *Gay American History* (New York: Thomas Crowell, 1976), pp. 16-19.

10. Between 1580 and 1680 the age at which most men married was 27 to 30, after they had accumulated enough capital to set up an independent household, but the aristocracy and upper gentry, already possessed of the necessary financial means, married younger. See Wrightson, *English Society* , pp. 66-70.

11. The excerpt from Francis Higgeson's journal is printed in Katz, *Gay American History*, pp. 19-20.

12. An equation between homosexuality and effeminacy is assumed in remarks on boy-actors and cross-dressing by Laura Levine, "Men in Women's Clothing: Anti-theatricality and Effeminization from 1579 to 1642," *Criticism* 28 (1986): 121-143; Stephen Orgel, "Nobody's Perfect: On Why Did the English Stage Take Boys for Women," *South Atlantic*

Quarterly 88 (1989): 7-29; and Marjorie Garber, "Fetish Envy" (paper delivered at the annual meeting of the Modern Language Association, 1989) and "Shakespeare as Fetish," *Shakespeare Quarterly* 41 (1990): 242-250, both papers incorporating material to be included in *Vested Interests: Cross-Dressing and Cultural Anxiety* (forthcoming).

13. Nicholas Breton, *The Good and the Badde, or Descriptions of the Worthies and Unworthies of this Age* . . . (London: George Purslowe, 1616), pp. 30-31.

14. *Troilus and Cressida*, 5.1.14-17, 27-31, in *The Complete Works*, ed. Stanley Wells and Gary Taylor (Oxford: Clarendon Press, 1986), p. 837. Further quotations from Shakespeare's plays are taken from this edition and are cited in the text by act, scene, and line numbers.

15. Alan Howard's interpretation of Achilles and Richard Jones Barry's of Patroclus (Royal Shakespeare Company, dir. John Barton, 1968) has set the pattern for most subsequent RSC productions, including one directed by Terry Hands (1981, with David Suchet as Achilles and Chris Hunter as Patroclus) that prompted one reviewer to find the relationship of Achilles and Patroclus "the only physically convincing relationship in the whole play" (David Nokes in the *Times Literary Supplement*, 17 July 1981, p. 810).

16. Jonathan Goldberg, "Colin to Hobbinol: Spenser's Familiar Letters," *South Atlantic Quarterly* 88 (1989): 107-126.

17. Thomas Heywood, *Pleasant Dialogues and Dramma's*, ed. W. Bang (Louvain: Uystpruyst, 1903), p. 101, ll. 3680-3681. Future quotations are taken from this edition and are cited by line number in the text.

18. *The Scourge of Villanie*, 3.55-66, 75-78, in *The Poems of John Marston*, ed. Arnold Davenport (Liverpool: Liverpool Univ. Press, 1961), pp. 112-113.

19. Transcribed from Beinecke MS Osborn b197 (Yale University), fols. 112-113, by Donald Foster, to whom I am grateful for bringing this poem to my attention and for sharing his transcription with me. The poem also appears, according to Foster, in Bodleian MSS Eng. Poet. c.50 (where it is entitled "On Jove [James I] and Ganymede [Buckingham] 1623"), Rawlinson Poet. 160, and Tanner 306. Subsequent references are cited in the text by line number.

20. On the ages of Carr and Villiers see Bingham, *James I of England*, pp. 81 and 159. Despite Villiers's age of 24 at the time he was created a Knight of the Order of the Garter, his portrait in his Garter robes "shows him as a tall young man with slender limbs and graceful proportions. Although he had been born in 1592 he still looks like an adolescent youth. He is clean-shaven and apparently smooth-faced" (Bingham, *James I of England*, p. 159).

21. Wrightson, *English Society*, pp. 66-70.

22. Ben Jonson, *Sejanus*, 4.373-380, 391-401, in *Ben Jonson*, 4, ed. C. H. Herford and Percy Simpson (Oxford, Clarendon Press, 1932): 431.

23. Reproduced in *Dido Queen of Carthage* and *The Massacre at Paris*, ed. H. J. Oliver, The Revels Plays (Cambridge, Mass.: Harvard Univ.

Press, 1968), p. 2. No evidence independent of the title page substantiates that *Dido* was in fact performed at court, but the subject, the style, and the message of the play are very much in the mode of John Lyly's comedies and other plays known to have been acted before Elizabeth. On these traditions, see Carter Anderson Daniel, "Patterns and Traditions of the Elizabethan Court Play to 1590" (Ph.D. dissertation, University of Virginia, 1965). My quotations from *Dido* and from Marlowe's other plays and poems come from *The Complete Works of Christopher Marlowe*, ed. Fredson Bowers, 2d ed., 2 vols. (Cambridge: Cambridge Univ. Press, 1979), and are cited in the text.

24. On the stage history of *Tamburlaine* and the play's vast influence on other playwrights, see Peter Berek, "*Tamburlaine*'s Weak Sons: Imitation as Interpretation before 1593," *Renaissance Drama*, n.s. 13 (1982): 55-82; Richard Levin, "The Contemporary Perception of Marlowe's *Tamburlaine*," *Medieval and Renaissance Drama in England*, 1, ed. J. Leeds Barroll (New York: AMS, 1984): 51-70; and Andrew Gurr, "Who Strutted and Bellowed?", *Shakespeare Survey* 16 (1963): 95-102. The stage history of *Edward II* is much sketchier. We have no more information than is stated on title pages of the earliest editions: that the play was performed in London by Pembroke's Men before 1593 and that it was revived by Queen Anne's Men between 1604-6 and 1617 at the Red Bull Theater—a socially less distinguished venue than the Globe or Blackfriars theaters that were home to the King's Men. Unlike *Tamburlaine*, which inspired dozens of rant-and-battle plays, *Edward II* did *not* inspire a series of plays with sodomite heroes, unless one accepts Richard II as a sodomite hero and Shakespeare's play as an answer to Marlowe's, rather than vice versa.

25. Michel Foucault, *The History of Sexuality*, vol. 1: *An Introduction*, trans. Robert Hurley (New York: Pantheon, 1978): 45.

26. Barbara J. Bono, *Literary Transvaluation: From Vergilian Epic to Shakespearean Tragicomedy* (Berkeley: Univ. of California Press, 1984), pp. 127-137.

27. Stephen Orgel, "Nobody's Perfect: On Why Did the English Stage Take Boys for Women," *South Atlantic Quarterly* 88 (1989): 7-29.

28. Bruce R. Smith, "Landscape with Figures: The Three Realms of Queen Elizabeth's Countryhouse Revels," *Renaissance Drama*, n.s. 8 (1977): 57-115.

29. Raphael Holinshed, *The Chronicles of England, Scotland, and Ireland* (London: Lucas Harrison, 1577), 2:849. Future quotations from Holinshed are taken from this edition and are cited in the text.

30. Jonathan Goldberg, "Playing the Sodomite" (paper delivered at the annual meeting of the Modern Language Association, 1989). In this paper Goldberg explicitly contrasts his view of sodomy as a breach of social hierarchy with a view of sodomy as a breach of gender distinctions in the arguments of Laura Levine and Stephen Orgel. See note 12, above.

31. *De casibus* tragedy takes its name from Boccaccio's widely read,

widely printed, and widely translated compendium *De casibus virorum illustrium* (1358), in which the lives of history's famous men are shown, one by one, to have followed the turning of Fortune's wheel. On the importance of Boccaccio's model to English tragedy see J. M. R. Margeson, *The Origins of English Tragedy* (Oxford: Clarendon Press, 1967), pp. 85-111.

32. Friedrich Hegel, *Aesthetics: Lectures on Fine Art* (1835), trans. T. M. Knox (Oxford: Clarendon Press, 1975), 2:1196: "a single action will under certain circumstances realize an aim or a character which is one-sidedly isolated in its complete determinacy, and therefore . . . will necessarily rouse against it the opposed 'pathos' and so lead to inevitable conflicts. The original essence of tragedy consists then in the fact that within such a conflict each of the opposed sides, if taken by itself, has *justification;* while each can establish the true and positive content of its own aim and character only by denying and infringing the equally justified power of the other. The consequence is that in its moral life, and because of it, each is nevertheless involved in *guilt.*"

33. Stephen Greenblatt, *Renaissance Self-Fashioning* (Chicago: Univ. of Chicago Press, 1980), pp. 193-221. "Marlowe's protagonists rebel against orthodoxy, but they do not do so just as they please; their acts of negation not only conjure up the order they would destroy but seem at times to be themselves conjured up by that very order" (p. 210, echoing Karl Marx in *The Eighteenth Brumaire of Louis Bonaparte,* "Men make their own history, but they do not make it just as they please").

CHAPTER SEVEN

1. Horace, Odes 4.1.29-40, trans. Henry Rider in *All the Odes and Epodes of Horace* (London, 1638), pp. 93-94. Selected odes had been translated and published by John Ashmore in 1621, but the homoerotic poems are not among them. On Horace's reputation and influence in the sixteenth and seventeenth centuries see Gilbert Highet, *The Classical Tradition* (Oxford: Oxford Univ. Press, 1949), pp. 244-250, and Valerie Edden, "'The Best of Lyrick Poets,'" in *Horace,* ed. C. D. N. Costa (London: Routledge & Kegan Paul, 1973), pp. 135-159.

2. T. W. Baldwin reaches this conclusion by noting that Shakespeare's allusions to Horace incorporate elements of Lambin's commentary. See *William Shakspere's Small Latine & Lesse Greeke* (Urbana: Univ. of Illinois Press, 1944), 2:497-525.

3. *Shakespeare's Sonnets,* ed. Stephen Booth (New Haven: Yale Univ. Press, 1977). In addition to a lightly edited text Booth provides a facsimile of the 1609 quarto and a full commentary. In that commentary sexual puns figure prominently.

4. *In Q. Horatium Flaccum . . . Commentarii,* ed. Denys Lambin (Frankfurt: Andreas Wechel, 1577), 1:214: "posteaquam multis verbis ostendit, se iam ad amorem esse ineptum, atque (ut ita dicam) mancum, denique iudicio tandem, ac voluntate ab huiusmodi deliciis, ineptiis, ac

nequitiis abhorrere: nunc vi amoris coactus fatetur se, quamvis aetate iam ingravescente a tali mollitie, ac nequitia remotissimus esse debeat, amore Ligurini pueri incensum tamen ad pristinas lascivias revocari." The copy of Wechel's edition now in the Alderman Library of the University of Virginia was once owned by Philemon Holland, the translator into English of Plutarch's *Moralia* and Suetonius's *Lives of the Caesars*.

5. Christoforo Landino and Hermanus Figulus in *Quincti Horatii Flacii Venusini, Poetae Lyrici elegantis, Opera* (Basel: Henricus Petrus, 1580), cols. 801, 798-799. Earlier editions had been published by Petrus in 1545, 1555, and 1570. Among the commentators who pass over passages like this in silence is Henri Etienne. Cf. Horace, *Opera*, ed. Henri Etienne, 2d ed. (Paris: Henri Etienne, 1588), p. 90.

6. The remarks of Steevens and Malone are quoted by Joseph Pequigney, *Such Is My Love: A Study of Shakespeare's Sonnets* (Chicago: Univ. of Chicago Press, 1985), pp. 30-31. For an overview of how "The Question of Homosexuality" was addressed by critics during the nineteenth century and the earlier part of the twentieth century, see Shakespeare, *The Sonnets*, ed. Hyder Rollins, New Variorum Ed. (Philadelphia: Lippincott, 1944), 2:232-239. Stephen Booth begs the question by quipping, "William Shakespeare was almost certainly homosexual, bisexual, or heterosexual. The sonnets provide no evidence on the matter" (*Shakespeare's Sonnets*, p. 548).

7. The grudging agreement that Pequigney's book has received is typified by Robert M. Adams's review in *The New York Review of Books*, 33 (1986): 50: "This is certainly a book that had to be written, that will make impossible any return to the old vague euphemisms, but that, after reading, one will be glad to keep distant in one's memory if one wants to enjoy the sonnets themselves—which also, by their sustained rhetoric, distance the very topics that Pequigney wants to lift into the foreground."

8. Quoted in Pequigney, *Such Is My Love*, pp. 79-80.

9. C.L. Barber and Richard P. Wheeler, *The Whole Journey: Shakespeare's Power of Development* (Berkeley: Univ. of California Press, 1986), p. 171: "The sonnets to the mistress make clear that genital relationship with her was crucial, if conflictual. W. H. Auden, a particularly trustworthy witness in this matter, mocked the eager claims of 'the Homintern' on the Sonnets; he described the love for the young man as 'mystical' and observed that such passionate devotion, enthralled by a special type of mortal beauty, rarely survives physical union."

10. Heather Dubrow, *Captive Victors: Shakespeare's Narrative Poems and Sonnets* (Ithaca: Cornell Univ. Press, 1986), pp. 171-190.

11. Michel Foucault, *The History of Homosexuality, 1: An Introduction*, trans. Robert Hurley (New York: Pantheon, 1978): 63. See also Antony Easthope's brilliant application of Foucault's ideas in "Foucault, Ovid, Donne: Versions of Sexuality, Ancient and Modern" in *Poetry and Phantasy* (Cambridge: Cambridge Univ. Press, 1989), pp. 47-62.

12. First suggested by Philippe Ariès, these are the three causes isolated and studied by various authors in *A History of Private Life*, vol. 3: *The Passions of the Renaissance*, ed. Roger Chartier, trans. Arthur Goldhammer (Cambridge, Mass.: Harvard Univ. Press, 1989). On the three forces individually see Yves Castan, "Politics and Private Life," pp. 21-67; François Lebrun, "The Two Reformations: Communal Devotion and Personal Piety," pp. 69-109; and Roger Chartier, "The Practical Impact of Writing," pp. 111-159.

13. Orest Ranum, "The Refuges of Intimacy," in *A History of Private Life*, 3:207-263. Other sites include walled gardens like the one that figures in Simon Foreman's erotic dream about Queen Elizabeth. (See chapter 1, above.)

14. *The Diary of Sir Simonds D'Ewes 1622-1624*, ed. Elisabeth Bourcier (Paris: Didier, 1974), p. 92. The occasion of this sharing of secrets, and the secrets themselves, are described in chapter 5, above.

15. In addition to the illustration on page 226, see examples pictured in the Victoria and Albert Museum handbook on *English Cabinets* (London: Her Majesty's Stationery Office, 1972). Such pieces of furniture were not restricted to rich people. A simple wooden version, its surface painted to look like fancy inlay work, is in the collection of the Agecroft Hall museum, Richmond, Virginia.

16. *The Diary of Sir Simonds D'Ewes*, p. 93.

17. Patricia Fumerton, "'Secret' Arts: Elizabethan Miniatures and Sonnets," rpt. in *Representing the English Renaissance*, ed. Stephen Greenblatt (Berkeley: Univ. of California Press, 1988), pp. 93-133.

18. Anne Ferry, *The "Inward" Language: Sonnets of Wyatt, Sidney, Shakespeare, Donne* (Chicago: Univ. of Chicago Press, 1983), pp. 1-30.

19. According to Ann Baynes Coiro, "Seventeenth-Century Commonplace Books and the Structure of Poetic Sequences" (paper delivered at the annual meeting of the Modern Language Association, December 1989), the 1620s and '30s witnessed, not the decline of manuscript culture that we might expect from the proliferation of printed books in the seventeenth century, but a fresh flourishing. With the rise of Puritan political power, manuscript culture acquired a distinctly royalist identity, especially in Oxford colleges. Coiro's argument was confirmed by Arthur F. Marotti, "The Poetry of Feargod Barbon, Edward Bannister, Nicholas Burghe, Peter Calfe, Sir Humphrey Coningsby, Margaret Douglas, John Finet, Lewison Fitzjames, John Lilliat, Andrew Ramsey, John Ramsey, Richard Roberts, William Skipwith, Henry Stanford, Thomas Wenman, and Others" (paper delivered at the annual meeting of the Modern Language Association, December 1989).

20. Francis Meres, *Palladis Tamia. Wits Treasury* (1598): "As the soule of *Euphorbus* was thought to live in *Pythagoras*: so the sweete wittie soule of *Ovid* lives in mellifluous & hony-tongued *Shakespeare*, witnes his *Venus* and *Adonis*, his *Lucrece*, his sugred Sonnets among his private friends, etc." Reprinted in C. M. Ingleby, *et al.*, *The Shakespere Allusion-Book: A Collection of Allusions to Shakespere from 1591 to 1700*, ed. John

Munro (London: Chatto & Windus, 1909), 1:46.

21. Sonnet 77, line 3 in *Shakespeare's Sonnets*, ed. Stephen Booth (New Haven: Yale Univ. Press, 1977), p. 69. All my quotations from the sonnets are transcribed in the original orthography from the facsimile of the 1609 quarto that Booth prints on pages facing his edited modern-spelling versions. Further quotations are cited in the text by sonnet number and line number.

22. *The Tragedy of Hamlet, Prince of Denmark*, 1.3.58-60, in William Shakespeare, *The Complete Works*, ed. Stanley Wells and Gary Taylor (Oxford: Clarendon Press, 1986), p. 742. Further quotations from Shakespeare's plays are taken from this edition and are cited in the text and by act, scene, and line numbers.

23. I follow Stephen Booth, and most other readers of sonnet 122, in assuming that the table's leaves are blank and that "thy record" in line 8 refers to what is "full characterd with lasting memory" in the poet's brain, not to anything that has been written down in the tables by the friend himself. See Booth's notes on the possible ambiguity, *Shakespeare's Sonnets*, pp. 412-413.

24. For this distinction between the two very different uses of verses in manuscript I am indebted to Mary Ellen Lamb, "Thomas Why-thorne's *Autobiography* and the Social Contexts of Manuscript Transmission" (paper delivered at the annual meeting of the Modern Language Association, December 1989).

25. Joel Fineman, *Shakespeare's Perjured Eye: The Invention of Poetic Subjectivity in the Sonnets* (Berkeley: Univ. of California Press, 1986).

26. "Sidney can only achieve the inner *through* the outer, the private *through* the public, the sincere self *through* self-display. One could argue that his private self is, therefore, not at all private since it is dependent on the public. But one could counter that it is intensely private since it is unrepresentable. Perhaps we might best propose that Sidney's and Hilliard's artifice of secrecy constitutes the first step or threshold ushering in the 'modern' idea of self at a distance from public expression" (Fumerton, "'Secret' Arts," p. 126).

27. Ferry, *The "Inward" Language*, pp. 170-214.

28. The surviving seventeenth-century manuscripts that include poems by Donne, almost all of them dating from the 1620s and '30s, are cataloged in Peter Beal, *Index of English Literary Manuscripts, 1450-1625*, (London: Mansell, 1980), 1.1:243-568. Poems by Donne were transcribed more often than those of any other British poet of the sixteenth and seventeenth centuries.

29. The twelve manuscripts, which like those containing poems by Donne date mostly from the 1620s and '30s, are cataloged and described in Beale, *Index of English Literary Manuscripts, 1450-1625*, 1.2:452-453. Part of this evidence is studied by Gary Taylor, "Some Manuscripts of Shakespeare's Sonnets," *Bulletin of The John Rylands University Library of Manchester* 68.1 (1985): 210-246.

30. *The Passionate Pilgrim* (1599), facsimile edition ed. Joseph Quincy

Adams (New York: Scribners, 1939). My quotations from *The Passionate Pilgrim* are taken from Adams's edition and are cited in the text.

31. Arthur F. Marotti, *John Donne, Coterie Poet* (Madison: Univ. of Wisconsin Press, 1986), pp. 3-24.

32. J. W. Saunders, "From Manuscript to Print: A Note on the Circulation of Poetic MSS in the Sixteenth Century," *Proceedings of the Leeds Philosophical and Literary Society* 6 (1951): 523.

33. Detective by detective, century by century, Samuel Schoenbaum provides an amusing narrative of these attempts in *Shakespeare's Lives* (Oxford: Clarendon Press, 1970).

34. *The Autobiography of Thomas Whythorne*, ed. James M. Osborn (Oxford: Clarendon Press, 1961), pp. 40-41. For this reference I am indebted to Mary Ellen Lamb, "Thomas Whythorne's *Autobiography* and the Social Contexts of Manuscript Transmission" (paper delivered at the annual meeting of the Modern Language Association, December 1989).

35. On the price of quartos see F. R. Johnson, "Notes on English Retail Book Prices 1550-1640," *The Library*, 5th ser. (1950): 83-112.

36. John Hart, "The Opening of the Unreasonable Writing of Our Inglish Toung" (1551) [BL MS Royal 17.c.VII], ed. Bror Danielsson in *John Hart's Works on English Orthography and Pronunciation* (Stockholm: Almquist & Wiksell, 1955), p. 162.

37. George Wyndham made this argument in his edition of Shakespeare's *Poems* (1898). For an account of the 1609 text and a summary of responses to Wyndham's argument see Shakespeare, *The Sonnets*, ed. Rollins, New Variorum Ed., 2:1-18. Booth remarks on the quarto's orthography in his preface to *Shakespeare's Sonnets*, pp. xiv-xviii, and in an extended note on sonnet 129, pp. 447-452.

38. *Epithalamium*, ll. 383, 398-403, in Edmund Spenser, *The Works*, 8, ed. C. G. Osgood and H. G. Gibbons (Baltimore: Johns Hopkins Univ. Press, 1947): 251.

39. Booth, *Shakespeare's Sonnets*, pp. 431-432.

40. Plutarch, *Moralia* 767, trans. Philemon Holland in *The Philosophie* (London, 1603), fols. 1132-1133. Further quotations are cited in the text by folio number. Connections between the sonnets and the plays with respect to the scenario of two male friends parted by a woman are explored in Cyrus Hoy, "Shakespeare and the Revenge of Art," *Rice University Studies* 60 (1974): 71-94.

41. John Donne, Elegy "To his Mistris Going to Bed" and "The Sunne Rising," in *The Elegies and The Songs and Sonnets*, ed. Helen Gardner (Oxford: Clarendon Press, 1965), pp. 14, 72.

42. Booth, *Shakespeare's Sonnets*, pp. 98-99.

43. Pequigney, *Such Is My Love*, pp. 209-210, summarizing the argument he has made in earlier chapters.

44. Booth, *Shakespeare's Sonnets*, pp. 175-178.

45. Michel Foucault, *The History of Sexuality*, vol. 2: *The Use of Pleasure*, trans. Robert Hurley (New York: Pantheon, 1985): 187-225.

46. Heather Trexler Remoff, *Sexual Choice: A Woman's Decision* (New

York: Dutton, 1984), pp. 3-11. The same observation about the expendability of males is made by Walter J. Ong, *Fighting for Life: Contest, Sexuality, and Consciousness* (Ithaca: Cornell Univ. Press, 1981), pp. 52-56.

47. Puttenham defines love poetry, like other forms of verse, according to its original use: "There were an other sort, who sought the favor of faire Ladies, and coveted to bemone their estates at large, & the perplexities of love in a certain pitious verse called *Elegie*, and thence were called *Eligiack*: such among the Latines were *Ovid, Tibullus, & Propertius*." *The Arte of English Poesie*, ed. Gladys Doidge Willcock and Alice Walker (Cambridge: Cambridge Univ. Press, 1936), p. 25. Sidney has these origins in mind when he sets up his criterion as to whether a love poem is good or not: "But truly many of such writings as come under the banner of unresistible love, if I were a mistress, would never persuade me they were in love: so coldly they apply fiery speeches, as men that had rather read lovers' writings . . . than that in truth they feel those passions, which easily (as I think) may be bewrayed by that same forcibleness or *energia* (as the Greeks call it)." *Defence of Poetry*, ed. J. A. Van Dorsten (Oxford: Oxford Univ. Press, 1966), pp. 69-70.

48. Sir William Cornwallis, *Essayes* (London: Edmund Mattes, 1600), sig. E3ᵛ.

49. *The Book of Common Prayer 1559: The Elizabethan Prayer Book*, ed. John E. Booty (Charlottesville: Univ. of Virginia Press, 1976), p. 297. Further quotations are cited in the text. Booth's remarks on Ephesians 5 occur in connection with sonnet 36, pp. 192-195.

50. The reference in sonnet 134, though addressed to the mistress, still concerns the poet's male love: "So now I have confest that he is thine,/And I my selfe am morgag'd to thy will,/My selfe Ile forfeit, so that other mine,/Thou wilt restore to be my comfort still" (134.1-4). The allusion to "one flesh" in sonnet 135 ("Who ever hath her wish, thou hast thy *Will*") leaves St. Paul and spiritual concerns far behind.

51. Pierre Bourdieu, *Outline of a Theory of Practice*, trans. Richard Nice (Cambridge: Cambridge Univ. Press, 1977), pp. 72-95.

52. C. S. Lewis, *English Literature in the Sixteenth Century Excluding Drama* (Oxford: Clarendon Press, 1954), p. 505.

53. Barber and Wheeler, *The Whole Journey*, p. 195.

54. Pequigney, *Such Is My Love*, pp. 202-207.

55. Dubrow, *Captive Victors*, pp. 221-222.

56. A full account of the critical reception of the 1609 quarto and of Benson's edition is offered by Sidney Lee in the introduction to his facsimile edition of *Shakespeares Sonnets . . . The First Edition 1609* (Oxford: Clarendon Press, 1905), pp. 51-62.

57. Margreta de Grazia discusses Malone's canonization of the quarto sonnets and the effect of his apparatus on subsequent readings in *Shakespeare "Verbatim": The Reproduction of Authenticity and the 1790*

Apparatus (Oxford: Oxford Univ. Press, 1990), chapter 3, "Individuating Shakespeare." See also her essay "Locating and Dislocating the 'I' of Shakespeare's Sonnets," in *William Shakespeare: His World, His Work, His Influence*, ed. John F. Andrews (New York: Scribners, 1985), 2:433-444.

INDEX

Main discussions are indicated in boldface.

Notes are indicated in italics.

Chapman, George, 93, 134, 183

Chartier, Roger, 130, *285, 290, 298, 301, 311*

Chaucer, Geoffrey, 59, 70, 97, 161, *276*

Chauncey, George, Jr., *272, 273, 288*

Childe, John, 52, 75

chivalry, 59, 128–132, 136, 154, *297*

Christianity (*see also* morality and moral discourse, sin), 3, 11–12, 14, 20, 21, 24, 37, **40–48**, 50–51, 52, 53, 66, 83, 87, 98, 127, 129, 131, 147, 156, 167, **172–176**, 177, 184, 191–192, 219, **232–234**, 259, **264–265**, 266, *271, 273, 274, 276, 278, 280, 281, 282, 290, 303*

Christmas (*see also* carnival), 14, 23, 113, 126, 128

Cicero, 36, 40, 97, 115, 257, *279*
De Amicitia 36, 84, *279*

class (*see* social class)

Clifford, James, *277*

Cochrane, Lydia G., *285*

Cockburn, J. S., *282, 283*

Coghan, Thomas, 87, *291*

Cohen, Walter, *301*

Coiro, Ann Baynes, *311*

Coke, Edward, **49–51**, 53, 73, 75, 166, 177, 186, 235, *283, 290, 302, 304*
A Booke of Entries, 51, *283, 290*
Institutes, 49, 50, 166, *283, 302*

colleges (*see also* inns of court, schools, universities), 66, **82–87**, 126, 144, 180, 193, 202, *292, 311*

concubinage, 47

Coote, Stephen, 101, *289*

Copland, Robert, *286*

Cornish, Richard, 194

Cornwallis, William, 261, *280, 314*

Coryate, Thomas, 148, 149, *299*

Costa, C. D. N., *309*

courtly love, 103, 109, 253, 258, 260, 264, 266, 268

courts and court records (*see also* crime, laws and legal discourse, statutes), 24, **48–53**, 156, 193, 194, 195, *283*

courtship, 59, 63, 64, 76, 124, 237, 249, 252, 259, *287*

Couse, William, 194, 195

Cousin, Gilbert, *280*

Craigie, James, *273*

Cressey, David, *285*

crime (*see also* courts and court reords, laws and legal discourse, statutes), 3, 18, 35, 42, 43, 46, 48–53, 76, 130, 134, 165, 220, *271, 278, 281, 297, 302*

Crompton, Louis, *275, 280, 281, 289, 303*

cross dressing, 126, 141–142, **147–155**, 161–163, 168, 170–171, 183–184, 199, *299, 300*

Cullen, Patrick, *292*

Culler, Jonathan, *278*

Cunnington, Phillis, *290*

Cupid, 5, 105, 125, 140, 266

Curtius, Ernst Robert, *289*

dancing, 23, **123–125**, 130, 156, 157, 173, 196, 200, *295*

Danckerts, Johan, 160

Daniel, Carter Anderson, *308*

Daniel, Samuel, 229, 231

Danielsson, Bror, *313*

Dante, 259

Darwin, Charles, 5

Davenport, Arnold, *305, 307*

Davis, Natalie Zemon, 85, *291*

Davy, Meredith, 118, 157

de Grazia, Margreta, *314–315*

de la Sale, Antoine, 32, 65, 164, *286*

de Maupassant, Guy, *295*

De Mause, Lloyd, *291*

de Montaigne, Michel (*see* Montaigne)

De Rougemont, Denis, 19, 20, *276*

de Worde, Wynkyn, 32, *286*

Della Casa, Giovanni, 166

Desan, Philippe, *276*

D'Ewes, Simonds, 48, 176, 234, *282, 304, 311*

Diana, 151, 212, 247

Diogenes Laertius, *305*

disguise, 34, 65, 68, 82, 124, 126, 140–146, 150, 152, 153, 155, 179, 199, 222, 228, *299, 300*

Donne, John, 27, 102, 103, 161, 162, 164, **174–176, 178–179**, 181, 182, 185, 186, 198, 213, 235, 239, **241**, 242, 252, *294, 304, 310, 311, 312, 313*
Satires, 103, 174–176, 178–179, *304*
Songs and Sonnets, 103, 241, *313*

Dover, K. J., *302*

Drakakis, John, *287, 300*

155, 179–180, 184, 186, 189, **191–
193**, **195–197**, 199, 201, 202, 205,
206–209, 211, 213, 223, 228, 232,
299, 305, 307
Garber, Marjorie, *299, 307*
Gaselee, Stephen, *295*
"gay," **9–12**, **18**, 26–29, 114, 171, *272,
273, 275, 277, 281, 284, 288, 294,
303, 306*
Gerard, Kent, *272, 284, 288*
Gesner, Carol, *295, 300*
Gesta Grayorum, 294
Gilbert, Arthur N., *273*
Ginsberg, Allen, 26
Girouard, Mark, *297*
Goldberg, Jonathan, 74, 97, 199, 215,
288, 290, 293, 307, 308
Golden Age, 81, 93, 98, 246
Goldhammer, Arthur, *290, 301, 311*
Golding, Arthur, 191–193, 197, 205,
289, 305
Goldmann, Lucien, *276*
Goodich, Michael, *282, 302*
Gorboduc, 103
Gorer, Geoffrey, 75, *288*
Gosson, Stephen, 196
Gray's Inn (*see also* inns of court), 102,
107, 113, *293–294*
Grazia, Margreta de, *314–315*
Greece 10, 14, 20, **35–37**, 41, 59–60,
103, 120, 125, 139, **167–169**, 170,
193, 203, 221, *271, 289, 295, 300,
302, 303*
Greek language, 19, 20, 88, 103, 120,
245, 247, *280, 290, 303*
Green, Martin, 54, 230, *284*
Greenberg, David F., 10, 18, 76, 166,
167, *272, 275, 289, 294, 302, 303,
306*
Greenblatt, Stephen, 222, *271, 277,
278, 309, 311*
Greene, Robert, **136–140**, 143–145, 152,
156, 157, 161, 216, *298*
Greenlaw, Edwin, *293*
Greville, Fulke, 143, *298*
Griswold, Wendy, *276*
Grosart, Alexander, *293, 294, 298*
Gunn, Thom, 26
Gurr, Andrew, *308*

Hakluyt, Richard, *271*

Hales, James, 143
Hales, Lady, 143
Hales, Nancy, *300*
Hall, Stuart, *278*
Halperin, David M., 10, *272, 302*
Hands, Terry, *307*
Hanna, Judith Lynne, 124, *295*
Harrison, William, 193
Hart, John, *313*
Harvey, Gabriel, 97, 199
Harvey, Richard, 124
Hawkes, Henry, 3–4, *271*
health (*see also* medicine and medical
discourse), 14, 15, 86, 87, 150,
291
Heffner, Ray, *292*
Hegel, Friedrich, 221, *309*
Hekma, Gert, 76, *272, 284, 288–289*
Heliodorus, 120, 136, *295*
Henderson, Robert W., *301*
Henry VIII, 43–47, 50, 52, 131, *281,
282, 283, 297*
Herbert, Mary Sidney, Countess of
Pembroke, 143, *298*
Hercules, 25, 97, 141, 210, 211, 220
heresy, 11, **42–44**, 47, 131, 165, 173, *301*
Herford, C. H., *290, 305, 307*
Hermes, 97
Herrup, Cynthia B., *283*
Heywood, Thomas, 150, 201, 202, 205,
303, 307
Higgeson, Francis, *306*
Highet, Gilbert, *309*
holidays (*see* carnival)
Holinshed, Raphael, 190, 213, 214, 216,
217, 220, *308*
Holland, Philemon, 38, 40, 170, *280,
298, 303, 306, 310, 313*
Hollar, Wenceslas, 160, *302*
Homer, 59, 120
homophobia, 42, 73, 171, 172, *275, 280,
281, 289, 302, 303*
homosociality, 33, 56, 73, 248, *279, 303*
honor, 47, 59, 65, 129, 198, 208, *286,
287, 297, 298, 306*
Horace 83, 161, 163–164, 168–169, 175,
179, 184, **228–230**, 231, 252, 254,
257, 264, 267, *302, 309, 310*
odes, 228–230, 231, 252, 254, 257, 264,
267, *309, 310*
satires, 161, 163–164, 168–169, 175,

Main discussions/other references/*notes*   325

248; *sonnet 12*, 246; *sonnet 13*, 246, 248, 249; *sonnet 15*, 246, 247–248, 257; *sonnet 16*, 246; *sonnet 18*, 246; *sonnet 19*, 248–249; *sonnet 20*, 226, 227, 230, **248–251**, 252, 253, 255, 256–257, 258, 262, 269; *sonnet 21*, 238, 250–251, 253, 256–257, 262; *sonnet 22*, 263; *sonnet 23*, 253–254, 256; *sonnet 25*, 255; *sonnet 26*, 252, 254, 260–261; *sonnet 27*, 254–255; *sonnet 28*, 254; sonnet 33, 261; *sonnet 34*, 261, 263; *sonnet 36*, 255–256, 262–263; *sonnet 37*, 262; *sonnet 39*, 263; *sonnet 40*, 252; *sonnet 42*, 263; *sonnet 46*, 254; *sonnet 48*, 252, 254, 255; *sonnet 52*, 252, 254, 255; *sonnet 54*, 245; *sonnet 57*, 254, 260–261; *sonnet 58*, 260–261; *sonnet 62*, 233, 263; *sonnet 63*, 254; *sonnet 64*, 252; *sonnet 65*, 254; *sonnet 67*, 245; *sonnet 75*, 252; *sonnet 77*, 236–237, 254, *312*; *sonnet 78*, 252; *sonnet 82*, 238, 262; *sonnet 86*, 238; *sonnet 87*, 252, 261; *sonnet 88*, 256; *sonnet 89*, 256; *sonnet 90*, 256; *sonnet 93*, 262; *sonnet 94*, 260–261, 262; *sonnet 95*, 245; *sonnet 97*, 262; *sonnet 98*, 245, 252; *sonnet 99*, 252; *sonnet 106*, 257–258; *sonnet 109*, 245, 252, 263; *sonnet 110*, 252, 260; *sonnet 112*, 256; *sonnet 113*, 268; *sonnet 114*, 261, 265, 268; *sonnet 115*, 268; *sonnet 116*, 263–264; *sonnet 120*, 256; *sonnet 121*, 256; *sonnet 122*, 236–238, 268, *312*; *sonnet 125*, 266, 268; *sonnet 126*, 265, 266; *sonnet 129*, 252; *sonnet 134*, 252, 263, *314*; *sonnet 135*, 252, 263, *314*; *sonnet 136*, 252; *sonnet 138*, 240, 257; *sonnet 142*, 252; *sonnet 143*, 252; *sonnet 144*, 240, 249, 265; *sonnet 151*, 252; *sonnet 153*, 266; *sonnet 154*, 252, 266
The Taming of the Shrew, 150, 151, *286*
Troilus and Cressida, 59, 64, 75, 197, 198, 203, 204, *285–286, 307*
Twelfth Night, 22, 67, 69, 71, 125, 151, 152, 154, 161, 183, 243–244, *300*
Two Gentlemen of Verona, 67, 69, 70, 140, 151

The Two Noble Kinsmen, 69–72, 123, 140, *295*
Venus and Adonis, 134–136, 240, *311*
The Winter's Tale, 67, 69, 98, 99, 101, 140
Shapiro, Michael, 149, 150, *299, 300, 305*
Sherzer, Joel, *285*
Shrove Tuesday (*see also* carnival), 85
Sidney, Mary (*see* Herbert, Mary Sidney)
Sidney, Philip, 17, 22, 24, 25, 99, 109, 136, **139–145**, 152, 157, 161, 216, 228, 229, 231, 235, 238, 245, 259, 260, *274, 298, 311, 312, 314*
Arcadia, 25, **139–143**, 152, 154, 161, 216, 228, *298*
Astrophel and Stella, 99, 109, 228
Simon, William, 16, 21, 100, *274, 293*
Simpson, Evelyn, *305*
Simpson, Percy, *290, 305, 307*
sin (*see also* Christianity, morality and moral discourse, vice), 3, 8, 11, 50, 51, 74, 98, 100, 107, *302*
Singer, Irving, *279*
Skretkowicz, Victor, *298*
Slack, Paul, *291*
Smith, Bruce R., *292, 297, 308*
Smith, Rowland, *295*
social class, 21, 23, 83–84, 102, 167–169, 210, 215, 216, 257, 269, *276*
Socrates, 35, 95, 159, 161, 211, *279*
sodomy, 3, 8, 11, 14, 18, 20, 35, **41–53**, 56, 70, 74–76, 87, 114, 131, 154, 161, 165–167, 173, 174, 177, 176, 178, 180, 182, 186, 191, 194, 196, 202, 206, 209, 216, 220, 222, 223, 230, 234, 266, *272, 273, 282, 283, 284, 288, 289, 302, 308*
Somerset (*see* Carr, Robert)
sonnets (*see also* Shakespeare, William, Sonnets), 21, 23–26, 54, 99, 103, 109–111, 151, 226, 228–242, 244, 245, 246–270, *277, 284, 309, 310, 311, 312, 313, 314*
sorcery (*see* magic)
Spenser, Edmund, 25, 27, 92, **94–99**, 104, 107, 109, 110, 199, 218, 229, 231, 246, 247, 251, 265, 266, *288, 290, 292, 293, 307, 313*
Amoretti, 109, 266
Epithalamion, 247, 251

Weimann, Robert M., 126, *296, 300*
Weissbourd, Bernard, *283*
Wells, Stanley, *272, 279, 289, 295, 307, 312*
Wheeler, Richard P., 231, 265, *310, 314*
Whitman, Walt, 26
Whitsuntide (*see also* carnival), 82, 124, 127, 128, 137, 151, 156
Whittaker, William Joseph, *281*
Whythorne, Thomas, 243, *312, 313*
Wilde, Oscar, 170, 211, 230
Wiles, David, 104, 121, 126, 207, 209, *295, 297*
Willcock, Gladys Doidge, *292, 314*
Willett, C., *290*
Williams, Clare, *299*
Williams, Richard, 194, 195, *306*

Williamson, Marilyn L., *287*
Wilson, F. P. *287, 297*
witchcraft (*see also* magic), 14, 43, 47, 173
wooing ceremony (*see also* folk drama), 125
Woollacott, Janet, *278*
Worde, Wynkyn de, 32, *286*
Wordsworth, William, 269
Wrightson, Keith, 83, *286, 289, 306, 307*
Wroth, Mary, 148, 149, *299*
Wyatt, Thomas, 235, *311*
Wyndham, George, 245, *279, 313*

Yates, Frances, *297*
Yeandle, Laetitia, *294*